PROPAGANDA FOR WAR

PROPAGANDA FOR WAR

The Campaign against American
Neutrality, 1914-1917

BY

H. C. PETERSON

☆ ☆
☆

University of Oklahoma Press
NORMAN · 1939

First Printing, April 25, 1939

Second Printing, June 15, 1939

Third Printing, September 25, 1939

Fourth Printing, October 28, 1939

TO EDITH AND ROY

PREFACE

THE enduring effects of the enlistment of American sympathies during the World War are demonstrated more clearly each year. Emotion instead of reason continually governs our thinking in relation to foreign affairs. Incidents which are distressing enough without exaggeration continue to be interpreted almost hysterically. Concepts which grew out of the wartime propaganda are still being accepted even though they are fundamentally inaccurate. As a result the United States seems to have become a partisan to all the world's troubles.

In the light of these circumstances it seems more than desirable that Americans candidly reconsider the origins of their thinking about the recent World War and that in the light of this re-evaluation they develop a cooler approach to disturbing events and individuals in other parts of the world. Surely before American leaders pursue a course which will lead to tragedy for millions of Americans and privation for other millions, they should be certain that they are not being dazzled by the brilliance of their own platitudes, that they are not mistaken as to the causes of international difficulties, and that they suffer no illusions as to what can be achieved by American intervention.

The attempt has been made in the following pages to trace the development of British influences in the United States in the years of neutrality. The British propaganda organizations, their theories and practices, are treated in their relation to public opinion in the United States. In addition consideration is given to the various economic influences — influences which were propaganda of the highest order. Finally the results of the propaganda are considered. The last year of the period is treated separately because of the change in situation and because of the rather definite change in attitude of President Wilson.

The limiting of this study to the propaganda of one nation tends in itself to show that nation's enemies in a more favorable light than they deserve to be shown. It must be remembered that German propaganda arguments, or the propaganda arguments of any nation in wartime, will not stand a very critical examination. A thorough consideration of the enemy propaganda is not included here because of the lack of space, because it has been treated rather extensively elsewhere, and because it is not as important as that of the British. After all, it was the British who succeeded and it was their arguments which became the American arguments.

It is impossible to express appreciation to all who have assisted in the preparation of this study. However, thanks must be extended to the librarians in the manuscript division of the Library of Congress, the Hoover War Library, the Clark University Library, the British Museum, and the British Imperial War Museum. I am also deeply indebted to Miss Mildred Ann Cooper, Miss Euphanelle Hendrix, and above all, to Miss Mary Alice Larson for their loyal assistance in the preparation of the manuscript. For advice, criticism, and encouragement I am more than grateful to Dr. W. H. Cooke, Dr. Russell M. Story, Dr. J. P. Bretz, and several others. To those who have given me access to manuscripts — one or two of which are quoted but, of necessity, not cited — I am deeply appreciative. The errors, omissions, and opinions are exclusively those of the author.

H. C. PETERSON

TABLE OF CONTENTS

Preface   vii

PART I. FROM THE OUTBREAK OF THE
WAR TO THE *SUSSEX* CRISIS

     I. Introduction   3

    II. British Propaganda Organizations   12

   III. British Propaganda   33

   IV. The Propaganda of Economics   71

    V. The *Lusitania*   109

   VI. German Propaganda and Sabotage;
More Grist for the Propaganda Mill   134

  VII. Reactions: American Newspapers   159

 VIII. Reactions: American People   169

   IX. Reactions: The Administration   180

    X. Who Kept Us Out of War?   210

PART II. THE LAST YEAR OF PEACE

   XI. Propaganda of the Last Year of Neutrality   229

  XII. Pressure of Economics in the
Last Year of Neutrality   248

 XIII. The Election of 1916   273

 XIV. The Race between a Negotiated Peace
and Unrestricted Submarine Warfare   283

  XV. Decision for War   306

 XVI. Conclusion   326

Appendices   333

Bibliography   345

Index   355

LIST OF ILLUSTRATIONS

Sir Gilbert Parker FACING PAGE 20

A page from the *American Press Résumé* 36

A letter from Sir Gilbert Parker 52

Sir Edward Grey 84

Armed Ship Cartoon 116

Franz von Papen 148

William Randolph Hearst 164

Count von Bernstorff 212

Sir William Wiseman 244

Woodrow Wilson and Colonel E. M. House 292

Captain Guy Gaunt 308

PART I ☆ FROM THE OUTBREAK OF THE WAR TO THE *SUSSEX* CRISIS

"Then when the working folk collected from the country, they did not perceive that they themselves were being bought and sold. But since they were without the food they loved, they sat looking at those who spoke. These fellows, well-knowing that the poor people were sick and lacked grain, pitchforked the goddess Peace out with their cries, although she often appeared because of her love for the country. And they shook down your rich and wealthy allies, laying accusations against them, saying 'This fellow has pro-Brasidas leanings.' Then you people would tear him to pieces like a pack of hounds. For the city, sitting ill and fearful, greedily ate up any slander anyone offered to her. . . . and without your perceiving it, Greece was left desolate and ruined." — ARISTOPHANES.

CHAPTER I ☆ INTRODUCTION

IN the history of the American people there are few scenes more striking or more pregnant with the hopes and fears of mankind than the reading of the war message to Congress by the American President on April 2, 1917. A rainy night with cavalry patrolling Pennsylvania Avenue and with rumors of bombings, it was exciting in itself. To Europeans it was the culmination of a race between the defeat of the Allies and American participation in the war. To Americans it was an assertion of rights and the participation in a fight which they would have preferred to have left alone. In addition, this scene represented the appearance of a leader in a struggle that had been devoid of leadership. The United States produced at the right moment "a man, who like Washington or Lincoln, easily dominated a colossal situation as spokesman of the highest ideals, whilst British and French [and German] demagogues could not rise above the rhetoric of the prize ring. . ."[1]

The decision of April 2 was of especial importance to the British; it was only natural that they should have hoped for it and have done all in their power to bring it about. Winston Churchill, in discussing the secret treaties of 1915, said: "Locked in the deadly struggle with the danger of Russian collapse staring them in the face, and with their very existence at stake neither Britain nor France was inclined to be particular about the price that they would pay [from their enemy's pocket] for the accession to the alliance of a new first class power."[2] By 1917 they were even less particular, for the need was greater than ever before. It is true that vast supplies of money and war materials were being obtained from America and it is true that the blockade of the Central Powers was becoming effective, but military matters were not so satisfactory. The Allies won battles, but they were gener-

---

[1]George Bernard Shaw.

[2]Churchill, Winston S., *World Crisis 1915* (New York: Charles Scribner's Sons, 1923), 343. Mr. Churchill was referring specifically to Italy. See also Seymour, Charles, *The Intimate Papers of Colonel House,* II (Boston: Houghton Mifflin Co., 1926), 133. Hereafter referred to as *Intimate Papers.*

ally of a negative character. They "stopped" the Germans at the Marne, they "did not let them pass" at Verdun, they "prevented" the German fleet from coming out again after Jutland. To offset these limited gains, however, the Allies saw the Germans win very tangible victories. In 1915 Russia was knocked down, Serbia was knocked out, and Great Britain was ignominiously defeated at the Dardanelles. In 1916 France was bled white at Verdun, Russia's armies were decimated, and Roumania was overrun. In 1917 Russia dropped out of the war, Italy suffered an overwhelming defeat at Caporetto, there were mutinies in the French army, and England was within six weeks of starvation.[3] The accession of a new first class power to the alliance was absolutely imperative.

The British campaign to induce the United States to come to their assistance affected every phase of American life; it was propaganda in its broadest meaning. News, money, and political pressure each played its part and the battle itself was fought not only in London, New York, and Washington, D. C., but also in American classrooms and pulpits, factories, and offices. It was a campaign to create a pro-British attitude of mind among Americans, to get American sympathies and interests so deeply involved in the European war that it would be impossible for this country to remain neutral.

The first problem confronting the directors of any such campaign was that of winning the sympathy of the general public. When Lord Northcliffe visited this country he remarked of Americans: "They dress alike, they talk alike, they think alike. What sheep!" Although he was not entirely correct, he was right in that the American public, like any public, demands uniformity of thought and conformity of action.[4] In so far as Americans were sheep they had to be reached through their emotions. Although every public thinks with its hopes, its fears, and its affections, the pre-war American public was especially sentimental, excessively turbulent in comparison with European, and finally, was subject to waves of emotion, apathy, interest, and boredom. The work of the British propagandist was to harness these feelings and put them to work for the Allies.

[3]Cruttwell, C. R. M. F., *A History of the Great War, 1914-1918* (Oxford, 1936), 384.

[4]Pareto, Vilfredo, *The Mind and Society* (New York, 1935), II, 664.

The British propaganda campaign naturally had to be based upon ideas Americans already had concerning the belligerent nations. In the first place it was soon found that people in the United States had but slight interest in countries other than those in Western Europe. Any "educational" efforts had to turn upon those lands west of the Vistula and north of the Danube. Among these, Germany was held in high esteem, but, fortunately for the Allies, this esteem had been diminished by certain actions of the German government after 1870. By the turn of the century, in some quarters, this had developed into positive dislike. The visit of Prince Henry, the Kaiser's brother, in 1902, occasioned somewhat of an outburst against Germany, but "it is interesting to note that the papers most vigorously assailing the Prince were often those of undisguised British sympathies."[5] France was neither liked nor disliked. Her underdog position and the fact that she had assisted this country during the Revolutionary War created some sympathy but, to the average churchgoer, the French seemed a trifle wicked. Belgium was practically unknown, which was an advantage. England, up to 1914, had been the most popular enemy of Americans. People in the United States enjoyed disliking her, but it was the dislike of first cousins. The distinct advantage, in so far as Anglo-American relations were involved, was that Americans thought they and the English were members of the same cultural scheme. The language factor here played a tremendously important part.[6] Among many elements in the country there existed a tendency to be very friendly toward England, and even among those who disliked the British there was to be found a feeling of respect for "our English cousins."[7]

[5]Schieber, C. E., "The Transformation of American Sentiment Towards Germany, 1870-1914," *The Journal of International Relations,* XII (July, 1921), No. 1, 72.

[6]"Americans unconsciously borrow their thoughts and ideas from England, because it is the only nation whose literature and Press are accessible to them in the original tongue. . . . Before the outbreak of the Five Years War, the majority of Americans already looked upon the Germans, however unconsciously, through the optics of the English Press and English literary publications." Count von Bernstorff, *My Three Years in America* (New York: Charles Scribner's Sons, 1920), 18.

[7]Count Keyserling has said: "Whenever I meet one of the representatives of this people I am shocked by the contrast between the dearth of their talents, the limitation of their horizon and the measure of recognition which every one of them exacts from me, as from everybody else."

The problem of gaining the sympathy and support of the American public turned upon the attitude of American newspapers. Here the British were greatly assisted by pre-war relations between the American press and the press of Great Britain. "For years the American public had received its day-by-day picture of Europe through a distinctly British perspective. Few American newspapers at that time maintained European staffs of their own; while those which did found few trained American foreign correspondents to man them. There were one or two capable American newspapermen in Berlin, but there were probably none at all in St. Petersburg, while even the Paris correspondents concentrated mainly upon social and artistic news rather than political reporting. Both our newspapers and press associations tended to cover European politics from London. Their London bureaus had general supervision over the correspondents on the Continent; the news was largely assembled in the London bureaus and forwarded by them. It was often heavily filled out with information or 'background' material derived from the British newspapers and magazines simply because they had so much better sources than the American staffs. . . . The New York *Times,* which perhaps gave more serious attention to European events than any other American newspaper, had an Englishman, Mr. Ernest Marshall, as the head of its London bureau, and his subordinates were largely Britishers. Its Berlin correspondent, Mr. Frederick William Wile, was an American, but the *Times* shared him with Northcliffe's *Daily Mail,* a leader in the anti-German propaganda in England. The New York *World's* London correspondent was an Irishman who had never worked in the United States; his staff, like Mr. Marshall's, was largely composed of British newspapermen. So was that of the *Sun.* Those correspondents who were American citizens, moreover, had often lived so long abroad as to absorb the British viewpoint. The dean of the American correspondents in London, Mr. Edward Price Bell of the Chicago *Daily News,* had arrived fresh from college, to remain there for the rest of his active life, and it was naturally impossible for the others not to reflect the atmosphere by which they were daily surrounded."[8] The result was "that the American view of Europe

[8]Millis, Walter, *Road to War, America 1914-1917* (Boston, 1935), 43 f. There is no reason to suspect that the British made any attempt to bribe American papers

was normally and unavoidably colored very deeply by the British attitude."

The problem of the press within the United States was much more complicated and much more important. American newspapers in the first two decades of the century were the dominant factor in controlling opinion. They comprised the sole reading material for ninety per cent of the American people. German propagandists informed their home office that "everything must be communicated to the American public in the form of 'news' as they have been accustomed to this, and only understand this kind of propaganda."[9] Propagandists probably also realized that the American newspapers deal only incidentally with news — that their principal commodity is sensation. In case of a foreign war, the support of the press would tend to go to the side which provided the best sensations. This, of course, meant that newspapers were very undependable. Like the public, the American press is a volatile force.[10]

Another, and in many ways the most important, factor to be considered was that American newspapers are primarily commercial undertakings. They exist largely for profits and they maintain policies friendly to the economic interests of the locality or the nation over and above any other interest. To secure or maintain a standing in the world of American newspapers requires a great deal of money. A metropolitan daily might be worth from five to twenty-five million dollars. A small town newspaper might be worth from five to twenty-five thousand dollars. Whether the amount be in the thousands or in the millions, it is put forward by people of wealth. Consequently, newspapers do not express

---

with money. In the United States such a course would have been futile and dangerous. Of course in such places as France or Italy where newspapers are notoriously venal, it may have been done. British propaganda headquarters reported the rumor in 1916 that the French had sent eighteen million francs to Roumania to buy up the press. Great Britain, *Daily Review of the Foreign Press Confidential Supplement,* April 19, 1916. Hereafter referred to as D. R. F. P. If a supplement is cited, it is so indicated.

[9]Great Britain, Foreign Office, *American Press Résumé,* September 10, 1915, *Supplement.* Hereafter referred to as *A. P. R.*

[10]The British propaganda bureau warned the British cabinet to beware "the danger of interpreting American opinion by the American press without making allowances for the characteristic volatility of both." *A. P. R.,* July, 18, 1917.

the opinions or ideas of their editors or reporters, but the opinions of those who control the purse strings. The independence of the newspaper writer is a fiction. These men must satisfy the publisher and the publisher must satisfy the owners of the stocks. When the stockholders do not force policies upon the newspapers, there is pressure, expressed and unexpressed, of the advertisers to direct the paper's attitude.[11] Newspapers appear to speak for the people; actually their policies are in large measure directed by dominant economic interests. "The voice is Jacob's voice, but the hands are the hands of Esau."

Finally, it should be borne in mind that the press bureaus and the great Eastern dailies exert a disproportionate influence on the American press as a whole. During the war years there were about twenty-five hundred daily papers in the United States. About a thousand of these were affiliated with the Associated Press and most of the rest were connected with the United Press or one of the other press organizations — all of which were dominated by prominent New York editors. The foreign news which came through these bureaus was primarily composed for the New York newspapers, so, in the last analysis, the control of the New York press practically meant the control of the entire American press.

The immediate problem for the British propagandists at the outset of the war was to obtain the support of the leaders of American life. In this regard they were very fortunate. The American aristocracy was distinctly Anglophile. To assume a pro-British attitude was the "thing to do" among cultured Americans. "Politicians might placate an Irish constituency or stir our bumptious nationalism with a little tail-twisting now and then; but those more cultivated elements which dominated our intellectual, political and financial life still found in London their unacknowledged capital."[12] This was accentuated by the fact that the economic aristocracy did most of its foreign business through London. Nearly all foreign banking was handled through the English capital. One of the Morgan partners stated: "Like most of our contemporaries and friends and neighbors, we wanted the Allies to

---

[11]See the magazine *Time,* August 26, 1925, on the Public Utility Bill.
[12]Millis, *op. cit.,* 41.

win the war from the outset. We were pro-Ally by inheritance, by instinct, by opinion."[13]

The intellectual leaders of the United States were also sympathetic toward England, largely as a result of the similarity of language and the fact that England was the one foreign country with which most of them were acquainted. College professors, ministers, and above all, public school teachers, saw in England all that they thought was missing from America; consequently they lavished upon her a great deal of affection.[14]

The problem of winning the support of the political leaders of the United States appeared to be even less difficult than that of gaining the adherence of the economic, social, and intellectual leaders. Primarily politicians are reflectors of opinion, and the opinions they reflect are usually those given in the press. In the case of President Wilson it was somewhat different, but even here the British had little to worry about.

Woodrow Wilson was of Scotch-Irish descent, the son of a minister. He was reared in the South during the period of reconstruction, and consequently the evils, the hatreds, the fruits of war, were not lost upon his impressionable mind. Out of this background and heritage, Wilson developed into something of a preacher, an idealogue — and a crusader. When he became head of Princeton University, this crusading spirit made him fiercely attack the aristocratic attitude in that once humble and democratic institution. Defeated here, he became Governor of New Jersey where he attacked political evils. As a result of the great opposition he aroused in the governorship, and for other reasons, he was "kicked upstairs" to become the Democratic presidential candidate. Then came another turn of fate — the Republican Party split — and the Democratic candidate, the crusader, became President.

As an individual Wilson was one of the most admirable men ever to be President of the United States. He was thoroughly honest, he was governed by a strong sense of right and wrong, and he was not unintelligent. But in addition, he was a sensitive

[13]*Time,* January 20, 1936, 36.
[14]See Sullivan, Mark, *Our Times,* V (New York, 1933), 73, for the effect of American schooling on our international sympathies.

person, peculiarly intense, and very stubborn, which qualities made him especially susceptible to idealistic propaganda. He also had a tendency to claim a divine justification for his own opinions and actions. "He was able, as are all very religious men, to attribute unto God the things that are Caesar's."[15] One Englishman called him the "theocrat of the White House." The most vulnerable point in Wilson's makeup was his tendency to go to extremes. He was constantly attempting to obtain more than came within the realm of possibility. At Princeton this created trouble for the college: at Washington it created trouble for the United States; at Paris it created trouble for the world.

A confusing thing about President Wilson is the fact that he was an aristocratic liberal. Since he lived on the fringe of the East's high society, his instincts were all on the side of the upper classes. Superimposed on this conservatism was a limited number of advanced western ideas. The combination of progressivism, conservatism, and idealism resulted in a most peculiar phenomenon. Neither the eastern conservatives nor the western liberals trusted him completely. Lord Bryce asked one correspondent, "I wonder what you think of W. W. Even in the United States people seem puzzled." Henry Watterson wrote: "Nobody knows just what Wilson will do or where he will land. He is a queer fish, has no close friends, and disdains counsel. His Cabinet is a lot of errand boys."[16]

Although the British reflected this feeling of uncertainty regarding the American President, they need have had no alarm. Wilson's background was all pro-British. Nearly all of his political ideas were of English origin, and his first and only important book was written with one eye on the British government. His sympathy was gained long before that of the public. In addition, the British could be sure that any propaganda effective with the American public would be effective with Wilson. At the White House a very elaborate system of sifting editorials was carried on in order to keep track of "movements of opinion" and the Lansing papers reveal that articles and editorials from papers throughout the country were referred to the Department of State

[15]Nicolson, Harold, *Peacemaking 1919* (Boston and New York, 1933), 53.
[16]Henry Watterson Papers, January 3, 1915.

by Wilson's secretary, Tumulty.[17] If British propagandists could reach the American press, they could reach the American President.

From almost every point of view the British had the advantage in attempting to win American sympathy. It was only in transmuting the sympathy into positive action that their problem became difficult.

[17]Lawrence, David, *The True Story of Woodrow Wilson* (New York, 1924), 195 ff. In 1919 Wilson mentioned how anxiously he watched "movements of opinion in this country during the months immediately preceding our entrance into the War." (September 20, 1919, at Los Angeles.)

CHAPTER II ☆ BRITISH PROPAGANDA AGENCIES AND ORGANIZATIONS

THE agencies and organizations by means of which the British influenced the thinking of the American people were many and varied. Some, such as censorship and intelligence groups, were formally organized, but many of the most effective agencies were independent and connected with no responsible propaganda department. It would be impossible to list all the groups which spread British ideas about the war because, in the last analysis, all people who had been propagandized were doing this work. However, it is possible to deal with the major sections, or units, which were fighting the war of words.

The first propaganda organization to be set in motion was that of censorship. On August 5, 1914, the British cut the cables between Germany and the United States.[1] No other means of rapid communication existed between these two nations, and as a result, the most effective instrument of propaganda, the news, was suppressed at the most crucial time in the history of the war — the time when first impressions were being made, when opinions were being established. Even after the inauguration of trans-Atlantic wireless, late in 1914, with its limited facilities for the transmission of news, German dispatches were slower than the British so that even the later, less important British interpretations of events became the accepted versions in America.

In November, 1917, an official of the State Department wrote to President Wilson advocating a censorship of the American press. His principal argument was that "the *first publication* is that which is *formative of public opinion* and which affects public emotion."[2] By controlling these first impressions all the opponent could do was to "retrieve part of the unfortunate effect" created by the original publication, and, in words of one British prop-

[1]Wireless censorship went into effect on August 1, 1914. Brownrigg, Sir Douglas, *Indiscretions of the Naval Censor* (London, 1920), 9. There are reasons for believing that cable messages were censored on August 1.
[2]Breckinridge Long Papers, Library of Congress.

aganda agent, "no contradiction, no retraction, can quite overcome the harm of the first printing."[3]

The cutting of the cables between the United States and
Germany was the first act of censorship and the first act of propaganda. These Siamese twins of public opinion were from that
time to dictate what the American people were to think. The
second move in the same endeavor was the censorship of the press
of England. This was done under the Defense of the Realm Act,
the famous DORA, which gave control over "all statements intended or likely to prejudice His Majesty's relations with foreign
powers." The year before the war there had been formed a Joint
Consultative Committee of Admiralty, War Office, and Press for
the purpose of planning censorship. This Press Censorship Committee was replaced in August, 1916, by the Press Bureau with
its duty to "supervise, largely on a voluntary basis, issue of news
to and by the press."[4] Sir John Simon, the Home Secretary, was
responsible to the Cabinet, while in direct charge was F. E. Smith,
the later Lord Birkenhead. He was replaced on September 3,
1914, by Stanley Buckmaster.[5] It must be remembered, of course,
that in addition to this committee, nearly every department of the
British government maintained its own separate intelligence and
censorship bureau.

As a matter of fact, the Press Bureau "was only a shield and
recording angel for the naval and military censors who acted
under direct instructions from the Admiralty and War Office."[6]
As one Englishman remarked, it was "the imaginative department, the body which dresses up the facts for presentment to the
public, a most important function and one leaving scope for in-

[3]*A. P. R.,* February 25, 1916.

[4]Dearle, N. B., *Dictionary of Official War-Time Organizations* (London,
1928), 310.

[5]Buckmaster was replaced by Sir Frank Swettenham, who, in turn, was replaced by Sir Edward Cook.

Because of the leaks of news during the war of 1870 the French were more
strict than other nations. It was more of a prohibition than it was a censorship.

At the outset of the war the French, at the urging of Viviani, appropriated
twenty-five million gold francs for "la Bureau de la presse" which controlled the
news. Under this group was a "syndicat des journalistes" which was an "association de defense et de discipline professionelle." De Chambure, A., *Quelques guides
de l'opinion en France pendant la grande guerre 1914-1918* (Paris, 1918), xv.

[6]*Lord Riddell's War Diary 1914-1918* (London, 1933), 116.

dividual imagination."[7] This censorship bureau in Great Britain must be considered a determining factor in controlling American opinion, because the news which it passed was the version which the American press released.

With their German source of information cut off, American newspapers had to secure their war news where it was available — and that was from England. The only way they could get even partially complete European news was to buy the advance sheets of London newspapers. Otherwise they were limited to official communiqués from the British or French governments. News obtained from other European countries also had to be filtered through the British censorship, so it can be seen that it was truly the British news that became American news.[8] The American correspondents in Europe did attempt to send unbiased news to their papers. They struggled against the restrictions imposed upon them by the British, but to no avail — they were helpless victims of circumstance. "Schreiner of the Associated Press estimated that at this time [1915] nearly three-quarters of the dispatches written by American correspondents in Central Europe were perishing under the shears of the British censors."[9]

The censorship of mail, similar to censorship of press and cable, served to control information passing between Europe and America. It also served as a source of information for the propagandists. The British mail censorship started on August 29, 1914, with fourteen persons on the original staff. By Easter of 1916 it had a force of approximately two thousand. Early in 1917 there were thirty-seven hundred persons in London alone censoring mail, and fifteen hundred in Liverpool.[10] Colonel G. S. H. Pearson was Chief Postal Censor from 1914 to 1918. The main office of this group was in Salisbury House in London but most of its work was done at the Liverpool branch. There were also censors at Gibralter, Alexandria, and Folkestone. In each case

[7]As quoted by Squires, James D., *British Propaganda at Home and in the United States From 1914-1917* (Cambridge: Harvard University Press, 1935), 35.

[8]"From September the New York *Times, Tribune* and *World* (and other papers) regularly bought the advance proofs of the London *Chronicle, Morning Post,* and *Daily Telegraph,* using the material in their own news columns and syndicating it throughout the United States." Millis, *op. cit.,* 63.

[9]*Ibid.,* 147.

[10]Wanderscheck, Hermann, *Weltkrieg und Propaganda* (Berlin, 1936), 70.

the censorship bureau consisted of a military and naval room, a cable department, and an issuing department. This last had charge of information to be turned over to the press.

Utilizing this censorship with great intelligence, the British were able to keep tab on all their enemies and the friends of their enemies. The censor summarized all information of interest which his organization intercepted and sent his reports to the departments which would be interested in the particular intelligence. It can readily be seen that such a source of information would be invaluable for every phase of propaganda work. It is also apparent that the elimination of information would cripple enemy propaganda. Occasionally the *Confidential Supplement* of the *Daily Review of the Foreign Press* would include information taken from "intercepted letters."[11]

One British measure of immense importance to the propagandists, indirectly connected with censorship, was the interception of wireless messages to and from Germany. Eventually the staff taking care of this work grew to about fifty "and as many as 2,000 intercepted messages were often received and dealt with in 24 hours." "In 1916 the Germans contracted a habit of changing the key of the principal Naval Signal Book every night at 12 o'clock, but the deciphering staff of Room 40 had by that time become so expert that the changes caused the night watch no serious embarrassment."[12] The work was done by the Naval Intelligence Department under Admiral Sir William Reginald Hall; the man in direct charge was Sir Alfred Ewing. The intelligence intercepted in this way was invaluable to propagandists as well as to statesmen and enabled the British government to anticipate many of the moves of her enemies.

The foregoing censorship controls could be called negative propaganda; they made it possible for the positive propaganda

[11]Note the report in the *American Press Résumé* of December 23, 1916, under the heading "Correspondent in Germany" in which a Chicago *Daily News* reporter has his private correspondence quoted to the British Cabinet and to British propagandists. At one time the censor revealed that someone in the United States had been opening private mail before it reached him. He stated "other cases have also been observed of letters having been tampered with before reaching the censorship," i.e., the mail was tampered with before he had a chance to tamper with it. *D. R. F. P., Confidential Supplement,* June 12, 1916.

[12]*The Times,* London, August 1, 1935.

to achieve a more complete victory. In fact, it is difficult to see
how the propagandists could have operated without the censor.

In September, 1914, Charles Masterman was authorized by
the British Foreign Office to form a War Propaganda Bureau.[13]
Installed in Wellington House, the office of an insurance firm, it
began to issue the propaganda which was soon to flood the United
States.[14] Developing by leaps and bounds, it became the principal
outlet for books, pamphlets, and other instruments of British
propaganda. Each branch of the work was controlled by a separate department under the direction of some individual of considerable prominence. Mr. Eric Maclagan was in charge of
propaganda for France; Mr. William Archer directed the department for the Scandinavian countries; while Sir Gilbert
Parker supervised the one which took care of propaganda for
the United States — the American Ministry of Information.
Parker had as his assistants Professor Macneile Dixon of Glas-
gow University, Mr. A. J. Toynbee of Balliol College, and others.
Starting out with nine men, by 1917 he had fifty-four.

"The mailing list of Wellington House (as a whole), being
carefully compiled was expanded till it contained 260,000 names
of influential persons throughout the Union."[15] Sir Gilbert Parker's list was made after consulting the American *Who's Who*.
From this compilation he made separate groupings of prominent
Americans, according to their profession, supposed intelligence,
or standing in the community.[16]

[13]Squires, *op cit.*, 26. In France the "Bureau de la presse" or "maison de la
presse" headed the various bureaus for the issuance of propaganda, such as chambers of commerce, travel offices (a favorite of the British), and other special
agencies. Vic, Jean, *La littérature de guerre* (Paris, 1923), 687 ff.

M. Ponsot was the first head of the "Bureau," followed by M. Berthelot,
while a M. Fournal ran the "services de propagande." The heads of various
agencies were M. Robelin of "l'union des grandes associations francaises," the
major organization after 1917, M. Chaix of "le centre d'action de propagande"
and M. Klobukowske of "le commissariat de l'information." Bornecqui, Henri
and Drouilly, J. Germain, *La France et la guerre — formation de l'opinion publique pendant la guerre* (Paris, 1921), 9.

The English maintained a daily two-hour telephone service with the French
propaganda headquarters. Wanderscheck, *op. cit.*, 29.

[14]Under Masterman was Sir Claude Schuster and later Sir Ernest Gowers.

[15]Sprott, Mary Esther, "A Survey of British War-Time Propaganda in America Issued from Wellington House," Master's Thesis, Stanford, 1921.

[16]Squires, *op. cit.*, 57. Sometimes enclosure cards were sent from the British
government.

Nicholson has stated that "Wellington house was . . . concerned with the production, translation and distribution of books, pamphlets, government publications, speeches[17] and so forth dealing with the war, its origin, its history and all the varied and difficult questions which arose during its development; the production and distribution of special pictorial papers; assisting in the placing of articles and interviews designed to influence opinion in the world's newspapers and magazines, especially in America; the wide distribution of pictorial matter, cartoons, pictures and drawings, photographs for insertion in newspapers and periodicals and for exhibition; the production and distribution of cinematograph films; personal correspondence with influential people abroad, especially in America; arrangements for the interchange of visits, of personal tours to neutral and allied countries and of visits of distinguished neutrals and of representatives of the Allies to this country; the production and distribution of maps, diagrams, posters, lantern slides and lectures, pictures, postcards, and all other possible means of miscellaneous propaganda."[18]

Sir Gilbert Parker has remarked that "besides our private correspondence with individuals we had our literature sent to a great number of public libraries, Y. M. C. A. societies, universities, colleges, clubs, and newspapers."[19]

Among the authors who wrote for Wellington House were many distinguished people, such as James M. Beck, William Archer, James Bryce, G. K. Chesterton, Conan Doyle, Sir Edward Cook, J. W. Headlam, Cardinal Mercier, E. J. Trevelyan, A. Maurice Low, Mrs. Humphrey Ward,[20] Alfred Noyes, Hilaire

[17]"The Allied propaganda, moreover, enjoyed the inestimable advantage of being self-financing. Our public clamored for the books, articles and motion picture films which conveyed it. Old established American publishing houses found it profitable, and did not think it so unpatriotic, to enter into agreements with the Entente governments for the distribution of propagandist war books, and there was a huge trade in volumes on French life from the French and British standpoint. Those who voiced the German side of the case found no such markets." Millis, *op. cit.*, 202.

[18]Nicholson, Ivor, "An Aspect of British Official War-time Propaganda," *Cornhill Magazine,* May, 1931, 594.

[19]From the material found in the Hoover War Library, it appears that Masterman's organization issued 45 publications in 1914, 132 in 1915, 202 in 1916, and 469 in 1917.

[20]Mrs. Ward, a British authoress, was thought to be very influential with

Belloc, and J. M. Robertson.[21] The naval censor tells of calling on Joseph Conrad, Rudyard Kipling, Alfred Noyes, and many others to popularize the British cause, and in one way or another they all responded.[22]

The operations of Wellington House were kept amazingly secret from Englishmen as well as Americans. When the Prime Minister was asked about the activities of Mr. Masterman, he replied that the latter was "continuing certain work which he was requested by the Government to undertake at the beginning of the war. The work is of a highly confidential nature, and much of its efficiency depends upon its being conducted in secret. . . ." Even many officials in the English government did not realize that there was such a thing as British propaganda.[23]

Although most of the formal propaganda came from Wellington House, there was a large amount produced by scores of unofficial or voluntary groups and organizations. One list of them is as follows:[24] (1) The faculty of the Oxford University issued the

---

Americans. Theodore Roosevelt advised the British to secure her support by being kind to her. They did.

[21]In the last year of neutrality, this appeal of big names was utilized in a series of interviews given to the American press at the instigation of Wellington House. The names on their list included Lord Runciman, Lord Robert Cecil, Bonar Law, Lord Cromer, Mrs. Humphrey Ward, and Mr. Archibald Hurd. Americans placed on this list by the British propagandists included George Burton Adams, Frederick Palmer, and of course, James M. Beck.

[22]Practically every well known writer in France was engaged in propaganda of one sort or another. It is interesting to note the group of professors from the University of Paris who were officially engaged in this work. Among these were Bedier, Lavisse, Aulard, Andler, Durkheim, Seailler, Ferrero (an Italian), Ribot, Rageot, Bougle, Camille Jullian, Barthou, and others. Early in the war the Germans mobilized their professors and issued a statement of the German "intellectuals." An American propagandist, who was also a college professor, said he was "profoundly humiliated" by this degradation of his profession. One wonders what his thoughts were on seeing the works of the French scholars or the later statement of the British "intellectuals" or even the writings of some American professors, not excluding himself.

[23]Squires, op. cit., 48 ff. "In order more thoroughly to appreciate the British activities all matters of definition should be cleared up. What is propaganda? It is the statement of a case in such a way that others may be influenced. In so far as its use against any enemy is concerned, the subject matter employed must not be self-evidently propagandist. Except in special circumstances its origin should be completely concealed." Stuart, Sir Campbell, Secrets of Crewe House (London, 1921), 2.

[24]Squires, op. cit., 17. See Wanderscheck, op. cit., 26.

Oxford pamphlets "often distinguished by authentic information." In "the majority of cases the authors were able to give a patriotic bias to the apparently objective presentation of material;"[25] (2) The Parliamentary Recruiting Committee; (3) The Cobden Club; (4) A nameless group of Anglican clerics; (5) The Council of Loyal British Subjects of British, Austrian, or Hungarian birth; (6) The United Workers; (7) The Atlantic Union; (8) The Victoria League; (9) The Union of Democratic Control;[26] (10) The Central Committee for National Patriotic Organizations.

This last organization was a good example of the volunteer propaganda groups. It was located at 8 Carlton House Terrace, London, and was established by G. W. Prothero and Harry Curl. It started work in August, 1914, was formally organized November 21, 1914, and soon had voluntary local organizations in England with sub-committees to take care of propaganda in other parts of the British Empire and throughout the world. Its report states: "The supply of literature and information to the United States of America was early in the war transferred, for special and imperative reasons, to a separate committee." It had affiliated societies in all neutral countries. In the words of their report, "other channels . . . have been the numberless national and international societies, associations, leagues, unions, and alliances . . . public reading rooms, social clubs, workingmen's clubs, officers' messes, seamen's institutes, hotels and casinos." British chambers of commerce were used as distributing centers. Students from neutral countries and British nationals abroad were exploited in the same manner.[27] They had two hundred and fifty speakers who had, by 1916, conducted fifteen thousand meetings. They distributed eight hundred and fifty thousand leaflets to school children[28] and nine hundred thousand to industrial dis-

[25]A complete list of eighty-seven titles is given in G. W. Prothero, *Select Analytical List of Books Concerning the Great War* (London, 1923). Squires has a brief comment on the publications of each of these groups.

[26]"The publications of the Union of Democratic Control and of its affiliate, the National Labor Press, indicate on very many questions it was possible even during war-time to write with discernment and a fair approximation of present-day verdicts." Squires, *op. cit.,* 17 ff.

[27]*Report of the Central Committee for National Patriotic Organizations* (London, 1916), 18 ff. The 1916 report was the only one issued to the public.

[28]Wellington House also issued propaganda for children.

tricts through libraries. They sent two hundred and fifty thous-
and pamphlets, booklets, and other publications to the neutral
world.

Perhaps the most interesting procedure of this particular
organization was its system of exploiting the friendships and business connections of leading Britishers. It obtained lists of important Americans who had dealings with people in England and
sent propaganda to them. The Americans naturally thought the
material was from their friends in England. The Committee's
report states that by "this means very many important commu-
nities — philosophical, educational, religious, scientific, philanthropic, artistic, legal, medical, commercial, industrial, mining,
agricultural, engineering, banking, athletic, etc. . . . have been
reached."[29]

The foregoing central propaganda groups directed their work
from England. This was practicable because of English control
of the seas. Such control eliminated the necessity for subordinate
offices outside Great Britain. Wellington House, of course, could
not take the risk of operating a propaganda bureau within the
United States. Sir Gilbert Parker, in charge of this work, had to
operate from Europe. Agents were sent to this country as well as
to other countries, but only on special assignments.[30] Mr. Kenneth Durant was perhaps Parker's best American helper, although he states he was not in Parker's employ. The *American
Press Résumé* constantly referred to him as "our valued and
careful correspondent."[31] There were, of course, many other

[29] *Report of the Central Committee, op. cit.,* 18.

[30] As far as is known, the Russian and Italian governments carried on no
propaganda in the United States. If they made any efforts, there is no proof of
their success. It is known that the Czech revolutionary organization accomplished
a great deal under the leadership of Masaryk, but this group was financed by
Great Britain and should be classified as British. The French spent at least a part
of the millions they appropriated in 1914 and 1916 for propaganda in this country.
Who did this work or how it was done remains untold. The Belgians were rather
effective, and in all probability, more credit should be given to them for the growth
of war feeling in the United States. One of their propagandists in the United
States, Lalla Vandervelde, was offered a position as propagandist in South America, which would seem to imply that there was something in the nature of an
organization in the United States. Vandervelde, Lalla, *Monarchs and Millionaires*
(London, 1925), 50 ff.

[31] *A. P. R.,* July 8, 1915, *et seq.* See also Viereck, G. S., *Spreading Germs of
Hate* (New York: Liveright Publishing Corporation, 1930), 130.

SIR GILBERT PARKER

"correspondents." The *American Press Résumé* of April 7, 1916, stated: "Sir Gilbert Parker has received the following report from Mr. John Masefield, who has lately finished a lecturing tour in the United States." Masefield wrote: "I have the honor to present to you my report of things noticed during my stay in the United States between the 13th of January and the 18th of March."

Von Papen, the German military attaché in Washington, has asserted that on August 23, 1914, there was a conference which took place in the offices of J. P. Morgan "in which the British propaganda service adopted a definite policy in the matter of coloring the American press, and whereon it was determined to appoint English editorial writers on forty American newspapers."[32] There is no evidence confirming this statement, and von Papen was probably wrong. But there is every indication that the Morgan firm did engage in propaganda work in connection with the floating of loans.[33] One cablegram sent to London referred to the "usual idiocy of newspapermen" stating "it might take some little time to set the stage and prepare properly" for a loan.[34]

A certain conversation recorded by the French historian, M. Gabriel Hanotaux, provokes considerable curiosity. In this interview a former Morgan partner, Mr. Robert Bacon, remarked: "In America . . . there are 50,000 people who understand the necessity of the United States entering the war immediately on your side. But there are 100,000,000 Americans who have not even thought of it. Our task is to see that the figures are reversed and that the 50,000 become the 100,000,000. We will accomplish this."[35] It would be very interesting to know just what he did to fulfill his promise.

Even if the Morgan firm did not attempt to influence public opinion, its retention by the British government as its agent was

[32]Carnegie Endowment for International Peace, *Official German Documents Relating to the World War,* II (New York, 1923), 1313.

[33]Mr. Lamont has stated that the Morgan firm and the Morgan partners possessed no stock in newspapers. United States Senate, *Hearings Before the Special Committee Investigating The Munitions Industry,* Seventy-fourth Congress, second session, pursuant to S. Res. 206 (73rd Congress). Government Printing Office (Washington, 1937), Part 26, 7917. Hereafter referred to as *M. I.*

[34]*M. I.,* Part 26, 7839.

[35]Hanotaux, Gabriel, *Histoire illustré de la guerre de 1914,* IX (Paris, 1919), 56.

in itself propaganda of the highest degree.[36] It would have been impossible for one of the greatest financial houses in the United States to establish such an affiliation without having an effect upon the American business world.

A vital part of the British propaganda organization was its information service. The traditional information agents, ambassadors, and consuls, naturally sent in regular reports. In addition, the Morgan firm kept British officials informed as to conditions in the United States. At one time the British Chancellor of the Exchequer requested that Mr. Davison keep him acquainted with the state of American opinion. One or two of the resulting reports were made available to the Munitions Investigation Committee.[37]

Special means of obtaining information in order to assist in the development of propaganda appeals were evolved by Sir Gilbert Parker. He "utilized the friendly service and assistance of confidential friends" to secure reports from important Americans on American opinion. In other words he secured reports on the reactions of Americans as to what propaganda was succeeding and what was not succeeding, what would probably succeed better, and what measures of repression could be safely pursued. All unfriendly statements were carefully reported and measures were taken to counteract them, or to win their authors to the cause of the Allies. In addition, long and detailed analyses of the American newspapers were made each week. In these, special attention was paid to unfriendly remarks.[38]

[36]A certain Lord Fairfax wrote to an American business man that the appointment of the Morgan firm as agent for the British government was an excellent thing "because of their being able to influence sentiment." *M. I.*, Part 26, 7853.

[37]One report of the Morgan partners is as follows: "Immediately upon my return I started inquiries in various parts of the country to ascertain present sentiment regarding attitude of people toward belligerents. Replies are without exception to effect that purely American sentiment almost unanimously pro-Ally. . . ." *M. I.*, Part 25, 7539. When quizzed concerning Mr. Davison's source of information, Mr. Morgan professed ignorance of it.

Because of their irritation with Senator Stone's opposition, Davison undoubtedly pleased the British when he cabled them: "Have information United States Senator Stone for years intimate with German Government, who now probably inspiring his activities." *M. I.*, Exhibit 2053, January 26, 1915, 7539.

[38]The chief British propagandists insisted that members of their department should keep in closest touch with things published in the neutral countries. Mitchell, P. C., *Report on the Propaganda Library*, Great Britain War Office, Sec. V. 43.

Each division of the propaganda ministry kept a separate record of events in its own field, and used select arguments in its propaganda to be distributed. The *Daily Review of the Foreign Press*[39] which was the comprehensive report of the entire ministry, contained little more than condensations of foreign news. This was probably a result of the fear that this widely circulated report might reach the public. Its *Confidential Supplement,* on the other hand, contained material intended only for information of high officials. There were also more detailed, localized reports, such as: *Summary of the British Press* (1916 to 1917); *Summary of the Provincial Press and British Papers Published Abroad* (1916 to 1917); *Summary of the Weekly Press* (September 13 to December 31 of 1916); *Report on Austrian Papers* (October 23, 1915 to April, 1916); *Report on the French Press* (June 3, 1915 to January 16, 1916); *Weekly Report on German Papers* (May 8, 1915 to December, 1916).[40]

One report, much more important than any of the above, as far as the United States was concerned, was the *American Press Résumé*. It was issued weekly or bi-weekly from April 12, 1915, to August 8, 1917. The *Résumé* was printed on blue paper, as was the *Confidential Supplement* of the *Daily Review of the Foreign Press,* and varied from six to twenty-five pages in length, with occasional supplements of equal size. Although "printed for the use of the cabinet," it was also probably distributed to a few of the more important propagandists. It was stamped "confidential" or "strictly confidential."[41] The *American Press Résumé* was prepared by Sir Gilbert Parker's American Ministry of Information, the department of Wellington House which took care of propaganda for the United States. It was apparently the central report upon which all efforts to educate American opinion were based.

The weekly analyses of opinion in the *Résumé* were of espe-

[39]Referred to in the footnotes as *D. R. F. P.*

The French issued a report on the newspapers of all countries under the name of *Bulletin Periodique de la Presse,* which was apparently compiled in the same way with the same purpose in mind.

[40]The dates given are incomplete. Undoubtedly some of these reports were continued over a longer period of time.

[41]In 1917 some of these *Résumés* were headed "Issued by the General Staff, War Office." See illustration facing p. 36.

cial importance in so far as they revealed the range and influence of propaganda within the United States. One column in the
Résumé was headed "Influencing the American Press." It varied
from week to week, but the following excerpts are typical:
"Amongst the thoroughly satisfactory articles upon the British
offensive may be mentioned Mr. Frederick Palmer's article in
Collier's Weekly"; "The *Literary Digest* published long extracts
from Dr. Taylor's report on the 'Wittenberg Camp' '"; "Articles
by the following writers have appeared: Mr. Archibald Hurd,
Alfred Noyes, Gilbert Murray, and James M. Beck"; [42] "The pro-
Ally Philadelphia *Public Ledger* writes an editorial upon the pam-
phlet 'Treasury Romances' prepared by Wellington House."[43]

Besides the weekly tabulation of American newspaper opinion, the *Résumés* contained reports of individuals in the United
States. Parker has told how he secured "reports from important
Americans," and how "by personal correspondence with influential and eminent people of every profession," he "built a backing for the British cause."[44] The *Résumés* are a detailed account
of these maneuvers, as well as an analysis of the American Press.

The letters of wide interest which Parker received were
printed in the *Résumé,* in which form they served as a guide for
the propagandists. As an example, after a particular group of
atrocity stories were favorably received, the *Résumé* of a few
weeks later revealed that efforts were made to expand this attack.
Then the *Résumé* reported that "atrocities are again widely discussed in the United States." When there was received a statement such as, "The American mind shows signs of being almost
surfeited with atrocities," the ensuing reports evidenced a change
of emphasis to the evil war aims of the Germans, or to the illegality and brutality of German naval policy. One letter commented
on the fact that the American newspapers were dissatisfied because British leaders would not give out statements to the press.

[42]*A. P. R.,* September 13, 1916.
[43]*A. P. R.,* November 8, 1916.
[44]Parker, Sir Gilbert, "The United States and the War," *Harpers Monthly
Magazine,* March, 1918, 522. Parker wrote to Americans stating: "My long and intimate association with the United States through my writings gives me confidence
to approach you, and I trust you will not think me intrusive or misunderstand my
motive." From the Hoover War Collection, dated March 6, 1916. See illustration
facing p. 52.

In succeeding issues there were reports of a veritable flood of interviews with British officials.

Just as they used natives in Africa and Asia, the British did all in their power to enlist Americans as propagandists to overcome the resistance of Americans. One distinguished English expert in this field wrote: "Better than any pumped-in propaganda abroad was [the] . . . method of making the leaders of the Imperial, neutral or Allied press themselves the propagandists when they returned home."[45] In doing this the British did not attempt bribery. Instead, the "method chosen was that of direct personal approach." Most educated Englishmen are socially delightful and in this phase of propaganda they were able to put their charm to work to good advantage. There is a compulsion in friendship which makes disagreement very distasteful and before long the British had eliminated "disagreement" from their American friends.

Sir Gilbert Parker has stated that he "advised and stimulated many people to write articles" and "asked . . . friends and correspondents to arrange for speeches, debates and lectures by American citizens." Especially did he utilize the "friendly services and assistance of confidential friends."[46] Here was the real genius of British propaganda organization. In other circles this procedure would be called a "confidence game." Eventually, as a result of the propaganda and the campaign to get the friendship of American leaders, almost all articulate Americans were taken into the Allies' camp, to become Crusaders for England.[47]

The first of the "native" propagandists were newspapermen. Their enlistment was, in origin, quite accidental. In order to make the stifling of news more acceptable to the dissatisfied cor-

---

[45]Beaverbrook, Lord, *Politicians and the Press* (London, 1927), 12.

[46]Parker, *loc. cit.*, 522.

[47]The name of James M. Beck has already been mentioned in the list of Wellington House writers. Jusserand gives a more extended list of authors advocating the cause of the Allies. Among others it includes Owen Wister, Richard Harding Davis, Herbert A. Gibbons, Alexander Powell, Elbert Baldwin, Owen Johnson, Robert Herrick, William R. Thayer, Henry Van Dyke, Will Irwin, and Gertrude Atherton. Jusserand, J. J., *Le sentiment américain pendant la guerre* (Paris, 1931), 49 ff.

To these should be added Gellett Burgess, Mildred Aldrich, Herbert Adams Gibbons, and Helen Gibbons. Irwin, Will, *Propaganda and the News*, 148.

respondents, an "official eye-witness" at the front had been appointed by the British.[48] His efforts pleased no one. In March and April, 1915, a step forward was made when parties of British correspondents were taken on a tour of the battlefields. In doing this it was discovered that the news writers could be pacified and at the same time be made to serve as propagandists. By stationing the reporters at the various army headquarters, and by making them personal friends, they became apologists for the British cause. In June, 1915, when the British General Headquarters received one American (Frederick Palmer) and six British correspondents, this system of propaganda was formally started.[49]

After this, the British propagandists constantly had the American newspapermen in mind. Nicholson has stated that Wellington House was vitally interested in "helping to provide information and facilities to London correspondents of neutral, especially American, papers." In 1916 Wellington House endorsed the recommendations of one of its agents that "special correspondents from this country [the United States] ... should be sent to the front and be allowed to see actual fighting." Explaining, he stated: "The French have, on the surface, done no propaganda work of any kind" but have been very cordial to American correspondents in France "and these correspondents have come back here and written the most enthusiastic articles for France. The last and most convincing ... is to be found in the visit of Frank Simonds."[50] The British went even further; they entertained all people of importance who visited France. "Editors, novelists, political experts, essayists, statesmen, university presidents, and men of importance in all walks of life, especially Americans, were given tours of the front. A visitor's chateau was provided for them and there the cuisine was excellent, while food rationing in England tightened under the growing submarine menace. They were chaperoned by most attentive and diplomatic reserve officers who had notes in hand from the Foreign Office about the standing and character of each visitor which made ingratiating hospitality the easier on the part

[48]This was Major E. D. Swinton. He did his work from September 14, 1914, to July 15, 1915. Riddell, *op. cit.*, 17.

[49]Neville Lytton had general charge of them on the British front.

[50]*A. P. R.*, May, 25, 1916.

of hosts. The guests were shown what was good for them to see. . . ."[51]

Back in England, "American journalists, publicists, authors, statesmen, greeters, and munition-makers" were courted assiduously. "Clubs were open to them, teas and dinners were given for them." "The American wives of Englishmen, who had already given their proof that blood is thicker than water, led by Lady Astor, formed a battalion of solicitude lest Americans in London become homesick."[52]

John St. Loe Strachey had a meeting of American correspondents each week at his home in London. There reporters were given the opportunity to meet some important personage, such as a cabinet member or a military leader. Men formerly aloof and inaccessible to reporters became very cordial. The personal contacts established at these meetings made censorship less distasteful to the correspondents, and also made it more difficult for those attending to give any but a British interpretation of news — even if it had been possible to get such a version past the censor. The same type of meeting was held by the foreign editor of the London *Times*.[53]

In order to exert the same influence over American press bureaus, the British Naval Censor kept "in closest touch" with the British agents of the Associated Press (Mr. Collins) and the United Press (Mr. Keen).[54] The European press bureaus had, of course, already been turned into propaganda agencies. The British had Reuters while the French used Havas. Even the German colonies had to copy their news from the dispatches of these two organizations.[55] Reuters sent out more than a million words a month, making up every week approximately four hundred articles.

In conducting such a propaganda system of native workers, it was necessary to go beyond those important individuals whom they could reach in Europe. In order to influence those small

[51]Palmer, Frederick, *With My Own Eyes* (New York, 1934), 332.

[52]*Ibid.*, 315.

[53]"There were Saturdays at Wickham Steed's where newspapermen, officers, and diplomats ... used to meet." Capek, Karel, *President Masaryk Tells His Story* (London, 1935), 251 f.

[54]Brownrigg, *op. cit.*, 125.

[55]See Wanderscheck, *op. cit.*, 21.

newspapers in the United States which had no press service and
no correspondents abroad, Sir Gilbert Parker "supplied three
hundred and sixty newspapers in the smaller c ies of the United
States with an English newspaper which [gav a weekly review
and comment of the affairs of the war."[56]

Few opportunities to influence writers w   left unexploited
and although newspaper people objected strongly to the control
which was placed upon them, their resistance was unavailing.
News was essential to the success of their papers and in order to
secure news they had to conform — which they did. The almost
complete capture of American newswriters resulted in a press
consistently friendly to the Allies. The American division of the
British propaganda ministry made a weekly analysis of this success for the information of the Cabinet. A terse statement such
as, "The week supplies satisfactory evidence of the permeation
of the American press by British influence"[57] means a great deal
more in this connection than would seem at first glance. It means
that even British propagandists were satisfied with their control.[58]

But newspaper people were not the only Americans who were
enlisted to fight Britain's battles. Appeal was systematically
made to all classes. One discussion of this problem divided Americans first as to "particular faiths"; second, "particular nationalities"; third, "labor"; fourth, "intellectuals"; and fifth, the
"average man." In all these cases it should be remembered that
the motive was to secure the active support of the leaders of that
particular class.

Some of the most extended efforts were made in the religious
field.[59] Wellington House sent appeals to all religious sects but
specialized on Episcopalians and Catholics. They popularized
and almost canonized Cardinal Mercier. A vast amount of literature was sent to American priests and preachers and many news
stories seem to have been composed especially for their benefit.

[56]Parker, *loc. cit.*, 522.

[57]*A. P. R.,* October 11, 1916.

[58]The "corpse factory" story man wrote: "It does not matter what happens
in neutral countries, except America, and there we are already served by the correspondents here and by our American visitors." Charteris, John, *At G. H. Q.*
(London: Cassell & Co., Ltd., 1931), 167.

[59]Abrams, Roy H., *Preachers Present Arms* (New York, 1933).

In securing the support of the various national groups in America, Wellington House had considerable difficulty. Many reports reveal the worry caused by the failure to obtain the active support of the Jews. They were eventually won over to the British cause by the promise of Palestine. Of more immediate concern was the problem of the Irish in America. They simply refused to sympathize with th British at all. Their memories were entirely too vivid. Many e   ts were made to influence the leaders of nationalities which desi el independence from Austria-Hungary and Germany. Thus the desires of the Poles, Czechs, and Serbs, were given serious attention. Partially as a result of these efforts the nations of Poland, Czechoslovakia, and Jugoslavia were constructed after the war.

It was in the group known as "intellectuals" that the best body of propagandists was enlisted. Sir Edward Grey wrote Theodore Roosevelt in September, 1914, that he was sending over J. M. Barrie and A. E. W. Mason "to meet people, particularly those connected with the universities, and explain the British case as regards this war and our view of the issues involved."[60] Later, with the same purpose in mind, many other writers were sent over. John Masefield was one of the 1916 contingent. Masaryk also "got in touch with the universities, particularly with historians and economists." The Central Committee for National Patriotic Organizations kept up the attack on the professors, reporting that "practically every professor of every faculty has received . . . private packets of literature in his own language." The result of this work was the enlistment of most of the leaders of intellectual life in America. Headed by such men as Lowell of Harvard and Hibben of Princeton, it was an imposing propaganda group. Dutifully bringing up the rear were the intellectual proletariat, the American school teachers.

In making an appeal to the "average man" it was found that this meant an appeal to the politicians. Among these, naturally the President was the most important. Some difficulty was encountered in attempting to reach Mr. Wilson. But it was accomplished by gaining the friendship of his personal adviser, Colonel House, who was early enlisted in the cause of the Allies. The first

[60]Grey, Viscount of Fallodon, *Twenty-Five Years, 1892-1916,* II (London, 1925), 138.

to insinuate himself into the confidence of House was the British naval attaché, Captain Guy Gaunt. Another was Sir William Wiseman. Both of these men were agents of Admiral Hall, chief of British naval intelligence. Sir Edward Grey also captivated the mysterious Colonel and hence, indirectly, President Wilson. In addition, he developed friendships of convenience with House, Page,[61] and Roosevelt.

In order to gain the assistance of leaders of the average man, it became essential to obtain the support of politicians out of power as well as those controlling the administration. If both the "outs" and "ins" were enlisted, possibilities of political attacks, especially in election years, would be eliminated. The chief politician out of power in the war years was a former president, Theodore Roosevelt. He was badly in need of a political issue and was deeply stirred by the Allies' sensational campaign. As a result he was easily won over and became chief of the American volunteer propagandists. Every man of importance among the leaders of the Allies made it a point to gain Roosevelt's friendship. Edward Grey wrote to him sentimentalizing about their bird walks together and sympathizing with him whenever Roosevelt made the remark, "now if I had been president." The enlistment of Roosevelt as propagandist for the Allies meant that the great body of his followers were the more easily "educated."

One of the most strident political supporters of the Allies was James M. Beck, who had been Assistant Attorney General of the United States during Roosevelt's administration. Beck was constantly in the public eye and was most vehement in defending the Allies and attacking anyone who did not also defend them. President Wilson told Tumulty, "I think . . . [Beck's] criticisms and his whole attitude before we went into the war were abominable and inexcusable."[62]

The personal appeal for the enlistment of native propagandists did not end with newspapermen, preachers, teachers, and

[61]Page was so thoroughly taken in that President Wilson became convinced that the British had exerted "improper influence on our ambassador." From *War Memoirs of Robert Lansing* (copyright 1935, used by special permission of the publishers, The Bobbs-Merrill Co.), 170. Hereafter referred to as Lansing, *Memoirs*.

[62]From *Woodrow Wilson as I Knew Him*, by Joseph P. Tumulty (copyright 1921, by Doubleday, Doran & Co., Inc.), 364.

politicians, but was used wherever contact could be established with a person of importance. The result of this enlistment of articulate Americans can be noticed even in post-war years.

An outstanding result of the practice of capitalizing on friendships was the development, by Americans, of organizations for defense or other purposes, but which actually became centers of pro-Ally propaganda. One of the most important groups in this category was the violently pro-Ally Navy League. The roll call of this League demonstrates the effectiveness of Britain's friends in securing the leaders of American economic life to back moves beneficial to the Allies. Among others it included: J. Pierpont Morgan; Thomas W. Lamont (Morgan); Elbert H. Gary (U. S. Steel); Harry P. Whitney (Guaranty Trust Company — agent of Atlas Powder Company and Hercules Powder Company); S. H. P. Pell (International Nickel Company); Cornelius Vanderbilt (Lackawanna Steel Company); Ogden L. Mills (Lackawanna Steel Company); Frederick R. Coudert (National Surety Company); Francis L. Hine (Bankers Trust Company); Daniel G. Read (Guaranty Trust Company — H. P. Whitney); Frank A. Vanderlip (President National City Bank — Standard Oil); L. L. Clark (American Locomotive Company); and Percy Rockefeller. It would be difficult to assemble a more influential group of native propagandists in any country, and these were only a few of the financial leaders who, through these defense leagues, gave their "sympathy" to the Allies. Robert M. LaFollette commented on this list: "Shades of Lincoln! What a band of patriots — with their business connections covering every financial and industrial center in the United States. Owning newspapers, periodicals, and magazines, and controlling through business relations the editorial good will of many others. . . ."[63]

Closely allied in origin and objective to the Navy League was the National Security League. This organization was particularly involved in the propaganda of preparedness. There was also the American Defense Society of which Theodore Roosevelt's friend, General Wood, was "the patron saint, the guide and inspiration."[64] It must be borne in mind that members of these groups

[63]*LaFollette's Magazine*, November, 1915.
[64]Hagedorn, Hermann, *Leonard Wood, A Biography* (New York, 1931), 155.

did not realize that in addition to their work for defense, they were also assisting British propagandists.

Among the groups which dealt exclusively with propaganda was the Pilgrim's Society in England, under Harry Brittain. This organization fostered the "hands-across-the-sea" movement which made a very strong appeal to Americans. The Pilgrims Club was similarly effective and received the commendation of Sir Gilbert Parker.[65] An example of the local organizations was the "British American League" in Southern California. A traveling agent of the British propaganda ministry reported that when this was started it "brought forth such a stormy campaign from the Germans that it forced these good British-Americans to seek immediate cover." However, this did not mean discontinuance of the work. The agent informed Parker that "the purpose and activities of the earlier organization are now concealed and conducted under the guise of an 'Allies' Aid Association,' an avowedly philanthropic body, of which Mr. Edmund Mitchel is the prime and ardent mover."[66]

The great success of British propaganda in the United States should not be attributed to a professional group of propagandists but to native Americans — volunteer propagandists. These were individually enlisted in some cases, but in the main were regimented into "soldiers of the king" by a process of eliminating, or at least curtailing, enemy interpretations of the war and by dominating the news with exaggerated and warped pro-Ally accounts of what was happening or had happened. Once these natives had acquired the "correct" frame of mind, they were enlisted for the "duration of the war." The formal propaganda groups acted merely as connecting and reinforcing elements of the British propaganda organizations. The real propagandists were Americans — our preachers, teachers, politicians, and journalists.[67]

[65]The *Alliance Française* was one of these structures. Their bulletin was started on November 1, 1914. Within five months it was printed in nine languages and had 70,000 readers; by March of 1916, 200,000 copies were issued bi-weekly. Thimme, Hans, *Weltkrieg Ohne Waffen — Die Propaganda der Westmächte gegen Deutschland, ihre Wirkung und ihre Abwehr* (Stuttgart, 1932), 6.

[66]This investigator reported to Sir Gilbert Parker: "Mr. Percy Morgan in San Francisco and Mr. Edmund Mitchel in Los Angeles, to whom you sent me, were extremely courteous and helpful." *A. P. R. Supplement,* January 28, 1916.

[67]Some of the material in this chapter is included in an article by the author in the *American Political Science Review,* for February, 1937.

CHAPTER III ☆ BRITISH PROPAGANDA

THE primary objective of a political propaganda campaign is to establish an attitude of mind, a climate of opinion. When such a campaign is successful, the point of view which it has created acts as a censor or interpreter of news and turns those propagandized into propagandists. The specific objective of British propaganda in the years of neutrality was to create a climate of opinion which would cause the United States to assist the Allies in fighting Germany. The hope, of course, was that this assistance would eventually take the form of actual participation in the war.

There were a number of factors which contributed to the great success of Sir Gilbert Parker and his associates. In the first place, there was a pro-British attitude among leading Americans at the outbreak of hostilities. Secondly, their propaganda was unobtrusive and artistically presented. In the third place, their principal enemy was a new-rising nation with all the unpleasant characteristics nominally encountered in the newly rich and newly powerful. Finally, their control of the conventional channels of American opinion made it unnecessary for them to compete on an equal footing with the Germans. Great Britain performed before the footlights — her enemy could only shout from behind the wings. The German actor also had to make himself heard not only above the down-stage declamations of John Bull, but above the persistent chants of the chorus of Americans who were echoing the British blank verse.

The immediate task of British propagandists was to make an ordinary political power struggle appear to be a fight between the forces of good and evil. Beyond this, they must make the Allies' cause appear to be America's cause — there must be developed a belief in the identity of interests between the United States and Great Britain.

In developing the idea that this new war was a holy war the British were very fortunate. The struggle between weary old England and boisterous new Germany readily adapted itself to the stereotype of virtue versus iniquity. The new expanding German power aroused all the usual opposition to change. The British government, on its part, had the customary support of that great majority who believe that that which is is sacrosanct. In addition, throughout the war years and the pre-war years the Germans were constantly doing things which angered the entire world, and these the propagandists exploited to the full. Such conduct was a natural result of conditions accompanying the rise of the Reich, a late comer to the scene of European power. Other nations strenuously objected to giving her a "place in the sun," especially as this could be done only at their expense. The Powers to the west had all the colonies, the United States had most of North America and forbade expansion into South America, and there was but small relief through immigration. In the face of unrelenting opposition, the virile German expansionist spirit became an explosive force; the Germans themselves became loud and truculent.

Every country on the way up puts a premium on effectiveness and as a result gives position and power to many crass, aggressive, and disagreeable people. The peculiar situation which faced Germany accentuated this natural phenomenon. Her youthful impatience caused her to substitute direct action for the more involved methods which characterize good politics. Her statesmen, unaccustomed to great power, played their new part badly, and her ordinary citizens were so preoccupied with their own progress that they disregarded the feelings of other peoples. All displayed a lack of restraint, a heavy-handedness which made their conduct appear wrong even on occasions when justice was on their side. In contrast to the gracious gentility of the British, the bad political manners of the Germans seemed to be unregenerate villainy.

The British, for their part, seemed to have gone to the other extreme. For a long time they have been accused of adopting an attitude of self-righteousness even while engaged in practices which they would utterly condemn in any other nation.[1] The phrase "perfidious Albion" is quoted in many countries. One

[1]Styron, Arthur, *The Cast Iron Man* (New York, 1935), 64.

"The catalogue of crusades is a British compilation which to neutral nations has long been as tiresome as the Homeric catalogue of ships." Tansill, Charles Callan, *America Goes to War* (Boston, 1938), 163.

American writer, in a sentence destined to become classic, remarked that "one of the greatest qualities which have made the English a great people is their eminently sane, reasonable, fairminded inability to conceive that any viewpoint save their own can possibly have the slightest merit."[2] Of course, the British are not the only ones who act in a pharisaical manner, but they probably do it more intensively than other nations. At least they did during the World War.

The attempt to identify the interests and ideals of the United States with those of England dominated all British propaganda. Every possible effort was made to make Americans feel that the war was "our fight." Every possible point of similarity between the two countries was stressed and re-stressed. The news and other printed matter released in the American press was so written that the reader would feel that his interests and hopes were in some way involved in the war. The British propaganda ministry always gave great prominence in their reports to such American headlines as "England's Defeat, Our Defeat."[3] At one time it was cheerfully reported that the pro-Ally newspapers "believe that Great Britain is fighting America's battle, that the future of democracy is at stake, and that the United States will have to fight for it, if not now, then hereafter. . . ."[4] The implications are clear. A vital part of these arguments was the contention that Great Britain and the United States were sister democracies. This later developed into the argument of democracy versus autocracy. Eventually the idea became current that for an American to be pro-Ally was patriotic and for him to be pro-German was to be anti-American. In other words, the British captured the American flag and waved it in front of themselves.

Aided by the realities of submarine warfare, the contention was made that the United States was actually menaced by Germany. The success of this argument is demonstrated in the statement of Senator Lawrence Y. Sherman who remarked, "I do not

[2]Millis, *op. cit.*, 64. The following is a note dated September 25, 1916, taken from Colonel House's diary: ". . . we resented some of the cant and hypocrisy indulged in by the British; for instance, as to Belgium." *M. I.*, Part 28, 8493.

[3]*A. P. R.*, May 19, 1916. This came as the result of an interview of Mrs. Humphrey Ward with Lord Cromer.

[4]*A. P. R.*, February 5, 1916. In a more despondent tone, they added, "But it is the view of only a minority."

think we embarked in the war in a humanitarian crusade. It was for self defense."[5] The "our fight" idea culminated in the assertion that the Monroe Doctrine would be violated if the Germans were victorious.[6]

Although this propaganda was remarkably successful, at one time Wellington House was advised that these arguments were having adverse effects. It was said that there was a growing irritation among most educated Americans at "the suggestion that they are entirely actuated by commercial motives," at the "paternal attitude," and at the "long lost brother" or the "call of the blood" fake.[7]

The corollary of the attempt to identify the British cause with American interests and ideals was the effort to make the German and his manners and morals appear foreign. The Germans in the United States unconsciously furthered the attainment of this objective. Their speech and group feeling were different from those of their neighbors. It was easy to exaggerate these differences and make them appear evil.[8] By making the foreign characteristics undesirable or even repulsive, citizens of this country were induced to believe that the Germans were alien to all America stood for. There was also created among Americans a desire to identify themselves with the more "civilized" English. A natural and very helpful by-product of this propaganda was the tendency of Americans to revile other Americans who did not believe such an interpretation to be true.

The effort to excite hostility against German foreignness was, of course, highly successful. The anger of any people is easily aroused against anything foreign, and in time of great emotional

[5]June 26, 1919, in the Forster Papers, New York Public Library.

[6]The attempt to identify the economic interests of the United States with those of the Allies goes far beyond the field of propaganda and must be considered in connection with the British economic warfare. George B. M. Harvey, the American Ambassador in London in 1923 remarked that the United States "did not enter the war for unselfish motives of any sort but for self-protection and self-interest."

[7]*A. P. R.,* March 3, 1916. This went so far that Parker felt the need of reassuring the British cabinet in his report: "I am sure that the interest which America feels in the war has a more idealistic basis than that of the Almighty Dollar. When the time comes, if come it must, she will be ready with her sacrifice." *A. P. R. Supplement,* January 28, 1916. This is apparently quoted from some agent in the United States.

[8]The recent German propaganda against Jews is of the same type.

Printed for the use of the Cabinet.

CONFIDENTIAL.

AMERICAN PRESS RÉSUMÉ.

(JUNE 3, 1915.)

(Including extracts from American newspapers issued between the dates May 15 and May 22 inclusive; American news cabled to London newspapers up to and including June 2.)

(1.) The British Coalition Cabinet.

The changes in the British Ministry have aroused universal interest in the United States of America, and the press has discussed in detail their probable causes and possible effects.

Although the pro-German newspapers have made comparatively little capital out of these events, yet the crisis has naturally attracted attention to any shortcomings discoverable in the Government's previous conduct of the war.

On the 20th May the Washington *Post* opens an article as follows :—

> "The announcement by Premier Asquith that the British Cabinet is to be reconstructed is sufficient evidence that bitter animosities have been engendered as a result of war operations. Naturally Mr. Asquith is doing his best to prevent the details of the quarrel from becoming public, but the resignation of Admiral Fisher, First Sea Lord, gives a clue to the division in the Cabinet."

And the Philadelphia *Public Ledger* of the 20th May is all the more severe for its absence of malice :—

> "On more than one occasion costly errors have been made. An unintelligent censorship has given ground for much dissatisfaction. The futile attempt to deal with the drink problem has excited derision."

Yet, while it is assumed on all hands that there must have been "something wrong" to precipitate the crisis, there is comparatively little tendency to draw far-reaching conclusions of a nature damaging to British prestige.

The New York *Tribune* of the 22nd May prints a long article on "DISSENSIONS AT THE ADMIRALTY," in which it criticises, without bias, the official relation between the First Lord and the First Sea Lord, but carefully emphasises the personal merits of the late holders of these two posts.

The New York *World* of the 21st May, on the other hand, dwells on the personal causes, and makes a sharp attack on both Mr. Churchill and Lord Kitchener :—

> "KITCHENER AND CHURCHILL.
>
> "The British Cabinet has broken down where it was least expected to break down. Kitchener and Churchill, representatives of blood and iron, have fallen short.
>
> "For months Lord Kitchener has been little less than the dictator of Great Britain. He has had his way about everything. He has

[501—7]   B

A PAGE FROM THE *AMERICAN PRESS RÉSUMÉ*

stress this is particularly true. The success of such propaganda is due to the fact that appeal is made to fundamental beliefs — the basic habits of a people.[9]

In carrying out their work the propagandists followed certain general lines which might be called techniques. In part these were as follows: (1) they told only that part of the truth which benefited their cause; (2) they utilized background material to imply things for which there was no evidence; (3) they exploited to the fullest the emotions and ideals of those being educated; (4) they gave their propaganda an aura of authority by using big names, by quoting their enemy, or by appealing to legality; (5) they made their arguments simple and eliminated all qualifying statements; (6) they used endless repetition.

One recent writer has stated that "the art of persuasion consists largely in *directing attention* to those aspects of [the news] ... which will influence the mind of the person to be persuaded."[10] It was this which the British were doing throughout the entire period. Falsehoods were used, but they were comparatively unimportant. It was much easier and much safer to give warped interpretations. By taking the regular news events and minimizing or eliminating those parts which would have reflected any credit upon the enemy it was possible to damage the enemy's cause. By exaggerating those parts of the story which redounded to the credit of the Allies, the prestige of the Entente Powers was greatly enhanced. The elimination of all arguments which tended to warrant German entry into the war, and the accentuating of all those which justified French and English participation, aided in establishing the concept of war guilt. In the propaganda of the conduct of war, the same practice was followed of suppression, selection, and exaggeration. By omitting mention of good Germans or good actions by Germans, these people were made to appear unregenerate. And, by omitting reference to evil Englishmen, the Germans, by contrast, were made to appear even worse. This technique of exploiting part-truths is characteristic of all propagandists. At the hands of the British it became high art.

An ever present technique of the British was the use of im-

[9]One development of this procedure was the effort made to ostracise the Germans socially. This amazed Bernstorff.

[10]Lowell, A. L., *Public Opinion in War and Peace* (Cambridge, 1923), 26.

plication. For instance, a destroyed village would be described in great detail, and the reader was left to assume that this destruction was the result of willful maliciousness on the part of the Germans. It was left to the reader to imply that wrecked buildings had been willfully demolished, that dead children had been deliberately killed, that maimed civilians had been mutilated by sadists. Many of the stories given in the Bryce Report, when analyzed, were not atrocities at all. Instead they were the usual barbarous aspects of war which were so pictured that the reader would interpret them as atrocities. When these interpreting backgrounds were added to exaggerated versions of actual events, distinctly anti-German impressions were created in the minds of readers.

All propaganda arguments made direct appeals to the emotions. In the last analysis, emotion is the common denominator of propaganda.

Emotional appeal was made in every major section of British propaganda, and even legal arguments were fundamentally based upon emotionalism. The effort was constantly made to arouse fear and hate of the Germans, and pity, love, and admiration for the British and French. A most important phase of this technique was the practice of exploiting idealism. The British did all they could to identify British and American ideals and to picture German actions as attacks upon democracy — the symbol of American idealism. The almost hysterical reaction in the United States to British propaganda demonstrates very clearly the effectiveness of such appeals. The fact that it was especially influential among the highly educated seems to indicate that learning is not an impregnable defense against appeals made to the emotions.

A large part of the effectiveness of propaganda depends upon its appearance of accuracy. The British took care of this in the first place by utilizing as many famous names as possible.[11] It did not matter what was the nature of the fame of the individual, for to the public an authority on one thing is an authority on all things. In addition to the appearance of authority gained by using the names of famous Englishmen it was realized that the same results could be obtained through utilizing the names of neutrals or enemy nationals. In such cases the individuals quoted

[11]*Supra,* pp. 17 f., 31. Also see footnotes 22 and 50 of Chapter II.

need not be especially prominent. Wellington House published many of the writings of Germans who attacked the German government, and of Americans who presented a pro-British point of view. One of the most popular publications of German authorship was Dr. Richard Grelling's *J'accuse*[12] which was translated into many languages. Another, the memoirs of Prince Lichnowsky, the German Ambassador in England at the outbreak of the war, enjoyed an even wider distribution. It has been asserted that four million copies of this book were issued. The writings by Americans, of course, appeared in an almost endless stream.

The final method used to lend authority to the propaganda arguments was the appeal to legality. This was supposed to have been especially effective in the United States because it was said that Americans base their judgment of right and wrong on the question of whether or not a rule has been broken rather than on the justice or injustice of a particular event. Although there is little validity to this generalization, it is true that the British took every advantage of legal arguments. Spring-Rice wrote home of "the necessity of employing a good, competent lawyer to state our case from the point of view of American precedents."[13] Even before this, there appeared James M. Beck's *The Evidence in the Case,* which applied this treatment to the origins of the war. This legalistic approach was also used in connection with atrocities, the invasion of Belgium, the execution of Edith Cavell and Captain Fryatt, the sinking of the *Lusitania,* and most of the other propaganda arguments. In some cases a good defense of the British case was evolved; in others opposing arguments were just as strong; in some the contentions were indefensible or irrelevant. Naturally, the basis for this propaganda was the supposition that the enemy and only the enemy broke the law. It is only necessary to mention the Anglo-French invasion of Greece, the placing of food on the contraband list, or the Order in Council of March 11, 1915, to recognize that this was incorrect.

Limitations which always had to be borne in mind were that the propaganda must be simple and it must be positive. It was, of course, well known that the great mass of the people can be

[12]This was brought out by the Central Committee for National Patriotic Organizations.

[13]*The Letters and Friendships of Sir Cecil Spring-Rice* (Boston: Houghton Mifflin Co., 1929), 257.

reached most effectively through obvious phrases such as "war guilt," "poor Belgium," or through slogans such as "make the world safe for democracy." These phrases and slogans, as well as most of the British propaganda arguments, were not half-statements which might give rise to doubts. Instead they represented simple, uncomplicated ideas which could be understood by almost anyone.

In spite of the necessity for simplicity, propagandists realized that for a campaign as broad as that being conducted in America, there had to be a wide range of arguments. The main ideas could be few, but different classes of people would require different presentations. There had to be serious arguments for intellectuals and pseudo-intellectuals, exciting, sensational stories for those easily moved by hate and anger, dramatic and pitiful incidents for that great mass of people who wish to worship or to weep.

Out of the idea that all arguments should be simple came the one most important technique of propaganda — repetition. To make a few concepts become an integral part of the persons propagandized it was essential to ring the changes on all the arguments upon which the concepts were founded. There had to be iteration and reiteration. The arguments had to be drummed into the consciousness of the people being propagandized with a never-ending repetition.

The propaganda department in each of the belligerent nations developed varying methods of procedure for carrying on its work.[14] Although British organizations were not under one head their methods were surprisingly similar. The list of argu-

[14]The French spoke of their propaganda in the following words: "It had for its object the making known of all the *weaknesses* of the enemy, the *powers* of friends, the great *moral reasons* that caused the formation of our alliances, the *universal desire to aid us* to secure a just victory in the name of liberty menaced." "And then propaganda ... [made] clear to the neutrals and to the Allies themselves the *power* and *disinterestedness* of the French effort." "The information services ... [undertook] the supreme task of making France and her Allies *loved,* of making Germany and her accomplices *hated;* of building up *hope* among the French." "It ... [made] *hate* necessary, *friendship* useful...." Bornecqui and Drouilly, *op. cit.,* 7 ff. Hanotaux gave as explanation for the issuance of the French "yellow book": *"Le gouvernement français a pris soin de la rendre accessible à tous et l'envoyer jusqu'en Amérique pour que l'opinion universelle soit saisie et éclairée."* Hanotaux, Gabriel, *Pendant la grande guerre* (Paris, 1916), 231.

ments developed by Wellington House[15] was almost identical with those used by the lesser organizations. The list prepared by P. Chalmers Mitchell of Wellington House, which purported to be an analysis of German propaganda, was included in the report of the Central Commmittee for National Patriotic Organization[16] and is the basis for the study of British propaganda in *The Times History of the War.*

The practical application of these procedures was, naturally, quite individual. The British, for instance, in their propaganda of "exaltation of selves and damnation of the enemy" did all they could to emphasize the personal element by featuring heroes and villains. Early in the war they made extended efforts to place Edward Grey on a pedestal. Only a slight degree of success rewarded this effort. The two military individuals who were lauded to the skies were Lord Kitchner and General Joffre. The latter was the special property of the French propagandists. Among the non-military heroes fabricated by the propaganda departments were Cardinal Mercier and Edith Cavell. It would have been desirable to make a popular idol out of the captain of the *Lusitania* but certain circumstances made this impossible. Among the minor heroes developed by the propaganda ministries were Haig, Petain, King Albert, Nivelle, and Diaz. Some success was had in exalting Lloyd George. Although some of these individuals merited their "elevation," to the propagandist this was irrelevant. The only question in his mind was, "will this person make a presentable hero?"

The principal success in creating a villain was with the Kaiser — an ordinary man with an extended ego. To a large extent the German Emperor was a European version of Theodore Roosevelt. His chief fault, that he was a man before he was an emperor, made it possible to picture him as the emblem of aggression. By ridiculing his conceit in such phrases as *me und Gott,* it was easy to imply that he was personally responsible for the war. His up-

[15](a) causes of the war; (b) manner Germans carried on the war; (c) attack on German colonial methods and exaltation of the British colonial policy; (d) attack on German aims especially when compared with the aims of the Allies; (e) friendship with America.

[16](a) certain victory; (b) a war of defense; (c) outrageous conduct of the enemy; (d) exaltation of selves; (e) victory would be good for the world; (f) need of expansion; (g) cupidity.

turned mustaches were a Godsend to British propagandists. They came to be the symbol of *militarismus*. George III in the American revolution, Jeff Davis in the Civil War, and "Butcher" Weyler in the Spanish-American War, were similar scapegoats, but the art of publicity had not been developed at that time to the extent to which this civilized era has seen it advance. No one of these earlier popular villains approached the mythical figure which the propagandists created in "the Kaiser." The secondary villain in the Hohenzollern family, the Crown Prince, was primarily satisfactory as an object of attack because of his weak appearance. Where the Kaiser was portrayed as a monster, the Crown Prince was pictured as a weak, treacherous, contemptible wretch.[17]

An integral part of all the British propaganda was the claim that they were bound to be victorious. One agent in reporting his work in California stated: "It is important . . . that confidence should be sustained and stimulated in the belief that the defeat of Germany is attainable." The "idea (which I fear is increasing) that the Allies may not be able to win anything more than a stalemate out of the contest appeared to be the one great defect in the general sentiment along the 'coast.' " "If you have in mind any special propaganda for California, I would urge that it be directed . . . to stimulate confidence."[18] It was, of course, realized from the outset that the bandwagon is always popular and the tendency noticed in California was fought vigorously and successfully.

The attempt to make it appear that the Allies would win was, at times, carried too far and acted as a boomerang. Victory was never very certain but "the truth was, of course, kept back from our people as it was from the British people lest it encourage the enemy and discourage us."[19] The leaders in American life were thoroughly convinced that victory for the Entente Powers was merely a question of time. After the United States had entered

[17]For the writings against the Hohenzollerns including William II, see Weltkriegsbücherei, *Bibliographie zur englischen Propaganda im Weltkrieg* (Stuttgart, 1935) (Edited by Hermann Wanderscheck), 27 ff.

[18]*A. P. R. Supplement*, January 28, 1916.

[19]Palmer, *op. cit.*, 335. Palmer reported Lord Kitchener as saying to the correspondents: "There is nothing for you to write about, nothing cheerful to report." *Ibid.*, 309.

the war, it became necessary to acquaint these individuals with the fact that it was not certain victory but certain defeat that confronted the Allies. Ambassador Page was "aghast" when he was told the truth.[20] McAdoo stated, "We had a distinct impression that it might be too late to save the Allied cause." It is not known what President Wilson's immediate reactions were to this information. There are reasons for believing that it was broken to him gradually, since it was quite late before he realized the gravity of the situation. Lloyd George has spoken disparagingly of Wilson's reluctance to take an active part in the war, not realizing that that reluctance was based upon faith in the British propaganda argument that the Allies were winning the war. After April 4, 1917, the British had to make special efforts to overcome the belief among Americans that the Germans were being defeated. In other words, by that time the victory propaganda was too successful.

Propaganda on the origin of the war, or war guilt, was Great Britain's principal contribution to war-time "education." Here was developed the thesis that sole responsibility for causing the war rested with Germany. The objective was the establishment of the belief that the Central Powers, and Germany in particular, had deliberately fomented the war for the purpose of gaining world dominance. J. P. Morgan's testimony before the Nye committee represents the final product of this propaganda. He stated, "The whole German Nation had started out on the war with the cry of world domination or annihilation."[21]

Intellectually, the establishment of belief in German war guilt was a difficult task. However, with the appeal being made to emotion rather than intellect fewer difficulties were presented. Primarily it called for omission of the consideration of certain actions by Serbia, Russia, France, and England. For instance, the responsibility of the Serbian government for the tragedy at Sarajevo was ignored or written down. Russian mobilization was discounted as soon as British censorship went into effect. French encouragement of Russian pugnacity was not revealed.[22] The

[20]Hendrick, Burton, *The Life and Letters of Walter H. Page,* II (New York: Houghton Mifflin Co., 1922, 1925), 275.

[21]*M. I.,* Part 25, 7438.

[22]France, for instance, gave Russia a series of blank checks, when the latter was most bellicose. These now appear as little short of incitement to war. See *Un*

British failure to attempt to curb the belligerent attitudes of France and Russia was hidden behind the publicity given to Grey's attempts to hold back Austria-Hungary. On the other hand no attention was given to the very real danger to Austria-Hungary from the nationalistic propaganda of the Balkans while the understandable German fear of France and Russia was completely ignored.[23]

The attempt to prove Germany's guilt also called for the removal of the causes of the war from the Balkans to Berlin. This was done by placing emphasis on the events after Germany and France had declared war rather than on those preceding this step. An hiatus was created between July 25 and August 1. Thus by a process of transmutation the consideration of origins of the war was made to turn upon events occurring upon the western rather than the eastern front. J. P. Morgan, who was certainly an intelligent man, could say in 1936 that "the war was begun by Germany by the unexpected and criminal invasion of Belgium."[24] This whole attitude must in some degree be attributed to the effects of British propaganda.

Perhaps the most persuasive arguments of the British on the origins of the war were based upon the contention that they en-

---

Livre Noir — Diplomatie d'avant-guerre d'apres des documents des archives Russes (1910-1917) Paris. Telegrams #195, July 27, 1914, Izvolsky to Sazonov, II, 281; #1551, July 29, 1914, Sazonov to Izvolsky, II, 289. See also the actions of Poincaré and Paleologue in Fay, Sidney B., *The Origins of the World War,* II (New York, 1928), 277 ff.

The moves of the French government even disturbed the British Ambassador in Paris, for he wrote home: "The French instead of putting pressure on the Russian Government to moderate their zeal expect us to give the Germans to understand that we mean fighting if war breaks out." *British Documents on the Origins of the War 1898-1914,* XI (London, 1926), 203, July 30, 1914.

[23]Early in July, 1914, we know that the German government gave Austria-Hungary what amounted to a "blank check" in her dealings with Serbia. This, however, was not a "blank check" to start a world war for the purpose of acquiring territory. When the results of the clash between Austria-Hungary and Serbia became perceptible, late in July, we know that the German government did try to put a brake on the actions of the Dual Monarchy. Telegram #174, July 28, 1914, and Telegram #192, July 30, 1914, from the Imperial Chancellor to the Ambassador at Vienna. *Kautsky Documents* #323 and #395.

To some extent these measures were blocked by the mobilization of the Russian army. "But it was primarily Russia's general mobilization, made when Germany was trying to bring Austria to a settlement, which precipitated the final catastrophe, causing Germany to mobilize and declare war." Fay, *op. cit.,* II, 555.

[24]*M. I.,* Part 25, 7483.

tered the war to protect Belgium, i.e., in defense of Belgian neutrality. It was made to appear convincing by ignoring the whole series of events between 1901 and 1914, and by omitting from the published documents certain vital correspondence. It was possible that England might come to the assistance of some small nation such as Belgium even if British interests were not involved. However, British participation in the war had been guaranteed by steps taken long before German troops crossed the Belgian frontier. "Page admitted that the British would have been found fighting with France even if France had violated Belgium."[25] The chief value of this propaganda was, of course, its dramatic quality.

The invasion of Belgium was only the first of the reprehensible, wartime acts committed by the Germans. Like those that followed, it was of great assistance to the opposing propagandists. This particular act was exploited most successfully by dwelling upon the fact that it involved the breaking of a treaty which had guaranteed Belgium's neutrality. This the British publicized throughout the world with the "scrap of paper" propaganda. But Germany was not the only nation which violated its written agreements. The King of Greece issued the following statement: "It is the merest cant for Great Britain and France to talk about the violation of the neutrality of Belgium and Luxembourg, after what they themselves have done, and are doing here. . . . Just look at the list of Greek territories already occupied by Allied troops — Lemnos, Imbros, Mitylene, Castellonza, Corfu, Salonica, including the Chalcidice Peninsula, and a large part of Macedonia. . . . They plead military necessity. It was under constraint of military necessity that Germany invaded Belgium and occupied Luxembourg. It is no good claiming that the neutrality of Greece was not guaranteed by the Powers who are now violating it, as was the case in Belgium, for the neutrality of Corfu is guaranteed by Great Britain, France, Russia, Austria and Prussia, and yet has not made any difference to their action."[26] Occasionally Americans questioned the propaganda based upon Belgian neutrality by referring to the violation of Greek neutrality. Wellington House at such times reported: "The situation in Greece has again prompted unfortunate ques-

25*Intimate Papers*, II, 319.

tions in the American press."[27] Fortunately, however, "the American press as a whole has consistently treated the Greek situation with partiality to the Allies."[28]

Ray Stannard Baker quoted Theodore Roosevelt as saying that "no treaties were ever effective unless backed by guns. He [Roosevelt] cited instances of how all the great nations had recently abandoned or broken over solemn treaties."[29] After the war President Wilson stated that France and Italy had "made waste paper of the treaty of Versailles," and the Germans always were of the opinion that Wilson had done the same thing with the Fourteen Points. There also seems to be no question that the American government was "cavalier" in its respect for treaties with the Indians. The American Secretary of the Interior in 1914 remarked to a friend, "Talking of Belgium, I was referred the other day to . . . the attack on Copenhagen by England in 1808, [sic] in which the Ministry justified its ruthless attack upon a neutral power in almost precisely the same language that von Bethmann-Hollweg used in justifying the attack on Belgium."[30] Bernard Shaw was even more unkind when he said, "If our own military success were at stake, we would violate the neutrality of heaven itself."[31]

Of great importance in the war guilt literature was the propaganda of militarism. Both the British and the French attacked the Germans as warlike and militaristic, stating that this spirit was responsible for the war itself and for the atrocities in the war. Similar to the other propaganda arguments, this one had a certain basis of fact. The army enjoyed great respect in Germany. It was the force which had made possible the unification of the Reich. It had to be strong to accomplish this unification in the very center of Europe. It had to push aside powerful estab-

[26]Clipped from the London *Times* of January 21, 1916, for the "War Aims File" of the British Foreign Office.

They were "simply acts of state dictated solely by the presumed interests of their authors under the same maxim invoked by Bethmann-Hollweg on August 4th, 1914: 'Necessity knows no law.'" Cruttwell, *op. cit.,* 232.

[27]*A. P. R.,* April 4, 1917.

[28]*A. P. R.,* August 30, 1916.

[29]August 14, 1914. Baker, R. S., *Woodrow Wilson Life and Letters,* V (New York, 1935), 198.

[30]Lane, Franklin K., *The Letters of Franklin K. Lane* (New York, 1922), 169.

[31]The New York *Times,* November 11, 1914.

lished nations instead of the savage tribes which opposed British
and French expansion. As the army grew in strength and prestige, Germany's position in the world likewise grew. It is not to
be wondered that the Germans had a high opinion of their army.
The propaganda dealing with militarism started from this point
and exaggerated the importance and influence of the army within
Germany. It also underrated the influence of the military in other
nations. It attempted to establish the belief that this militaristic
attitude was characteristic of all Germans and of no one else.

It is, of course, true that militarism is to be found in Germany. But it is not absent from other countries. France, for
instance, had been at war 367 out of the 713 years previous to
1914.[32] She had produced Louis XIV and had also given to the
world that symbol of militarism, Napoleon Bonaparte. "La guerre est pour elle une industrie." With England it was not greatly
different, but here it was navalism rather than militarism. It was
not an accident that the word "jingo" originated in England.
Bernard Shaw once remarked, "We cannot shout for years that
we are boys of the bulldog breed, and then suddenly pose as
gazelles." The United States also has had its militarists. Certainly there is a striking parallel between the jingoism of Leonard
Wood and Theodore Roosevelt and that of their contemporaries
in Central Europe.[33] It also should be noted that present day navalism in all countries is based upon the ideas of Captain Mahan,
an American. The Germans were and are militaristic, partially
as a result of geographic factors, but so are other peoples. The
fact that they were especially dependent upon their army in this
period was merely incidental to the origins and conduct of the
war. Militarism was actually a symptom of European political
unrest rather than a cause of it. But this, of course, did not injure
the effectiveness of the propaganda of militarism.

An argument which made this militarism propaganda seem
especially convincing was the contention that Germany was prepared for the war while other nations were not. It was true that
the German military machine was in excellent condition. However, the other phase of this argument, the unpreparedness of the

[32]Demartial, Georges, *La guerre de 1914, Comment on mobilisa les consciences* (Paris, 1922), 64.
[33]See contemporary comments by such men as Cobb of the New York *World*.

Allies, was not true. The successful use of this contention was made possible by the inferior quality of military leadership of England, France, and Russia — a mediocrity which continued throughout the war.

The most interesting aspect of the propaganda of militarism lay in the fact that it was not so much action as it was appearance which made it successful. The suddenly achieved position of Germany and of Germany's army had an especially bad effect upon the military leaders of the Reich. Their success went to their heads and was responsible for a hauteur which was very obnoxious.[34] The propagandists readily saw that to the democratically minded Americans this attitude could be made to appear as proof of every kind of villainy. Consequently, they attacked German officers in nearly all their writings. Before long it came to be assumed that these people were "almost as bad as the Kaiser." Even more effective were the attacks upon the German goose- ✓ step. How this particular step could be responsible for anything was, of course, irrelevant to the propagandists. It appeared arrogant and made Americans willing to believe that soldiers must be evil if they marched in such a way.

The material issued on this militaristic phase of propaganda by Wellington House was very broad. An especially convincing part of it was the group of German books which were reissued in English. This included parts of the writings of Clausewitz, Nietzche, Fichte, and Hegel.[35] The propagandists were especially fortunate in having at hand a book by Bernhardi. Wellington House distributed this throughout the United States by the millions, although in Germany "only 6000 copies . . . had been printed and not all sold."[36] It appeared under titles such as *Germany and the Next War, How Germany Makes War,* or *Britain as Germany's Vassal.*[37] Another book of the same type was a military manual which bore the title *The War Book of the German*

[34]See Weltkriegsbücherei, *op. cit.,* 30.

There were numerous attacks upon the brutality of German officers. It is interesting to note that Frederick Palmer quotes an Alsatian as saying, "German officers are better than French officers. They look after their men better. They know their business better." Palmer, *op. cit.,* 322.

[35]Wanderscheck, *op. cit.,* 74.

[36]Bowers, Claud G., *Beveridge and the Progressive Era* (New York, 1932), 463.

[37]These appeared in 1914.

General Staff.[38] It was also widely distributed. Perhaps the most effective of these German books used as British propaganda against German militarism were those by Treitschke. One edition carried an introduction by the Right Honorable Arthur James Balfour, the British Prime Minister, with a foreword by A. Lawrence Lowell, President of Harvard University.[39]

The propaganda material on the origins of the war published during the years of neutrality reached unbelievable proportions.[40] Each government issued collections of "selected" documents,[41] which served as source material for amateur propagandists. They were "widely quoted but never read" and as far as adding to the store of knowledge about the origins of the war they should have been neither quoted nor read. In addition to this official literature there were a great many books and magazine articles which dealt with this controversial matter. Into the United States there came a veritable flood of this war origins literature and nearly all of it presented the British point of view. Books by Americans and Germans which attacked Germany were featured by Wellington House, but there were also many publications of English or French authorship. Undoubtedly the most effective of all these war guilt writings was that vast body of newspaper articles which, after being edited by the British censor, were published throughout the United States. In most cases these articles were written by reporters with but the scantiest knowledge of what had occurred. Almost without exception they were attempts at simplified interpretations of complicated situations. They were written in haste, with their authors deeply moved by the anguish of the war. They were written from the heart and not from the head, and appealed only to the heart of America. They were so successful that even today, a quarter of a century after the events, historians must tear down this false scaffolding before they can see clearly what the actual structure is.

[38]Published by McBride, Nast, and Co., New York, March, 1915.

[39]Published by Macmillan in 1916. Among other editions was one published by McBride, Nast and Company in 1915.

[40]Including the propaganda writings, there have been over two million books and articles dealing with the cause of the Great War. Weltkriegsbücherei, *op. cit.*, 31 ff.

[41]These became known as the rainbow series because of thier varicolored bindings.

The war guilt propaganda was a triumph of the early days of the war when interest in Europe was high and when German defense was almost entirely eliminated. It placed Germany on the defensive from the beginning and made it possible to start discussion of later events from the basis of original German guilt. Without question it was the outstanding propaganda success of the war.

Directly related to the origins or war guilt propaganda was that of war aims.[42] Most of the British writings on the German participation in the war implied or openly stated that the Germans had some very reprehensible ambitions to be realized at the eventual peace conference. Undoubtedly Germany did have ambitious desires. The implication, however, in all these arguments was that the Allied nations had no questionable motives, that they were merely fighting for peace, international law, humanity, and democracy. On January 5, 1915, Lloyd George said, "Nor are we fighting to destroy Austria-Hungary or to deprive Turkey of its capital, or of the rich and renowned lands of Asia Minor and Thrace, which are predominantly Turkish in race." This denial of selfish aims was issued just before the completion of the secret treaties of London in which the Allied nations began the division of the spoils.[43] Later understandings provided for additional gains at the expense of the Central Powers. The Treaty of Versailles is ample evidence that the war aims of Great Britain and her allies were not the result of complete disinterestedness and that their propaganda attacking German war aims might justly be termed hypocritical.[44]

One part of the war aims propaganda — that relating to colonial problems — served a double purpose. It not only condemned the Germans for their treatment of natives but provided an ex-

[42]Weltkriegsbücherei, op. cit., 36 f.

[43]For instance, article IV of the Treaty of London states, "By the future treaty of peace Italy shall receive the Trentino; the whole of Southern Tirol, as far as its natural and geographical frontier, the Brenner ..." Again in article IX, "France, Great Britain, and Russia recognize ... [Italy's] right to take over when Turkey is broken up, a portion equal to theirs in the Mediterranean ..." In article XII, "In the event of an extension of the French and British colonial possessions in Africa at the expense of Germany ..." Italy is to get compensation.

[44]Up to 1917 the Foreign Office kept a file of published statements on war aims, probably for the purpose of aiding their propagandists. This is now the property of the British War Imperial Museum.

cuse for the Allies to deprive Germany of those colonies at the peace conference.[45]

The British propaganda on the conduct of the war was primarily based upon the appalling political stupidities committed by the Germans. Starting with the invasion of Belgum and ending with the Zimmerman note, the Germans committed a series of political blunders which were simply incomparable. New to the field of world power they had no appreciation of the fact that their acts had to be governed by political expediency. They had not learned that being effective was only a minor part of political technique. They stumbled out of one error into another — to the utter joy of their opponents. The German political ability has never been high — in these years it reached bottom. It is true that the British issued a number of accounts of terrible events attributed to the Germans which were purely fictitious, but the vital part of the "conduct of the war" propaganda was the treatment given to the actual events of the war. Indeed one of the most interesting aspects of the entire war propaganda was the methods used to exploit these German blunders. By judicious editing and rather specialized emphasis, they were turned into veritable acts of frightfulness.

The most extreme phase of this propaganda was that which went under the name of the atrocity drive. This classic campaign of defamation provides an extraordinarily clear example of the way part-truths were utilized. The police records of any large city will bear out the contention that barbarous actions do occur, especially where large bodies of people are thrown together. In time of war, when the restraints of church and family which ordinarily operate are eliminated, there is naturally a great increase in such acts of violence. Also in "every large army there must be a proportion of men of criminal instincts whose worst passions are unleashed by the immunity which the conditions of warfare afford."[46] It would be very surprising if under these conditions atrocities did not occur. General Sherman once said, "You take the best lot of young men, all church members, if you please . . . put them into an army . . . let them invade the enemy's country,

[45]Weltkriegsbücherei, *op. cit.*, 48 ff.
[46]Lord Bryce, *Report of the Committee on Alleged German Outrages* (London, 1915), 25.

and live upon it for any length of time, and they will gradually lose all principle and self-restraint to a degree beyond the control of discipline."[47]

The propaganda of the British continued in this phase of the work the same practice already noticed in propaganda dealing with war origins. The censor eliminated all reference to actions by soldiers of the Allied countries which might be considered uncivilized.[48] On the other hand the propagandists gave wide publicity to all incidents which showed the enemy as brutal and barbarous. When these stories were treated in the sensational manner characteristic of American "yellow journalism" some astounding results were obtained. They gained much of their appearance of authority because of the fact that the armies of the Entente nations were fighting upon their own soil. Naturally these soldiers would commit but few atrocities against their own people. On the other hand the armies of the Central Powers were operating upon enemy soil in the midst of an hostile population. It was a perfect situation for unspeakable acts to be committed.

The tales of German barbarity were in answer to the desire of the Allies to believe that sort of thing of the Germans, and after appearing, served as a reason for believing the Germans were barbarous. They were the beginning and the end of the story; born of desire they served as reason. On August 7, 1914, Lord Bertie, the British Ambassador in Paris, wrote in his diary: "Of course each side will accuse the other of brutalities and atrocities." On the tenth of the same month he was believing those very atrocities, and by May, 1915, he reacted as the propagandists would have desired. He stated, "I began by not believing in German atrocities, and now I feel that I myself would, if I could, kill every combatant German that I might meet."

The original basis for the atrocity stories was provided in the early days of the war, especially between August 4, and August

[47]*The Reminiscences of Carl Schurz,* III (copyright, 1906-7, by Doubleday, Doran and Co., Inc.), 133. When the subject of atrocities was brought to the attention of Kitchener he exclaimed "What is the good of discussing that incident? *All war is an outrage!*" Riddell, *op. cit.,* 53.

[48]"I have examined impartially all the legends which grew up during the war. I have been convinced that atrocities were committed by all parties, even though they were committed to different degrees." Nitti, Francesco, *They Make a Desert* (London, 1924), 41. See Demartial, *op. cit.,* pages 15 ff. for examples of atrocities in former wars.

From
SIR GILBERT PARKER.

20, CARLTON HOUSE TERRACE,

LONDON, S.W.,

ENGLAND.

16 MAR 1915

Dear Sir,

I am well aware that American enterprise has made
available reprints of the official papers relating to
the present European war; but the original British prints
of these publications may not be accessible to those
persons of influence who would study them for a true
history of the conflict. I am venturing to send to you
under another cover several of these official documents.
I am sure you will not consider this an impertinence,
but will realise that Britishers are deeply anxious that
their cause may be judged from authoritative evidence.

In common with the great majority of Americans,
you have, no doubt, made up your mind as to what country
should be held responsible for this tragedy, but these
papers may be found useful for reference, and because
they contain the uncontrovertible facts, I feel that
you will probably welcome them in this form.

My long and intimate association with the United
States through my writings gives me confidence to
approach you, and I trust you will not think me
intrusive or misunderstand my motive.

With all respect,

I am,

Yours very truly,

Gilbert Parker

A LETTER FROM SIR GILBERT PARKER

30, 1914. The period was one of turmoil and excitement. War was
new to everyone involved, soldiers as well as civilians. The raw
German levies marched into Belgium not yet accustomed to strict
obedience. On the other hand the Belgian civil population did not
fully appreciate the nature of modern warfare. It was not surprising that patriotic Belgian civilians did their utmost to assist
their cause by killing German officers and soldiers. In addition,
the Germans apparently confused the actions of civilians with
those of soldiers and punished the civil population unjustly.[49]
With snipings occurring in an area in which there was a large
civilian population and a new and nervous enemy army, it is not
surprising that the actions of the Germans were inordinately
severe. Hostages were taken, buildings were destroyed in reprisal, and occasionally in retaliation, individuals, or groups of people, were executed. The method adopted by Wellington House in
dealing with these events was to remove or discount any mention
of the actions which prompted the Germans to punish the Belgians.[50]

In addition to the numerous single atrocity stories issued,
several of the propaganda agencies issued compendiums or collections of these tales. As early as September 16, 1914, the Belgian government presented its report to the American press. The
report included stories of mutilated bodies at Louvain and of
girls "burned alive in Aerschot." The greatest of these atrocity
reports, however, was that issued by the committee under Lord
Bryce dealing with the atrocities in Belgium.[51] The report was a
collection and not an analysis. A large percentage of the events
making up the report was based upon second and third hand information. Rumors and opinions were included uncritically. It is
not impossible that many of the statements used were the product
of leading questions. Incomplete versions of actual events were

[49]"The invaders appear to have proceeded upon the theory that any chance
shot coming from an unexpected place was fired by civilians." Undoubtedly the
Germans confounded "legitimate military operations with the hostile intervention
of civilians." *Bryce Report, op. cit.*, 26.

[50]"There had been instances of harsh treatment of Belgian nationals, but this
severity had been attended by extenuating circumstances." *F. R. S.*, 1914 Supplement, 799-801.

[51]The Bryce Committee was officially the "German Outrages Inquiry Committee." It was appointed by the Prime Minister in December, 1914. Dearle, *op.
cit.*, 56.

the basis of the report. In addition, this official report of the
British government dignified a great many old wives' tales and
considerable barrack-room gossip. Mr. Bryce's biographer, H.
A. L. Fisher, states that the main body of the report has not been
disproved and insists that each story be considered true until it
is proved false. It would seem to be more fair to place the burden
of proof upon Lord Bryce.

Throughout the stories are references to drunkenness among
the German soldiers. This condition, although exaggerated, perhaps accounted for some of the things which actually occurred.
To counteract any conviction that these occurrences were merely
the result of drunkenness the Bryce committee hastened to state
that "the excesses . . . . [were] too widespread and too uniform
in their character to be mere sporadic outbursts of passion or
rapacity."

The destruction of property likewise offered opportunities for
exaggeration. Numerous stories in the Bryce report told of little
pastilles which the German soldiers threw into buildings to set
them in flames. For instance, "they plastered the walls with in-
flammable pastilles about the size of a penny, which they rubbed
with the hand and ignited." Very possibly these tales of the destruction of buildings were correct. It is, of course, impossible to
say what motivated the acts, and the accounts of the Bryce committee led one to believe that justifiable motives did not exist.
Destruction of property, however, is oftentimes necessary to
avoid the destruction of armies. The stories were effective largely
because the civilian population of the world was totally ignorant
of war and its necessities.

The utilization of Belgian civilians as shields for German
soldiery furnished material for several good stories in the report.
It is impossible to state whether or not this was done, but it is not
completely unreasonable. Soldiers might wish to do this regardless of their nationality. The shield stories, however, were only
of minor importance in the atrocity literature.

Sex stories in the report were among the most effective and
were given wide circulation by the American traveling-salesmen
public.[52] The supply did not approach the demand. Although

[52]Sex stories are traditional material for war propagandists. The story of the
Olivette in the Spanish-American war reveals a nineteenth century version of such

many of the alleged events were colorful enough, variations and additions enriched the original work of the Bryce Committee. Some of these Bryce sex stories were very good as propaganda, depending upon the people to whose attention they were directed. A few quotations will show this quite clearly:

> Immediately after the men had been killed, I saw the Germans going into the houses in the Place and bringing out the women and girls. About twenty were brought out. They were marched close to the corpses. Each of them was held by the arms. They tried to get away. They were made to lie on tables which had been brought into the square. About fifteen of them were then violated. Each of them was violated by about twelve soldiers. While this was going on about seventy Germans were standing round the women including five officers (young). The officers started it. There were some of the Germans between me and the women, but I could see everything perfectly. The ravishing went on for about one and one-half hours. I watched the whole time. Many of the women fainted and showed no sign of life. The Red Cross took them away to the hospital.[53]

This story is undoubtedly the work of someone's feverish imagination. If it were not the work of one of Bryce's clerks or atrocity collectors, it was probably an ordinary barrack-room classic.

Occasionally the sex stories would be combined with sadistic aberrations:

> As I looked into the kitchen I saw the Germans seize the baby out of the arms of the farmer's wife. There were three German soldiers, one officer and two privates. The two privates held the baby and the officer took out his sword and cut the baby's head off . . .

This, of course, is but a rewrite of a standard wartime atrocity story. Senator Allen of Nebraska used it in 1898. He stated that it had been "conclusively established that Spanish soldiers had

---

propaganda. The following story from the American Revolution might be the grandfather of some of the World War atrocities: "A couple of Hessians rape two American girls in the presence of their father and brother, as a result of which one of the girls commits suicide and the other 'is suddenly seized with a violent convulsion attended with hickups, that in a few minutes put an end to her existence.'" Heilman, Robert B., *America in English Fiction 1760:1800* (Baton Rouge, 1937), 185.

[53]*Bryce Report,* P 11.

in one or more instances taken little infants by the heels, held them up, and hacked them to pieces with the deadly machete in the presence of the mothers and fathers themselves."[54] The account continued as follows:

> We saw the officer say something to the farmer's wife, and saw her push him away. After five or six minutes the two soldiers seized the woman and put her on the ground. She resisted them and they then pulled all her clothes off her until she was quite naked. The officer then violated her while one soldier held her by the shoulders and the other by the arms. After the officer each soldier in turn violated her, the other soldier holding her down.... After the woman had been violated by the three the officer cut off the woman's breasts.[55]

The cutting of women's breasts seemed to be the most popular of the sadistic touches. For instance:

> We met a woman whose blouse or dress was torn open in front and she was all covered with blood. Her breasts had been cut off, the edges of the wounds being torn and rough. We spoke to the woman. She was with us for ten minutes, but it was impossible to understand what she was saying as she was *folle*.[56]

Another very popular story told with many variations was the spitted child:

> One of the Germans took a rifle and struck her a tremendous blow with the butt on the head. Another took his bayonet and fixed it and thrust it through the child. He then put his rifle on his shoulder with the child up it, its little arms stretched out once or twice.[57]

> They were singing and making a lot of noise and dancing about. As the German soldiers came along the street I saw a small child, whether boy or girl I could not see, come out of a house. The child was about two years of age. The child came into the middle of the street so as to be in the way of the soldiers. The soldiers were walking in twos. The first line of two passed the child; one of the second line, the man on the left, stepped aside and drove his bayonet with both hands into the child's stomach, lifting the child into the air on his bayonet and carrying it away on his bayonet, he and his comrades still singing.[58]

[54]Quoted by Millis in his *Martial Spirit*, 70.
[55]*Bryce Report*, P 12.
[56]*Bryce Report*, P 74 d 89.
[57]*Bryce Report*, P 32 d 130.
[58]*Bryce Report*, P 32 d 4.

Less extreme stories of sadism still contained propaganda value:

> We saw a boy of about twelve with a bandage where his hand should be. We asked what was the matter, and were told the Germans had cut off his hand because he clung to his parents, who were being thrown in the fire.[59] Personally, I only saw the bandage. We also saw a mother and her little girl with a bandage on the latter's head. The mother told us the child's ear had been cut off by the Germans. . . .[60]

> We saw a German soldier come out of the wood and fire three separate times at a little girl of from four to six years of age who was at the point marked A [on a sketch of the place]. Seeing that he failed to hit the child by firing at her and that she stood quite still, he ran at her and bayonetted her in the stomach.[61]

Among the purely fictitious tales of classic fame, was that of the "crucified Canadian." This unfortunate individual was sometimes a Frenchman, and sometimes a Belgian. He appeared in many uniforms and with varying personalities.[62] An American reporter asked an Englishman if the "crucified Canadian" story were true and was told that it was not but "it had an excellent effect on Canadian recruiting."[63]

The version which was included in the Bryce Report is as follows:

> On September tenth we came to the village of Haecht, and I and some others were sent out as a patrol: we passed a river and came to a farmhouse. On the door of the farm I saw a child — two or three years old — nailed to the door by its hands and feet. . . . In the garden of the same house I saw the body of another child — a little girl of five or six; she had been shot in the forehead.[64]

In order to exploit the intense feeling created by the sinking

[59]"We know now that no babies whose hands were cut off by German soldiers have ever been identified." Palmer, Colonel Frederick, *Newton D. Baker America at War*, I (New York, 1931), 38.

[60]*Bryce Report*, P 5 a 14.

[61]*Bryce Report*, P 76 d 94.

[62]See Charteris, *op. cit.*, 75, for one story of the origin of the "crucified Canadian" and of the "Angel of Mons." Also see Ponsonby, Arthur, *Falsehood in War-Time* (New York, 1928), 91 ff.

[63]Palmer, *With My Own Eyes*, 322.

[64]*Bryce Report*, P 79 d 107.

of the *Lusitania,* Sir Gilbert Parker rushed the atrocity report to completion and issued it five days after the tragedy off Old Kinsdale Head. By taking advantage of this event a great deal of attention was directed toward the report.

It was with this particular project that Sir Gilbert Parker's organization had its happiest utilization of "authority." Among men with reputations for reliability there could have been secured no better one than Bryce to influence the people of the United States. His *American Commonwealth* and other works very justly gained for him a reputation as a scholar and his services as British Ambassador to the United States had made many friends for him. He was spoken of as "Wilson's old friend" and the St. Louis *Republican* said, "If there is a man in the entire British Empire whom the people of this nation are prepared to believe implicitly, it is James Bryce." Wellington House could report: "Even in papers hostile to the Allies, there is not the slightest attempt to impugn the correctness of the facts alleged. Lord Bryce's prestige in America put scepticism out of the question, and many leading articles begin on this note."[65]

Frederick Palmer, a pro-British writer of war days, now says, "One could forgive Lord Bryce, so simple, so benign and ingenuous — this great liberal — for believing the evidence of extreme instances [of atrocities] which was shown him."[66] "We may look back on Lord Bryce's signing of the atrocity report as a venerable statesman's 'bit' when, in the name of its beloved dead and wounded, every combatant nation realized that its future was to be signed and sealed by victory or defeat at arms."[67] This is, perhaps, the nearest thing to an excuse that can be made for Lord Bryce. His report is one of the most extreme examples of the definition of propaganda as "assassination by word." It was in itself one of the worst atrocities of the war.[68]

[65]*A. P. R.,* May 27, 1915.
[66]Palmer, *With My Own Eyes,* 322.
[67]Palmer, *N. D. Baker,* Vol. 38.
[68]The *Bryce Report* was supported by J. H. Morgan in his book *Germany's Dishonored Army.* Morgan interrogated in hospitals and field lazzerettes, two or three hundred officers and soldiers, representing almost every regiment of the British army. He also took the testimony of the French and Belgian soldiers when it was possible. German cruelty was supposed to be one of habit, and carefully thought out and characteristic of Germany. Examples: carriers of telegrams found burned with coal oil, soldiers whose faces had been caved in by boot heels, the

The atrocity stories which were issued under the official seals of the various governments were but a fraction of such literature.[69] There were any number of other stories based primarily upon alleged German diaries and letters. "We know that many of the letters . . . were faked."[70] The largest body of these stories appeared as news items or as anecdotes of public lecturers.

Many of the propaganda stories in the World War were not new merchandise but were merely the stock-in-trade garnered by former war propagandists. Removed from the shelves where they had been placed after previous wars, they were dusted off, newly labeled, and advertised as new stock. Unfortunately some of the shopworn goods did not appeal to the public.

The standard prison propaganda[71] was not very successful in the United States because it had been too thoroughly exploited in the Civil War. Instead, stories which were more oriental in character, i.e., more extreme and unbelievable, were found to be most effective with the sensation-craving public. One of the most popular of the stories not included in the collections was that of the corpse factory. Here was told the tale of the horrible Huns who sent the bodies of dead soldiers back to Germany to be boiled down into soap. There were several versions of this anecdote. Although intended for the oriental market, it was most successful in the United States.[72]

The propagandists composed a number of "modernistic" atrocity stories such as tales of infecting wells with bacteria. Wellington House reported quite cheerfully that the distinguished American novelist, Gertrude Atherton, was spreading the story of innoculating exchange prisoners with tuberculosis germs.[73]

A somewhat unusual handling of an atrocity story is to be found in the tale of the Belgian baby without hands. Apparently

---

soldier whose body showed many bayonet wounds, made at the time he tied up a bullet wound. The Morgan report was widely read and made a good impression upon American readers. Wanderscheck, *op. cit.*, 133.

[69]The Committee for National Patriotic Organizations issued a supplement to the magazine, *The Field*, on atrocities. They also issued books on the subject.

[70]Palmer, *N. D. Baker*, I, 38.

[71]See Weltkriegsbücherei, *op. cit.*, 50 f.

[72]See Ponsonby, *op. cit.*, 102 ff. for the origin and the more detailed account.

[73]In 1914 Mrs. Carrie Chapman Catt came home with some especially gory tales. After the United States entered the war the Reverend Newell Dwight Hillis also made some contributions to this literature.

the chopping off of a child's hands did occur, only the incident happened in Africa and the Belgians rather than the Germans did the mutilating. This particular story had a number of amusing repercussions.[74] Among other standard stories are those of the mutilated nurse, the baby of Courbeck Loo, little Alf's stamp collection and the tattooed man.[75]

It is true that these fictitious tales were effective in creating anti-German feeling. However, the bald-faced falsity of the yarns has created indignation among certain liberals and has caused them to exaggerate the importance of these fabrications. The major portion of the atrocity stories was not based upon lurid imaginings but upon truths presented to the public in warped or distorted fashion. Actual occurrences with vital incidents omitted in the telling, and with incorrect interpretations of the things told, created an impression in the minds of the public which was totally false.

One of the best known stories based on real occurrences was that of the destruction of Louvain. The problem of handling large hostile populations behind their lines troubled the Germans throughout the war. At Louvain they were convinced of the co-operation of the Belgians in the town with an attacking body of Belgian soldiers. They were very probably correct. In retaliation the Germans executed some of the civilians and destroyed about one-eighth of the city. As a study in Belgian heroism the events at Louvain would have been good material for the propagandists, but in transforming them into an atrocity story by omitting discussion of the acts of the Belgian civilians, by exaggerating the destruction carried out, and by throwing in an occasional fictitious human interest story, Louvain became one of the classic bits of propaganda literature.[76]

One of the very fine opportunities for Wellington House came with the firing upon Rheims Cathedral. The Bryce Report men-

[74]Ponsonby, *op. cit.*, 78 ff.

[75]Ponsonby, *passim*.

[76]The Louvain story is included in most of the longer wartime propaganda books. Wartime writings dealing with it exclusively are listed in Weltkriegsbücherei, *op. cit.*, 46.

The Louvain library "had not been fired by official order but in soldier wantonness, which is excusable on your side and deliberately official on the other." Palmer, *With My Own Eyes, op. cit.*, 305.

tions that "In many instances the soldiers of the Allied armies used church towers and private houses as cover for their operations." In the case of Rheims, the French apparently could not resist the opportunity of utilizing the towers of the church for observation purposes. The Germans found confirmation of this practice in French and English periodicals.[77] Consequently thinking only of military necessity and with complete disregard of the propaganda value to the enemy of such an action, they fired upon the cathedral and caused considerable damage to it. It was but one more case in which the Germans stumbled into the arms of the Allies' propagandists. Wellington House and *la maison de la presse,* were able to exploit their blunder very satisfactorily. All that was necessary in this case was to ignore the use to which the French had been putting the building and to enlarge on the damage done to it. The story awakened the sympathy of many non-religious people in the United States because of the fact that pictures of this cathedral were popular etchings in the living rooms of the lower middle class. Also public school teachers had a habit of speaking of Rheims as the outstanding example of the beauties of European architecture. In all probability the complete destruction of other equally beautiful structures would have had much less propaganda value.

The emphasis on the fearful plights of "women and children" characterized all British propaganda, but Wellington House realized that this procedure could reach perfection only if it were made less abstract. It may have been the desire to create another Joan of Arc, or perhaps an Evangelina Cisneros, which caused them to publicize Edith Cavell. Whatever the motive, this English nurse was made the personification of innocent people who were crushed under the German war machine. The tragedy of Edith Cavell, when given artistic treatment, came to be the second ranking atrocity story of the war.

In the various wars in history women have played a more or less aloof part. The British disposed of Joan of Arc, the American government hanged Mrs. Surratt, and other women have been executed from time to time, but on the whole they have secured a kind of immunity. During the World War, the French

[77] Kriegsministerium, *Die Beschiessung der Kathedral von Rheims* (Berlin, 1915).

shot a number of women, one of them for aiding prisoners to escape.[78] Edith Cavell was engaged in the same practice in Belgium under cover of her mission as a nurse. Between November, 1914, and July, 1915, she assisted some two hundred and fifty men in getting through the lines.[79] She was executed along with others in a general clean-up of the spies of the Allies behind the German lines. She apparently did not engage in espionage work herself but her aid in getting agents in and out of the country must have been invaluable.

The question naturally arises as to why this particular execution of a woman should have been such an effective bit of propaganda. When Jusserand approached Lansing on the matter, the latter wanted to know "why so much more sympathy for the women than for the men?" But suffering women are a stereotype in the thinking of most Anglo-Saxons. Women and children served as especially fine objects of propaganda throughout the war. It was easy to make people weep for these "defenseless" human beings when equally defenseless men could gain little sympathy. The Germans took no advantage of the opportunity in the case of Marguerite Schmidt, and it is quite apparent that the puritan-minded Americans would never have become excited over the execution of such a woman as Mata Hari. Edith Cavell, on the other hand, was an exceptionally good figure to publicize. In the first place, she was a woman of the middle class; secondly, she was a nurse — a profession of high dramatic appeal to women; and she apparently displayed considerable heroism in going to her death.

Because certain American officials were involved in the Cavell affair (albeit inappropriately), propagandists were able to represent the United States as a party to the incident — an excellent example of the propaganda of identification. Wellington House noted with satisfaction that James M. Beck demanded "the dismissal of the officers who flouted, deceived, and mocked the representatives of the United States."[80] An American correspondent

[78]Marguerite Schmidt, March 24, 1915. Nine women spies were condemned to death by the French. Aston, Sir George, *Secret Service* (London, 1930), 153.

[79]Got, Ambroise, *The Case of Miss Cavell* (London, 1920), 73.

[80]*A. P. R.*, November 5, 1915. The incident also served to stop some peace talk. *A. P. R.*, October 29, 1915.

of Sir Gilbert Parker wrote to him that the Cavell case "gave us occasion for another outburst of real sentiment."[81]

Under the treatment of able journalists, the combination of heroic appeal and repulsion of an atrocity made her case one of the most effective in the wartime propaganda. Wellington House reported: for its effect in America, the Cavell case "can only be paralleled by the *Lusitania* outrage or the conquest of Belgium."[82] Innumerable newspaper articles, magazine articles, and even books were issued on the subject. Wanderscheck lists in his *Bibliography* twenty-eight books or pamphlets which dealt exclusively with Edith Cavell and he does not attempt to enumerate those which treated her incidentally.

The execution of Captain Fryatt was also given considerable attention but it was never a successful bit of propaganda material. Although similar to the *Lusitania* case the casualties were too limited to attract wide attention, while the fact that the victim was a man made it impossible to induce the public to shed many tears over his fate.

The first chance to exploit fully the propaganda value of the use of new methods of warfare was with the introduction of gas at Second Ypres. This enabled Wellington House to publicize the "inhuman" methods employed by the enemy. Some of the heat in this controversy may have resulted from professional jealousy, for the French had been working on a gas and were not yet ready for its trial. When they did perfect it, there was a good deal of satisfaction expressed in the newspapers over the just retaliation. Very soon there was an easing up on the talk about "inhuman warfare" in regard to the use of gas, because the prevailing winds favored the Allies, and they found gas a most useful weapon. The British propaganda department report on disclosures of German activities in the United States contained the interesting remark: "The memorandum [one of the papers from the Albert portfolio] discloses that England and France have been in the market for liquid chlorine since September, 1914, through the agency of an Italian, Dalbrun."[83] Months before

---

[81]*A. P. R.*, December 3, 1915.

[82]*A. P. R.*, October 29, 1915.

[83]*A. P. R. Supplement,* September 10, 1915. "The French were the first to consider the use of poison gas." Palmer, *N. D. Baker,* I, 38.

this gas attack, the French had used liquid fire which was apparently more frightful than gas.[84]

Another event which offered an opportunity to Wellington House to become hysterical in damning the Germans was the new method of fighting in and from the air. England has been very fortunate in her history in being able to do most of her fighting in foreign lands. Many times she has had to spend only money and no blood. With the introduction of aircraft she was suddenly brought face to face with actual warfare at home. It was a frightful shock. But the raids did serve a good purpose by providing the propagandists an opportunity to exclaim to Americans about attacks on defenseless towns and the killing of women and children. Wellington House was able to report, "The American press condemns almost unanimously Zeppelin raids."[85] It should be mentioned, of course, that in the last year of the war British air raids alone over Germany were "five times greater than the total number of German air raids on Great Britain during the four years of the war." In the thirteen months preceding the armistice there were 709 raids into Germany, 374 on large defenseless towns.[86]

The attacks upon German methods of war might be given greater consideration if it were not for the fact that they applied also to the other warring powers. A Frenchman has stated that the "reproches à l'Allemagne s'appliquent aussi bien à la France et à ses alliés."[87] Lord Fisher, an Englishman, has remarked: "The essence of war is violence, moderation is stupidity." In 1912 André Tardieu declared: "I will have nothing to do with a moderation or suppression of air warfare or submarine war. Innocent people, churches, in fact, all objects of value must be destroyed in order to gain a final victory."[88]

Directly in line with the Allies' atrocity campaign and overlapping it in many cases was the appeal to American compassion. For over four years appeals for sympathy for "poor France" and "poor Belgium" were constantly directed at the American public.

[84]Cruttwell, op. cit., 153.
[85]A. P. R., February 25, 1916.
[86]Allen, William C., War! Behind the Smoke Screen (Philadelphia, 1929), 63.
[87]Demartial, op. cit., 10.
[88]Bomert, E. A., Truth, A Path to Justice and Reconciliation (London, 1926), 182.

The depths of pathos were plumbed, providing a daily emotional catharsis for sentimental Americans. "It was the propaganda of love as contrasted with the propaganda of hate; and . . . although slower in effect, was yet powerful."[89]

One English writer has said that "the Congo scandal had made Belgium a stench in the nostrils of the world." It was this same Belgium with the evil reputation which now became the primary subject of the pity campaign. A combination of two propaganda methods is to be found in this procedure. In the first place emotion was enlisted on the side of the Allies. Secondly by persuading Americans to participate in the relief work they were unconsciously made to identify the Allies' cause as the cause of Americans.

There were numerous national and local relief organizations in the United States which served to spread the propaganda of the Allies' "holy war." In Louisville, Kentucky, the famous editor, Henry Watterson, became head of the local Belgian Relief Committee at the behest of the Belgian Prime Minister, Havenith. Prominent men of other towns were beseiged for their support either for the Belgian Relief Committee, for the Permanent Blind Relief War Fund, or for some similar organization. Much newspaper space was bought for the relief funds, much was contributed by the papers, and more was paid for by large firms. It was arranged that the relief money would be spent locally in each case, so that the merchants would profit and at the same time would be serving charity. Each of these drives served to emphasize the propaganda of pathos. Each served to enlist the sympathies of all those Americans who contributed.

Americans in Europe who were engaged in this work of mercy were likewise exploited. The ambulance units which went to France and Belgium were thoroughly publicized and the Red Cross hospitals set up with American funds contributed their bit toward propaganda. "Secretary Bryan . . . on one occasion sent a query as to whether this American hospital service was taking care to succor German wounded as well as French. By a remarkable coincidence it was discovered that there was not a German in the hospital; but the Ambassador rushed out one of his military attachés with a searching party, and by good luck they

[89]Irwin, *op. cit.*, 148.

found three mangled but still living Germans. One died on the way in and was dumped unceremoniously upon the roadside; the other two survived, and Mr. Herrick was able to telegraph Washington that they were caring for Germans."[90]

Above all was the work of the American relief organizations in Belgium a vital bit of propaganda. The best example of the effectiveness of this appeal is the publicity given to Herbert Hoover, who headed Belgian relief. Articles dealing with the war activities of any American would have been popular, but when that American had a very important position, his news value, and hence his propaganda value, was greatly enlarged. One interesting sidelight on this relief propaganda is told by a Belgian woman who came to this country to appeal for money. Apparently she was a cheerful soul and had not realized how "pitiful" she was supposed to be, so she wore her gay little frocks and told her straightforward story. Soon she awakened to what was expected of her, dyed all her clothes black, and made the rest of her appeals in mourning. Later this same woman wrote, "I was amused and gratified to have a cable from the Belgian Prime Minister asking me to go to Brazil and the Argentine Republic as an official propagandist. On the advice of Mr. Roosevelt and of Sir Cecil Spring-Rice, I declined the mission."[91]

An effective part of the "poor Belgium" propaganda was the publicity given to Cardinal Mercier's letter of defiance to General von Bissing. This was a fake concocted by two journalists. It was cribbed from Anatole France's *L'anneau d'amethyste* in his *Histoire contemporaine*. The hoax was discovered but naturally did not interfere with the circulation of the story. Wellington House reported: "The charge . . . appears to be correct, judging by internal evidence. Whole passages are taken verbatim."[92]

The effectiveness of the "poor Belgium" propaganda cannot be questioned. The American people lost their heads completely and could discuss no phase of the war in which Belgium was involved without throwing reason to the winds. The secretary of a Pittsburgh munitions plant wrote to the Secretary of State:

[90]Millis, *op. cit.*, 75.
[91]Vandervelde, *op. cit.*, 52.
[92]*D. R. F. P.*, May 26, 1916.

"Never forget for a moment that there are a million — or millions — of Germans in our country working night and day to force us to declare war on Belgium — the little ruined nation of Belgium."[93] An American correspondent now writes that the "propaganda of Belgium had much to do with bringing the United States into the war," and yet admits that he himself wrote it "in the illusion of the moment."[94] Arthur Balfour could say, "How fortunate it was for the sake of our relations with America, that we had the outrage of Belgium."[95] A typical British propaganda report stated: "It is remarkable how quickly the American press responds to any appeal on behalf of the Belgians. Belgium has become almost an American charge and the fate of Belgium seems still to make the strongest appeal for American sympathy."[96]

The culmination of British "educational efforts" in the first twenty months of the war was found in the propaganda of damnation. Propaganda in all its phases tended to create as evil a picture of the enemy as could be contrived. The appeal to pity, the atrocity campaign, and the war guilt literature all united in showing that the "foes were not only defiant, vainglorious men, but malign spirits steeped in depravity and lewdness."[97] A book issued by Wellington House stated: "The behaviour of the German Red Cross was vile and the German women were horrible."[98] In cartoons the German was pictured as a cross between a gorilla and Simon Legree. The classic villainies of Richard III or Iago would hardly compare with the lurid acts of the enemy of the British. One phase of this propaganda to assassinate the character of the enemy was in the writings about German culture and ideals. The writings which had formerly been praised for their thoroughness and realism were now widely attacked and were offered as proof of the evil character of the Germans.[99]

In the work of enemy damnation in the Bryce Report there was a peculiar conflict. It was desired to show the enemy in the worst possible light and yet by recording examples of individual

[93]Lansing Papers, Library of Congress.
[94]Palmer, *With My Own Eyes*, 306.
[95]*Ibid.*, 309.
[96]*A. P. R.*, February 25, 1916.
[97]Playne, Caroline E., *Society at War 1914-1916* (Boston, 1931), 95.
[98]*The Quality of Mercy* by Kible Howar, quoted in Sprott, *op. cit.*, 28.
[99]Weltkriegsbücherei, *op. cit.*, 25 ff.

malevolence it was feared that the German government would appear to be innocent. Hence, although numerous instances of crimes were recorded which could only have been personal, the effort was constantly made to show that they were instigated by the German government.[100] On the American scene the effort was made in certain districts to exonerate the German people and to place all blame on their government. Although to be found in the earliest of war writings, this Janus-like procedure was to gain its greatest fame in the phrase of Woodrow Wilson: "We have no quarrel with the German people."[101]

Probably as effective as all the formal propaganda of anathematization was a group of phrases which were used in much of the newspaper writing. The incorrectly quoted phrase of Bismarck, "blood and iron," was used with propaganda of German militarism. The title of the German national anthem, *Deutschland, Deutschland, über alles,* was glibly interpreted as the German desire to rule the world rather than as an expression of German patriotism. The devout phrase, *Gott mit uns,* was interpreted as an expression of conceit — "God is on our side" — rather than as an expression of supplication — "God be with us" or "God is with us."

In addition to phrases there was also developed a stirring group of anti-German epithets. Any small boy can testify to the efficacy of strong words as a substitute for weak arguments. The strong words eliminate the necessity of arguing. The Germans were branded as "cowardly, grasping, lying, cruel, inferior, and criminal."[102] Evil names such as "Huns, beasts, barbarians," were attached to them, and other words such as Prussianism, Absolutism, Kaiserism, and Pan-Germanism, were used. This was so effective that eventually the word German itself came to signify all that was base. With the establishment of the anti-German mental climate among the American people it came to be impossible for an individual to analyze the war critically without exposing himself to a barrage of these words. He was

[100]Some months after the declaration of war, M. Durkheim, in his *L'Alle-magne au-dessus de tout* claimed that atrocities were a part of the German war plan. Bornecqui and Drouilly, *op. cit.,* 45.

[101]The *Outlook,* the *Independent,* and *Harper's Weekly,* among others used this approach. House recommended the idea to Wilson.

[102]Wanderscheck, *op. cit.,* 19.

immediately damned with the superlative of these epithets —
pro-German.[103]

The picture of the Germans painted by British propagandists
was fantastic, but it was accepted as long as the peoples propagandized were kept away from Germans in the flesh. Newspapermen who toured Belgium behind the German lines failed to
find any evidence of atrocities. Their famous telegram to the
Associated Press read as follows: "In spirit fairness we unite in
declaring German atrocities groundless as far as were able to
observe. After spending two weeks with German army accompanying troops upward hundred miles we unable report single
instance unprovoked reprisal. Also unable confirm rumors mis-
treatment prisoners or non-combatants. . . . Numerous investi-
gated rumors proved groundless. . . . Discipline German soldiers
excellent as observed. No drunkenness. To truth these statements we pledge professional personal word."[104] An English minister reported: "I have on my table letters from almost every
camp in England, from Scotland, Egypt and the front. I search
in vain for one bitter or angry word against Germany."[105] Just
before the Bryce Report was compiled an American visited the
front and reported as follows: "People told us that the Germans
behaved very well during their short occupation [of Amiens] of
about eleven days." "One thing that has struck me forcibly since
coming to the front is the universal respect which the army itself
has for the German army. I have heard nothing but praise concerning them, for their bravery, their valour, and their wonderful
machine training."[106]

At the time of the Peace Conference the American Commission was informed that soldiers in the army of occupation were
getting along with the Germans better than they were with the
French. An officer returning from Coblenz stated: "The United
States Army of Occupation will come back from Germany con-

[103]After the United States entered the war this was responsible for the Ang-
licization of many German names.

[104]September 3, 1914 — Roger Lewis (A.P.), Irvin S. Cobb (*Saturday Evening Post*), Harvey Hansen (Chicago Daily *News*), O'Donell Bennett, and John
T. McCutcheon.

[105]Playne, *op. cit.*, 57. The propaganda, of course, was primarily effective
among civilians.

[106]November 21 and 29, 1914. The Squier Diary in the Library of Congress.

vinced that we fought on the wrong side — that the German is a
better citizen than the Frenchman." His investigation disclosed
the following American complaints about the French: (1) The
French rob the Americans on every occasion; (2) "The French
are dirty in their persons, in their houses, in their towns. Also,
they are an immoral lot;" (3) "The French army after the spring
of 1918 held back as much as possible, giving the United States
army all the hard work to do."

These complaints, though probably not justified, were fairly
widespread among Americans of the army of occupation and resulted in the fact that "French officers were practically never
saluted by United States enlisted men." "The effect on a German
of a French officer walking through groups of American enlisted
men, with never a salute, is obvious."[107] The remedy suggested
was more propaganda.

In comparing war guilt, as far as such a thing is relevant, it
seems clear that Germany was more responsible than France or
Great Britain. In comparing war conduct one is also impressed
by the fact that, as far as we can tell, German actions were worse
than those of most of her enemies. In both cases it is evident that
the statesmanship of the Germans was distinctly inferior to that
of her principal enemies. These facts seem fairly incontestable.
But the British version of them — and the version current in the
United States — makes a very different story, and a totally false
story. The acceptance of this British interpretation by American
leaders is important in considering events of the neutrality years
because it was this interpretation which prompted these leaders
to direct their actions in such a way as to lead to war.

[107]Confidential Report of J. C. Grew, January 17, 1919. Henry White Papers,
Library of Congress.

CHAPTER IV ☆ THE PROPAGANDA OF ECONOMICS

THE British campaign to gain American economic assistance was strikingly similar to their education campaign and, as far as results are concerned, must be considered a part of it. Where propagandists tried to establish the identity of British and American idealism, agents directing the economic maneuvers attempted to fuse the industrial and financial systems of the two countries. Likewise, where the censor eliminated news coming from Germany, the British economic agents destroyed all business connections between the United States and the Central Powers. British propaganda and British economic warfare supplemented and complemented each other. The one operated primarily upon American feelings, the other upon American interests.

The merging of American and British economic interests turned upon several factors. The first of these was British naval policy which made American foreign trade dependent upon the actions of the British government. It also caused the Germans to retaliate and thus come in conflict with the American government. The second was purchases in this country which meant high wages and higher profits for thousands of people in American industry. The third was British loans. These gave Americans a vested interest in the Allies' cause. All three combined to create good will between the United States and Great Britain and, indirectly, to create ill-will between the United States and Germany. Each step was propaganda in the most practical meaning of the word.

The conscription of American industry and commerce by the British was made possible by the elimination of business connections between the United States and Germany. According to international law, trade between a neutral and warring power could be completely stopped only in cases where an actual blockade was maintained. Under the law of nations, however, it is possible to stop a vessel at sea and bring its captain before a

prize court under certain conditions.[1] Utilizing this legal tech-
nicality, the British began to set up what was in actuality a
blockade. The most effective means of stifling trade with the
Central Powers was to claim that material being sent to those
nations was contraband. This was done by extending to fantastic
proportions the meaning of the word contraband. The first requisite was to transfer to the list of "absolute contraband" (i.e.,
specific war munitions) every article of peace-time commerce
which was thought could be included without too much risk of
protest from the United States. Everything else was made "conditional contraband." Every "two or three months fresh notifi-
cations were sent to the neutrals" of additions of these two lists.[2]

When the outcry against these measures became too strong,
certain commodities were temporarily removed from the contraband list. For instance, on October 25, 1914, cotton was again
allowed to go through to Germany, but as soon as the price of
cotton went up and the southern planters were finding sufficient
markets among the Allies, it was reclassified as contraband. "The
[British] Ambassador gave assurance on November 1, 1914,
that the British Government then had no intention of interfering
with turpentine and rosin. On December 22 he informed the
Department of State that his Government had decided to add
turpentine and rosin to the list of absolute contraband."[3]

The second part of this procedure was in the extension of
the meaning of the phrase "conditional" contraband. "Conditional
contraband could be confiscated only upon proof of its destination to the armed forces of the enemy." By placing almost every
essential article on the conditional contraband list, it became
possible at a later time to transfer even these articles to the
classification of absolute contraband.

These British restrictions created a difficult situation in Germany. In order to husband their resources, and to prevent profi-

[1](1) If they offer resistance to search; (2) if they carry contraband; (3) if
they render aid to the enemy; (4) if they attempt to infringe a blockade. Guichard,
Lieut. Louis, *The Naval Blockade, 1914-1918* (New York, 1930), 7.

[2]As Sir Edward Grey expressed it: "It would be politic for us not to make the
list too large at first."

[3]United States, Department of State, *Policy Of The United States Toward
Maritime Commerce In War,* State Department Publication #835, (Carlton Savage, editor), II (Washington, 1936), 36. Hereafter cited as Savage.

teering, the Germans placed food under government control.[4] Using this as an excuse, the British immediately added food to the contraband list. The American government voiced its objections and quoted Lord Salisbury as saying: "Foodstuffs, with a hostile destination, can be considered contraband of war only if they are supplies for the enemy's forces. It is not sufficient that they are capable of being so used; it must be shown that this was in fact their destination at the time of the seizure."[5] The Germans tried to have this British order in council revoked. "The [American] Department of State received formal assurances from the German Government on February 8 that foodstuffs imported into Germany directly or indirectly from the United States, would not be used by the German armed forces or by Government authorities. Furthermore, the German Government expressed its willingness to have food from the United States distributed by American organizations."[6] Naturally, the British gave no serious consideration to this suggestion.

In order to enforce these tortured interpretations of the laws of contraband, and to gain more complete control over sea-going commerce, measures were taken to force all ships to direct their courses through English waters. On November 5, 1914, an Admiralty announcement stated: "All ships passing a line drawn from the northern point of the Hebrides through the Faroe Islands to Iceland, do so at their own risk." Later, by forcing all ships to enter British ports for examination rather than permitting them to be searched on the high seas according to the usage of international law, even the commerce permitted by the new "British" international law was practically eliminated. "Even a vessel which was finally permitted to proceed on her voyage was often detained so long a time that the profits were eaten up."[7] In cases where the cargo was suspected of being contraband, shippers were forced to appear before British prize courts. "The inordinate costs and delays which they were able to impose upon

---

[4]It has been claimed that shipments of food were stopped as early as August 20, 1914. Seymour, Charles, *American Diplomacy During The World War* (Johns Hopkins Press, 1934), 34.

[5]*Papers Relating To The Foreign Relations Of The United States* (Washington, 1928), 1914 *Supplement*, 230. Hereafter referred to as *F. R. S.*

[6]Savage, *op. cit.*, II, 15.

[7]Lansing's *Memoirs*, 123.

the 'suspected' shipper merely in bringing his case to trial were a sufficient weapon in themselves" and it was the British courts which passed upon the proof.

These restrictive measures were but the preliminary attempts to obtain a blockade where the legal right to blockade did not exist. The Germans were so disturbed by these actions that in retaliation they declared a war zone around the British Isles and threatened to sink all ships which entered those waters. This provided the English with exactly the excuse for which they were looking. In counter-retaliation, on March 1, 1915, the following declaration was made: "The British and French Governments will therefore hold themselves free to detain and take into port ships carrying goods of presumed enemy *destination, ownership* or *origin.*"[8] "The [American] Secretary of State commented on this declaration in cables of March 5 to the American Ambassadors in Great Britain and France.[9] He stated that the apparent intention of the two powers to interfere with and take into custody all ships trading with Germany was in effect a blockade of German ports. ... Furthermore, the first sentence of the declaration claimed a right pertaining only to a state of blockade and the last sentence proposed a treatment of ships and cargoes as if no blockade existed. The two together presented 'a proposed course of action previously unknown to international law,' and as a consequence neutrals had no standard by which to measure their rights or to avoid danger to their ships and cargoes. The Secretary believed that the British and French Governments ought to assert whether they relied upon the rules governing a blockade or the rules applicable when no blockade existed." "The declaration of the Allies was made effective by a British order in council of March 11, 1915,[10] and by a French decree of March 13."[11] The

[8]Savage, *op. cit.*, II, 16.
[9]*Ibid.*, 273, Document 53.
[10]*Ibid.*, 274, Document 54.
[11]*Ibid.*, 16 f. The British order in council stated: "1. No merchant vessel which sailed from her port of departure after the 1st March 1915, shall be allowed to proceed on her voyage to any German port....2. No merchant vessel which sailed from any German port after the 1st March, 1915, shall be allowed to proceed on her voyage with any goods on board laden at such port....3. Every merchant vessel which sailed from her port of departure after the 1st March, 1915, on her way to a port other than a German port, carrying goods with an enemy destination, or which are enemy property, may be required to discharge such goods in a British or Allied port." *Ibid.*, 276 f.

order in council itself avoided the use of the word "blockade." In the covering note it was stated that they were "initiating a policy of blockade." Consequently by March, 1915, the British were able to put into operation a blockade in spite of the fact that they had no legal right to do so under international law.

In an effort to force the United States to assist in these restrictive measures against Germany, Great Britain next delicately threatened to forbid the shipment of certain essential raw materials from the British colonies to the United States. "In October and November, 1914 the British Government placed embargoes on the exportation from Great Britain and its colonies . . . of rubber, wool, hides, jute, plumbago, manganese, ferromanganese, chrome, tungsten ore, and other ingredients of steel which were absolutely essential for manufacturing interests in the United States who depend on British colonies for their sources of supply in those materials."[12] This pressure immediately brought the American government to terms, causing it to establish new rules of questionable impartiality. According to the arrangement finally worked out between the United States and Great Britain, the former "would (1) take steps to insure the correctness of manifests of outgoing cargoes; (2) rescind an order which prohibited the publication of manifests of cargoes until thirty days after the vessels carrying the cargoes had cleared from a port of the United States; and (3) decline to support claims of exporters who consigned shipments 'to order.' In return the British government would gladly negotiate for the grant of permits for the 'exportation from Great Britain and its colonies to the United States of rubber, hides, jute, plumbago, manganese, ferromanganese, chrome, tungsten ore, and other ingredients of steel,' on receiving assurances against the exportation of these articles and against the exportation of products derived from some of them to destinations objectionable to the British Government."[13]

"It is to be particularly noted . . . that the British Government insisted not only on restricting the exports of any articles manufactured from the raw materials imported from the British Empire to such countries as they might designate or approve, but

[12]*M. I.*, Part 27, 8258.
[13]Savage, *op. cit.*, II, 14.

they also managed by their partial control of the sources of this raw material, by wielding that club, to compel American manufacturers who were dealing with them to agree not to export any articles to any except approved countries, no matter where the raw material had been obtained. In other words, the British not only controlled articles manufactured from the raw materials obtained in the British Empire, but also controlled and exercised the right to control the shipment of manufactures from any raw materials, wherever obtained."[14] "The British, by this agreement, asserted and obtained control over the manufacturers of countries which imported anything from the British Empire, even as to their own domestic trade." American manufacturers "could not deal with any neutral country without permission of the British authorities. They could not even deal with domestic concerns in this country in intra- or interstate commerce within the boundaries of the United States without permission of the British Government."[15] In other cases the British exerted direct pressure against American industries. For instance, they "told the American copper producers that if they continued to sell copper to Germany, we [Great Britain] should buy none from them ourselves, but should hold up all their European consignments."[16] This and the threat of the British directed at the small neutrals in Europe forced even the Guggenheim people into line. "By March of 1915 [the British] had control of 95% of the exportable copper in the United States."[17]

In order to make sure that supplies did not reach the Central Powers through the neighboring neutral countries, in October, 1915, these small nations were placed upon a quota basis and their imports were controlled by British-dominated syndicates. The first of these was in Holland, the *N. O. T.*, or the *Nederlandsche Overzeetrust Maatschappij,* which was established in December, 1914. In October, 1915, a government agency was established in Switzerland for this same purpose. It was the *S. S. S.,* the *Société Suisse de Surveillance.* Different arrangements were made with other small neutrals to guard against the possi-

---

[14]*M. I.,* Part 27, 8259.
[15]*M. I.,* Part 27, 8262.
[16]*War Memoirs of David Lloyd George, 1914-1915,* II (London, 1933), 664.
[17]*Ibid.,* II, 665.

bility of anything getting through to Germany. This amounted to almost complete British control of the domestic and foreign commerce of these small European nations, including commerce with the United States, and kept the domestic products of neutral countries from being used to provision Germany.

The legal aspects of the economic warfare as carried on by Great Britain are well described in the wartime phrase, "Britain rules the waves and waives the rules." British agents consistently reported the American point of view that Great Britain was guilty of "indefensible illegalities."[18] On February, 18, 1916, they quoted the New York *Post,* saying that "England, even in the view of impartial jurists, like Professor Woolsey, has violated every canon of International Law."[19] In the American note of March 30, 1915, the activities of the British were referred to as "an almost unqualified denial of the sovereign rights of the nations now at peace." At another time Lansing asserted these restrictions were "not justified by the rules of international law or required under the principle of self-preservation." He claimed, "The British naval authorities had violated more rules of international law than the Germans. . . . For a year and a half we had made protest after protest to London because of the illegal practices."[20] Albert Bushnell Hart supported the view of the State Department in an interview in The New York *Times.* He wrote: "If it is a blockade, then it includes the blockade of Norway and Denmark, and there is no such thing as the 'blockade' of a neutral. If it is not a blockade, it is a violation of the recognized principle of the freedom of the sea for the commerce between a neutral and a belligerent."[21] Colonel House has claimed that the

---

[18]*A. P. R., Supplement,* January 28, 1916.

[19]*A. P. R.,* February 18, 1916. At one time it was remarked: "When it was first reported that a strong effort would be made in Parliament to make the Anglo-French blockade legal, the news was favorably received in the United States." *A. P. R.,* February 25, 1916.

From the American scene came the report to Sir Gilbert Parker that "an attempt to justify British naval policy upon the grounds of military necessity ... is summarily rejected. They point out that such a course is precisely the one which Germany pursued." *A. P. R.,* December 3, 1915.

[20]Lansing's *Memoirs,* 110.

[21]*A. P. R.,* March 17, 1916.

"Great Britain has not the legal right to blockade [these neutral ports] and ... therefore, it is presumed she has no intention of claiming to blockade [them]." Savage, *op. cit.,* II, 285.

United States would not again stand for such a blockade, and even Charles Seymour has admitted "that the United States did not, and would not, recognize the legality of the Allied pseudo-blockade."[22]

It is hardly beyond question that the British economic warfare was contrary to international law and that their defense of these maneuvers was not greatly different from the German defense of the invasion of Belgium. The Lord Chancellor, Viscount Haldane, told Page: "We have necessity on our side; you have the law — what is left of it — on your side; we'll not seriously quarrel."[23] The British Prime Minister remarked, "Under existing conditions there is no form of economic pressure to which we do not consider ourselves entitled to resort."[24] A more typically British defense was reported by Sir Gilbert Parker as follows: "I understand, I think, the technical difficulties under international law in the term 'blockade.' These niceties are dwelt upon by men who take the narrow view of international law and American interests and by well-meaning theorists."[25] Although the British referred to their critics as "well-meaning theorists," they themselves became indignant when their enemies were guilty of infractions of law. They maintained an attitude of outraged virtue toward German illegalities even though those illegalities were in retaliation to their own acts, which were outside the law.

Aside from the legal aspects of British and German economic warfare, it must be admitted that the situation was governed by higher rules than international law. In spite of the hypocrisy of the British and the bad taste of the Germans, there was considerable moral justification for their actions. The great war was a struggle of nations for their very existence and it naturally follows that each belligerent had to attempt the annihilation of its enemy's fighting ability. It was not a case of professional armies fighting each other. It was nation against nation. This meant that economic as well as military destruction of the enemy was legiti-

---

[22]Seymour, Charles, *American Neutrality, 1914-1917* (New Haven, 1935), 6.
[23]Baker, *op. cit.*, V, 263.
[24]Seymour, *American Diplomacy*, 28.
[25]*A. P. R.*, February 25, 1916.

mate. In carrying out this economic warfare, illegality was of but slight moment. The United States desired to maintain the rights of its citizens to travel in the zones of war and to sell merchandise to the belligerents. Great Britain and Germany were striving for national preservation. The "higher law" was definitely on the side of the belligerents.

Probably neither Great Britain nor Germany saw much justification in American objections to their illegal actions, but the British, at least, realized the political importance of these complaints and kept a very close watch upon them. They used their ambassadorial, economic, and propaganda agencies to obtain reports on American reactions to this economic warfare. For instance, Sir Gilbert Parker wrote a prominent Southern editor: "I should like you to tell me in confidence whether there is much opposition, or whether there is going to be much opposition, to the cotton contraband; also whether the British Orders in Council are still provoking anything like widespread comment. . . ."[26]

The reports which streamed in to the British government in reply to their inquiries made it possible for them to know just how far they could go. In themselves, these reports are very revealing. One American agent commented: "If the British Government continues to antagonize a number of exporters in this country, it will be quite possible to arouse a real wave of anti-British sentiment. . . . After all, this country has the whip hand if it wants to exert pressure, so far as the Allies are concerned."[27] If pressure had been exerted by the American government, it is quite clear that the British would have been forced to stop some of their illegalities. Sir Edward Grey has stated: "The Allies soon became dependent for an adequate supply of munitions on the United States. If we quarreled with the United States, we could not get that supply. It was better, therefore, to carry on that war without blockade, if need be, than to incur a break with the United States about contraband and thereby deprive the Allies of the resources necessary to carry on the war at all or with any chance of success. The object of diplomacy, therefore, was to

[26]September 2, 1915, Henry Watterson Papers. Library of Congress.
[27]*A. P. R.*, August 6, 1915.

secure the maximum of blockade that could be enforced without a rupture with the United States."[28]

In June, Sir Gilbert Parker reported to the Cabinet that "the strong disapproval of British naval policy has not abated. This is a matter of real American feeling and not of German agitation."[29] He stated, "The principal parties aggrieved by the British blockade appear to be: (a) meat packers (b) cotton growers (c) importing and exporting firms generally."[30] Later reports, however, demonstrated that these American remonstrances could be ignored. The meat packers did not wish too strong a line taken "lest the British government would withdraw its patronage, and leave them worse off than ever." Also some meat for the United States had to be shipped from Argentina in British ships. Complaints of the cotton growers, they reported, likewise could be ignored "since the price of cotton [had] ... improved" and "the protests ... [were] less numerous and bitter. ... Moreover, England is the South's best customer, and its sympathies naturally lie with its customers."[31] The complaints of the exporters and importers were found to merit less attention than those of the meat packers and cotton growers.[32]

The agents not only obtained reports on the status of American opinion; they also gave advice as to what additional pressure could be safely exerted. Early in 1916 one of his American correspondents wrote to Sir Gilbert Parker: "I have always thought, as I told you before, that the simplest plan was to extend the contraband list to include everything. There would, of course, be

[28]*M. I.*, Part 27, 8271.

[29]*A. P. R.*, June 23, 1915.

[30]*A. P. R.*, July 22, 1915. The Department of State sent the following note to the British Government on September 26, 1914. "Not only is the situation a critical one to the commercial interests of the United States, but many of the great industries of this country are suffering because their products are denied long-established markets in European countries which, though neutral, are contiguous to the nations at war. Producers and exporters, steamship and insurance companies are pressing, and not without reason, for relief from the menace to trans-Atlantic trade which is gradually but surely destroying their business and threatening them with financial disaster." *M. I.*, Part 27, 8262.

[31]*A. P. R.*, November 5, 1915.

[32]Lansing stated that "there grew up the suspicion in many quarters that the British authorities desired to make trade between American and the Scandinavian neutrals unprofitable as well as difficult." Later was found widespread belief in American quarters that the censorship was utilized to permit British firms to get business away from American concerns.

a great objection to that over here, but the objection could be met on grounds of technical legality."[33] A little later the advice was even more specific. Here, says the individual from the American front, are "some suggestions I have to make. These are the summing up of conferences with several important men, strong friends of England, and may be taken almost *as a message* from your friends fighting your battles in Congress:

"1. Repeat the *Dacia* maneuver [having France and Italy take the blame for breaking international law.] 2. Extend your list of contraband just as far as you like and seize everything going in to neutral ports on the 'continuous voyage' theory, and seize everything coming out of Germany through neutral ports on the theory of 'enemy property' as we seized cotton in the Civil War when found.[34] 3. Let little things come through if it will stop criticism. 4. Finally, do not make it hard for your friends who are zealously fighting your battles, to do so." In the last case he was referring to congressmen and senators who were fighting a munitions embargo. He wrote: "Lodge is the most virulent fighter of these measures."[35]

Included in the reports on American reactions to British economic warfare, was a whole series of opinions as to "what the United States may do." Late in 1915 it was stated: "But the New York *World* does not suggest that anything is really to be done. . . . With the exception of the Washington *Post,* no American paper contemplates the possibility of war with Great Britain. . . . Most papers speaks of prolonged negotiations, and ultimate resort to arbitration." It was then remarked that the United States had two possible weapons against Great Britain: an embargo and a refusal to grant further loans. Parker assured the Cabinet, however, that these would not be used. It was possible for him to say that the press generally "does not refer at all to what may happen if Great Britain proves obdurate."[36]

[33]*A. P. R.,* February 18, 1916.
[34]See Savage, *op. cit.,* II, 38. Six weeks later, on April 13, 1916, the British government openly abandoned the distinction between absolute and conditional contraband.
[35]*A. P. R.,* February 25, 1916. Some months before the war, Philander Knox wrote to William Howard Taft: "Lodge's view is a snobbish view. It is the London society view." Philander Knox Papers, Library of Congress.
[36]*A. P. R.,* December 3, 1915.

The weekly reports of February, 1916, reveal the source of the confidence with which the British pushed their economic warfare harder and harder. On the twelfth, Parker reported: "But upon the steps which the United States intends to take in order to enforce its views, the press, as a whole, is discreetly silent. [And though strong notes may be written] there is no evidence, in the press at any rate and at present, that more serious things are contemplated."[37]

On the eighteenth an American correspondent wrote: "I don't think that the Allies will suffer in this country by any action on the part of the British Navy which will bring stronger pressure to bear on Germany, even if the navy oversteps the bounds of International Law, provided all disputes with shippers here can be settled as quickly as possible and with as much civility as possible, and also with every kind of consideration for the American shipper. The whole thing is, in fact, a commercial rather than a legal question and a great deal can be done by making payments where payments are possible, and a few kind words.... The country must be kept prosperous at all costs, so that although there is and will be a good deal of talk in Congress against the Allies and [the] blockade nothing will be done, nor will Wilson desire to bring about any action."[38]

A little later — February 25 — the Cabinet was reassured that the American press "generally does not discuss the steps which the Administration might take against England. Where it does so it usually suggests a protest now, and a claim for indemnity after the war."[39]

All the reports were not favorable, and in such cases the British found it necessary to exercise care, but on the whole Wellington House was able to report quite consistently that Great Britain need have no fear for anything the American government might do to oppose British infractions of international law.

It must not be thought that British trade restrictions were originally devised for the purpose of influencing the United States. It was probably quite late that the propaganda value of these acts was understood. The primary objective was to injure

[37] *A. P. R.*, February 12, 1916.
[38] *A. P. R.*, February 18, 1916.
[39] *A. P. R.*, February 25, 1916.

Great Britain's enemies. The British policy looked to the use of every possible weapon, legal and illegal, by which the Central Powers could be starved out. It sought, according to Winston Churchill, to treat "the whole of Germany as if it were a beleaguered fortress, and avowedly sought to starve the whole population — men, women, and children, old and young, wounded and sound — into submission."[40] In 1937 the First Lord of the Admiralty, Mr. Alfred Duff Cooper, stated: ". . . we did everything in our power to starve the women and children in Germany!"[41] Walter Hines Page stormed: "It would take several years to kill that vast horde of Germans, but it will not take so long to starve them out."[42] The policy, however, was not limited to one of starvation; it was a warfare of economic annihilation. The British newspapers openly stated that they desired the "lasting ruin of German trade."[43]

Ultimately the entire outcome of the war depended upon the success of British attacks on the German economic structure. Actions which would embroil the United States and Germany were in the last analysis subordinate to, and dependent upon this campaign. But the ramifications of the British economic warfare were such that they touched upon every phase of German-American and Anglo-American relations. The destruction of economic connections between the United States and the Central Powers served to eliminate any possibility of sympathy arising as a result of mutuality of interests. As the censor worked to prevent the American public from hearing the German side of the news, so the British Navy worked to destroy economic relationships which might create good will between the United States and the Central Powers. On the other hand British purchases and loans in the United States served as a positive means of joining the economic interests of the two countries.

The structure of Anglo-American economic interdependence was started during the very first days of the war. After ties had been created which effected an actual Anglo-American unity of material interests, it became much more easy for Wellington

---

[40]Churchill, *op. cit.*, 215.
[41]*Time,* August 2, 1937, 17.
[42]Hendrick, *op. cit.*, I, 331.
[43]Runciman, the New York *Times,* December 24, 1915.

House to persuade Americans that there was also a unity, or identity, of moral and spiritual interests. Throughout the period of neutrality there was a growing inter-penetration of the British and American economic systems. Step by step the fate of America became tied with that of the Allies. Sir Edward Grey has stated that Great Britain and France became dependent upon the United States for the supply of munitions. But, in addition, they became dependent upon the New World for many other things which their overtaxed nations found it impossible to produce. Nor was the dependency limited to belligerents. The United States found her prosperity inextricably entwined with the success of the Allies. Defeat for Great Britain came to signify disaster for American financial and commercial interests.

During the first half of 1914 there was a slight depression in the United States and with the outbreak of hostilities in Europe economic conditions immediately became worse. An unprecedented array of selling orders was cabled overnight from Europe to New York, but the stock market was closed on August 1, thus preventing a severe panic. The price of wheat fell and the crisis in the cotton trade was still more formidable.[44] "Absolute ruin of the cotton-planters was predicted" which caused a movement to have non-users "buy a bale of cotton." A pessimistic Morgan report states: "The catastrophe of the war fell during a period of hard times that had continued in America for over a year. Business throughout the country was depressed, farm prices were deflated, unemployment was serious, the heavy industries were working far below capacity, bank clearings were off."[45]

On August 3, 1914, the French made a request to J. P. Morgan and Company for a loan of at least a hundred million dollars. Morgan replied that such a transaction was impossible at that time because of the objections of the United States government. In his cable he expressed the belief that "after little while might be very possible and excellent thing to do and shall hope take up question with you soon as possible."[46] France was not satisfied with this refusal and on August 8 again requested a loan. The Paris firm of Morgan, Harjes and Company cabled:

[44]Noyes, Alexander D., *The War Period Of American Finance, 1908-1925* (New York, 1926), 64.

[45]*M. I.*, Part 29, Exhibit 2791, 9227.   [46]*M. I.*, Part 25, Exhibit 2031, 7489.

SIR EDWARD GREY

"If you cannot see your way to arrange big loan previously cabled about would it not be possible to at least begin such an operation by means of France Treasury bill say for six or twelve months for . . . perhaps $10,000,000 which could be increased or converted as the situation with you might permit. . . . **Fear that** if we do not forestall others it is provable [probable?] that such houses as Kuhn, Loeb & Co. may try to do something for other nation."[47]

These efforts to secure aid from the United States displayed at the outset that the French, at least, were cognizant of the propaganda effect of economic ties and expressed the desire that Germany be forestalled in obtaining the allegiance of the American money market. On the next day, August 9, Morgan and Company reported that there was not much prospect of floating a loan. They did however hold out some promise for the future, stating: "Will . . . make careful investigation and cable you further . . . soon as possible."[48]

Immediately after these cabled communications a Morgan representative went to the American State Department to see whether the government would permit the issuance of a loan.[49] Apparently no satisfaction was gained from that source. On the thirteenth, Morgan, Harjes and Company cabled New York: "As to loan, fully appreciate the difficulties you explain, but earnestly hope you will be able to oblige Government here to extent of $20,-000,000. . . . The moral effect would be excellent all around and also would undoubtedly be of great value United States later on."[50]

These frantic calls from the French apparently leaked out. Morgan cabled Paris as follows: "In view publicity, which we deplore . . . we have issued statement today stating French Government have not applied to us for loan but that private interests have asked if we would consider making loan in case French

[47]*M. I.*, Part 25, Exhibit 2032, 7659.

[48]*M. I.*, Part 25, Exhibit 2033, 7660.

[49]"We are consulting our Government here as do not wish take any action under present strained circumstances which will be offensive to them, although we understand there is no legal objection to loan suggested." *M. I.*, Part 25, Exhibit 2035, 7499.

This was in connection with a further French request dated August 11 for a $20,000,000 loan. *M. I.*, Part 25, Exhibit 2034, 7660. See also Exhibit 2037.

[50]*M. I.*, Part 25, Exhibit 2036, 7661.

Government would desire."[51] This equivocal statement marks
the end of the original effort to ally American moneyed interests
with the fate of France. The episode was definitely terminated
with the statement by Bryan on the issuance of loans to belligerents.

On August 10, 1914, William Jennings Bryan, the Secretary
of State, sent an important letter to President Wilson in connection with these attempts to float a loan for France. He remarked:
"Money is the worst of all contrabands because it commands everything else. . . . If we approved of [such loans] . . . our citizens
would be divided into groups, each group loaning money to the
country which it favors and this money could not be furnished
without expressions of sympathy. These expressions are disturbing enough when they do not rest upon pecuniary interests —
they would be still more disturbing if each group was pecuniarily
interested in the success of the nation to whom its members had
loaned money. The powerful financial interests which would be
connected with these loans would be tempted to use their influence through the newspapers to support the interests of the Government to which they had loaned because the value of the
security would be directly affected by the result of the war. We
would thus find our newspapers violently arrayed on one side or
the other, each paper supporting a financial group and pecuniary
interest. All of this influence would make it all the more difficult
for us to maintain neutrality as our action on various questions
that would arise would affect one side or the other, and powerful
financial interests would be thrown into the balance."[52]

On August 15, 1914, Bryan wrote to J. P. Morgan and
Company a letter which was made public stating that loans to
belligerent nations would be inconsistent with the true spirit of
neutrality. On January 20, 1915, in a letter to Senator Stone,
Chairman of the Senate Foreign Relations Committee, he reiter-
ated this policy.

During the months of August, September, and October, 1914,
there was but slight improvement in the economic status of the
United States. By the end of the year most of the European holders had thrown onto the market American stocks which amounted

[51]*M. I.*, Part 25, Exhibit 2038, August 14, 1914, 7661.
[52]*M. I.*, Part 25, Exhibit 2046, August 10, 1914, 7517.

to $2,400,000,000. It was confidently stated that the United States was ruined financially, but early in December figures of the "outlaw market" revealed that prices were almost up to the July level. As a result, the stock market was opened on December 11. Measures had been taken by various organizations to ameliorate conditions created by the war. There was also a beginning of heavy buying of American products by the belligerent nations. Grain was one of the first commodities to show increase in price, for with a blockade of Russia, immense orders converged on America.

The British government sent Sir Richard Crawford to the United States as its commercial advisor. He began to place large orders for war materials and was soon followed by agents representing the other belligerents. Later he was replaced by Sir George Paish who took charge of most of the buying for Great Britain. The Federal Reserve began to operate on November 16 and by that time normality in exchange had been reached. The effect of this upturn of economic conditions upon agriculture, the cotton industry, and manufacturing, became plainly evident. "The American community welcomed, with a feeling of relief, orders coming from Europe. . . . As our foreign trade grew, unemployment decreased and pay rolls increased."[53]

The improvement of business conditions had hardly started before there developed pressure to overthrow the State Department restriction upon loans. Mr. R. L. Farnham of the National City Bank (Standard Oil) and Messrs. Willard Straight, and W. H. Davison of J. P. Morgan and Company began to "inquire into the possibility" of such a change being made. On October 16, 1914, rumors appeared in the newspapers that certain loans might be permitted. Mr. Vanderlip has explained that "there was a large amount of idleness. There was great dullness in our industries, there was every reason for us to stimulate those industries with an export business, if we could."[54] On October 23 a vice president of his bank, the National City Bank, wrote to Robert Lansing, the Counsellor of the State Department: "The critical time for American finance in our international relations is during the next 3 or 4 months and, if we allow these purchases

[53] *M. I.*, Part 29, Exhibit 2791, January 15, 1936, 9227.
[54] *M. I.*, Part 25, 7530.

to go elsewhere, we will have neglected our foreign trade at the time of our greatest need and greatest opportunity." He then suggested that his bank be permitted to extend temporary credit to the warring powers.[55]

On October 23 Lansing interviewed President Wilson in order to obtain a revision in the loan policy by making a distinction between loans and credits.[56] Wilson agreed to this arrangement, but in order to avoid criticism of the administration, it was decided to dissuade bankers from embarrassing the government by requesting permission to arrange such credits.[57] Immediately after the conference with Wilson, Lansing informed Straight of Morgan and Company of the change in policy, and two days later he advised Farnham of the National City Bank.[58] On October 25 the French Ambassador in Washington informed Mr. McRoberts of the National City Bank: "I think it is appropriate for me to confidentially tell you that from information, the accuracy of which I cannot doubt, you will find the competent authorities ready, not of course to grant a 'permission' which is neither asked for nor

[55]*M. I.*, Part 25, Exhibit 2045, October 23, 1914, 7664. This vice president is probably Mr. McRoberts.

[56]"From my conversation with the President I gathered the following impressions as to his views concerning bank credits of belligerent governments in contradistinction to a public loan floated in this country. There is a decided difference between an issue of Government bonds, which are sold in open market to investors, and an arrangement for easy exchange in meeting debts incurred in trade between a government and American merchants.... The acceptance of Treasury notes or other evidences of debt in payment for articles purchased in the country is merely a means of facilitating trade by a system of credits which will avoid the clumsy and impractical method of cash payments. As trade with belligerents is legitimate and proper it is desirable that obstacles, such as interference with an arrangement of credits or easy method of exchange, should be removed." *M. I.*, Part 25, 7518 f.

[57]"The question of an arrangement of this sort ought not to be submitted to this Government for its opinion, since it has given its views on loans in general, although an arrangement as to credits has to do with a commercial debt rather than with a loan of money. The above are my individual impressions of the conversation with the President, who authorized me to give them to such persons as were entitled to hear them, upon the express understanding that they were my own impressions and that I had no authority to speak for the President or the Government."

The foregoing is an extract from the memorandum prepared by Lansing immediately after his interview with President Wilson. *M. I.*, Part 25, 7519.

[58]*M. I.*, Part 25, 7519.

wanted, but to abstain from objections."[59] The Morgan firm notified its Paris representative that "Washington [i.e., the State Department] did not wish to be placed in a position approving or disapproving" these financial transactions.[60]

Thus on October 23, 1914, the starting of the "blood soaked boom" was made possible by making a technical distinction between loans and credits — a distinction which Mr. J. P. Morgan admitted did not exist.[61] This action marked the first step away from Bryan's strict neutrality. The decision on the part of Lansing and Wilson to change the loan policy, at the same time evading responsibility for the change, does not reflect credit on either of them.

On January 8, 1915, William J. Stone, Chairman of the Foreign Relations Committee of the Senate, wrote to the Secretary of State concerning accusations of the unneutrality of the American government. Among other items he referred to "change of policy in regard to loans to belligerents."[62] On January 20 the State Department replied, giving the very definite impression that there had been no change in the policy of the government, which did little to clarify the government's position. On March 31, 1915, however, the State Department issued a public notice of the change in policy which had been adopted in October of the previous year. This announcement read as follows: "The State Department has from time to time received information directly or indirectly to the effect that belligerent nations had arranged with banks in the United States for credits in various sums. While loans to belligerents have been disapproved, this Government has not felt that it was justified in interposing objection to the credit arrangements which have been brought to its attention. It has never approved these nor disapproved — it has simply taken no action in the

[59]Mr. Vanderlip apparently is of the opinion that Mr. Bryan was a party to this change in policy. *M. I.*, Part 25, 7511. *M. I.*, Part 25, 7528.

There is no other evidence to bear out his contention. Senator Clark remarked: "In view of Secretary Bryan's later letter to Mr. Stone there is no indication that Bryan knew anything about the fact that Lansing had communicated to the bankers, as Lansing said he did, this differentiation between loans and credits." *M. I.*, Part 26, 7884.

[60]*M. I.*, Part 27, Exhibit 2339, March 29, 1915, 8340.

[61]*M. I.*, Part 25, 7501, *et seq.*

[62]*M. I.*, Part 25, Exhibit 2048, October 25, 1914, 7524.

premises and expressed no opinion."[63] Thus was taken another step forward in the gradual breakdown of the American policy of strict neutrality.

Within a week after this official statement, the National City Bank extended a credit of ten million dollars to France. This "credit" had been under consideration for some time. On October 9 the National City Bank had written to Ambassador Jusserand that they stood ready to dispose of ten million dollars worth of one year Treasury warrants "not to the public, but to large institutions *to whom an appeal could be made on other than strictly investment lines.*"[64] Following the grant of credit to France a twenty-five million dollar credit was extended to Russia in January, 1915.[65] On March 30, J. P. Morgan and Company, National City Bank and the First National Bank, all of New York City, had arranged another fifty million dollar credit for France.[66]

On May 1 there was carried through a ten million dollar credit to Russia and following it were considerable negotiations concerning another credit to France. The French desired to capitalize on the feeling aroused by the sinking of the *Lusitania,* and later on, Morgan had similar thoughts in connection with the sinking of the *Arabic.*[67] On May 17, 1915, Morgan's French representative telegraphed the New York office: "In view of recent events [i.e., the sinking of the *Lusitania*] Minister of Finance suggests that public opinion in U. S. A. likely more favourable to belligerents' position than few weeks ago and that consequently some financial arrangement with France might now have better chance of success. . . . Although recognizing lack of urgency, Minister of Finance *naturally desirous of taking advantage of*

[63]*M. I.,* Part 27, Exhibit 2342, March 31, 1915, 8198.

This public announcement was precipitated by the negotiations over the credit extended to the French government on the first of April.

[64]*M. I.,* Part 25, Exhibit 2042, October 9, 1914, 7663. Italics mine.

The distribution of this French loan lasted from November 4, 1914, until April of the following year. Both the National City Bank and J. P. Morgan and Company insist that they did not make any loans or credits previous to the change of policy by the State Department. *M. I.,* Part 25, 7508, 7532. *M. I.,* Part 26, 7823.

[65]*M. I.,* Part 25, 7537.

[66]"Germany had one public and one private issue in the spring of 1915." *M. I.,* Part 26, 7811.

[67]"We have feeling that since sinking S. S. *Arabic* conditions may have improved slightly toward favoring unsecured loan. . . ." *M. I.,* Part 26, 7874.

any good opportunity."[68] This loan was carried through to the extent of $44,436,395. Also at this time there was evidence that France was attempting to obtain credit by "urging manufacturers here take payment for material in 5-percent Treasury notes."[69]

With the possibility of obtaining credits (i.e., loans) in the United States, purchases by the Allies began to increase by leaps and bounds. "For the 19 weeks . . . [preceding] the 4th of December [1915] the average excess of exports over imports was $17,000,000 per week."[70] With the increased purchases there developed considerable dissatisfaction with the results being obtained. Consequently there were started negotiations between J. P. Morgan and Company and the British government, with the object in mind of designating the Morgan firm as the controlling purchasing agent for the British government. These negotiations were completed January 15, 1915, and Edward R. Stettinius was placed in direct charge of buying for the British.[71] Somewhat later in the year the Morgan firm also became the purchasing agent for the French government.

As early as the end of the year 1914 "the traffic in war materials with the Allies had become deeply entrenched in America's economic organization, and the possibility of keeping out of the war by the diplomacy of neutrality, no matter how skillfully conducted, had reached the vanishing point. By October, perhaps earlier, our case was lost."[72]

In the spring of 1915, the purchases of the Allies in the United States grew to startling proportions. The Bethlehem Steel Company, under the guiding hand of Charles M. Schwab, received a one hundred million dollar order for Lyddite shells and shrapnel. During April the first boom reactions were appearing with "wild fluctuations in Bethlehem Steel," mostly upward, and with "cotton prices rising to new high levels."[73] On April 22 was announced an order from Russia for $21,724,400. On the first of May, West-

[68]*M. I.*, Part 27, Exhibit 2354, May 17, 1915, 8350. Italics mine.
[69]*M. I.*, Part 27, Exhibit 2385, December 3, 1914, 8216.
[70]*A. P. R.*, January 7, 1916.
[71]*M. I.*, Part 25, 7552. The Morgan firm was in "no way connected with questions of finance or credit."
[72]Baker, *op. cit.*, V, 181.
[73]The New York *Times*, April 11 and 15, 1915.

inghouse secured an order worth twenty-eight million dollars, and the boom kept on in an ever increasing stream of orders — from the Allies.

During this early period, Charles M. Schwab accepted an order for the construction of British submarines. When the news leaked out, there appeared considerable adverse criticism. The Philadelphia *Public Ledger* said it was "legal but not righteous." The New York *World* agreed. Eventually the administration felt called upon to act and requested that the order be cancelled. Shortly thereafter newspapers carried an announcement that this advice had been followed. Sir Douglas Brownrigg has intimated, however, that these underseas boats were delivered in spite of the cancellation notice.[74]

May, 1915, was the turning point of so many phases of the war that it is not surprising to find in the United States that the real boom began during that month. This was caused by the fact that Lloyd George became Minister of Munitions and initiated a program of buying high explosives, limited only by the capacity of accessible producers. "This meant unlimited requisition on American manufacturers."[75] "The excess of domestic merchandise exports over imports jumped from $435,758,368 on June 30, 1914 to $1,042,008,725 on June 30, 1915."[76] "The total exports of merchandise . . . [were] about $2,300,000,000."[77] "Trade with Allied countries increased approximately 141 percent from 1914 to 1915. . . ." "The net outstanding indebtedness of the Allies in the United States . . . [was also] increasing by leaps and bounds."[78]

As early as the spring of 1915 the British Chancellor of the Exchequer told his government that it was going beyond its ability to pay. He was instructed to keep this information to himself.[79] But all the government officials must have known that the huge purchases in the United States could not be continued unless

[74]Brownrigg, *op. cit.*, 80 f.

[75]Noyes, *op. cit.*, 111. It was possible for the London *Times* to say as early as May 10, 1915, "It is pointed out that as things stand the United States is invaluable to the Allies as a peaceful base of military supplies."

[76]*M. I.*, Part 28, 8498.

[77]*M. I.*, Part 28, 8700.

[78]Some firms were, at first, quite hesitant about expanding their plants to the extent necessary for the handling of this business. *M. I.*, Part 25, 7565, 7569; Part 27, 8272.

[79]*Lord Riddell's War Diary, op. cit.*, 105.

funds were forthcoming to pay the bills. In the last analysis the only place where sufficient money could be arranged for was in the United States and it was to the American financial community that the British turned for help.

In addition to the assistance obtained by means of the financial arrangements permitted by the American government, efforts were made to obtain new sources of credit. Certain governors of the Federal Reserve Board, including Benjamin Strong, an intimate friend of J. P. Morgan, were attempting to get the Board to change its policy in regard to a kind of paper known as acceptances. Colonel House added his influence to secure the change. He recorded in his diary an interview on August 3 with Charles Hamlin, one of the governors of the Federal Reserve Board. House stated: "We went into the question of broadening credits and I found he was not impressed with the importance of this as were Delano and Strong. I, therefore, endeavored to straighten him out in this direction. He [Hamlin] said the Board's counsel thought acceptances could not be made for longer than six months and the comptroller agreed with this decision. I pointed out the actual wording of the law and said the Board's ruling prevented it but the law itself did not. Therefore, in my opinion, all that was necessary was for the Board to rescind their former action and make a new ruling. He promised it should be done in a way not to restrict credits and so our foreign trade should go on uninterrupted."[80]

Certain members of the Board, especially Mr. Warburg and Mr. Miller, strenuously objected to this change. At this time Secretary of the Treasury McAdoo and President Wilson entered the lists for the Allies. On August 27, 1915, House wrote to Wilson as follows:

"Dear Governor: You know, of course, there is trouble brewing in the Federal Reserve Board.

"I sympathize with McAdoo's view in regard to foreign acceptances and I hope there may be some way of bringing it about without a public rupture. . . . It is unfortunate that any controversy has arisen among the members and, if I were in your place, I would caution McAdoo to go slow.

[80]*M. I.*, Part 27, Exhibit 2419, August 3, 1915, 8398.

"Miller might be gotten out a little later, and then, perhaps, Warburg would leave of his own volition. I am inclined to think he would."[81]

In this letter it can be seen that House favored removing members of the Federal Reserve Board in order to get their policies changed for the benefit of the Allies. Mr. Wilson answered Colonel House on August 31: "You are right about the Reserve Board imbroglio. And I think McAdoo thinks so too now. Indeed I think he raised the question about the action of certain members of the Board about that meeting only *to get a leverage for something bigger* than the proper handling of acceptances and discounts."[82]

In these negotiations there were a number of things of considerable importance about which the Federal Reserve Board was not at first informed. Later "the Board was very much concerned [when it learned] that some of these acceptances were credits guaranteed by the Bank of France."[83] This "acceptance" transaction was summarized in the following comments before the Munitions Investigation Committee:

MR. RAUSHENBUSH: "Do we get the story correctly, then, that the Federal Reserve regulations were changed to allow the rediscount of a kind of paper that was called acceptances, but which were not really acceptances because they had government securities behind them, and then after that regulation was changed to allow $135,000,000 worth of financing, the United States Treasury had to bail out the people who held them to the extent of $120,000,000?"

MR. BROWN: "That is the story as the documents revealed.
. . . "[84]

The relaxation of American policy on credits brought about in 1914, and the change in policy on "acceptances" in 1915, were a help to the Allies, but the situation had developed beyond the point where such expedients would suffice. It was essential to raise huge sums of money in the United States and, to do that, the Bryan policy on loans had to be completely eliminated. From

[81]*M. I.*, Part 27, Exhibit 2420, August 27, 1915, 8398.
[82]*M. I.*, Part 27, Exhibit 2421, August 31, 1915, 8399. Italics mine. Undoubtedly he was referring to the half billion dollar loan being considered.
[83]*M. I.*, Part 27, 8235.
[84]*M. I.*, Part 27, 8235.

June to September, 1915, measures were being taken by J. P. Morgan and Company and the British government for the accomplishment of both these ends. Early in the summer the British made insistent inquiries of Morgan as to the possibility of floating a large loan in the United States. At the outset Morgan expressed considerable pessimism as to whether such a loan could be absorbed in this country.[85] As a consequence of his hesitancy the British began to look elsewhere for an agent.[86] This apparently caused Morgan to adopt a more cheerful attitude. On July 23, 1915, he cabled his London partners "that a financial loan was imperative, and that the market has much improved."[87] On August 9 he wrote: "It is our opinion that properly handled, properly secured loans could be placed here to an amount of $500,000,000, possibly more."[88]

On August 17 Morgan issued a "feeler" in the American press as to the possibility of floating such a loan. This turned out to be most discouraging. He cabled London: "As you know, when intimations of this kind are made, applications come from all parts of the country if business attractive. We have received but 3 or 4 inquiries as result this item, which does not encourage us very materially."[89] However, he had come to the conclusion that it would be possible to place a loan of one hundred million dollars.

Up to this date there had been no consultation with the American State Department. But apparently there was no anxiety about receiving permission in spite of the Bryan pronouncement. In order to gain complete reversal of the loan policy, the British now began to consider means of exerting pressure against the American government.

In August, 1915, the British and French officials held a conference to decide on the methods to be used to force the American government to permit a loan. It was decided that a sum of two hundred million dollars in gold would be prepared for shipment to the United States. "Merely the announcement of this shipment would dispose the banks to promise their assistance in a loan because they would fear that such an influx of gold could

[85]*M. I.*, Part 26, 7843 ff.
[86]*M. I.*, Part 26, 7850.
[87]*M. I.*, Part 26, 7846.
[88]*M. I.*, Part 26, 7847.
[89]*M. I.*, Part 26, Exhibit 2213, August 18, 1915, 8121.

only raise all prices and create business troubles."[90] The intention of the British was, by means of this threat of inflation, to compel indirectly the American government to change its stand. The plan here developed was never executed. It was found that the exchange situation provided a better lever.

Late in July, 1915, preliminary steps were taken to prepare the ground for the plan to force the American government to change its policy on loans. On July 27, Morgan's friend, Strong, and Mr. Delano, both of the Federal Reserve Board, called upon Colonel House. At that time they succeeded in convincing him of the possible dire consequences of an exchange crisis and of the necessity of forestalling it by granting assistance to the Allies. As a result of this conference, House wrote the following letter to President Wilson: "Delano and Governor Strong of the New York Federal Reserve Bank were here yesterday to see me concerning the serious condition that confronts us in regard to foreign exchange. They believe that unless the Federal Reserve System broadens its basis of credits that another month or two will bring about a crisis and almost a complete breakdown of our foreign trade. They told me that three of the Reserve Board are in favor of broadening the credits, but that two are opposed to it. They did not give the names for it was not necessary. [Miller and Warburg?] My advice was that while we were living under abnormal conditions we should have the courage to meet them in a way that will redound to the advantage of our country, and that credits should be broadened as far as perfect safety would permit. I hope this view meets with your approval."[91]

Following this preparation, on August 13, J. P. Morgan and Company withdrew its support from the market, and sterling began to sag ominously. To accentuate the crisis, the Morgan firm also continued to sell sterling.[92] This threat was almost terrifying to American financial interests. Immediately after the withdrawal of support from the British pound, Governor Strong addressed a letter to Colonel House: "Referring to our conversation of a week ago. You have doubtless observed that matters are develop-

[90]*M. I.*, Part 26, 7887 f. See also Ribot, Alexandre, *Lettres à Un Ami, Souvenirs de Ma Vie Politique* (Paris, 1924), 98 f.
[91]*M. I.*, Part 27, July 28, 1915, 8225 f.
[92]*M. I.*, Part 27, 8151.

ing along the lines of our discussion. Sterling exchange sold yesterday below 4.71."[93]

A little later Governor Strong appealed to the Secretary of the Treasury.[94] Mr. Morgan also sent one of his partners to see Mr. McAdoo in order to emphasize the danger of the exchange crisis. He reported this visit in a cable to his London office: "We have today sent word to the Secretary of Treasury that we regard the exchange situation as very serious from the point of view of our commerce, in order that the Administration may be fully informed and with hopes that they might in some way be helpful."[95] Mr. Morgan was later asked: "When your partner went to talk to the Secretary of the Treasury about the seriousness of the exchange situation, did you tell him that you had not been supporting the exchange market for three days, after you had supported it for months prior thereto?"[96] Mr. Morgan was unable to answer.

It should be remembered that previous to this time the British government, through J. P. Morgan and Company, had spent millions to bolster exchange. The prospect of a slight drop from time to time had created considerable nervousness. Yet at this time there was little apparent anxiety. Mr. Brown of the Munitions Investigation Committee queried the Morgan partners: "Now we find a few weeks before you were worried about a 3-cent break in the market. This break goes down almost 20 cents, if I remember right. And there were no expressions of concern to the Bank of England or to the British Treasury about where their exchange is going. The expressions of concern go to the Secretary of the Treasury of the United States."[97]

The members of the Munitions Investigation Committee were interested in knowing who pulled the props from under sterling. Mr. Morgan was quite insistent that his firm was not responsible, stating, "It is foreign to our traditions, and we never did such a thing in our lives."[98] Senator Clark was of the opinion that regardless of who was to blame, "the firm of J. P. Morgan & Co.,

[93]*M. I.*, Part 26, 7861.
[94]*M. I.*, Part 26, 7878 ff. Exhibits 2233, 2235.
[95]*M. I.*, Part 26, Exhibit 2213, August 18, 1915, 8122. See also 7886.
[96]*M. I.*, Part 26, 7858.
[97]*M. I.*, Part 26, 7870. See also 7891.
[98]*M. I.*, Part 26, 7873.

on the instruction and at the request of the British Government, did peg the exchange market and hold it there throughout the remainder of the war; and that so far from being out of funds at that time to support the exchange market if it wanted to, the British Government, in the last year, did expend some 4 or 5 hundred million dollars in supporting the exchange market at that figure."[99]

Exchange on sterling reached bottom (4.51) on September 1. The next day there was an announcement of the coming of the Anglo-French Commission. Exchange shortly began to recover and afterward the British did not leave it unsupported.[100]

In the midst of this crisis brought about by the removal of support from sterling, and after Strong and Davison had urged the Secretary of the Treasury to obtain a reversal on the American policy on loans, Mr. McAdoo joined the forces against the policy of financial neutrality. On August 21 he wrote a long letter to President Wilson advocating the scuttling of the American loan policy in order to permit the flotation of a large loan to Great Britain and France:

> Great Britain is, and always has been, our best customer. Since the war began, her purchases and those of her Allies (France, Russia and Italy) have enormously increased. . . . The high prices for food products have brought great prosperity to our farmers, while the purchases of war munitions have stimulated industry and have set factories going to full capacity throughout the great manufacturing districts, while the reduction of imports and their actual cessation in some cases, have caused new industries to spring up and others to be enlarged. Great prosperity is coming. It is, in large measure, here already. It will be tremendously increased if we can extend reasonable credits to our customers. . . . Our prosperity is dependent on our continued and enlarged foreign trade.

[99]*M. I.*, Part 28, 8580.

In reply to the statement that no pressure was exerted on the American government to change the loan policy, Senator Clark stated: "After the Morgan Co. stepped out from under exchange and allowed exchange to drop . . . that was an exertion of a very considerable amount of pressure." *M. I.*, Part 26, 7885.

[100]*M. I.*, Part 28, 8583. "The British saw fit from August 13 until the announcement of their British delegation, to leave the exchange market unsupported, on the theory that when the announcement was made that they were shipping $100,000,000 of gold, and that their committee was coming over here; that it would have the effect of stabilizing the market." *M. I.*, Part 26, 7892.

To preserve that we must do everything we can to assist our customers to buy. . . .

It is imperative for England to establish a large credit in this country. She will need at least $500,000,000. She can't get this in any way, at the moment, that seems feasible, except by sale of short-time Government notes. Here she encounters the obstacle presented by Mr. Bryan's letter of June 20, 1915, to Senator Stone in which it is stated that "war loans in this country were disapproved because inconsistent with the spirit of neutrality" etc., and "this Government has not been advised that any general loans have been made by foreign governments in this country since *the President expressed his wish that loans of this character should not be made.*" The italicized part is the hardest hurdle of the entire letter. Large banking houses here which have the ability to finance a large loan, will not do so or even attempt to do so, in the face of this declaration. We have tied our hands so that we cannot help ourselves or help our best customers. France and Russia are in the same boat. Each, especially France, needs a large credit here.

The declaration seems to me most illogical and inconsistent. We approve and encourage sales of supplies to England and others but we disapprove the creation by them of credit balances here to finance their lawful and welcome purchases. We must find some way to give them needed credits but there is no way, I fear, unless this declaration can be modified. Maybe the *Arabic* incident may clarify the situation! I should hate to have it modified that way.[101]

On August 17, 1915, a Mr. James B. Forgan of the First National Bank of Chicago wrote to the Federal Reserve Board as to the possibility of floating a loan for the Allies in the United States. Following this there was a series of letters between various government officials[102] which eventually resulted in the addition of the new Secretary of State, Lansing, to the group exerting pressure to have the loan policy changed for the benefit of the Allies. On August 25 Lansing wrote to the President: ". . . . we must recognize the fact that conditions have materially changed

[101]*M. I.*, Part 26, Exhibit 2219, August 21, 1915, 8123 ff.

[102](1) Mr. James B. Forgan to F. A. Delano of the Federal Reserve Board, dated August 17, 1915; (2) Secretary McAdoo to Secretary Lansing, dated August 23, 1915; (3) Charles Hamlin of the Federal Reserve Board to Secretary of State Lansing, dated August 24, 1915; (4) Secretary Lansing to the President, dated August 26, 1915; (5) President Wilson to Secretary Lansing, dated August 26, 1915. *M. I.*, Part 26, Exhibits 2220-2225, 7864 ff.

since last autumn when we endeavored to discourage the flotation of any general loan by a belligerent in this country. The question of exchange and the large debts which result from purchases by belligerent governments require some method of funding these debts in this country."

The exchange crisis and the personal pressure which had been exerted against Wilson through Lansing, McAdoo, and others, were enough to convince him of the necessity for abandoning the loan policy. On August 26 the President acceded to Mr. Lansing's recommendation using as his answer one of the quotations suggested in the original letter from Forgan to the Federal Reserve Board. The quotation read: "Parties would take no action either for or against such a transaction." In addition Wilson informed Lansing that "this should be orally conveyed . . . and not put in writing."[103] In other words the same evasive method was used for the final overthrow of the loan policy which had been used in gaining permission for the granting of so-called credits.

Although it apparently had been decided on August 26 that the Allies were to be permitted to float a huge loan in this country, there were additional negotiations after this date. On September 5 in a letter from Lansing to the President there is a complete statement of the problem. Lansing wrote as follows:

My Dear Mr. President:

Doubtless Secretary McAdoo has discussed with you the necessity of floating Government loans for the belligerent nations, which are purchasing such great quantities of goods in this country, in order to avoid a serious financial situation which will not only affect them but this country as well. . . .

If the European countries cannot find means to pay for the excess of goods sold to them over those purchased from them they will have to stop buying and our present export trade will shrink proportionately. The result would be restriction of outputs, industrial depression, idle capital and idle labor, numerous failures, financial demoralization, and general unrest and suffering among the laboring classes. . . .

I believe that Secretary McAdoo is convinced, and I agree with him, that there is only one means of avoiding this situation, which would so seriously affect economic conditions in this country, and

[103]*M. I.*, Part 26, 7865.

that is the flotation of large bond issues by the belligerent governments. . . .

The difficulty is — and this is what Secretary McAdoo came to see me about—that the Government early in the war announced that it considered "war loans" to be contrary to the "true spirit of neutrality". . . .

The practical reasons for the policy at the time we adopted it were sound, but basing it on the ground that loans are "inconsistent with the true spirit of neutrality" is now a source of embarrassment. . . .

Can we afford to let a declaration as to our conception of the "true spirit of neutrality" . . . stand in the way of our national interests which seem to be seriously threatened?

Secretary McAdoo considers that the situation is becoming acute and that something should be done at once to avoid the disastrous results which will follow a continuance of the present policy.[104]

The explanation of the duplicate request for a change in policy and a duplicate agreement for the change on two different dates is not exactly clear. As far as end results are concerned, the Lansing letters of August 25 and September 5 are identical, as are the Wilson replies of August 26 and September 6. If it had been the intention of Mr. Lansing to have the more complete letter of September 5 go down in history as his part in gaining this change in policy, he did not make a happy choice of words when he asked the question "can we afford to let . . . the true spirit of neutrality . . . stand in the way of our national interests?"

On September 5, the same day that Lansing wrote his long letter to Wilson, he also had an interview with the President and it was apparently decided to go ahead with the change in policy as worked out on August 26.[105] The method of avoiding responsibility for granting permission for the flotation of loans also seems to have been confirmed.

An announcement had been made on September 2 of the coming of the joint Anglo-French Commission for the handling of the exchange and credit difficulties. The Commission left Europe on the fifth and arrived in New York on the tenth of September. Some dissatisfaction was expressed with its personnel, and the

[104]*M. I.*, Part 26, 7883.
[105]*M. I.*, Part 26, Exhibit 2237, 7884.

members did have some misconception as to what they might accomplish. At first it was desired to raise a billion dollars. Subsequently the amount was set at a mere one-half billion. A syndicate was formed for the flotation of the loan. This included J. P. Morgan and Company, the National City Bank, and the First National Bank. Naturally the Morgan Company was the dominant member of this trio.

After the decision had finally been made to permit a loan, the same individuals continued to act to make that loan a success. The biographer of the British Ambassador wrote: "When it became apparent that a loan was necessary in order to give a credit for American exports to Europe, many secret forces began to act in its favor." "Government and newspapers did their best to convince the people that there was no politics in the loan and that it was merely business."[106] Not only was there "no opposition from the administration," government officials rendered open support. "The Comptroller of the Currency openly urged the banks to use their swollen cash reserves by lending to the Allies."[107] His chief contribution was a new policy which permitted the Federal Reserve banks to invest heavily in these bonds. In answer to queries as to the legality of such investments, he wrote: ". . . this office had been advised by counsel that governments are not 'corporations' or 'persons' within the meaning of section 5200, and that investments made by national banking association in Government securities, such as Government bonds, in excess of 10 percent of the unimpaired capital and surplus of the association, would not be in violation of that section."[108] On September 11 "McAdoo wrote Lansing requesting his help to make Anglo-French mission of bankers to negotiate a loan in the United States a success."[109] And the State Department assured people it would not be unneutral to buy the bonds.

On September 17 the President wrote to McAdoo that he should advise Senator Chamberlain of Oregon "of the real significance of the loan, namely, the maintenance of international exchanges, whose breakdown would be absolutely disastrous to

[106]Spring-Rice, *op. cit.*, II, 281.
[107]Van Alstyne, *loc. cit.*, June, 1933, 183.
[108]*M. I.*, Part 27, 8152.
[109]*M. I.*, Part 27, 8255.

the United States."[110] "The Vice President, Marshall, a little later made a speech along much the same lines."[111] It can be seen from Wilson's letter to Chamberlain that he had been greatly impressed by the exchange situation which he probably did not know was a fake crisis created by the British.

It can be seen from the foregoing that the Secretary of the Treasury, the Comptroller of the Currency, the Secretary of State, and the President of the United States were all assisting in the war financing of foreign belligerent governments. "It is a comment upon the essential unneutrality of these acts ... that Germany's agreement to moderate her submarine policy was accompanied by [these] new developments, financial and economic, of crucial advantage to the Allies."[112]

In addition to the assistance of various government officials, the pro-Ally newspapers immediately rallied loyally to the cause. The Memphis *Journal* said, "if the loan does not succeed, England and France will not be able to buy and pay for the amount of cotton that otherwise they would use." The New York *Herald* added its bit: "Failure to borrow would result in wholesale curtailments of orders all the way down the list from the least to the greatest of exports, with the single exception of munitions of war." "The New York press, with the notable exception of the Hearst and German-language papers, gave the loan stalwart support. But the country as a whole was distrustful."[113]

Long before the Commission came to the United States and before permission was granted for the loan, it was realized that its success was dependent in large measure on the state of public opinion. "Setting the stage" was essential. It could only be done "after press propaganda" had prepared the field. In the Munitions Investigation this was brought out very clearly:

MR. CLARK: "In other words, you felt that before you could undertake to be responsible for the flotation of this loan ... that very definite preparation should be made by campaigns, so to speak, of propaganda?"

MR. MORGAN: "Not propaganda, education."[114]

[110]*M. I.*, Part 26, 7905. See Baker, *op. cit.*, V, 383.
[111]*M. I.*, Part 26, 7917.
[112]Baker, *op. cit.*, V, 383.
[113]Van Alstyne, *loc. cit.*, 184.
[114]*M. I.*, Part 26, 7837, 7908.

One group of people who were propagandized were the munitions makers. Considerable pressure was exerted to induce them to subscribe to the loan.[115] Morgan also recommended that commercial houses in England cable American individuals and firms with whom they carried on business in order to induce them to invest in these bonds.[116] In other words, as one of the members of the senatorial investigation expressed it, Morgan suggested "putting the heat on those people."[117] Individuals in England, however, had a better conception of the possible results of any such action. They cabled to Morgan: "Have discussed the question of approaching commercial houses with the Governor of the Bank of England and feel it would be exceedingly difficult to get any comprehensive action taken on lines suggested without a certain number of parties talking about the matter and thus enabling enemy sympathizers to spoil success of the underwriting. We will, however, further consider the matter."[118]

The total of the underwriting secured from manufacturers in this country was about $90,000,000.[119] The munitions makers purchased slightly under $10,000,000 worth of the Anglo-French bond issue.

Among the more legitimate means used to sell these bonds was straight advertising sent to brokerage houses and bankers throughout the country by the Guaranty Trust Company.[120] In the advertising, the Wellington House method of enlisting the support of distinguished American leaders was followed. Among the names obtained to affix to these circulars were those of James J. Hill, Howard Elliott, Henry L. Higginson, Theodore N. Vail, Robert T. Lincoln, and Seth Law [Seth Low?].[121]

Mr. Lamont, a Morgan partner, has stated that there was a "quite spontaneous outburst of publicity from all over the country." However, the support given the loan was far from being "spontaneous." "Thoroughgoing measures had to be employed to make effective an educational campaign throughout the coun-

[115]*M. I.*, Part 28, 8525.
[116]*M. I.*, Part 26, Exhibit 2268, September 27, 1915, 7910. See also 7913.
[117]*M. I.*, Part 26, 7911.
[118]*M. I.*, Part 26, 7912.
[119]*M. I.*, Part 26, 7915.
[120]*M. I.*, Part 27, Exhibit 2310, 8332.
[121]*M. I.*, Part 27, Exhibit 2310, 8332.

try.”[122] And even then the result left the "trio" quite disappointed. On November 3 Morgan cabled London: "For your further information, remaining British and French commissioners here express bitter disappointment over slow sales of loan, total sales to public being less than $10,000,000, over and above the $260,-000,000 withdrawn by participants, thus leaving $230,000,000 to be sold to the public. Sales proceeding so slowly that practically no chance before dissolution of syndicate December 15 of being able to dispose of any large amount.”[123] Mr. Whitney testified: "It was a tremendous, a terrific job, and very serious intensive work was done to organize the underwriting.”[124]

Some of the difficulty in floating the loan turned upon the fear that if the Allies lost the war the debt would be repudiated. Even after the loan had been marketed, Wellington House had continued its work of educating the American people to the fact that the credit of the Allies was beyond question.[125] They were horrified when the Hearst papers published what purported to be an interview with Rudyard Kipling in which Kipling suggested that there should be a repudiation of war debts.[126] Wellington House reported: "Its effects have been dreadful. Protests arise from every side." The following protest which was published in the St. Louis *Globe-Democrat* was considered particularly disturbing: "Certainly such Americans as invested in the so-called 'first mortgage on the British Empire and France and all her colonies' will not be in a mirthful mood if the bonds are repudiated."

It was possible to float such a loan only by insuring good profits to the bankers and brokers who marketed it. These firms required generous compensation and in the words of Senator Clark, Morgan and Company had to " 'sweeten the pot' to make

[122]*M. I.*, Part 26, 7917, 7923.

[123]*M. I.*, Part 27, 8165.

[124]*M. I.*, Part 27, 8167.

[125]Sir Gilbert Parker noticed with apparent uneasiness the attention given to the financial condition of the Allies. At the same time he reported "practical interest [in the U. S.] is concerned with the means to secure permanently for the United States after the war something like the industrial supremacy possessed by the country at the present." *A. P. R.*, December 24, 1915.

[126]In a later report, Parker stated he had interrogated Kipling, who said of the interview: "It is largely distorted, and the financial part is a misrepresentation." The original interview supposedly came from the London *Morning Post* of January 25, 1915, but a search of the *Post* of this date showed no interview with Kipling.

it worth while for them."[127] Or, as Mr. Lamont expressed it, an additional amount had to be paid "to overcome the ignorance with regard to its [the loan's] goodness."[128]

"When $512,000,000 of underwriting was obtained . . . it was obtained only because a lot of investors . . . came in at the underwriting price."[129] The bonds did not sell easily and even after several months they were "largely held by the original underwriters."[130]

The total subscribers, companies and individuals, amounted to 1567. These sales were distributed among forty-one states, but *1458 of the sales were made in fourteen eastern states.*[131] New York headed the list with 665 subscribers (465 in New York City alone); Pennsylvania came next with 223; Massachusetts had 217. These figures clearly demonstrate the sectional nature of its success. Only five and one-half million dollars worth of the bonds were sold in Chicago.

Following the original one-half billion dollar Anglo-French loan there were five additional loans or credits marketed up to April 1, 1916. They totaled $281,000,000.

The money raised by the Allies in the United States made it possible for them to make enormous additional purchases. This brought great additional prosperity and created a demand for more loans to be floated in order to continue the American industrial expansion. The Secretary of the Treasury wrote the President in 1915: "Our credit resources are simply marvelous now. They are easily five to six billion dollars." The combined exports of the United States to Great Britain and her allies grew from $824,000,000 in 1914 to $1,991,000,000 in 1915. Meanwhile the exports to the Central Powers decreased from $169,-000,000 to approximately $12,000,000, and in the following year were to drop to slightly over one million dollars.[132] The purchases of industrial and commercial products created a pros-

127*M. I.*, Part 26, 7844.
128*M. I.*, Part 26, 7852.
129 *M. I.*, Part 27, 8167.
130*M. I.*, Part 28, 8518 f. See also Part 27, 8177. "The United Kingdom notes are still largely held by friendly banking institutions." December 28, 1916. *M. I.*, Part 28, Exhibit 2663, 8620.
131Van Alstyne, *loc. cit.*, 189.
132*M. I.*, Part 28, 8701.

perity which began to be felt throughout the country. It spread from east into the middle west and in 1916 was to reach the far west. Bankers were pleased, merchants were pleased, farmers began to be pleased. "The Wilson Administration was not unpleased to have business looking up. A Congressional election was approaching and the sign of the full dinner pail would help keep Democrats in power. Keeping Democrats in power was deemed for the good of the country, by Democrats."[133] (See Appendix A for analyses of financial and trade operations.)

But all these economic extravagances had more than a local or domestic effect upon the United States. The London *Times* of October 13, 1915, spoke of the Anglo-French loans as a "valuable financial stroke, with political value, in the widest sense into the bargain." A British propagandist wrote: "The moral effect of this loan in creating a sympathetic effect in America for the Allies has been great. This is the aspect in which I am chiefly concerned."[134] The loan further united American business interests with the Allied governments and reflected the close intimacy into which the industry of the country had already been drawn with the Allies' cause. "Prices had risen enormously. Profits had swollen tenfold. The Allies had become the *sole* customer of the United States. Loans the Allies had obtained from New York banks swept the gold of Europe into American coffers. From that time on, whether desired or not, the victory of the Allies became essential to the United States. The vacillations of Wilson's policy only made this necessity more apparent."[135]

A correspondent of Sir Gilbert Parker wrote: "Within earshot of my own house 16,000 workmen are busy, day and night ... making munitions for England. Other factories of ... [munitions?] and other war supplies are being enlarged or built new in this one city of New Haven."[136] Could it be other than that these thousands of workmen and people dependent upon them

[133]Beard, Charles A., *The Devil Theory of War* (New York, 1936), 25.

[134]"Exchange is falling again now that the loan is through," "that is all the more reason why no stone should be left unturned to protect interests of the Allies in this country and to prevent a loss of financial or moral reputation." *A. P. R.,* October 29, 1915.

[135]Tardieu: *France and America,* 150 and 151, as quoted in *M. I.,* Part 28, 8500.

[136]*A. P. R., Supplement,* January 28, 1916.

should be friendly to the British and anxious to have them win —
even if it finally took American assistance?

A Wellington House report early in 1916 displayed how economic connections of the British had tied the United States'
financial world to the cause of the Allies. It stated: "American
banking is so intimately connected with the American Stock Exchange that the opinion of the latter may fairly be said to represent those of the whole financial community. From the beginning
of the present war, prices in Wall Street have risen regularly in
response to any military successes of the Allies, and fallen with
equal regularity when the Central Powers achieved successes."[137]

Each dollar invested in British or French bonds made friends
for the Allies, and when the safety of that investment became
dependent upon the success of the Allies, American interest in
that success became much more than academic. American prosperity came to depend upon continued purchasing and loaning
by the Allies. Also it depended upon those supplies reaching
Europe.

The economic warfare as a whole made the United States a
financial, if not a political ally of Great Britain and France. In
addition it threatened the Central Powers with the national destruction which the armies of the Allies were found unable to
accomplish. As soon as the Germans struck back at the blockade
and the utilization of the New World as a base of supplies, they
found themselves confronted not only by the might of Great
Britain and her allies, but also by that of the United States. As
far as the economic warfare was concerned, the American declaration of war took place in 1915. It was only natural that the
military warfare should eventually follow. During the World
War, as during the years of peace, the flag followed the dollar.

[137]*A. P. R.*, January 7, 1916.

CHAPTER V ☆ THE *LUSITANIA*

THE British economic warfare looked as though it would result in starving Germany into submission. Rather than permit such a thing to happen the Germans chose to wage an economic warfare that was even more ruthless in an attempt to starve England into submission. The weapon used for this purpose — the only one available — was the submarine. While the chief immediate purpose "was to bring pressure upon the Allies in order to compel them to relax their blockade," as soon as the effectiveness of the submarine became apparent, it was decided "to strike at the general economic capacity of the British to continue the war."[1] In other words, the economic warfare as ultimately carried on by both sides was for the complete destruction of the enemy's home front.

The inauguration of German economic warfare was of immense importance to the British in their campaign to create an anti-German climate of opinion within the United States. In line with their policy of exploiting actual events the sinking of ships by the U-boats was highly advertised. The loss of lives and property directly affected this country and made it possible for Wellington House to use the "identity of interests" arguments very extensively. Not only did the submarine warfare bring the war home to Americans, it brought it home in its most distressing aspect and made it possible for the Allies' protagonists to claim that this was proof of their other claims as to German barbarity.

The inflexibility of the Germans in carrying out their attacks on Great Britain was of especial help to the propagandists. The Germans failed to realize that the war was above all a political matter and that pliability, which is the essence of politics, had to govern all important phases of the actions of the belligerents.

[1]Seymour, *American Neutrality*, 58.

Admiral Koch defined the purpose of the submarine campaign as an attempt "to deliver a vigorous cut at the arteries of England's economic existence in order to disgust England with its operations at long range against Germany ... and to show England that, just as the throttling process worked against ... [Germany] the constant gnawing at the source of England's economic life worked against her." *Official German Documents*, I, 618.

They were abrupt in their actions and stubborn and unbending in the face of disapprobation. Above all they had an unhappy faculty for committing acts which were dramatic. Their methods of waging economic warfare compared with those of the British as the work of an apprentice compares with that of a skilled craftsman.

On November 3, 1914, the British Admiralty had announced that the entire North Sea must be considered a "military area" and that after November 5 all ships entering therein did so "at their own peril."[2] The Scandinavian neutrals in protesting against this war zone declaration attempted to obtain the support of the United States. The American government, however, declined to protest against this British action.

The Germans started their economic warfare by a similar act. Their proclamation of February 4, 1915, declared that all waters surrounding Great Britain and Ireland, including the English Channel, comprised a war zone.

Their proclamation stated:

> Since the beginning of the present war Great Britain has carried on a mercantile warfare against Germany in a way that defies all the principles of international law. . . . The British Government has put a number of articles in the list of contraband which are not or at most only indirectly useful for military purposes and, therefore, according to the London declaration as well as according to the universally recognized rules of international law, may not be designated as contraband. She has further actually abolished the distinction between absolute and relative contraband. . . . She does not even hesitate to violate the Paris declaration. . . . The neutral powers have generally acquiesced in the steps taken by the English Government. . . . For her violations of international law Great Britain pleads the vital interests which the British empire has at stake, and the neutral powers seem to satisfy themselves with theoretical protests. . . . Germany must now appeal to these same vital interests to its regret. . . . Just as England has designated the area between Scotland and Norway as an area of war, so Germany now declares all the waters surrounding Great Britain and Ireland including the entire English channel as an area of war, and thus will proceed against the shipping of the enemy.
>
> For this purpose beginning February 18th, 1915, it will en-

[2]Savage, *op. cit.*, II, Document 31, 226.

deavor to destroy every enemy ship that is found in this area of war without its always being possible to avert the peril that thus threatens persons and cargoes. Neutrals are therefore warned against further entrusting crews, passengers, and wares to such ships. Their attention [is] also called to the fact that it is advisable for their ships to avoid entering this area, for even though the German naval forces have instructions to avoid violence to neutral ships insofar as they are recognizable, in view of the misuse of neutral flags ordered by the British Government and the contingencies of naval warfare their becoming victims of torpedoes directed against enemy ships cannot always be avoided... The German Government . . . expect[s] that the neutral powers will show no less consideration for the vital interests of Germany than for those of England and will aid in keeping their citizens and the property of the latter from this area.[3]

Just as the British had stated that the new conditions of warfare called for new methods, especially in relation to definitions of contraband, rules of blockade, and searching of ships on the high seas, the Germans now claimed that these same new conditions — and especially the British illegalities — made it necessary for them to adopt a new weapon, the submarine. In other words, both maintained that new conditions made existing international law inapplicable.

In reply to the German war zone proclamation the American government took an unyielding stand. Its note of February 10, 1915, declared:

If the commanders of German vessels of war . . . should destroy on the high seas an American vessel *or the lives of American citizens,* it would be difficult for the Government of the United States to view the act in any other light than as an indefensible violation of neutral rights which it would be very hard indeed to reconcile with the friendly relations now so happily subsisting between the two governments.

If such a deplorable situation should arise, the Imperial German Government can readily appreciate that the Government of the United States would be constrained to hold the Imperial German Government to a *strict accountability* for such acts of their naval authorities and *to take any steps it might be necessary to take* to safeguard American lives and property and to secure to

[3]*Ibid.,* II, 265, Document 48.

American citizens the full enjoyment of their acknowledged rights on the high seas.[4]

It will be noticed that in this note the American government made no distinction between American ships and those of the belligerents. In other words, it maintained that the presence of an American on a belligerent ship gave that ship an immunity which the belligerent government itself could not have claimed. "It is thus apparent that the first American protest on submarines . . . with its challenging 'strict accountability,' was founded on the false premise that the United States was privileged to speak not only for American vessels and their personnel but also on behalf of American citizens on Allied and other vessels. No other neutral country appears to have fallen into this error."[5] This "confusion of ideas and legal conceptions" was eventually to be most expensive. The distinguished student of international law, John Bassett Moore, has recently stated: The more the evidence is studied "the clearer it becomes that what most decisively contributed to the involvement of the United States in the war was the assertion of a right to protect belligerent ships on which Americans saw fit to travel and the treatment of armed belligerent merchantmen as peaceful vessels. Both assumptions were contrary to reason and to settled law, and no other professed neutral advanced them."[6]

Even assuming the rights claimed by Lansing were legal, the American government did not approach the situation in a manner which would have provided for a solution. It took an uncompromising stand which left the Germans with but one choice if they were to escape war with the United States and that was complete submission. It meant surrender of the illegal submarine warfare without gaining any modification of the illegal British blockade.

[4]*Ibid.*, II, 268, Document 49. Italics mine.

Lansing interpreted "strict accountability" to mean "that the German government must make full reparation for the act of their naval force and must also repudiate the act, apologize for it and give ample assurance that it will not be repeated." *Ibid.*, Document 74, May 5, 1915, II, 306.

This makes the note more extreme than it appears to be on the surface. It is worth noting that although a similar phrase was considered in connection with the infractions of international law by the Allies, it was not used.

[5]Borchard and Lage, *Neutrality For The United States* (New Haven, 1937), 183.

[6]Moore, John Bassett, "America's Neutrality Policy," the New York *Times*, May 17, 1937.

The decision to reject the war zone concept was taken far too hastily and reflected the same rashness and disregard of opposing points of view which characterized Wilson's handling of the Vera Cruz incident. Presented with demands such as were embodied in the American note of February 10, no government could have yielded. Certainly the German government in the midst of a difficult war would have been unable to accept such a diplomatic defeat. And yet Lansing and Wilson were quite naïvely puzzled when the Germans did not immediately abandon the submarine warfare. At no time did they think of what the economic warfare meant to the Germans. On June 1 Lansing wrote a querulous note to Wilson remarking that the Germans showed "an inflexible purpose to continue a course of action which this government [i.e., the United States] has frankly asserted would be illegal and inhuman."[7]

This lack of understanding continued throughout the period. After the second *Lusitania* note, Wilson wrote to Lansing that two things were plain to him: first, that the American people wanted a definite settlement of the *Lusitania* issue; and second, they desired that he not hasten matters "or so conduct the correspondence as to make an unfriendly issue inevitable."[8] In spite of his realization that the American people desired a peaceful settlement of the issue, he, with the assistance of the equally stubborn Germans, had already so directed matters that such a result was unobtainable. The situation created by Wilson and Lansing and the Wilhelmstrasse provided for no way in which the American government could save its face except by the complete surrender of Germany, and no way in which the German government could save its position except by the complete surrender of the United States. Wilson and Lansing had assisted in driving the American nation into a blind alley.

After the exchange of notes between the United States and Germany, Americans continued to travel in the area restricted by the German note of February 4, and the commerce between the United States and British ports increased amazingly. Meanwhile the German efforts to destroy British commerce, including that

---

[7]Savage, *op. cit.*, II, 331. Document 94.
[8]*Ibid.*, 356, Document 102, July 13, 1915.

with the United States, also developed and were becoming more reckless each day.

According to international law, ships might be stopped on the high seas, inspected, and destroyed if their cargoes were contraband. However, no boats could be sunk without warning and without providing for the safety of passengers. The British had revised these rules by forcing ships to enter British ports for inspection. The Germans discarded them entirely. They interpreted their war zone proclamations as establishing a blockade area in which none of these rights existed. The British were partially responsible for the elimination of these rulings in that they instructed their merchant ships as well as war ships to destroy submarines when possible. Schwieger commented on the fact that "several British captains were decorated or otherwise rewarded for ramming or attempting to ram submarines."[9] Even the captain of the *Lusitania* "was sailing under orders, which, if he had attempted without success to carry out, would have made it lawful for the submarine ruthlessly to destroy his vessel with everyone on board."[10] As a result of their vulnerability, the U-boats "operated in constant fear of being fired upon or rammed."[11]

The use of neutral flags by British merchant ships added to the difficulties of the submarine commanders. The English liner *Lusitania* raised the American flag to hide its identity on a trip early in 1915,[12] and other ships misused neutral flags in order to

[9]Bailey, Thomas A., "The Sinking of the *Lusitania*," *The American Historical Review*, XLI, 60.

[10]*Ibid.*, 61. On February 10, 1915, the British Admiralty sent out secret orders to masters of British merchantmen: "If a submarine comes up suddenly ahead of you with obvious hostile intention, steer straight for her at your utmost speed, altering course as necessary to keep her ahead." In other words orders were given to attack before the enemy craft could give the warning prescribed by international law. *Ibid.*, 60.

"One vessel, the small collier *Thordis*, during heavy weather on the 28th (February, 1915), rammed a submarine off Beachy Head; Berlin admitted that she had injured the U-boat; the latter had, however, safely regained port." "Before the end of March, it was announced in the press that the *Thordis* had received a reward of £660 for this gallant action." Borchard and Lage, *op. cit.*, 212.

[11]Bailey, Thomas A., "German Documents Relating To The *Lusitania*," *The Journal of Modern History*, September, 1936, 321.

[12]On February 10, 1915, Bryan sent a note to the British government in which he remarked that it "would seem to impose upon the Government of Great Britain a measure of responsibility for the loss of American lives" in case the boat were sunk.

attack submarines. The U-boat commanders found it dangerous to approach neutral ships in a legal manner;[13] consequently they more and more tended to ignore legality.

As a result of the hazards encountered by the submarines, there was adopted a policy of treating all ships in the war zone as if they were enemy war vessels. Very few restrictions were placed upon the commanders in their efforts to prevent all commerce between the British Isles and the rest of the world. The German government had requested of the American government information concerning, and silhouettes of, American boats so that these would not be sunk. This seems to have been the only exception to the policy of unrestricted sinkings. The submarines were ordered to attack "transport ships, merchants ships, [and] war ships."[14] The *U-20,* for instance, was concerned primarily with sinking enemy transports, but it attempted to sink "sizable ships that came within striking distance."[15] Schwieger tried to sink a fifteen hundred ton Swedish steamer, a three thousand ton Norwegian steamer, a Danish passenger steamer, and a fourteen thousand ton *White Star* passenger liner.[16]

Previous to the German acceptance of the challenge to an economic conflict by proclaiming a war zone around Great Britain, there had been ships sunk by mines and by submarines. Some of these were fighting ships, such as the *Formidable,* which went down with six hundred men on January 1, 1915. But after the war zone order went into effect on February 18, the campaign against merchant ships began to be truly appreciated. On March 14 the papers carried headlines:

GERMANS TORPEDO 8 SHIPS IN 3 DAYS
BRITAIN HAS LOST 137 TRADE VESSELS
In March the sinking of the Allies' ships reached about 80,000 tons. In April only about 60,000 tons were sunk but in the next

[13]Schwieger noted that there was no danger to be expected in "approaching on the surface so small a vessel as a 99-ton schooner." Bailey, *J. M. H., loc. cit.,* 330.

[14]*Ibid.,* 325.

[15]*Ibid.,* 320, 322.

[16]*Ibid.,* 329, 331, 332. It would seem that the German government was not quite honest when it stated: "It is far from the German Government to have any intention of ordering attacks by submarines or flyers on neutral vessels in the zone which have not been guilty of any hostile act; on the contrary the most explicit instructions have been repeatedly given the German armed forces to avoid attacking such vessels." Savage, *op. cit.,* II, 328.

five months the rate was to range from 109,000 to 185,000 a month. As a result of these successes the Germans naturally wanted to redouble these blows at their enemies.[17] It could hardly be expected that the American demands for a cessation of this type of warfare would be heeded.

It was inevitable as a result of the extraordinary thoroughness of the submarine commanders, and as a result of the American stand of February 10, that some event would occur which would bring relations between the United States and Germany to a crisis. The first American casualty occurred on March 28 with the sinking of the *Falaba*.[18] On May 1 three American lives were lost when the American steamer *Gulflight* was attacked. This latter incident was the first and only case, up to the time the United States broke off relations with Germany, in which Americans lost their lives as the result of an attack upon an American ship. The boat was following two British patrol boats and, as a result, had given up the protection of the neutral flag. The Americans by this act had placed themselves and their vessel under the armed protection of one of the belligerents. "While such convoy lasted, their sole source of protection lay in the two British patrol boats — irrespective of what flag their own vessel was flying." "In the course of the resulting diplomatic correspondence the Germans

[17]See Gibson, R. H., and Prendergast, M., *The German Submarine War* (New York, 1931).

[18]The note from the German government on May 29 stated: "In the case of the sinking of the English steamer *Falaba*, the commander of the German submarine had the intention of allowing passengers and crew ample opportunity to save themselves. It was not until the captain disregarded the order to lay to, and took flight, sending up rocket signals for help, that the German commander ordered the crew and passengers by signals and megaphone to leave the ship within ten minutes; as a matter of fact he allowed them twenty-three minutes and did not fire the torpedo until suspicious steamers were hurrying to the aid of the *Falaba*." Savage, *op. cit.*, II, 328.

The American government replied: "With regard to the sinking of the steamer *Falaba*, by which an American citizen lost his life, the Government of the United States is surprised to find the Imperial German Government contending that an effort on the part of a merchantman to escape capture and secure assistance alters the obligation of the officer seeking to make the capture in respect of the safety of the lives of those on board. . . ."

Yet later in the note it was stated: "Nothing but actual forcible resistance or continued efforts to escape by flight when ordered to stop for the purpose of visit on the part of the merchantman has ever been held to forfeit the lives of her passengers or crew." *Ibid.*, 341.

J. N. DARLING IN DES MOINES REGISTER

ARMED SHIP CARTOON

WILSON: "Come on — you've a perfect right to stand here!"

offered compensation for the attack," but "any indemnity in this case which the United States may have succeeded in getting from Germany under the threat of the *Lusitania* ultimatum must clearly be regarded as a windfall; it was not legally due."[19]

The *Gulflight* did not sink but was towed into port, and the casualties resulted only incidentally from the submarine attack. "Wireless operator Short and Seaman Charpenta jumped overboard and were drowned." Captain Gunter died from heart failure.[20] In England there was apparently some thought of embalming the body of the captain of the *Gulflight* and sending the remains to the United States for propaganda purposes.[21]

Of much more importance from the view of public opinion was the sinking of the British liner *Lusitania* on May 7, 1915. Because of the fact that a major section of British propaganda in the United States was concerned with this incident it is essential to know the ramifications of what propagandists pictured as a clear-cut issue. In the first place the *Lusitania* was a British commerce steamer "constructed with Government funds as [an] auxiliary cruiser . . . [and was] expressly included in the navy list published by [the] British Admiralty."[22] The boat "was one of two specially subsidized naval reserve ships, the other being the *Mauretania*."[23] The *Lusitania* "was practically built for the admiralty . . . and had bases laid for mounting guns of 6 inch cal-

[19]Borchard and Lage, *op. cit.*, 229.

[20]Page to Lansing, May 7, 1915. "Diplomatic Correspondence," *A. J. I. L.*, XI, Special Supplement (1917) 76, 77, as quoted in Borchard and Lage, *op. cit.*, 221.

[21]Thompson, Basil, *Queer People* (London, 1922), 63 f.

[22]Borchard and Lage, *op. cit.*, 329. Captain Turner reported: "She was built to the Admiralty requirements and her construction was subsidized by the British Government." London *Times*, May 8, 1915.

[23]Admiral F. E. Chadwick to Henry White in the Henry White Papers: Library of Congress.

The *Boston Evening Transcript* of August 7, 1914, mentioned the sister ship of the *Lusitania* as follows: "It will be fitted out as *H. M. S. Mauretania* and prepared to destroy the hostile shipping of Germany." "Commerce destruction was the ultimate purpose for which the *Mauretania* was constructed." Malone Report, June 4, 1915.

In 1916 a picture of the *Mauretania* as a troop ship appeared in the rotogravure sections of the papers.

[24]Malone Report, June 4, 1915. "All the more valuable English merchant ships have been provided with guns, ammunition and other weapons, and reenforced with a crew specially practiced in managing guns." German reply to the first *Lusitania* note, May 28, 1915. Savage, *op. cit.*, II, 329.

ibre."[24] "All in all, there appears to have been considerable justice in the contentions of the German foreign office that the giant Cunarder, whatever its technical status, was not just an ordinary unarmed merchant vessel." "But these details do not alter the fact that technically the *Lusitania* was not a warship."[25]

The Germans also claimed that the *Lusitania* was armed. Though they may have been correct, there is no reliable evidence that guns had been mounted on her decks.[26] An individual in New York City asserted that he saw masked guns on this ship, but there was no verification of his statement, and the individual in question went to the penitentiary for his rashness.[27]

On May 1, the date on which the *Lusitania* sailed from New York, there was published in the newspapers the following warning:[28]

> Travelers intending to embark on the Atlantic voyage are reminded that a state of war exists between Germany and her Allies and Great Britain and her Allies; that the zone of war includes the waters adjacent to the British Isles; that in accordance with formal notice given by the Imperial Government, vessels flying the flag of Great Britain or any of her Allies, are liable to destruction in those waters and that travelers sailing in the war zone on ships of Great Britain or her Allies do so at their own risk.

This notice was issued by the German Ambassador — quite contrary to diplomatic usage — and in certain New York papers

[25]Bailey, *A. H. R., loc. cit.*, 58, 61. The consular report to the State Department commented that the *Lusitania* listed to starboard "because of the longitudinal warship character bulkheads."

[26]In Malone's report to McAdoo he remarked: "If any guns had been mounted, or there was any intention to mount guns on the *Lusitania* on her open bow or open stern deck, these guns would have been mounted on the stable gun bases provided for the purpose, and not upon any blocks or blocking or other alleged paraphernalia for this purpose." Savage, *op. cit.*, II, 338. See Borchard and Lage, 155 ff., for a questioning of the value of Malone's evidence.

[27]Although this man later recanted, he told a friend of his that he did this at the suggestion of his lawyer, and that in spite of his recantation he had seen the guns on the *Lusitania*. (See the Lansing Papers in the Library of Congress.) In all probability this individual was not a dependable witness.

[28]On the date this notice was issued and a week before the sinking of the *Lusitania*, Lansing wrote to Bryan and stated he was informed that this had been "prepared about a week ago." Savage, *op. cit.*, II, 303, Document 72.

Bernstorff later stated this notice had been prepared some time before it was actually released.

was placed in close proximity to the notice of the *Lusitania's* sailing. A member of the Cunard Company issued a public statement: "As for submarines, I have no fear of them whatever." Whether or not this notice reassured them, no passengers seem to have canceled their reservations on the *Lusitania*.

Many Americans have felt that, irrespective of circumstances surrounding the destruction of this particular ship, citizens of this country should not carelessly endanger the peace of the nation by traveling in war zones. In this connection it must be admitted that practically none of the passengers on the *Lusitania* had any serious reason for going abroad at that time. Those who did have legitimate reasons for undertaking the trip could have secured passage on an American boat leaving New York on the same day. Among the Americans on the passenger list there was a voice student, a governess, a mechanic, several salesmen of war supplies, an art dealer, an insurance broker, a millionaire, and others.[29] It would seem that the nation's right to have peace was more important than their right to travel.

Although the *Lusitania* carried only a small number of Americans, there was on board an unusually large number of Canadians.[30] This is probably accounted for by the fact that the Canadians were going to Europe to enlist. "Many Britishers residing in Canada on the outbreak of the war immediately proceeded over seas at their own expense and served with units of the British army."[31] The German government claimed the large number of Canadians included Canadian troops. However, in all probability, these men had not yet enlisted.[32]

[29]See the report of the Mixed Claims Commission. The reasons given by many of the Americans for going abroad seem almost frivolous today. It now appears almost impossible to justify their going.

[30]A news account of a few days after the sinking listed the passengers according to nationality as follows: 904 British subjects, 13 Scots, 39 Irish, 188 Americans, 52 Russians, 18 Persians, 5 Swedes, 6 Greeks, 6 French, 3 Dutchmen, 1 Belgian, 1 Finn, 2 Mexicans, I Italian, 1 Swiss. Toronto *Daily Mail and Empire*, May 8, 1915. [These figures are slightly inaccurate.]

[31]Major W. E. L. Coleman of the Canadian Office of National Defense, September 4, 1934, to the writer. In Malone's note to the Secretary of the Treasury, he said: "If any individual reservists of any nationality sailed on the *Lusitania* on this trip they did so as individuals, paying their own passage and receiving their individual tickets." Savage, *op. cit.*, II, 333.

[32]"No members of the Canadian Forces who served in France and Belgium went to these theaters of war privately...." Major Coleman to the author.

There was a number of reasons why this particular boat was chosen by people going abroad. In the first place it was the "Queen of the Atlantic," and was considered to be the safest boat on the high seas. Secondly, in British lands, the slogan of the day was "carry on." This influenced many people to disregard German warnings. Finally there was an element of defiance of the Germans, among Americans as well as among Englishmen.

The major part of the material shipped on the *Lusitania* was munitions of war. In the cargo were included twenty-four hundred cases of rifle cartridges shipped from the Remington A. U. M. C. Company (J. P. Morgan and Company), and twelve hundred and fifty cases of shrapnel shipped from the Bethlehem Steel Company (Charles M. Schwab) at Bethlehem, Pennsylvania. These munitions were consigned to the British Royal Arsenal at Woolwich, England. The shrapnel apparently did not contain the explosive charge although the eighteen cases of fuses which accompanied the shrapnel may have. The rifle cartridges contained an estimated ten or eleven tons of black powder.[33] These munitions if delivered to the Western Front were enough to kill a probable sixteen hundred, and a possible three million, one hundred and fifty thousand men.

Under the rulings of the Department of Commerce and Labor, these shrapnel and rifle bullets were not considered "high explosives" and hence it was possible, legally, to ship them on a passenger vessel. On the other hand it cannot be denied that this made the *Lusitania* a munitions ship, which was using a cargo of noncombatants, including women and children, to protect war supplies. A number of people have pointed out that "on land no American sitting on an ammunition wagon could prevent its being fired on on its way to the front" and consequently Americans traveling on a munitions boat could not be expected to give it immunity. In reply to the German contention that the *Lusitania* carried munitions, the American government took the position that the Germans were beclouding the issue. Wilson intimated that this was an irrelevant matter; others held a contrary point of view. It may have been legal to ship these death-dealing instruments on a passenger boat, but it was far from being ethical. The

[33]*The Nation*, January 3, 1923, 15. See Savage, *op. cit.*, II, Document 75, 307 f.

British and American governments, as well as the Cunard Company, would seem to have been culpable for allowing travelers to take passage on a boat with such a cargo.

The anger of the American people made it possible for the American and British newspapers to gloss over their own governments' shortcomings in this connection. After the first day the American press attempted to avoid discussion of the *Lusitania's* cargo, and when Senator LaFollette stated that the boat carried munitions, the indignant Anglophiles wished to throw him out of the Senate. "The prosecution of the Senator was dropped only when Mr. Malone [Collector of the Port of New York] offered to testify in his behalf."[34]

The fact that the *Lusitania* was sunk within nine miles of shore, and that the German Embassy had issued a warning on the morning of the sailing made many people believe that the sinking of the boat was deliberately premeditated. Although the *U-20* had been instructed to sink all enemy boats, as far as can be ascertained it had no instructions to sink this particular vessel. The fact that neither the liner nor the submarine was in its proper course indicates that the meeting of the submarine and the Cunarder was entirely accidental. Captain Schwieger was running low on fuel and consequently was plying in a location where he otherwise would not have been. The *Lusitania* was following a route which it had been specifically instructed to avoid. Even the commander of the *U-20* expressed surprise at finding his victim plying this course.[35] The meeting of the *U-20* and the *Lusitania* was an accident. It was, however, an accident which was bound to occur sooner or later.

Schwieger's diary reported his encounter with the *Lusitania* as follows:

> Ahead to starboard four funnels and two masts of a steamer with course perpendicular to us come into sight (coming from SSW it steered toward Galley Head). Ship is made out to be large passenger steamer.
>
> [We] submerged to a depth of 11 meters and went ahead at full speed, taking a course converging with the one of the steamer, hoping it might change its course to starboard along the Irish coast.

[34]*The Nation*, November 24, 1920, 579.
[35]Bailey, *J. M. H., loc. cit.*, 332.

The steamer turns to starboard, takes course to Queenstown, thus making possible an approach for a shot. Until 3:00 P.M. we ran at high speed in order to gain position directly ahead.

Clean bow shot at a distance of 700 meter (G-torpedo, 3 meters depth adjustment); angle 90°, estimated speed 22 knots. Torpedo hits starboard side right behind the bridge.

An unusually heavy detonation takes place with a very strong explosion cloud (far beyond front funnel). The explosion of the torpedo must have been followed by a second one (boiler or coal or powder?). The superstructure above the point of impact and the bridge are torn asunder, fire breaks out, and smoke envelops the high bridge.

The ship stops immediately and keels over to starboard very quickly, immersing simultaneously at the bow. It appears as if the ship were going to capsize very shortly. Great confusion ensues on board; the boats are made clear and in part are lowered to the water. In doing so, great panic must have reigned; some boats, full to capacity, are rushed and founder immediately. On the port side fewer boats are made clear than on the starboard side, on account of the [ship's] list.

The ship blows off [steam]; on the bow the name *Lusitania* becomes visible in golden letters. The funnels were painted black; no flag was set astern. Ship was running 20 knots [?]. Since it seems as if the steamer will keep above the water only a short time, we dived to a depth of 24 meters and ran out to sea. It would have been impossible for me, anyhow, to fire a second torpedo into this crowd of people struggling to save their lives.[36]

The account of Captain Schwieger states that the torpedo struck the boat "right behind the bridge." Some survivors have claimed that the torpedo struck the rear of the boat near the fourth funnel.[37]

The location of the point of impact becomes important because of the much disputed second explosion. Schwieger stated in his report that there must have been a second one. One survivor wrote: "A second explosion quickly followed."[38] Another said that after he reached the water there was another explosion

---

[36]*Ibid.*, 332, 335 f.

[37]The Mersey Report, which is quite undependable, states that the explosion occurred about fifty yards away from the bridge, which was directly over the hold in which munitions cargo was stored.

[38]Lauriat, Charles E., *The Lusitania's Last Voyage* (Boston, 1915), 8.

which sent up a shower of wreckage. One testified there was a second explosion about two minutes before the boat sank. Still another claimed it occurred just as the boat went under.[39]

The propagandists immediately attempted to make people believe that the second explosion was caused by a second torpedo, thus giving unquestionable proof of German barbarism. The Mersey Report claimed "a second torpedo was fired immediately. . . . The torpedoes struck the ship almost simultaneously." Some passengers claimed to have seen two torpedoes. Captain Turner testified that he saw two, but that only one struck the boat. A woman told a newspaperman that she saw three torpedoes and two submarines.

The attempt to exploit the second explosion soon encountered difficulties. The Germans contended that there was no second torpedo but that the munitions had exploded. This counter-statement caused the British to drop discussion of the second explosion, but interest in it has not disappeared. Bailey accepts it as a fact and, with Dudley Field Malone, considers it possible that "the intense heat generated by the torpedo explosion ignited the ten or eleven tons of powder in the cartridges."[40] "The exploding munitions theory gains further support when we note that the giant Cunarder which was equipped with devices to render her unsinkable, went to the bottom within eighteen minutes," while on other occasions "vessels not even one-fifth the size of the *Lusitania* did not sink at all . . . or sank slowly; or required a second torpedo or gunfire to complete their destruction."[41] Previous to the attack on the *Lusitania*, Captain Schwieger had found it necessary to use two torpedoes to sink a six thousand ton British steamer,[42] and had to use gunfire as well as a torpedo to sink a five thousand ton boat.

In addition to the rapidity of the sinking, the inefficiency of the crew contributed in no small measure to the heavy list of casualties. One survivor in speaking of the order to stop lowering

[39]When these conflicting stories were brought to the attention of the survivors interviewed, they were agreed in saying these accounts were untrue and that there was no second explosion.

[40]Bailey, *A. H. R.*, *loc. cit.*, 62.

[41]*Ibid.* The Mersey Report states the boat was afloat for twenty minutes after being struck.

[42]Bailey, *J. M. H.*, *loc. cit.*, 332.

the life boats commented on the fact that immediately afterwards the sailors disappeared. The crew was far from being
efficient in the handling of the life boats and in taking care of the
passengers during the short time available between the explosion
and the sinking. Part of this was due to the fact that there had
been no life boat drills on the trip across the Atlantic. The inefficiency of the crew is usually attributed to the fact that many
of the regular sailors had entered the navy and that consequently
the men on the *Lusitania* were inexperienced.

The ineffectiveness of the crew in all probability was largely
the fault of the captain. When the *Lusitania* sailed from New
York on May 1 it was under the command of a relief captain,
William Thomas Turner. Since the regular commander, Captain
Dow, signed the first sheet of the manifest, the change must have
been made shortly before the sailing date. After the explosion of
the torpedo "Captain Turner and Captain Anderson were both
calling in stentorian tones not to lower away the boats . . . saying
that there was no danger and that the ship would float."[43] Previous to this Mr. Turner had disobeyed many of the instructions
given him. He was plying a course which he had been instructed
to avoid. The ship was running at a reduced speed in a dangerous
area where speed would have made the difference between safety
and disaster, as proved by the unsuccessful attempts of the *U-20*
to sink fast boats.[44] The portholes were left open; the life boats
had not been swung out; and no life boat drills had been held.[45]
A contemporary writer has stated: "I submit that the man proved
himself mentally inadequate for such a command and guilty of
such grave mistakes in judgment in his disobedience of orders as
to render it absolutely certain that he jeopardized his ship unnecessarily and contributed to the disaster — unintentionally, of
course."[46] Captain Anderson, the second in command, went down
with the boat. Captain Turner was saved.[47]

[43]Lauriat, *op. cit.*, 9.

[44]"The slow speed of the U-20, approximately 12 knots, frustrated what otherwise might have been successful attacks on two faster steamers. These experiences
must have pointed to the futility of attempting to warn so swift a liner as the
Lusitania." Bailey, *J. M. H.*, *loc. cit.*, 322.

[45]*The Nation*, January 3, 1923, 15.

[46]Villard, O. G., "The True Story of the *Lusitania*," *The American Mercury*,
May, 1935.

[47]Captain Turner died June 23, 1933.

When the inefficiency of the captain and the crew was added to the work of the submarine commander and whatever may have caused the second explosion,[48] the sinking of the *Lusitania* became one of the major sea disasters. Seven hundred and eighty-five of the 1257 passengers, and 413 of the 702 members of the crew lost their lives. One hundred and twenty-eight of the 197 Americans were drowned.[49]

In spite of all the mitigating factors, the sinking of the *Lusitania* was the most damaging of all the political errors made by the Germans during the war. It was disastrous to Germany because it was a striking and dramatic event. The spectacle of the supposedly innocent passengers made victims of German ruthlessness outweighed any actualities of contributory responsibility of the United States, Great Britain, and the Cunard Company, or the dubious correctness of the American policy concerning traveling in the war zone. It branded Germany as the malefactor among nations.

The entire field of British propaganda was benefited by this incident. The most marked advantage was gained with the Americans who had been enlisted or drafted as British propagandists. The American newspapers which had been giving so much space to British interpretations of the war saw in this occurrence a complete justification of their attitude. The editors on the Atlantic seaboard lost their heads completely and all found it a type of sensation which sold their newspapers for them.

Quickly marshalling their forces, British propagandists took full advantage of their opportunity. A week after the disaster they rushed into print with the Bryce atrocity report. Next it was found that a German had designed a medal to commemorate the sinking of the *Lusitania*. This was not an official award and but few copies of it were in circulation in Germany. The British propagandists, however, reproduced the medal in large numbers and distributed it throughout the world. In doing this they spread the rumors abroad that it had been awarded to the crew of the *U-20* by the German government. Occasionally they would admit that

[48]"The foreman of the Queenstown jury protested that all the victims were not drowned. 'I have seen many of the bodies, and the people were killed; they were blown to pieces.' "

[49]The loss of the British and Canadians amounted to 61.8%, American 64.9%, others an even 50%.

the particular medal being distributed was a mere reproduction, but it is doubtful whether in the second or third telling, this part of the story was retained. Lord Newton has stated that he considered it one of their best pieces of propaganda. Certainly "the propaganda value of the medal was great. . . ."[50]

The British commission under Lord Mersey, which had been appointed to investigate the disaster, also did its utmost to capitalize on the feeling aroused by the event. The final report is a complete white-wash of everything and everybody connected with the British and American side of the case. Survivors report that the commission did not attempt to obtain information. Instead it converted itself into a sounding board of sensation for the newspapers. One man spoke of the inquest as a farce.

The American newspapers, already won to the British cause, aided in befogging the real issues. The subject of the cargo was dismissed or given but scant attention, and in order to play up community of interest between the Allies and the United States, there was apparently a deliberate attempt to induce people to believe that the boat was American. Finally, it was seldom made clear that Americans comprised but a small per cent of the casualties. For instance, the London *Times* of March 8, 1915, stated: "About four-fifths of her passengers were citizens of the United States."[51]

With the sinking of the *Lusitania* it quickly became apparent that a new phase of the war had been reached. The regicides are supposed to have looked at the French Revolution through the little window of Louis XVI's guillotine. After May 7, 1915, German-American relations could be conducted only through the

[50]"I asked a West End store if they could undertake the reproduction of it for propaganda purposes. They agreed to do so, and the medals were sold all over the world in neutral countries, especially in America and South America. After some initial difficulty a great success was achieved. I believe it to have been one of the best pieces of propaganda." As quoted by Ponsonby, *op. cit.*, 124, 125, from the London *Evening Standard,* November 1, 1926.

(1) No medal was given to the crew of the German U-boat; (2) no medal was struck in commemoration of the event by the German government; (3) the German government could not have withdrawn a medal it never issued; (4) a metal-worker in Munich designed the medal, which was always rare in Germany; (5) the large number of medals in circulation was due to the reproduction of Goetz's medal in Great Britain. *Ibid.,* 125.

[51]This rate would ordinarily have been correct. However, at this particular time the Canadians far outnumbered the Americans.

portholes of the *Lusitania*. People throughout the world were wondering whether it meant war. In England "the question upon everybody's lips was will the United States . . . join the Allies."[52]

President Wilson's first public speech after the tragedy was to occur in Philadelphia before several thousand newly naturalized foreign born citizens. Naturally people expected in this speech some expression of the government's intentions. In an otherwise harmless address, the President made the mistake of using the phrase "too proud to fight." Although this was of no particular significance in itself, it was taken to mean that the United States would not enter the war and would not condescend to fight Germany. Those people who were excessively sympathetic with the Allies became most indignant. The British jeered.

On May 13 the American government sent the first *Lusitania* note to Germany. Perhaps as a result of the unfavorable reaction to the "too proud to fight" speech, the note was more severe than it otherwise might have been. Garrison, then Secretary of War, is given credit for having made the note so threatening.[53] It embodied the view that the rights of Americans to trade and travel in European waters, war zone or no war zone, could not be abridged, When von Jagow read this, he laughed and said, "Why not the right of free travel on land in war territory?" The principal American argument was that the submarine could not be used at all "without an inevitable violation of many sacred principles of justice and humanity," and strongly implied that it would have to be abandoned as an instrument of war against merchant ships. The note was a challenge and a threat of war.

Prior to the sending of the first *Lusitania* note, Bryan had been making a continuous effort to eliminate the points of controversy between the United States and Germany. At the beginning of the argument over submarine warfare, he had tried to arrange a compromise between Germany and England whereby food could be sent to Germany in exchange for an abandonment of unrestricted submarine warfare.[54] The Germans wished all

[52]London *Times*, May 10, 1915.

[53]Lawrence, *op. cit.*, 150.

[54]After the sinking of the *Lusitania* the German government attempted to reach a compromise. Zimmerman told Gerard that "an agreement might be reached on somewhat the following basis: Germany and England both agree not to use gases. Food, cotton, copper, rubber, and such other raw material as does not di-

the illegal restrictions on their trade abolished. They felt that yielding on the food issue alone would give sanction to other British actions.[55] On the other hand, there was no desire on the part of the British to remove causes of friction between the United States and Germany. Winston Churchill remarked: "We were sure that . . . [the submarine war] would offend and perhaps embroil the United States; and that in any case our position for enforcing the blockade would be greatly strengthened."[56]

After failing to get the belligerents to agree to compromise, Bryan attempted to induce Wilson to make some concessions. Even as early at the *Falaba* incident, he was attempting to keep Americans from taking passage on belligerent ships entering the war zone. On April 2 he wrote to Wilson that "the American who takes passage upon a British vessel knowing that this method of warfare [i.e., submarine warfare] will be employed, stands in a different position from that occupied by one who suffers without any fault of his own. . . . It seems to me that the doctrine of contributory negligence has some bearing on this case."[57] The Counsellor of the State Department, Robert Lansing, had at that time joined Mr. Wilson in opposition to Bryan. On April 7 he wrote to his superior that either one of two courses seemed to be open: "(1) to warn Americans generally to keep out of the German war zone, if on board a merchant vessel, which is not of American nationality; (2) to hold Germany to a strict accountability for every American life lost by submarine attack on high seas."[58] He then went on to add that expediency, that is, a desire to keep out of war, "would favor the adoption of a policy resulting in the

---

rectly enter into manufacture of munitions of war to be allowed to enter Germany. Germany to stop torpedoing of merchant vessels without notice but England to agree that merchant vessels shall not be armed and shall not attempt to ram submarines." Savage, *op. cit.*, 324, Document 89, May 25, 1915.

[55] An adviser of the State Department expressed the opinion when this note was under discussion, that it also presented nothing which would be acceptable to the Germans. He stated: "The entire stoppage of food supplies on both sides would be much more serious to Great Britain than Germany and it does not seem reasonable that Germany would be willing merely for the sake of renewing its supply of food to open the way for an unlimited supply not only of food, but also of war materials to Great Britain if Germany was able to establish an effective blockade." Chandler P. Anderson to Lansing, February 19, 1915, in the Lansing Papers.

[56] Churchill, *op. cit.*, 292.

[57] Savage, *op. cit.*, II, 290.

[58] *Ibid.*, 296.

first course suggested," but that American dignity demanded the second.

After the sinking of the *Lusitania* Bryan again suggested to Lansing and Wilson that "Americans who took passage on a British vessel destined to pass through the German war zone did so in a measure at their own peril, and were not entitled to the full protection of the Government."[59] "If the authorities of a city are justified in warning people off the streets of the city in which they reside, surely a nation is justified in warning its citizens off . . . the water highways which belong to no nation alone, but to all the nations in common."[60] Lansing contended that for the government to adopt such a point of view would be impossible after the note of February 10, and would be an admission of partial responsibility for the American lives lost on the *Lusitania*. He insisted on maintaining the "legal rights" of Americans. The President, also, was of the opinion that it was too late to take such a position.[61]

There were others who held opinions similar to Bryan's, but they were not in a position to obtain a hearing for their views. Some in Congress "felt at once that those who had lost their lives were themselves primarily to blame for having traveled on a ship which they knew to be in danger."[62] Gerard wrote to Lansing: "When Americans have reasonable opportunity to cross the ocean why should we enter a great war because some American wants to cross on a ship when he can have a private bathroom." General Leonard Wood, in spite of his pro-British conduct, is supposed to have said: "You cannot cover 10,000 tons [*sic*] of ammunition with a petticoat."[63]

Meanwhile Bryan was bearing the brunt of the struggle with Wilson. He wrote to the President: "Germany has a right to pre-

[59]*Ibid.*, 56.

[60]Tansill, *op. cit.*, 330, Bryan to Wilson.

[61]"We defined our position at the outset and cannot alter it — at any rate so far as it affects the past." Savage, *op. cit.*, II, 314, Document 83.

[62]Hale, W. B., *Peace Or War*, 67.

[63]Senator LaFollette was one of the few who, after the sinking of the *Lusitania*, had the courage openly to oppose Wilson's policy. He stated: "The present Administration had assumed and acted upon the policy that it could enforce to the very letter of the law the principles of international law against one belligerent and relax them as to the other. That thing no nation can do without losing its character as a neutral nation and without losing the rights that go with strict and absolute neutrality." *LaFollette's Magazine*, April, 1917.

vent contraband from going to the Allies, and a ship carrying contraband should not rely upon passengers to protect her from attack — it would be like putting women and children in front of an army."[64] Wilson answered: "I am inclined to think we ought to take steps as you suggest to prevent our citizens from traveling on ships carrying munitions of war, and I shall seek to find the legal way to do it."[65] This, however, was but a passing thought. Immediately afterwards he returned to his unyielding stand and insisted that Americans must be protected in their rights to travel regardless of the nationality or cargo of the ships on which they were taking passage.

Bryan was greatly disturbed by Wilson's evident intention of taking a stiff attitude. He said to his wife, "Mary, what does the President mean? I cannot understand his attitude."[66] "One night . . . [Bryan] came home, his eyes shining. . . . The President had consented to the principle of arbitration." Mrs. Bryan records that "after the telegram had been drawn for communicating this statement to the German Government, the President directed that it not be sent because of information he had received through a newspaperman from the German Embassy."[67] The change was more likely a result of pressure from Wilson's other advisors. When Lansing received the revised telegram containing an agreement for arbitration, he, Tumulty, and Garrison, again besieged the President. As a result the note was sent unamended.

Still fighting for peace, Bryan got Lansing to prepare a notice that he had discussed with Wilson warning Americans against taking passage on belligerent merchant ships pending negotiations.[68] Wilson was dubious as to the wisdom of such a notice and told Bryan: "It weakens the effect of our saying to Germany that

[64]Bryan, W. J., *The Memoirs Of W. J. Bryan* (Chicago, 1925), 399 f.
[65]Wilson to Bryan, June 5, 1915. *Bryan* MS as quoted by Tansill.
[66]Bryan, *op. cit.*, 420.
[67]*Ibid.*, 421 f. A diplomatic denial of the postscript was made by Wilson on October 31, 1916.
[68]"The President in view of the present diplomatic situation requests that American citizens, intending to proceed abroad and to traverse waters adjacent to the coasts of Great Britain and France, will refrain from taking passage on vessels of belligerent nationality pending the exchange of views between this Government and the Government of Germany regarding the use of submarines in interrupting vessels of commerce in those waters." Lansing's comment was: "A request like this would be, in my opinion, almost, if not quite, as effective as an order, and presents no legal difficulties." Savage, *op. cit.*, II, 318.

we mean to support our citizens in the exercise of their right to travel both on our ships and on belligerent."[69]

As a result of the unwillingness of the administration to take a less belligerent stand in this controversy, Bryan decided to resign his office as Secretary of State. At first he had hoped the President would warn Americans to keep out of the war zone. In this he failed. Then he hoped that the "postscript," or secondary note, would be sent agreeing to arbitration. When this proposal was also rejected, he could do no other than resign at the first opportunity. He turned in his resignation rather than sign the second note to Germany. Many were surprised, saying that this second note was no worse than the first, but the reason Bryan openly broke with the President was because of the policy involved. He saw that it would lead to war, regardless of the effect of the particular note — and it did. Succeeding events proved his judgment to be prophetically accurate.

The first crisis over the *Lusitania* terminated with the German note of July 8 and the American reply of July 21. In the American note Lansing stated that "he could not consent to abate any fundamental American right because of a mere change of circumstances," and "that repetition by the commanders of German naval vessels of acts in contravention of these rights must be regarded by the Government of the United States, when they affect American citizens, as deliberately unfriendly."[70] This threat of war was the inevitable consequence of the American policy as propounded in the note of February 10, and in the first *Lusitania* note.

Ambassador Page and other strong partisans of the British expected another *Lusitania* to be sunk. Indeed, there seems to have been a desire on their part for such an occurrence. After the event of May 7, 1915, however, there was no recurrence of a disaster in which a great many American lives were lost. The Germans, quite belatedly, displayed some caution. Also there was a striking decrease in the number of Americans traveling in Europe. There were eighty per cent fewer American men who obtained passage to England in the year following the sinking of the *Lusitania* than there had been in the first year of the war.

[69]Bryan, *op. cit.*, 403.
[70]Savage, *op. cit.*, II, 363.

After the *Lusitania* crisis there were, of course, other sinkings which kept the submarine issue alive. On June 30, 1915, the *Armenian* was sunk; August 19 the *Arabic* went down;[71] November 7 the *Ancona* was destroyed in the Mediterranean. All these in one way or another affected the American government.

On September 1, 1915, after the crisis brought about by the sinking of the *Arabic,* the Germans promised to give warning before sinking merchant ships. Bernstorff advised the Secretary of State: "Liners will not be sunk by our submarines without warning and without safety of the lives of noncombatants, provided that the liners do not try to escape or offer resistance."[72] "A second German note was received on October 5 stating that orders to submarine commanders had been made so stringent that the recurrence of incidents similar to the *Arabic* case was considered out of the question. . . ."[73] On November 29, in a note concerning the *Frye* case, there was a complete statement of the new policy.

> . . . the German naval forces will sink only such American vessels as are loaded with absolute contraband, when the pre-conditions provided by the Declaration of London are present. In this the German Government quite shares the view of the American Government that all possible care must be taken for the security of the crew and passengers of a vessel to be sunk. Consequently, the persons found on board of a vessel may not be ordered into her lifeboats except when the general conditions, that is to say, the weather, the condition of the sea, and the neighborhood of the coasts afford absolute certainty that the boats will reach the nearest port. For the rest the German Government begs to point out that in cases where German naval forces have sunk neutral vessels for carrying contraband, no loss of life has yet occurred.[74]

The first phase of the controversy between the United States and Germany over the submarine was terminated by the *Arabic* incident. Out of it President Wilson gained a temporary victory which increased his prestige a great deal. Ultimately, of course, his policies would have to be backed up with force unless the

[71]It was claimed by the Germans that the *Arabic* attempted to ram the submarine.

[72]Savage, *op. cit.,* II, 378.

[73]*Ibid.,* 64.

[74]*Ibid.,* 429.

Germans found it possible to gain a decision without depending upon the submarine.

To the British the struggle between Germany and the United States was of tremendous importance. It not only meant increased difficulties for their principal enemy but it might mean that the United States would enter the war against that enemy. It is more than likely that they had this in mind when they tightened the blockade and made conditions even more desperate for the Central Powers.

In this advanced stage all the factors which had shaped American thinking were reinforced by German naval policy. The ideas which people in the United States had concerning the conflict now became vital factors in determining the course of events. It seems rather clear that if the propaganda had not been so successful and if American finance and industry had not had such a great stake in an Allies' victory the Americans would have found a way out of the difficulty. The ties with Great Britain, however, eliminated any desire for a solution which would have been unacceptable to the British.

CHAPTER VI ☆ GERMAN PROPAGANDA AND SABOTAGE; MORE GRIST FOR THE PROPAGANDA MILL

WHILE a thorough study of German activities in the United States does not come within the scope of this work, nevertheless it is essential to deal with them in so far as they aided British propagandists in creating an anti-German attitude in this country. And these activities were important in that they seemed to prove that German methods of making war were nefarious; they made the "identity of interest" or "our fight" arguments appear to be valid. They seemed to substantiate the British contention that Germany was an enemy of the United States as well as of the Allies.

At the outbreak of hostilities there was apparently no realization on the part of the German government of the important role that the United States would play in the war. Consequently no serious thought was given to the necessity of having a well-rounded organization to take care of German interests in this country. For instance, authorities in Berlin never fully appreciated the absolute necessity of counteracting anti-German feeling in the New World.[1] Propaganda was underestimated too long, the organizations which were handling it were inadequate, and the material issued was never sufficient.

The original advantages enjoyed by the Germans in any educational campaign within this country were greatly overshadowed by the disadvantages. There existed among the American people considerable respect for the German because of his industry and

[1] The importance of preventing the American entry into the war is expressed in the report of von Papen to Falkenhayn upon returning to Germany: "General, if you do not succeed in keeping the United States from joining the coalition of our enemies, you will lose the war; on this point there can be absolutely no doubt. The enormous material and moral resources at the disposal of the United States are so wholly underestimated here that in my opinion it is above all things essential to enlighten public opinion to an extent quite different from that which has hitherto been the case." Testimony of von Papen, *Official German Documents*, 1307. See Landau, Captain Henry, *The Enemy Within, The Inside Story of German Sabotage in America* (New York, 1937), Chapter I.

reliability. There was also a large body of people who were of German blood and who could be expected to have sympathy for the Reich. On the other hand, there prevailed a pre-war antagonism toward the German government. More important was the fact that as soon as the war broke out, the Central Powers were cut off from the rest of the world and hence could not gain a hearing in the United States. The final and most important handicap to German propagandists in the United States was the fact that their news was censored by the enemy. That German propagandists had to be constantly on the defensive, constantly explaining, reveals why they could never have hoped to succeed in winning American sympathy.

Being cut off from Germany and German news hampered German agents at every turn. It was positively disastrous to the propagandist. When, late in 1914, wireless communication with Germany was finally permitted, there was still no immediate improvement in the situation. At first there was time only for diplomatic and commercial messages; no propaganda could be sent.[2] Later in 1915 it was possible more and more to obtain information from the Central Powers, but even then the material sent was completely unsuited for the American public. When used it had to be rewritten — consequently, even then the propagandists were late with the news, and as before, were on the defensive rather than the offensive.[3] This lateness of news always partially invalidated German propaganda and oftentimes destroyed its effectiveness completely.

The German organizations in the United States operated almost without assistance from their home office. Their position was similar to that of a force behind the enemy lines, cut off from its base of supplies. The nominal head of all German agents working in this country was the Ambassador, Count Johann von Bernstorff, who acted as treasurer for the various enterprises. The individuals taking care of propaganda, purchases, or less respectable activities consulted with him from time to time, and on important matters his decision was probably final.[4] He attempted,

[2]Irwin, *op. cit.*, 129.

[3]The facilities to send material to the United States was an obvious advantage for the Allies. Having their own wireless stations as well as cables, they could send overseas five words to Germany's one. *Ibid.*, 137.

[4]Landau, *op. cit.*, 104.

of course, to keep in the background as much as possible, "his principal duty being to watch Congress and the President in order to prevent any political action unfavorable to Germany."[5]

The German propaganda office in Berlin, unlike Wellington House, dealt almost exclusively with the propaganda in Europe. Distance and inadequate communication facilities made it exceedingly difficult for the home office to handle propaganda in the United States. As a result the Germans decided they must create a special organization for America. One of the traditional legends of the war relates that the Germans had in this country a vast propaganda machine which had been organized and put into operation before the opening of hostilities in Europe, but there is no evidence to support this belief. The German propaganda organization in America was a makeshift gathered together after a hot July sun had precipitated the explosion so long awaited. It was composed of a chance-medley of individuals who happened to be available at that particular time. They were inexperienced, unacquainted with the American situation, and did not demonstrate abilities of any high order.

This propaganda department was known as the German Information Service. It was under the direction of Dr. Bernard Dernburg, who never had more than a dozen men in his organization. The personnel included consular agents, attachés, and business men stranded in New York at the outbreak of the war. M. B. Claussen, a New York press agent of the Hamburg-American Line, became Dernburg's assistant. On the advisory board, there were Dr. Fuehr, Dr. Mechlenberg, Dr. Heinrich Albert, Meyer-Gerhardt, Ewald Hecker, Herr Plage, and George Sylvester Viereck. Professors Muensterberg, Francke, and von Mach helped out from time to time. Realizing to a slight degree that only an American could fully understand the peculiarities of Americans, they employed one of them, a Mr. William Bayard Hale, to act as advisor. Mr. Hale was supposed to have been a friend of Woodrow Wilson, as well as the Kaiser.

The success of British propaganda rested largely upon its excellent service of information. It is in this respect that Dernburg's organization failed utterly. The individuals on his board of strategy collected some information and ideas, and obtained

[5]*Ibid.*, 9.

assistance from people of German descent in the United States,
but on the whole the bureau operated without the benefit of an
intelligence department. Nor did it receive adequate information
from abroad. Dernburg did not know what the American government was doing, what the British government planned to do, or
what his own government was considering. He had only the vagu-
est ideas concerning the activities of his own compatriots in the
United States. It has been said that an intelligence department is
the eyes and ears of an army; Dernburg's force was blind, deaf,
and dumb.

This bureau took care of the ordinary work of a propaganda
organization. It published pamphlets,[6] gave support to authors
desiring to publish books which were favorable to Germany, and
later arranged for the release of some newsreels. It was realized,
of course, that the newspaper was the only effective propaganda
medium in the United States. Consequently, much attention was
given to the problem of creating a more sympathetic attitude in
the press. The Germans were appalled by the attitude of American newspapers. The few friendly statements which were published were naturally unimportant in comparison with the flood
of articles which were unfriendly.

Unlike the British, the German propagandists were unable,
not only to control news in the United States, but to get their
versions of events before the American public at all. At the outbreak of the war various German officials attempted to counteract the effect of the British news which filled the press. Dernburg
was particularly successful in doing this. For a while the papers
clamored for his articles which offered a point of view totally new
to the American public. Ambassador Bernstorff also attempted to
assist by issuing statements from time to time. However, the pro-
Ally newspapers raised such a storm over these interviews that
the practice had to be discontinued. By the time it was possible
to obtain German news by wireless, the *Lusitania* incident had
occurred and the newspapers practically closed their columns to

[6]Among the authors of these pamphlets were Dernburg, von Mach, Kuno
Francke, and William Bayard Hale. Some of their most popular writings were:
The War Plotters of Wall Street, Thou Shalt Not Kill, and so on. Other best
sellers were: *The Truth About Germany, Germany's Just Cause, Germany's Hour
of Destiny, The Catechism of Balaam Jr.,* and so on. Viereck, George Sylvester,
Spreading Germs of Hate, 82 ff.

German news. Bernstorff notified his government: "Our propaganda in this country, has as a result of the *Lusitania* incident, completely collapsed."[7]

The leading newspapers which were friendly to the Central Powers were German-American and reached only the German reading public. To these should be added the group of unimportant Irish-American papers[8] owned by James K. McGuire. These backed the Germans because McGuire believed that Ireland's only hope lay in a German victory.[9] As far as influencing Americans was concerned, however, they can be completely discounted. Their editors wasted their ammunition on captured forts.

Among the regular American newspapers, the Milwaukee *Sentinel*[10] and the Washington *Post*[11] were the only ones which were, even for a while, consistently pro-German. The leading American papers which gave the Germans, as well as the British, a hearing were those of William Randolph Hearst.[12] Hearst, like a few other publishers, occasionally attacked Great Britain and hence assisted the Germans slightly. The Chicago *Tribune*, which like the Hearst papers, was rather anti-British, also printed some special dispatches from Germany.[13] A number of newspapers consistently opposed the British naval policy. These included the Cincinnati *Inquirer*, the Sacramento *Bee*, the Los Angeles *Times*, the St. Louis *Globe Democrat*, and the Cleveland *Plain Dealer*.[14]

[7]Bernstorff, *op. cit.*, 30.

[8]These were the *National Catholic* in New York City, the *Truth* in Scranton, and the *Light* in Albany.

[9]McGuire "seems to have sincerely believed that Germany would win the war and that Ireland's hope lay in Germany, and so he co-operated with Germany's representatives here as best he could." The testimony of Alexander Bruce Bielaski in United States Senate Judiciary Committee Hearings on *Brewing and Liquor Interests and German Propaganda, II* (Washington, 1919), 1397. Hereafter cited as *Brewing and Liquor Interests*.

[10]*A. P. R.*, August 6, 1915.

[11]When John R. McLean died and was succeeded by his son, Edward, the policy of the Washington *Post* was reversed.

[12]These included the New York *American*, and the New York *Journal*, the Chicago *Examiner*, and the Chicago *Evening American*, the Boston *American*, the Atlanta *Georgian*, the San Francisco *Examiner*, the San Francisco *Call*, and the *Examiner* and the *Evening Herald* in Los Angeles.

[13]These were offered to the forty newspapers which bought the *Tribune* press service.

[14]*A. P. R., passim*.

Most of their columns, however, were filled with news which was very satisfactory to the British and French censors.

The Germans made a number of attempts to gain a hearing in the American press. Their first serious effort was through the attempted purchase of the American Press Association.[15] They felt that control of this organization might make it possible to counteract partially the unfriendly reports of the major press bureaus. However, they were unable to complete this deal. Then in October, 1915, the International Press Exchange was organized, but it could not compete with the old established firms.

In 1916 a syndicate dominated by Dr. E. A. Rumely bought the New York *Evening Mail*. Unsuccessful attempts were also made through Samuel Untermeyer to purchase the New York *Sun*. The *International*, a monthly magazine of literature and comment, was bought in 1915. It, however, turned out to be an unsatisfactory investment. There is some suspicion that the Jewish paper *Die Wahrheit* was financed with German funds. The most successful of the investments was the *Fatherland*, a weekly magazine edited by George Sylvester Viereck.[16] But little was achieved by these efforts. The almost unanimous opposition of the American press could not be overcome.

Like the British, the Germans attempted to secure volunteer propagandists in the United States. A number of professional writers were induced to prepare articles and books for the German Information Service. In many cases these were distinguished men, but they were in large measure men of German blood. Unlike the imposing array of American writers who were issuing propaganda for Great Britain and France, the German list was made up primarily of professors, who can always be counted on to hold varying opinions, and Irish sympathizers whose bitterness toward England motivated their activities. The Germans also included among the writers friendly to them a group of individuals who were only incidentally or occasionally friendly.

---

[15]At a price of $900,000. See *Brewing and Liquor Interests*, II, 1978 ff.

[16]It had a circulation of 75,000.

Fair Play, published by a Hungarian, who was known at one time as a friend of Theodore Roosevelt, received at various times payments amounting to $10,000. The *American Independent* in San Francisco obtained $1,500 a month from the German Consul General.

These were men who were willing to concede that there were two sides to the war.[17]

In addition to the professional writers who were enlisted by Dernburg's organization, there was at first a large number of German-Americans who entered the lists. These volunteer propagandists continually injured the German cause. Their vociferous defense of Germany offended where it was supposed to have gained sympathy. "In their ardor to defend the German viewpoint and their own reputation as desirable American citizens, many . . . of them overstepped the bounds of discretion and common sense, and thus added new fuel to the flames."[18] After Bryan had left the administration, German-Americans flocked to his speeches *en masse* and by their presence made it possible to label him with the hated epithet "pro-German." Embargo and peace meetings were also ruined by their support. Their bombastic, brassy attitude made enemies for them right and left. The truth may have been on their side, but after hearing them expound it, Americans became advocates of error. It is very surprising that these people could have lived in the United States for years without ever understanding American ways of thinking. Their assistance was of no importance and the damage they did was incalculable.

The methods and materials of German propaganda were similar to those of the Allies. German interpretations, like those of the British, were based on part-truths. Attempts were made to cast an unholy light upon the motives of the Allies and to glorify those of Germany. Reports of the progress of the war featured the courage of the German soldier and the frustration of the Entente armies. It was the same partial treatment used by Wellington House.[19] Their arguments on the origins of the war attempted to picture the Allies as solely responsible. The great difference in the two campaigns was that the German war-guilt propaganda was almost entirely composed of defensive arguments. Consequently their contentions were taken to be merely excuses. They

[17]Such writers as Oswald Garrison Villard, David Starr Jordan, Israel Zangwill, Bertrand Russell, Ludwig Lewisohn, and Frank Harris.

[18]Wittke, Carl, *German-Americans and the World War* (Columbus, Ohio, 1936), 4.

[19]Mitchell classifies their propaganda as: (1) political and general; (2) pacifism; (3) the seas; (4) export of munitions; (5) finance; (6) atrocities.

really injured their cause by discussing war guilt after the successful British and French campaigns in this field. Late in 1915 they were instructed from Berlin to cease their attempts to place blame for the war on England alone and to cease criticising Belgian neutrality.

The German literature on atrocities was also but a pale imitation of the artistic creations of the British and French. All their arguments dealing with the damnation of the enemy were largely ineffective as a result of the successful British campaign of "identity of interests." The German-language newspapers also revived many incidents from the history of Anglo-American relations during the last century[20] in order to create bad feeling between England and the United States. Perhaps one of their poorest arguments was the discussion of German culture. After the very adequate handling by Wellington House, the word *kultur* was hardly one which would create sympathy for Germany.

A strong appeal was made to the American public by the German discussion of British interference with American trade and mails. It was successful because it dealt with something of importance to the United States. Thus for once the Germans utilized the British practice of dwelling on community of interests, and for a moment convinced the American people that their desires were identical with those of Germany. The only other really successful German propaganda was that directed against the export of munitions. This was kept up over a considerable length of time and Americans agreed that the munitions trade was not righteous.

As a result of Dernburg's defense of the sinking of the *Lusitania,* he was forced to give up his work in May, 1915, and Dr. Fuehr, who succeeded him, lacked his ability. The entire organization was destroyed in the winter of 1915 as a result of the British exposure of their activities. After that time there was no adequate German propaganda organization and the steps taken toward influencing the American public were haphazard and disorganized. In comparing the actual accomplishment of the British and German propaganda work in the United States, it must be borne in mind that the latter group operated but a scant year

[20]Wittke, *op. cit.,* 14.

while British organization was expanded and improved throughout the entire two and one-half year period.

Entirely aside from the many handicaps under which the German propagandists were operating, it must be conceded that their work would never have been too well received. Their propaganda was "insufficient in form and wrong psychologically." The salesman's trick of selling himself rather than his wares was a practice with which they were unacquainted. They were seldom able to charm foreigners to the extent of making them openly advocate the German cause. The personal appeal of Edward Grey and other Englishmen was beyond their comprehension. Indeed, many of them were personally offensive. At no time did they appeal to the fundamental emotions of hate, fear, love, or vanity. They did not invoke sentiment; they did not weep over women and children; they did not develop a villain among their enemies, nor a hero among themselves. They did not even create a martyr. Their truculent attitude actually created enmity rather than friendliness.

Laborious handling, or dullness, was the worst attribute of German propagandists. They made no attempt to take advantage of the American thirst for sensation and no efforts to excite the American populace. Instead they insisted on discussing "the truth about the war" or "the actualities of the case." One of von Mach's pamphlets bore the title *Facts — War or no war, you have to face the facts either now or later*. Among the books subsidized was a set of German classics. Apparently the Germans believed American strap-hangers would desire to read a volume of Kant, Hegel, or Klopstock on their way to and from work. They were totally blind to the fact that Americans could not be moved through an appeal to reason.

The British Ambassador must have been thinking of German propaganda when he wrote that "people here don't like to be preached at," for the Germans were constantly preaching.[21] They were both intemperate and pugnacious. Their work was characterized by excessive optimism and excessive pessimism; moderation was not one of their virtues. "They were far too open about

[21]One of the British propagandists was of the opinion that "the Germans cared much less about convincing other people than about convincing themselves." He called this a megalomania. Mitchell, *op. cit.*, 42.

their activity; far too obvious in their appeals; far too negligent of tact and finesse in spreading their message."[22]

German propaganda in the United States need not have been a complete failure. With a competent organization and adequate facilities, considerable success might have been achieved. But there was needed an individual treatment and a very skillful handling, which Dernburg, Fuehr, and their associates were unable to provide.[23]

The second phase of German activities in the United States was the purchase and transportation of supplies through the blockade to the Central Powers. This work was handled by a commission headed by Dr. Heinrich Albert.[24] Most of the hundred and fifty million dollars in German treasury notes which Bernstorff had been given for expenses in America was used to pay for the operations of this purchasing commission. But here again misfortune hounded the German agents. The appearance of this foreign money gave rise to rumors of vast sums being spent by the Germans for sabotage and propaganda. Needless to say the friends of the Allies exploited this rumor to the fullest.

The purchase and transportation of supplies for the Central Powers was, from the outset, very expensive. In order to evade the blockade, numerous expedients had to be worked out, all of which were costly. In addition to the difficulties of finance, such things as obtaining ships, securing insurance, and disguising consignees, had to be taken care of. The first ships to be utilized were German cruisers at liberty on the high seas at the outbreak of hostilities. Originally acting as raiders, they soon began to carry supplies and delivered shipments valued at $1,500,000.[25] Later Albert utilized Scandinavian, then American lines, but finally had to buy his own ships.[26] Although his agents were sending

[22]Squires, *op. cit.*, 45.

[23]Ambassador Bernstorff has attempted to defend the work of the Germans as follows: "If ... [German propaganda] had really been so clumsy or ineffective as the enemy press afterward claimed, the Entente and their American partisans would not have set in motion such gigantic machinery to combat it." Bernstorff, *op. cit.*, 43.

[24]Others on the commission included Isaac Strauss, Meyer-Gerhardt, and Captain Hecker.

[25]Hamburg-American Steam Packet Company *vs.* United States. These shipments were arranged by officials of the Hamburg-American Line.

[26]Bernstorff, *op. cit.*, 81.

most of the cargoes from New York, "they were [also] making tremendous shipments from Galveston and New Orleans and other Southern ports."[27] The goods were sent to neutrals in Europe, though sometimes it was possible to sell to British merchants and then have a Scandinavian or Dutch neutral repurchase the material.

A very important part of this work was the attempt of the German military attaché, Franz von Papen, to buy up certain products which the Allies needed very badly. Early in the war it had been suggested to the German government that it should buy up all the munitions plants in the United States. The seriousness of the failure to do so became increasingly manifest as the French and British were reinforced by a stream of steel from America. Von Papen, in 1915, went to work to make up for the failure to act in 1914. His maneuvers through the Bridgeport Projectile Company, were, temporarily, very embarrassing to the Allies. "The objects of the company were: (1) to tie up the output of machinery and tool manufacturers for several months to come with contracts, and yet word the cancellation clauses in such a way that acceptance could be delayed; (2) to hold up supplies for the Allies by accepting munitions contracts with such provisions in the agreements that no penalty would ensue if the contracts could not be fulfilled; (3) to pay abnormally high wages and thus unsettle labor, especially at the neighboring Union Metallic Cartridge Company in Bridgeport, which had large Allied contracts; and (4) to tie up powder supplies at certain factories by forward purchases over a long period of time, the orders ultimately to be cancelled or the powder to be sold to neutral countries."[28]

The Bridgeport Projectile Company bought up chemicals, powder, and other supplies necessary for the manufacture of munitions. Its agents offered such handsome amounts for materials that they were successful in making it impossible for the firms dealing with Great Britain and France to obtain necessary supplies. A brief panic was created in the munitions business by cornering the acid-proof container market. Approximately $3,400,000 was poured into its purchases through Albert's offices.

[27]*Brewing and Liquor Interests*, II, 2138.
[28]Landau, *op. cit.*, 99.

Over one million dollars was recovered by selling a portion of the supplies to the Spanish government, a neutral.

The same methods were used by the Bosch Magneto Company. This firm accepted huge orders for airplane magnetoes. Shipments were delayed for months, and finally cancelled, to the very great embarrassment of the Allies. Von Papen's agents further inconvenienced the American manufacturers intent upon selling to France and Great Britain by cornering vast quantities of benzol, necessary in the production of picric acid.

The twenty-seven million dollars spent in this "legal" sabotage work was the best investment the Germans made in the United States.[29] Not until the end of 1915 did the British discover what was holding up the deliveries of their orders. An article appeared in the New York *Times* saying, "British send agent to rush munitions . . . want to know why only forty-three percent of supply contracts have been delivered."[30] The difference between forty-three per cent and one hundred per cent of one's war supplies can be the margin between defeat and victory.

The seriousness of the situation created by shipments of American munitions to the Allies made it apparent to the Germans that new measures would have to be undertaken. More and more the Germans came to resent the provisioning being done by the United States. A German officer wrote: "We are at our wit's end to defend ourselves against American ammunition."[31] Bernstorff informed the Counsellor of the State Department: "Winchester Arms Manufacturing Company, New Haven, has delivered 500,000 rifles to the London Armory since August 5." He also stated that Russia had been buying powder and that Japan had been purchasing all available quantities of dynamite. As a postscript he added: "I further hear that a French general and a French senator are staying at the Bethlehem Club, Bethlehem, Pennsylvania, where they are ordering arms, etc., at the Bethlehem Steel Works."[32]

[29]Bernstorff, *op. cit.*, 96 ff. Also see von Papen's testimony in the Official German Documents, II, 1313 ff.

[30]The New York *Times*, January 2, 1916.

[31]Rintelen von Kleist, Franz, *The Dark Invader, Wartime Reminiscences Of A German Naval Intelligence Officer* (London, 1933), 61.

[32]*F. R. S.*, September 15, 1914, 572, 573.

This "new invisible enemy was the cause for the deepest gloom. It was no opponent who could be faced in the open field; it was no foe whose trenches could be taken by storm; it was a spectre, an intangible phantom, against which strategy, tactics, and all the courage of the German soldier were helpless."[33] Ambassador Gerard telegraphed in December, 1914: "Universal, very bitter, and increasing feeling in Germany because of reported sale by Americans of munitions of war, etc., to the Allies."[34] As a result of this situation, it was decided that steps must be taken in an attempt to stem this flood of American supplies.

In order to prevent the United States from being used as a base of supplies, in May, 1915, the German government sent Franz Rintelen von Kleist to the United States with orders to do everything in his power to check the shipment of munitions to France and Great Britain. There were practically no restrictions on him; he was to use any weapon available to combat American participation in the economic warfare against Germany.[35] Here again the Germans blindly struck out failing to realize that method usually determines the success or failure of political actions. Oth-

[33]Rintelen von Kleist, *op. cit.*, 66.

[34]*M. I.*, Part 27, 8365. Joseph V. Fuller recently pointed out: "Clearly enough, the Germans would not have minded so much the sale of goods clearly contraband of war to the Allies had they themselves been able to obtain freely foodstuffs, cotton, copper, and other materials of debatably contraband character directly or through their neutral neighbors. Conversely, they would not have minded so much the general blockade imposed upon them had it been partly equalized by an American embargo on the shipment of military supplies to their enemies."

[35]He operated independently of von Papen and other German agents in the United States. Bernstorff denies that he knew Rintelen was a German government agent, or that he financed Rintelen, saying that the latter secured $500,000 through Captain Boy-Ed, Naval Attaché at Washington. Bernstorff's telegrams to Berlin questioning the status of Rintelen remained unanswered. *Official German Documents*, II, 2564.

Zimmerman sent the following note to the Embassy in Washington:

"For Military Attaché. You can obtain particulars as to persons suitable for carrying on sabotage in the U. S. and Canada from the following persons: one, Joseph MacGarrity, Philadelphia, Pa.; two, John P. Keating, Michigan Avenue, Chicago, three, Jeremiah O'Leary, 16 Park Row, New York.

"One and two are absolutely reliable and discreet. Number three is reliable but not always discreet. These persons were indicated by Sir Roger Casement. In the U. S. sabotage can be carried out in every kind of factory for supplying munitions of war. Railway embankments and bridges must not be touched. Embassy must in no circumstances be compromised. Similar precautions must be taken in regard to Irish pro-German propaganda." Landau, *op. cit.*, 8.

ers besides Rintelen took part in the drive to prevent supplies from reaching the Entente Powers. Dr. Heinrich Albert, head of the purchasing mission, "was to handle the funds, also to act as the director of activities to tie up Allied munitions orders. Captain von Papen was to supervise an active army of spies and sabotage agents both in the United States and in Canada. Captain Boy-Ed was to direct sabotage on ships transporting munitions to the Allies, to arrange for coal and supplies for German warships and commerce raiders, and also to recruit spies to send to enemy countries in Europe, chiefly England. In this work these four chiefs were to be actively assisted by the various German consuls and consular representatives scattered throughout the United States."[36]

In the first fifteen months of the war, thirty-six ships were damaged or destroyed by fire from incendiary bombs. Rintelen was responsible for many of these.[37] He also claimed credit for explosions which crippled or destroyed munitions ships while they were on the high seas. This was done by means of bombs attached to the rudders of the boats before they left the New York harbor.[38] One of his more elaborate schemes even resulted in a profit. He set up a brokerage firm, and obtained large orders for supplying the Russian army with bridles, saddles, mules, munitions, and other incidental items. After being paid for these articles, he had them transported to Russia in ships on which he had placed a generous supply of bombs. The bombs did their work and the supplies destined for Russia were lost in mid-ocean.

Rintelen also succeeded in embarrassing the Allies by fomenting strikes. Due to the rapidly rising prices and the great demand for labor, he was for a time successful in fostering discontent

[36]Landau, *op. cit.*, 9.

[37]Rintelen used with considerable success the detonator of a German chemist, Dr. Scheele. The Scheele detonator consisted of a lead tube containing picric and sulphuric acids, which ignite upon contact. The two acids were separated in the tubing by a copper disc, and the graduations of thickness of the copper could be utilized as time fuses. It was a convenient, efficient instrument. The lead container melted in the resulting fire, so there was nothing but a little heap of lead, usually unnoticed, to betray the origin of the flame. One of these "cigars," as they were called, dropped into a crate of cotton goods often caused the destruction of a ship.

[38]Rintelen tells of rowing into New York harbor while one of his men swam to a munitions ship to plant one of the new toys. Within a few days the news arrived that the ship's rudder had been mysteriously blown off and that she was drifting aimlessly at sea.

among the dock workers in New York and a few other Atlantic port cities.[39] Grouping about him workers who were favorable to the German cause, he founded Labor's National Peace Council. Hanging out the shingle of the new union, he offered to pay full wages to any and all who would refuse to load munitions ships. This succeeded until the violently pro-British head of the American Federation of Labor, Samuel Gompers, rallied the old unions to oppose Rintelen's strike.[40]

These slight interferences with the munitions trade were all that Rintelen accomplished in the United States. Although they were somewhat effective, it must be conceded that the Allies suffered no permanent setback as a result. The sabotage carried on by other Germans, either official or unofficial, was even less effective. In fact, it is very possible that some of the explosions for which they were given credit were really accidents caused by the ignorance of employees who had been newly enlisted and hastily trained to handle explosives.

On May 30, 1915, a cargo of explosives was destroyed in Seattle Harbor. A group of Germans were arrested and charged with intentionally causing this explosion. The German consul in San Francisco, Franz Bopp was among those accused. Although the evidence was somewhat scanty, five of the men including Bopp were convicted.[41] On August 29, 1915, a small powder plant blew up in the east; DuPonts had an explosion on November 30; and on July 30, 1916, the chief loading docks for munitions in New York harbor, on Black Tom Island, exploded with great loss

[39]Before the Senate investigating committee on *Brewing and Liquor Interests and German Propaganda,* Mr. Bielaski spoke of "their [the Germans'] peace propaganda, their efforts to bring about strikes, and their efforts to induce Germans and Austro-Hungarians to withdraw from service in any factory engaged in the production of war materials" as quite effective.

[40]Gompers' biographer states: "The most considerable attempt at stopping the mighty streams of munitions and guns moving out of the country by 1915 was made by Captain Boy-Ed and Captain von Rintelen, who approached T. V. O'Conner, Dick Butler and Pasel Vocearelli of the Longshoremen with a proposition to place two million dollars in their hands to conduct a strike on the Atlantic Coast. The plan was to stop the shipment of ammunitions to the Allies for eight weeks, long enough for the Germans to administer a knockout on the Western Front; but this scheme together with similar ones ended in failure." Harvey, Rowland Hill, *Champion Of The Toiling Masses* (Stanford, 1935), 214.

[41]See Paxson, Frederic L., *American Democracy and the World War, Pre-War Years,* 1913-1917 (Boston, 1936), 264.

FRANZ VON PAPEN

of life and property.[42] On January 11, 1917, the munitions plant at Kingsland, New Jersey, was destroyed. The two latter cases are still being adjudicated.

A number of these sabotage efforts were extraordinarily clumsy. Before Rintelen arrived in this country, an individual by the name of Werner Horn had tried to blow up the Canadian-American bridge at Vanceboro, Maine.[43] This bridge could have been replaced in an afternoon. On December 18, 1915, the New York *Times* published a notice that von der Goltz and some accomplices had attempted to dynamite the Welland Canal.[44] Later Eric Muenther set off a bomb in the capitol building at Washington. What he could have hoped to accomplish by this is very questionable. Another bomb placed in the hold of the *Minnehaha* started a fire which was soon extinguished.

The German desire to embarrass Canadian participation in the war occasioned considerable difficulty for the official German agents in the United States. "On December 12, 1914, the following cipher telegram, Number 357, was sent from Berlin to von Bernstorff: 'Secret: The transportation of Japanese troops through Canada must be prevented at all costs if necessary by blowing up Canadian railways. . . .' "[45] On January 3, 1915, Zim-

[42]A certain Robert Fay was arrested and convicted on charge of a conspiracy to destroy factories making munitions for the Allies. He was sentenced to a long term at Atlanta.

"There was a deadly explosion on the night of July 29-30, 1916, at the Black Tom docks of the Lehigh Valley at Jersey City. Windows were shattered over a wide area, the shock jarred the Statue of Liberty on Bedloe's Island, and resulting fire did damage to life and property." Paxson, *op. cit.*, 267.

"In October, 1930, however, a Mixed Claims Commission disallowed the claim of the American Government for $40,000,000 damages, finding no evidence, in either case, to support the American contention that the explosions had been brought about by German agents." Hacker, Louis M. and Kendrick, Benjamin B., *The United States Since 1865* (New York: F. S. Crofts & Co., 1932), 500.

[43]"The name of Captain Boy-Ed, naval attaché of the German Embassy, was mentioned as Horn's paymaster, and stubs found later among the papers of Captain Franz von Papen, military attaché, indicated that Horn had received Imperial funds." Paxson, *op. cit.*, 267.

[44]"Hans Tauscher, whose name cropped up repeatedly in the spy rumors, escaped conviction, and was the only one of the operators whose name had even secondary meaning to the public. He was husband of Madame Gadsky, operatic star, whose performances and records made her many friends. Tauscher was acquitted in June, 1916, of a conspiracy to blow up the Welland Canal, which runs around Niagara Falls in Ontario." *Ibid.*, 267 f.

[45]Landau, *op. cit.*, 19.

mermann wired that "the 'General Staff is anxious that vigorous measures should be taken to destroy the Canadian Pacific in several places.' Therefore, a scheme was devised to employ Hindu coolies in the Canadian Northwest to dynamite railway bridges and tunnels, and von Papen personally paid Schulenberg $4,000 to buy a ton of dynamite and 50 rifles fitted with Maxim silencers to shoot any guards in the way."[46] These measures were completely unsuccessful.

In addition to standard sabotage, the Germans used the United States as a base from which they operated to undermine their enemies by means of revolution.[47] In an attempt to start another revolt in Mexico, Rintelen financed Huerta, whose mysterious death annoyed him because he suspected that the British had poisoned his revolutionary.[48] Some German agents in San Francisco tried to foster a rebellion in India, but here again, they only created trouble for themselves.[49] The movement for Irish independence under the leadership of Sir Roger Casement had some support from German agents in this country. Most of the assistance, however, came from Irish-Americans.[50] Not one of these revolutionary movements benefited the Germans, and the blunders which accompanied them brought Germany much undesirable publicity in the United States.

The most dramatic of the amateur terroristic activities in these years was the work of a teacher of German by the name of Eric Muenther.[51] Muenther, acting independently of officials in this country, apparently decided to kill the man he considered re-

[46]*Ibid.,* 32.

[47]German propaganda addressed itself to old-fashioned Americans, with Revolutionary traditions; the cotton growers of the South almost bankrupt by the blockade; the Irish with a grudge against England; the Jews with a grudge against Russia; and the German-Americans. Viereck, *op. cit.,* 46.

[48]Another German agent, von der Goltz, was actively engaged in Mexican affairs. Before operating in the New World he had been "directing revolutionary efforts in Russia." Lutz, Ralph H., *The Fall Of The German Empire,* II (Stanford, 1933), 81.

[49]*Brewing and Liquor Interests, op. cit.,* II, 1477.

[50]As early as 1915 or the first months of 1916 the secret Irish revolutionary party sent word to America that they intended to fight, and a new organization (Friends of Irish Freedom) which was controlled by the Clan-na-Gael, came into being. Viereck, *op. cit.,* 211.

[51]As an instructor in American colleges, he was known as Frank Holt.

sponsible for the munitions traffic. On July 2, 1915, brandishing a revolver in each hand, he gained entrance to the estate of J. P. Morgan where the financier was entertaining the British Ambassador, Sir Cecil Spring-Rice. Muenther claimed that he had not intended to kill Morgan but that he only desired to frighten him: "I went to the Morgan home in order to force him to use his great influence to stop the shipment of explosives. That is why I took some explosives with me, in order to be able to demonstrate to him, *ad oculos*, what the use of machines of murder means, but I did not wish to hurt anyone. I wanted him to be in the same danger (him and his family) that we are imposing on Europe. . . ."[52]

Thus ". . . for an instant the great financier was faced, in his own peaceful country home, by that death which he had been exporting in such quantity. . . . Was it impossible, perhaps, for America to munition one side in a world conflict without being brushed by the struggle? That the banker should suffer a few minutes of peril and some days of discomfort as his share of the titanic suffering which he was helping to promote seemed quite dreadful at the time."[53] Muenther was neither physically nor mentally strong and was easily overpowered. Before the trial he was found dead in his cell. He was said to have committed suicide.

German activities in the United States were in themselves of no great importance in accomplishing the objectives for which they had been designed. The propaganda convinced few people who were not already adherents of the German cause; purchases were too small to make any great difference to the economic warfare of the Central Powers; the sabotage only delayed — it did not stop the supplying of war materials to the Allies. These German operations were of consequence in that they gave British propagandists horrible examples in America which served to illustrate dramatically that the Germans were America's enemies and that they were as evil as they had been pictured. The true significance of the German activities in the history of this period lies in the fact that the publicity given to them augmented greatly the anti-German feeling among the American people.

The exposure of the things being done by the Germans was the work of the Secret Service agents of the British Admiralty.

[52]Millis, *op. cit.*, 201.　　　　[53]*Ibid.*, 201.

The person in charge in the United States was Captain Guy
Gaunt, the Naval Attaché at Washington. His chief assistants
were Sir William Wiseman,[54] Sir Geoffrey Butler, and Colonel
Norman Thwaites. No information is available concerning the
size of their organization, but to judge by results, it must have
been extensive.

The genius back of this work was Admiral Sir William Reginald Hall, head of the intelligence department of the British
navy. "Blinker" Hall remained in London, but the information
he was constantly obtaining made possible the successes of his
agents in America. Hall's deciphering bureau was able to decode
the messages sent by wireless from Germany and in this way he
obtained the names of all individuals of importance in the German organization in America.[55] Not only did he find the names
of the officials delegated to this work, but also the names of their
friends and assistants.

The same aid given to Gaunt by Admiral Hall in London was
rendered in the United States by the American Secret Service.
This organization tapped the telephone wires of the German and
Austrian Embassies and each night thereafter "a stenographic
report of every conversation, trivial and important, of the previous twenty-four hours"[56] was recorded. In addition, all the
German officials and their friends were constantly shadowed.[57]
It became impossible for them to do anything without the knowledge of the American Secret Service and Captain Guy Gaunt.

Another branch of Gaunt's intelligence department was the
Czech National Alliance. This organization, the creation of
Thomas G. Masaryk, included some eighty Secret Service men,
who, duplicating the work of W. J. Flynn of the American Secret
Service and Guy Gaunt of the British, also shadowed German
sympathizers in the United States. Their services proved so

---

[54]Wiseman later became a partner in the international banking firm of Kuhn,
Loeb and Company. At one time he was mentioned as buying half a million dollars
worth of bonds for himself.

[55]A list of agents who distributed German propaganda in Spain and South
America was available to British propagandists early in 1916, so it can be seen that
the United States did not alone have the benefit of the British secret service. *D. R.
F. P., Confidential Supplement*, April 1, 1916.

[56]*Liberty Magazine*, June 2, 1928.

[57]Von Papen recorded his resentment at being shadowed, but he was only
one of many. *Official German Documents*, II, 1314 f.

valuable that by the end of 1916 it was "arranged for [their] . . . expenses . . . to be put down officially to the account of the British Secret Service."[58] An individual by the name of Voska was in immediate charge of these Czechoslovakian G-Men.[59]

In order to exploit fully the information obtained by the various detective agencies, Captain Gaunt arranged with John R. Rathom[60] of the Providence (Rhode Island) *Journal* to give their disclosures the widest publicity. An agreement was also made with the New York *Times* for republishing much of the material under the heading "The Providence *Journal* Will Say Today." Each night Rathom was given some information on German activities. Occasionally it was true. At other times, as he has admitted, the revelations were figments of his own romantic imagination. "Mr. Rathom claimed to have his secret agents planted everywhere, even in the German Embassy itself; he produced damning code messages (of a curiously detective-thriller character) said to have been plucked from the ether by his own wireless operators."[61] Eventually Rathom went too far and the British agents in the United States found it impossible to save him.

With a horde of detectives trailing the Germans and an extended organization to take advantage of the secrets uncovered, it was not long before the Germans became the uncomfortable recipients of entirely too much attention.

Gaunt's first disclosures concerned the sending of reservists back to Germany. These reservists had to devise means of getting through to Holland or Denmark, and they accomplished this by using the passports of other nationals.[62] Ordinarily such ac-

---

[58]Masaryk, Thomas Garrigue, *The Making of a State, Memories and Observations, 1914-1918* (London, 1927), 243.

[59]The activities of the Czech National Alliance were of assistance not only in shadowing Germans, but in carrying on revolutionary propaganda which resulted in the creation of the Czechoslovakian State.

[60]John R. Rathom, Australian-born editor, turned his Providence *Journal* to a crusade of exposure, boasting later of the spies he planted in the offices of the Hamburg-American Line in New York and the German consulate in San Francisco." Paxson, *op. cit.*, 263.

[61]Millis, *op. cit.*, 204.

[62]"Hence a traffic in forged passports was begun, whereby persons seeking service against the Allies were screened by false statements. . . . One Richard P. Stegler, arrested in New York for passport fraud in February, 1915, owed his exposure to a jealous girl, and turned State's evidence. He told how he procured the name and birth certificate of an American citizen, and secured a passport on which he proposed to go to England as a spy." Paxson, *op. cit.*, 269.

tions would have been condoned as sporting ventures, but by placing the major emphasis on the falsification of passports, it was possible to make these reservists appear to be criminals.

At the outbreak of the war a number of German ships were stranded on the high seas. In order for them to reach neutral ports or to raid the Allies' shipping, Germans in New York arranged through the Hamburg-American Line to refuel these vessels. False clearance papers were necessary, and consequently another opportunity was afforded Gaunt to expose the Germans as violators of American law. Dr. Buenz, a distinguished old gentleman, formerly in the German consular service, was implicated and sent to Auburn Penitentiary where he was to die.[63]

The most effective of these disclosures resulted from the theft of the Albert portfolio by Frank Burke, an American Secret Service operator. Dr. Albert, an orderly individual, kept very complete records of his activities. It happened that these records were in his brief case, which he was taking home with him on the evening of July 24, 1915. He made the mistake of leaving the brief case in the subway, but then remembered and returned for it in time to see a strange individual, brief case under arm, disappear into a moving car. For a while the dismayed Albert hoped that it had been an ordinary thief who had purloined his secrets. But the thief was far from ordinary, and the portfolio was to spell disaster for all German agents in the United States.[64]

Secretary McAdoo, Burke's superior, released some of the papers in the Albert portfolio to the New York *World*. This file was published starting August 15, 1915. The letters and records in the portfolio furnished a fairly good outline of the propaganda and proposed sabotage of the Germans. However, they revealed nothing illegal. The revelations, nevertheless, were an excellent aid to the British. They made the American people believe firmly in all sorts of unholy actions being carried on by the Germans

[63]"He conceded that as early as July 31, 1914, he had been directed to equip and cloak a fleet of supply ships with which to provision and outfit German warships in the South Atlantic. Under these orders, he did not deny getting ready a dozen vessels, of which the *Berwind* cleared from New York August 5, with a false manifest. It was an expensive outfitting, for of twelve ships prepared only ten sailed, and of these only the *Berwind* managed to deliver its cargo to the *Cap Trafalgar* and the other members of the German squadron." Paxson, *op. cit.*, 266.

[64]"Dr. Albert was known for many years as the 'Minister Without Portfolio.'" Landau, *op. cit.*, 100.

and only by the Germans. Viereck has stated: "The loss of the Albert portfolio was like the loss of the Marne."[65]

Gaunt's next success was the Archibald affair. According to one version of this incident, the British Secret Service agents knew that a man by the name of Salzman was going to take some papers from the United States to Germany. They stopped him in a very clumsy way, but deliberately permitted him to get through. This encouraged the Germans to send papers with an American, J. F. Archibald.

Archibald has denied he was in the pay of the Central Powers. He has also denied he was in the employ of the British. Whoever his employer, or employers, may have been, it is known that he approached the Austrian Ambassador, Constantin Dumba, and a number of German agents, offering to transport documents into Germany for them. Dumba has stated that he was in the employ of the Austrian government. When he boarded the ship at New York, he carried with him certain gifts from Bernstorff and Prince Hatzfeldt, and letters from Dumba and von Papen. On reaching the British Coast he was searched and these documents were taken from him.

Dumba's official letters mentioned "his efforts to keep Austrian and Hungarian subjects out of the munitions factories,"[66] and also of "the preparation of disturbances in the Bethlehem Steel" plant. These revelations caused considerable annoyance among Americans, but some incidental remarks in the private correspondence incited real anger. Dumba referred to the "self-willed temperament of the President," while von Papen made the mistake of using the phrase, "these idiotic Yankees." These remarks angered the American people and President Wilson. Sir Edward Grey was highly elated and referred to the affair as of "inestimable value." Perhaps the recollection of the effect of the De Lôme letter added to his appreciation of the statements of Dumba and von Papen. "Motivated by a fine unselfishness, the British released the text of these to the press, and furnished the American Embassy with photostatic copies of the originals."[67]

[65]McAdoo, W. G., *Crowded Years, The Reminiscences of William G. McAdoo* (Boston, 1931), 330. With regard to the propaganda McAdoo says, "I'm morally convinced that the Allies were doing the same thing, but we had no documentary proof."

[66]Paxson, *op. cit.*, 271.   [67]Landau, *op. cit.*, 52.

President Wilson requested Dumba's recall stating that he had been guilty of a "flagrant violation of diplomatic propriety in employing an American citizen protected by an American passport as secret bearer of official dispatches through the lines of the enemy of Austria-Hungary." In his answer to this, Archibald remarked that he was not going through enemy lines. He was on a neutral ship going from a neutral port to a neutral port. And as for carrying messages, it was done consistently because there was no other means for officials of the Central Powers in America to communicate with their home governments. How much he was protected by his American passport is evinced by the fact that he was seized and searched by the British.

Ambassador Dumba returned to his native Austria. Since the German attachés, von Papen and Boy-Ed, had been implicated in these disclosures as well as in the trials of various German suspects, they also were sent home.[68] Additional profit was gained by this recall of German and Austrian officials, for when von Papen's boat approached England, Admiral Hall had it stopped and the German military attaché was deprived of his papers, accounts, and cancelled checks, which served to uncover additional proof of German intrigue."[69]

Admiral Hall, as might be expected, also administered the *coup de grace* to Franz Rintelen von Kleist. In August, 1915, Rintelen received the following telegram in a German cipher: "To the Naval Attaché at the Embassy: Captain Rintelen is to be informed unobtrusively that he is under instructions to return to Germany." Although Rintelen was in no way connected with the Naval Department, he apparently believed this telegram was

[68]"Of the spy directors whom von Papen left behind him, Paul Koenig was one of the most important." Landau, *op. cit.*, 61.

Ambassador Bernstorff threatened to leave at this time if he were, in the minds of the American people, involved in the activities of the two attachés. Lansing wrote to Bernstorff: "You are in no way included in this episode, and we should look upon it with extreme regret were you to leave us, because you are at present entrusted with those important negotiations." *Official German Documents*, I, 260.

[69]Wellington House was surprised by the reactions of the *Springfield Republican* which stated: "The seizure of the private papers will strike many people . . . as a mean performance. They actually prove nothing but they do increase the suspicion." *A. P. R.*, February 12, 1916.

genuine and sailed for home. When he approached England Admiral Hall paged him at sea, removed him from the ship, and interned him. He was later taken to the United States, where he was sentenced to a term in the federal penitentiary at Atlanta.

By the end of 1915 the German organization in the United States had been effectually crippled. In April of the following year the remnants of it were gathered in by the American Secret Service agents who raided the office of von Igel in New York City.[70] With the confiscation of von Igel's papers, the curtain was closed upon German activities in the United States. The drama had been a vigorous one; the characters had all been guilty, in the public mind, of villainy; and the American people were ready to believe anything about the Germans.

In September, 1915, Sir Gilbert Parker had commented that "if things go a little further, German intrigues may become the center of a very vigorous sweep of public indignation."[71] By the time the pro-Ally newspapers had finished sensationalizing these intrigues, Parker's prophecy had been realized, for the American people had become obsessed with the idea that German propagandists and *saboteurs* infested the country. President Wilson was ready to quell a German uprising if he could discover where it was to start.[72] So-called patriots became "spy mad" and indiscriminately accused people of being German agents whenever they refused to accept the Allies' propaganda. Lansing compared the mania for ferreting out German spies with the witch-hunting mania of the seventeenth century, and concluded that "certainly nine out of ten, and probably ninety-nine out of a hundred of these suspects were guiltless of any wrongful act or intention."[73]

Such high personages had been named in these disclosures that the British were certain the German government would suffer as a consequence. Parker wrote to the cabinet: "The publication of these revelations is bound to have a most beneficial effect upon the resentment felt, especially in the South, against British trade interference and may well put an end to the agita-

[70]The documents stolen from von Igel's office remained in the United States government hands because Bernstorff refused to acknowledge them as official Embassy records. *Official German Documents,* I, 258.

[71]*A. P. R., Supplement,* September 10, 1915.

[72]Baker, *op. cit.,* V, 388. August 25, 1915.

[73]Lansing *Memoirs,* 84.

tion for an embargo on the export of munitions."[74] He also noted that the publicity given to the names of pro-Germans would render useless their attempts to defend Germany. Henceforth the individual who tried to excuse any single German action became suspect. A letter intercepted by the censor revealed that German officials in the United States were "astonished" to find "that German-Americans of all classes are suddenly endeavoring to accentuate their American tendencies."[75]

The successful work of Captain Guy Gaunt and Admiral Hall capped the climax to Sir Gilbert Parker's "identity of interests" campaign. Americans were convinced that the enemy of the English and the French was also their enemy. After they had accepted this point of view, it was natural that they should believe that their welfare depended upon the defeat of Germany and that the United States must assist in that defeat.

[74]*A. P. R., Supplement,* September 10, 1915.
[75]*D. R. F. P., Confidential Supplement,* July 20, 1914, 94.

CHAPTER VII ☆ REACTIONS TO THE WAR, AUGUST 1914-FEBRUARY 1916: AMERICAN NEWSPAPERS

NEWSPAPERS in America during the years of neutrality represented the end-point of the British propaganda campaign. In almost all cases the American press accepted the British views as conceived by Wellington House and as released by the British censor. As a result American newspapers of those years should be viewed not as a mirror reflecting American reactions to the war, but as the principal medium through which the British influenced Americans. Newspapers are quite often far from picturing the desires and ambitions of the people. During the war, as one British agent expressed it, newspapers may have relieved the emotions of the American people, but they did not correctly represent the American mind.[1]

When Albert J. Beveridge first saw the German press reports, he commented: "This German news is very different from the English and French versions. I fear the American people know very little of what is going on."[2] The American people never did really find out what was going on, nor did the people in other countries.[3] American newsmen were in the same position. They had not expected the war to occur and found themselves off their guard. They were unable to assess coolly the events which were happening so rapidly. Their previous lack of attention to European affairs meant they knew little beyond what the governments told them of the immediate crisis. The tragic character of events

[1]There were a surprising number of editorials in the American press which revealed an understanding of the war — but Americans do not read editorials. It was the news columns which were important.

[2]Bowers, *op. cit.*, 459. "One of the first and most amusing pamphlets got out by the pro-Germans, *A Trip Through Headline Land*, reproduced with caustic comment, the newspaper headlines announcing almost daily the complete destruction of the German Army, while Germany was taking fortress after fortress in Belgium and in France." Viereck, *op. cit.*, 84.

[3]"Most persons did not know that France had been seriously invaded until the train service to Boulogne stopped and let the cat out of the bag." "Censorship in France," *The Outlook*, June 13, 1917, 258.

shocked them and encouraged them to let their emotions govern their thinking. "As the crisis rapidly deepened [editors] . . . jumped only the more rashly to unsound conclusions — which, by the fatal tradition of editorial 'consistency' were bound to influence the whole course of the papers' polices."[4] They quickly accepted the original British propaganda thesis — that Germany was guilty of starting the war. The news released by the censor appeared to prove it definitely, and later news seemed only to confirm first impressions; consequently the anti-German attitude of the American press increased. Before very long editors and reporters were looking for evil in the Germans. Naturally, they had no difficulty in finding it.

As the British began to impose restrictions upon the formerly lucrative American trade with Germany, it was natural that the newspapers — the spokesmen of economic interests — should voice strong objections. Nevertheless their objections were seldom overly bitter and promised little actual trouble for Great Britain.[5] After trade with the Allies had grown to such proportions that the German business was no longer essential, newspapers abated their attacks on British evasions of international law.

When the Germans started their economic warfare, the American press was prepared to give it an entirely different reception. Both sentiment and interest dictated a strongly antagonistic stand. Consequently editors, as well as the American government, took over the British propaganda argument that "British malpractices infringed only on property rights, while German malpractices endangered human rights." The adoption of this defense made it possible for them to appear consistent in advocating strict accountability in dealing with Germans, and lenient opposition in dealing with Great Britain.

It was customary during the years of neutrality to consider American opinion on geographical lines. In so far as newspapers were concerned, critics were unanimous in differentiating be-

---

[4]Millis, *op. cit.*, 36.

[5]*Supra*, 81 f. In February of 1916 Parker reported: "But upon the steps which the United States intends to take in order to enforce its views, the press, as a whole, is discreetly silent," and though strong notes may be written, "there is no evidence, in the press at any rate and at present, that more serious things are contemplated." *A. P. R.*, February 12, 1916.

tween the Atlantic seaboard attitude and that of the Middle and
Far West. The South as a unit was usually ignored. The newspapers along the Atlantic seaboard for a short time maintained a
pretense of neutrality, but their sympathies were most evident.
In this rock-ribbed Republican area, they soon enlisted almost
unanimously in the cause of the Allies. Wellington House consistently referred to Eastern papers as "strongly pro-Entente and
mainly Republican."[6] In addition to the thoroughly partisan news
articles, editorial comments likewise defended the Allies and attacked the Central Powers.

Perhaps it is to be expected that papers of the largest American city should be considered the most important in the nation.
At any rate that is the position given to those published in New
York City. In the first place they are the wealthiest papers and
have the largest circulations. In the second place foreign news is
written almost exclusively for them and is passed on to the inland
states only after having been released in New York. Finally, their
opinions are assumed — quite falsely — to be the opinions of the
American people. During the years of neutrality, New York newspapers seldom expressed views which would have been acceptable west of the Alleghenies. They were consistently partisan,
consistently pro-Ally. A typical report of the British propaganda
ministry stated: "As might be expected, the New York press is
the most satisfactory in its comment."[7]

The outstanding newspaper in New York City and in the
United States was the New York *Times*. It was a strong de-
fender of the capitalistic system and was to a certain extent a
backer of the Democratic party. British propagandists invari-
ably listed the *Times* as pro-Ally and even while the rest of the
United States was attacking British economic warfare, Wellington House reported that "the important New York *Times* . . .
deals very kindly with British naval policy."[8] Its partisanship
was so pronounced that Sir Gilbert Parker warned his organization and the British Cabinet that it was utterly naïve to suppose
that its opinions were those of the American people.[9] At another

[6]*D. R. F. P.*, February 2, 1917.
[7]*A. P. R.*, August 13, 1915.
[8]*A. P. R.*, February 12, 1916.
[9]*A. P. R.*, March 17, 1916.

time he commented, "The New York *Times* has been notable for its friendliness to the Allies, and reports what commercial circles think in New York, and not what agriculturists think in the West."[10]

The second most important New York newspaper in this period was the *World*,[11] although Wellington House reported that, since it was "the mouthpiece of the Administration," it was "perhaps the *most* important paper in the United States."[12] In spite of this opinion it is easy to see that the *World* followed the President more than it led him. At one time Parker reported that the *World* was "obviously awaiting the lead of the President."[13] Its connection with the administration was clearly shown when Secretary McAdoo permitted it to publish documents stolen from Dr. Albert. Although not so partisan as the *Times*, the *World* was "a firm friend and admirer of the Allies."[14]

Among other New York papers the *Tribune* was referred to by French propagandists as "notre principal allié aux États Unis." Wellington House stated it was "ardently pro-French."[15] James Gordon Bennett, the owner of the New York *Herald*, liked France so well that he made his home in Paris. Consequently it should not be surprising that British propagandists referred to the *Herald* as "ardently pro-Ally."[16] In referring to the *Post* and the *Sun*, Parker stated that they were "generally friendly."[17] The less important newspapers in New York City followed fairly closely the stands taken by these leading dailies.

The press in other Eastern cities did not differ greatly from that of New York. The Boston *Evening Transcript*,[18] the Boston

[10]*A. P. R.*, March 10, 1916.

[11]For some reason or other one British propaganda organization spoke of the *World* and the *Times* as "official." *D. R. F. P., Neutral Press Supplement*, February 9, 1917.

[12]*A. P. R.*, February 18, 1916.

[13]*A. P. R.*, March 10, 1916.

[14]*A. P. R.*, October 24, 1915.

[15]*A. P. R.*, March 10, 1916. The New York *Tribune* was a very conservative paper, one of its owners being W. H. Page. *D. R. F. P., Confidential Supplement*, August 19, 1916.

[16]*A. P. R.*, January 7, 1916.

[17]*A. P. R.*, February 18, 1916. For an analytic list of newspapers see the *A. P. R.*, March 24, 1916.

[18]*A. P. R.*, March 10, 1916.

Globe,[19] and the Springfield (Massachusetts) *Republican* were distinctly pro-Ally.[20] The Philadelphia *Public Ledger* was one of a group of papers which "support any British anti-German measure."[21] In speaking of the Providence *Journal,* Parker applied his usual expression, "ardently pro-Ally," which in this case was a charming bit of understatement.[22] The only leading papers in the East which Wellington House considered unfriendly were the Washington *Post* and the New York *Evening Mail,* and it was admitted that the latter was fair to the British when the issue was incontestable.[23]

The most noteworthy aspect of Western and Midwestern newspapers from 1914 to 1917 was the lack of attention given to the war. An agent reported to the British Cabinet: "Indeed, in the country districts, in small towns, and even in the larger cities of the Middle and Far West, the ignorance about the war, and lack of interest in it, are hardly believable."[24] The editors of the leading Atlantic Coast papers, as well as the English propagandists were enormously irritated by the idea of anyone's failing to join in their excitement over the war, and assumed that Midwesterners were pro-German when they refused to become adherents of the Allies' cause.

But at the same time that confirmation of the pro-Germanness of Middle Western papers seemed to be found in their editorial attacks on British naval policy, equal justification for the label "pro-Ally" might have been found in their news columns, which were filled with the identical pro-British dispatches published in the New York press. The real difference between the Western newspapers and those of the Atlantic seaboard lay in the fact that the former did not use their headlines and editorial columns to carry on a crusade against Germany. To say that they

[19]*A. P. R.,* January 7, 1916.

[20]*A. P. R.,* of February 12, 1916, speaks of this paper as "generally favorable to the Allies," and at another time used the phrase "even a paper so friendly as the Springfield *Republican.*"

[21]*A. P. R.,* February 12, 1916.

[22]This paper, which was owned by local industrialists who undoubtedly acquired war orders at an early date, was one of the leading anti-German papers.

[23]The *A. P. R.,* of October 25, 1916, reported that some articles in the New York *Evening Mail* showed no "pro-German bias."

[24]*A. P. R.,* January 7, 1916.

were pro-German means merely that they were not so strongly pro-Ally as were the New York *Times, Herald* and *Tribune.*

An agent of the British propaganda ministry traveling on the West Coast in 1916 commented on "the deplorable condition of the press in California." He was shocked by "her execrable newspapers." Later he wrote to Sir Gilbert Parker: "It took me some days to learn to read the San Francisco and Los Angeles papers. Yet after a little use and adjustment, I found them not nearly so terrifying as at first sight." The change in his attitude was brought about because he found that, in spite of the sensationalism and vigorous opposition to British naval policy, the large majority of the news carried the same pro-British interpretations demanded by the British censor.

The papers west of the Appalachians which were listed by the British as pro-Ally or friendly to Great Britain included the Louisville *Courier-Journal,* the St. Louis *Republican,* the St. Louis *Post Dispatch,* the Cleveland *Leader,* the New Orleans *Picayune,* the Chicago *Herald,* the Chicago *Daily News,* the Indianapolis *News,* the Dallas *News,* and the Portland *Oregonian.* British propagandists were especially pleased with a newspaper in Minneapolis by the name of the *Bellman.* Quite often they would refer to it as "perhaps the most important newspaper in the Middle West."[25] This was a weekly periodical issued by the publishers of the *Northwestern Miller.* An individual associated with this publication has written that "the *Bellman* never made money, but thanks to a certain amount of peculiar bookkeeping it never seemed to lose any." Why Sir Gilbert Parker's organization should have had so high an opinion of such an inconsequential paper remains a mystery.

The only newspaper in the Middle West which was classified as pro-German was the Milwaukee *Sentinel.* Those which Wellington House listed as "unfriendly" to Great Britain included the Chicago *Tribune,* the Cincinnati *Inquirer,* the Cleveland *Plain Dealer,* the Los Angeles *Times,* the Sacramento *Bee,* the San Francisco *Chronicle,* and the San Francisco *Call.*[26]

The one powerful American newspaper interest which was independent of the British censor was the chain controlled by

[25]*A. P. R.,* July 27, 1917.
[26]Parker commented that "no American newspaper dares to be anti-French."

WILLIAM RANDOLPH HEARST

William Randolph Hearst. Hearst, to the discomfiture of the British, did not leave undisputed the war guilt, atrocity, or war aims propaganda. It must not necessarily be assumed that his attitude was a result of his being able to see the truth in each case; rather was it a product of his dislike of the British. Hearst did print the same British propaganda which was to be found in the rest of the American press, but he also intimated that these dispatches from London contained only part of the truth. Such tolerance represented so great a menace to the British campaign in the United States that Hearst became one of the outstanding problems of British propagandists and their American allies.

In order to counteract Hearst's influence, they labeled him pro-German. They were so successful in doing this that one is surprised in checking over the Hearst papers of that period to find not only that it was untrue, but that British propagandists admitted it was untrue. A careful analysis demonstrated quite clearly that news items in the Hearst papers more often than not were British propaganda. One writer admitted in the *American Press Résumé* that "it is not fair to charge Hearst with pro-Germanism, without recognizing the conspicuous fact that he is ever ready to receive into his papers and to give prominent display to special articles of any and all partisanships whenever the interest of the subject, or the repute of the author make a fair claim upon him."[27] "To say that he [Hearst] is pro-German is at once to over-credit his integrity and to undervalue his importance. He is not pro-anything except Hearst. . . . He would just as easily be pro-Hottentot if that paid better. . . . No more do I believe that Hearst has been 'bought' by the Germans. I do not believe that Hearst can be bought in that sense; certainly I am sure that he would not be a safe or dependable bargain for any purchaser."[28]

This report was confirmed by a New York newspaperman in a letter which was purloined by the British censor. He wrote: "And about Hearst? I question if he cares a rap which side wins. He's a queer fish. His one and only concern is circulation for his papers. . . . And I don't for a moment believe that German money has gone to Hearst. . . . In all my years here [in the newspaper world] . . . I have never heard a whisper of money being able to

[27]*A. P. R., Supplement,* January 28, 1916.
[28]*A. P. R., Supplement,* January 28, 1916.

buy Hearst or his papers." After maintaining that out of all the New York press, only the Hearst publications contained occasional pro-German articles, he commented: "It impresses me you ought to be satisfied with that, if you are to admit at all that a question may have two sides. And throughout the country the percentage is much the same, or even greater on the Allies' side."[29]

Hearst's own defense, which was transmitted to the British Cabinet, included a list of pro-Ally writers whose articles were published in his papers. He wrote as follows: "In order to give the side of the Allies fully and clearly, I have bought the service of the London *Times,* the London *Daily Telegraph,* the London *News* and the services of other newspapers and press associations. I have also bought articles by Hall Caine, Sir Gilbert Parker, Conan Doyle, H. G. Wells, G. K. Chesterton, Bernard Shaw, Rudyard Kipling, Lord Northcliffe, Dr. E. J. Dillon, Colonel Ashmead Bartlett, Captain Granville Fortescue, T. P. O'Connor, Stanley Washburn, Frederick Palmer, Clemenceau, Pierre Loti, Sarah Bernhardt, Guglielmo Ferrero, Gabriele d'Annunzio, Camille Cinnafaura [?], C. F. Bertelli, and a long list of English, French and Italian writers."[30]

Speaking of the independent papers which bought his various services, he wrote: "The papers which buy our service buy the articles from all the long list of pro-Ally contributors enumerated above. . . . While I do not control the editorial attitudes of these papers, I surely have offered them every opportunity to print pro-Ally literature if they desire to do so."

The only newspapers not considered in the foregoing analysis are those of the German-language press, and they exerted but little influence in the United States. As was expected, the editors attempted to defend their homeland and their relatives. In doing

[29]This was listed by the censor as U. S. A. #11,057. *D. R. F. P., Confidential Supplement,* December 9, 1916.

"The Hearst papers . . . published in two years about four thousand columns of pro-German articles and ten thousand columns of pro-Ally articles." Grattan, Hartley C., *Why We Fought* (New York, 1929), 48.

[30]Also "I have published Hall Caine's 'King's' book in America, and devoted the proceeds to the charities of the Allies."

"In addition to that, I issued a moving picture called 'Fighting for France'; exhibited it in New York, Boston, Chicago, San Francisco and Los Angeles, and in hundreds of other cities and towns through the United States, and devoted the whole profits to the charities of the Allies."

so they became excited and adopted a most belligerent attitude, which diminished their effectiveness. The stigma of foreignness had already made them suspect and their defense of an unpopular cause only increased the belief that they represented un-American influences. In the last analysis these papers injured more than they benefited the German cause in the United States.

Previous to May, 1915, newspapers in all sections of the country made a display of neutrality. They expressed preference for one side or the other — usually the British — but did attempt to be just to the enemy. The following *Literary Digest* poll of partisan feeling gives an analysis of the situation that is probably accurate for the time — November 14, 1914:

POLL OF SYMPATHIES OF EDITORS

Pro-Ally	105	*Neutral*	242	*Pro-German*	20
Eastern	34			Eastern	1
Southern	47			Southern	5
Central	13			Central	10
Western	11			Western	4

POLL OF SYMPATHIES OF CITIES

Pro-Ally	189	*Neutral*	140	*Pro-German*	38
Eastern	52	Eastern	24	Eastern	2
Southern	71	Southern	28	Southern	4
Central	40	Central	66	Central	29
Western	26	Western	22	Western	3

At the time of the sinking of the *Lusitania* most American editors cast aside their appearance of impartiality. Most Eastern writers lost their heads completely and gave consideration only to the personal aspects. However, many of the Western and Midwestern editors continued their objections to British actions, although much of their opposition was friendly and at no time did they advocate the German cause.

Toward the end of 1915, after the various exposés of German activities in the United States, the antagonism of the press toward the Central Powers deepened perceptibly. In the case of the Eastern metropolitan dailies, the editors gave clear expression to their wrath against the Germans. More and more they adopted the Wellington House argument that this British and French war was "our war" and did all in their power to make the American people think the same way. Senator Sherman once suggested that in case of war there should be a conscription of all editors east of Pittsburgh. But most American newspapermen were already front line fighters in the Allies' campaign to get the United States into the war.

During the first twenty months of the war American newspapers displayed attributes which made them suspect among educated people. They were uniformly sensational and aggravated every crisis which arose. Snap judgments resulted in many errors which were never corrected. It is true that many of their mistakes were not intentional, but a more cautious approach would have eliminated some of them. The papers in the East acted in a provocative manner throughout the years of neutrality. They reflected the minority opinions of Eastern pro-British aristocracy and not the views of the vast majority of Americans who would have preferred a closer approach to impartiality. The papers in the West more nearly expressed the wishes of the American people, but, like the Eastern papers, they were so easily influenced by the news which they received from abroad that they also gave yeoman service in establishing a pro-Ally attitude of mind in this country.

CHAPTER VIII ☆ REACTIONS TO THE WAR, AUGUST 1914-FEBRUARY 1916: THE AMERICAN PEOPLE

THE first reaction of the American people to the war was one of revulsion and amazement; the conflict appeared "senseless," "insane," "utterly without cause."[1] In a very short time, however, there appeared on the surface that thread of violence which has been a continuous part of the history of the United States. In spite of their profound repugnance, Americans began to enjoy the fight. Responding to the stimulus of British propaganda, they thought of the French and Belgians as pathetic heroes, the British as gallant defenders of the right, and the Germans as deep-dyed villains. It was natural for them to reflect these views which they found dominating their newspapers. Americans could seldom remain neutral in any war; they have too many traditions of conflict. During the World War circumstances made it inevitable that their partisanship should be pro-Ally. It should be remembered that this partisanship arose before any difficulties existed in our relations with Germany.

The reactions to atrocity stories varied from district to district. New England and the Middle Atlantic States were perhaps the most receptive areas. In other parts of the United States, the interest in these incidents was spread by preachers, teachers, and other individuals who were continually giving public speeches. As the months passed, there developed a larger and larger public interest in such stories as those collected by Lord Bryce or in the more striking misinterpreted incidents such as the violation of Belgian neutrality, the burning of Louvain, the shelling of Rheims, and the execution of Edith Cavell.

The sinking of the *Lusitania* brought out the true state of American feeling toward the war as a whole. People in the East

---

[1]Americans in Europe also displayed a complete lack of understanding of the war. An Englishman commented on them as follows: "These ladies and gentlemen had never seen a war before, and they could not understand why it should be allowed to interfere with the elementary comfort of a neutral who was ready to pay liberally for everything." Thompson, *op. cit.*, 52.

were greatly excited, but only a few of the most rabidly pro-Ally individuals dared to advocate a declaration of war against Germany. Sir Gilbert Parker made a careful check of American feeling and found that from coast to coast less than six out of a thousand editors wanted war. Theodore Roosevelt was shouting fierce imprecations to the heavens, but he was going too fast even for the conservative moneyed interests. One Wall Street publication stated: "By his bombastic utterances, directly provocative of war, Mr. Roosevelt again shows what a self-seeking political adventurer he is."[2] The farther one proceeded from New York City, the less evidence there was of excitement over the sinking of the giant Cunarder. On the Pacific Coast, Secretary of Agriculture Houston noticed that only casual attention was given to the tragedy. There are those who state that the government should have entered the war after the sinking of the *Lusitania* and condemn Wilson for his failure to do so, but such a course would have been completely unacceptable to the country. Viewed as a whole, Americans were indignant and horrified, but the incident seemed so remote that no aggressive action was desired of the government. The British Ambassador regretfully informed Sir Edward Grey that the United States was "a long way from war with anybody." At a later time, Wellington House commented: "It is almost beyond doubt . . . that the country was not ready for war and any declaration of war against Germany might possibly have resulted in civil strife."[3]

The failure of the United States to enter the war engendered considerable anger in Paris and London.[4] Page wrote Wilson that "the unofficial feeling is that the United States must declare war or forfeit European respect."[5] Later when it became apparent that Americans failed to share this unofficial feeling, there developed the "profoundest depression" among the British. Lord Bertie, in Paris, expressed nonchalance about America's joining the Allies, but privately his remarks were just the reverse.[6] Kitch-

---

[2]*The Commercial and Financial Chronicle*, May 15, 1915.

[3]*A. P. R.*, April 25, 1917.

[4]Grey wrote to House in August, "There is I think disappointment that the feeling in America is not more combative." *Intimate Papers*, II, 67.

[5]Hendrick, *op. cit.*, III, 239.

[6]*Intimate Papers*, I, 441. Bertie wrote in his diary: "They are a rotten lot of psalm singing, profit mongering humbugs." *Ibid.*, 267.

ener said to House that he did not want Wilson "to think that Great Britain either made the request or had a desire for us to enter, but if we considered it necessary to do so, in his opinion it would greatly shorten the war and would save innumerable lives, not only of the Allies, but of the Germans as well."[7] By autumn the feeling among the British was one of open ridicule.[8] Page wrote to Wilson: "The English press, practically unanimously, makes sneering remarks about our Government."[9]

In the summer of 1915 revelations of German intrigue created considerable excitement in the Eastern industrial sections of the United States. It was hoped by the British that this would cause a warlike spirit to arise — especially in view of the anger still felt over the sinking of the *Lusitania*. In spite of the publicity given these incidents, however, British agents in the United States had to report that no desire for war had been aroused. On August 6 they stated: "There can be no doubt of the overwhelming sentiment which opposes anything in the nature of a break with Germany if such a break can be honourably avoided." On September 3 the national sentiment was described as "a very real and fixed though passive determination to avoid war at all costs."[10] At the turn of the next year it was stated that even sympathy among the commercial interests in the East was a static one,[11] and that "neither Republicans nor Democrats, with very few exceptions . . . [desired] war."

A report by one of Parker's American agents, at the beginning of 1916, gives a rather clear picture of the state of American opinion. It is as follows: "I should say that the bulk of the people throughout the country deliberately avoid any serious partisanship as regards the war. The partisanship of the newspapers — either way — does not reflect the popular mind; it might rather be described as relieving it. Even in the East, from what I hear, those who profess strong preference for either side are quite out

[7]*Ibid.*, I, 436.
[8]Hendrick, *op. cit.*, III, 250.
[9]*Ibid.*, II, 79.
[10]*A. P. R.*, September 3, 1915.
[11]"Just as an early peace, favorable to the Allies . . . [was] the object of the best hopes of legitimate American finance, so the avoidance of American intervention in the war . . . [seemed] also to be hoped for in Wall Street." *A. P. R.*, January 7, 1916.

of touch with the masses. In the Middle West and West they are obviously out of touch. . . . [He then spoke of 'neutralism' as a desire for national unity with a mixed population.] This neutralism . . . might quite conceivably be transformed into another phase of nationalism—viz. chauvinism—if, for instance, Washington were to give the signal for a national outburst against some foreign Power. . . . The essence of the outburst would not be partisanship for any country except the United States. . . . It may be unlikely that Washington will fly a signal of this sort, but there is no saying what will happen in an election year. . . . The national spirit of the Americans would now, as always, be more at ease in chauvinism than in neutralism."[12]

In March, 1916, after twenty months of hostilities, the propagandists had to admit that the keynote of the situation was "the desire of the great majority of the American people to avoid war, so long as it . . . [could] possibly be avoided."[13] The typical American was described as "neutralist" if not pacifist.[14] Wellington House quoted him as saying: "We do not understand the real facts of the situation in Europe" and "we do not want to have anything to do with it."

In order to gain a comprehensive view of American reactions to the war, one must consider the factors of race and geography. Persons in this country who were nationals or recent immigrants from Europe were, as might be expected, partisan to their home countries, but many of them exerted no influence upon the thinking of the public. There were very few Frenchmen in the United States, and the Russians and Italians were largely people of the lower classes who were unable to make their partisanship count for a great deal.

Immigrants recently from England naturally retained a regard for their homeland, but among the old English stock in the Middlewestern and Western districts of the United States, there was considerable antagonism to Great Britain. Along the Atlantic seaboard where the Irish and the South Europeans had quite outnumbered the old families of English origin, the people of English blood had revived their allegiance to the British king. These Anglophiles dominated society in Boston, New York, and the

[12]*A. P. R.*, March 3, 1916.   [14]*A. P. R.*, May 31, 1916.
[13]*A. P. R.*, March 3, 1916.

large cities of the East, and were impassioned in their attachment to the cause of the Allies.

The Irish must be considered on the side of the Central Powers because so many of them believed that the cause of Irish freedom would be benefited by the defeat of Great Britain. Their adherence to the German cause was not the result of love for Germany, but of deep hatred of England. The nationals in the United States from Austria-Hungary, Bulgaria, and Turkey, may be completely ignored. Few of them lived among socially important Americans, and those who did have a voice in American affairs had little or no interest in their native lands.

The most interesting of all these national groups were the German-Americans. At the same time that they maintained an unquestionable loyalty to the United States, they kept alive an affection for Germany and the German way of doing things. Carl Schurz expressed their feelings in the words: "Germania is our mother; Columbia is our bride." Unfortunately their retention of German customs and interest caused them to be criticized by one hundred per cent Americans who felt that there existed room for only one loyalty among citizens of the United States. Fostered by British propagandists, opposition to German-Americans was whipped up until "hyphenate" and "traitor" became synonymous. But loyalties are not necessarily exclusive; it is only among provincial people that they are so regarded.

As Germans in the United States saw their Fatherland fighting for its very life, they were naturally greatly disturbed. Their anxiety turned to anger as American papers day after day carried dispatches which pictured their relatives in the German army as monsters. The atrocity stories may have been convincing to Anglo-Americans, but they aroused only horror and indignation in the minds of German-Americans. Toward the end of 1915, after Gaunt's organization had uncovered and publicized the activities of Rintelen and von Papen, German-Americans found themselves vilified and discredited. Of all the people who suffered during the years of the war, few drank more deeply of the bitter dregs of humiliation and disgrace.

Their rôle after the United States joined the Allies was even more unhappy. They were forced to make war against the land of their birth,[15] and the *furor Americanus*,[16] in some instances, made life at home almost unbearable. "In Wisconsin, workmen were threatened with the loss of their jobs for failure to subscribe [to the Liberty loans]; 'councils of defense' appeared at the homes of farmers in the dead of night, threatened to break down the doors of farmhouses, and with personal abuse, violence and threats to 'get the rope,' compelled men to buy their quotas."[17] In other sections in which German-Americans lived, similar incidents occurred. "The country was honeycombed with a veritable army of officials and volunteers bent upon ferreting out treachery. There was hardly a community of any size which did not have, in addition to its regularly constituted officers of the law, some kind of 'Security League,' 'Loyalty League,' or 'Citizens Patriotic League.' These volunteer organizations sometimes operated on a national scale, employed detectives, and arrogated to themselves as extra-legal organizations more powers than the legally constituted authorities cared to exercise. In view of this fact, and the veritable 'German spy hunt' mania which swept the country, the remarkable fact is that so few German-Americans were convicted, or ever charged with disloyalty."[18]

In addition to classifying American sentiments according to nationality, it has been customary to observe that there existed within the United States geographic boundaries to wartime prejudices. The fact that the pro-Ally attitude so apparent along the eastern fringe of the United States was not also dominant in the West has caused students of the period to remark that while the East was pro-Ally, the West was pro-German. Nothing was further from the truth. The sympathy of all sections of the United States lay almost exclusively with Great Britain, France, and Belgium.[19] In January, 1915, one of the Morgan partners cabled London that "purely American sentiment almost unanimously

---

[15]"From ten to fifteen per cent of the troops of the American Expeditionary Force were of German birth or origin, and made excellent records." Wittke, *op. cit.*, 162.

[16]*Ibid.*, Chapter IV.

[17]*Ibid.*, 159.

[18]*Ibid.*, 143.

[19]The English Ambassador, Spring-Rice, wrote to Lord Grey in November of 1914: "The President told me that 90 percent of the American people are very strongly in favor of the Allies."

pro-Ally; perhaps 99% throughout country."[20] A year later one of Parker's agents wrote: "I am glad to be able to send you at the beginning of the new year this assurance that the American people from coast to coast are with you in approval and sympathy. I find ... [the Middle West] just a little more neutral than the East, a little less interested in the war," while the friendship of the Pacific Coast is "an asset of considerable value to the cause which has so overwhelmingly and conclusively won it. I should deplore any external attempts to make it more pro-Ally than it is."[21]

The only difference between the sympathies of the East and those of the West lay in the fact that Easterners were more extreme in their pro-Ally partisanship, more prejudiced, and desirous of entering the war. Westerners, on the other hand, were pro-Ally in sympathy, but they subordinated that sympathy to their concern for the welfare of the United States. Above all did they wish to keep the New World from being entangled in the Old World's trouble.

In the last analysis, opinion in America was divided not upon geographic lines, but upon lines of wealth and education; it was the country club versus the country. All classes were sympathetic with the Entente powers, but the upper classes including the rich, the powerful, the cultured, and the educated, were partisan to the extent that they were willing to assist in the defeat of Germany.

Starting as early as August, 1914, prominent men of America hastened to join a cause that was intellectually fashionable. Industrialists and financiers one by one took up the cudgels for the belligerents with whom they were doing so much profitable business. Preceding them came the imposing array of American society women. They swung into action with great gusto — at long last finding a cause worthy of their talents. Politicians, with the instinct of the chameleon, caught and reflected the popular shades of opinion. College professors and school teachers repeated with a great show of wisdom the arguments which had originated in Wellington House or in *la maison de la presse*. Close behind the educators came the ministers, and before long the American clergy was preaching a holy war, enlisting God and the Bible

[20]*M. I.*, Part 25, 7539.
[21]*A. P. R. Supplement*, January 28, 1916.

in the cause which newspapers told them was righteous. Just as strange as the enlistment of the clergy was the enlistment of liberals throughout the country. Usually such individuals spend most of their time talking about the value of peace. When it came down to hard realities, a large number of these people were found on the popular side assisting in establishing a climate of opinion favorable to war.

By February, 1916, Sir Gilbert Parker was able to report that the *articulate* people throughout the United States had joined the Allies.[22] The success of the British propagandists corroborates the statement that there are no limits to the field of propaganda. The only restrictions are on the manner of approach. The wealthy can be persuaded to support a cause by getting them to invest their money in it; educators can be controlled simply through controlling their reading matter; liberals and preachers are the easiest of all to enlist by the mere introduction of an idealistic flavor to the propaganda.[23]

It must not be assumed, however, that Americans who became adherents of the Allies were insincere. They honestly believed the interpretations of the news which were presented to them. They were convinced that here was something worth fighting for and that they would be unworthy of American ideals if they did not advocate the defeat of the Central Powers. Indeed, some of them were ashamed because the United States was not already in the war.

In contradistinction to the easy surrender of American leaders to war hysteria was the stubborn pacifism of the great mass of the people. The passionate belligerency of prominent Americans was not shared by the common people. They hoped that Germany would be defeated, but they did not desire to take part in the war in order to accomplish that defeat. The plain people clung to the belief that the war was not our fight and that the United States should remain neutral. Sir Gilbert Parker's official and unofficial agents in this country did all they could to label this pacifism contemptible and pro-German. As a matter of fact it was neither. It represented perhaps the most patriotic trend of thought which was current during that period, and British prop-

[22]*A. P. R.*, February 5, 1916.
[23]Abrams, *op. cit.*

agandists themselves conceded that it was "inaccurate to identify pacifism as pro-Germanism."[24] They had to admit that the pacifist sentiment was "a genuine American article."[25]

The first way in which the pacifism of the public expressed itself was in the movement for an embargo on war munitions. In August, 1914, the New York *Sun* ran an article opposing the sale of war supplies, stating: "Could anything be more rational than a refusal . . . to permit Europe to draw on this country further for the expense of the mad course on which it is about to embark?" Many people believed that the sale of munitions would establish connections which would tend to draw the United States into the war. Consequently "memorials which turned up against this business overflowed the capitol from all parts of the land." Congressman Vollmer declared in the House: "On the first day of the present session of Congress — December 7, 1914 — I introduced . . . [a resolution] to prohibit the exports of arms and ammunition. Since that time 3,000,000 American citizens have petitioned Congress to enact such legislation."[26] By the end of December, 1914, there were a half dozen measures pending in Congress to stop exportations of war materials.

People in every section of the country were supporting the campaign for an embargo. Although William Jennings Bryan[27] and the pacifists led the movement, widespread support came from many classes, including people of strongly pro-Ally sympathies. On the basis of legality, it was contended that the United States had recently placed an embargo on munitions to Mexico, that Great Britain had done likewise during the Russo-Japanese War, and that Sweden was already prohibiting the sale of munitions to the belligerents.[28] The most important arguments turned

[24] *A. P. R.*, March 7, 1917.

[25] *A. P. R.*, March 10, 1916.

[26] March 4, 1915. The leading bill was introduced by Senator Hitchcock of Nebraska.

[27] One Wellington House report states: "The papers constantly refer to . . . [Bryan], but usually with impatience; and his attitude is not considered to be of international importance." *A. P. R.*, July 14, 1915.

[28] A Frenchman has remarked that "Sweden took her neutrality very seriously and was [even] horror-struck at the very idea of her railroads carrying material for the Allies." Guichard, *op. cit.*, 133. In the case of Sweden the British government threatened reprisals if the Swedes did not put an embargo on munitions to Germany.

Germany wrote the American government stating that an embargo was the

on the unethical nature of the business. It was stated that it was positively unneutral for the United States to permit its territory to become the base of supplies for Great Britain, France, and Russia. Gerard wrote to House: "There is no doubt ... that a real neutrality would stop the sale, but would our people 'stand' for such a curtailment of American industry?"

The backing of German-Americans and the German government did a great deal to injure this effort to prevent the United States from becoming entangled in the European controversy. Several organizations were formed by Germans in this country to support these measures. They spent a quarter of a million dollars on the Embargo Conference alone. The natural outcome of their participation was that Americans ceased to give their support and those favoring England were able to label the entire movement pro-German. When the administration voiced its opposition, the embargo movement was defeated.

The individuals and groups desiring to keep the United States out of the war promoted a number of movements designed to bring an end to the European conflict. In this group there were William Jennings Bryan, Robert LaFollette, Jane Addams, David Starr Jordan and, for a while, Henry Ford. They desired that the United States intervene not as a partisan but as a neutral in an endeavor to stop the war. Immediately they came in conflict with the "identity of interests" propaganda, the claim that the war was "our fight." As a result they were branded by the Allies' protagonists as pro-German. The movement was attacked by the pro-Ally elements in the country at every opportunity. Roosevelt referred to Jane Addams' peace movement as " 'silly and base,' an effort of 'foolish and noxious' women."[29] The attempts of the pacifists to bring an end to the war were to suffer over-

---

only neutral course possible, as proved by Wilson's own words in regard to sending arms into Mexico. The President was quoted as saying that "because Carranza had no ports, while Huerta had them and was able to import these materials ... it was our duty as a nation to treat [Carranza and Huerta] upon an equality if we wished to observe the true spirit of neutrality as compared with a mere paper neutrality." April 4, 1915. *Diplomatic Correspondence with Belligerent Governments Relating to Neutral Rights and Commerce, 1915-1918,* I (Washington, 1923), 125.

[29]Millis, 127.

whelming defeat when Henry Ford's peace ship, the *Oscar II*, started on its unhappy cruise.

The fundamental intentions and aims of the American people were seldom clearly expressed in the writings or speeches of the neutrality years. The newspapermen, politicians, preachers, and ordinary lecturers — the war hawks of 1914 — expressed merely their own ideas, and not those of their listeners. The thinking of the commonalty was dominated throughout these years by an obstinate desire to keep out of the war. Subordinate to this was the desire to see the Allies win. The protagonists of Britain and France did their best to make this secondary wish the primary one. But throughout the period there persisted the passive, unyielding determination on the part of the vast body of ordinary citizens, to remain detached from the European struggle.

CHAPTER IX ☆ REACTIONS TO THE WAR, AUGUST 1914-FEBRUARY 1916: THE ADMINISTRATION

THE attempt of the British to win the sympathy and support of recognized leaders in all spheres of American life was especially successful among powerful individuals in the field of politics. Some of the most prominent politicians in the United States were actively engaged in fighting Britain's battles on the American political front. The growing American investment in the Anglo-French cause offered them positive reasons for this partisanship, the consequences of which are clearly discernible.

American political leaders during the years 1914-1917 were governed largely by their emotions. They did not possess knowledge adequate for the understanding of European affairs. However, their unquestioning acceptance of the British view of the war, which made them adopt the dangerous policy of benevolent neutrality resulted primarily from the propaganda which engulfed all of America. In perfect accord with desires of the British propagandists, Democrats and Republicans alike refused to judge the actions of the Allies by ordinary standards of criticism, while, on the other hand, they were hypercritical in their dealings with the nations of the Central Powers. The friendship of these controlling individuals in American politics was exceedingly helpful to Great Britain, but resulted in compromising the United States in its efforts to maintain peace.

One of the popular misconceptions of the American people has been that Woodrow Wilson, from 1914 to 1917, was completely impartial in thought and deed, and that he entered the war only when the Germans forced him to do so. The President himself undoubtedly considered his actions perfectly correct. He, like most other articulate Americans of that time, believed so many of the British propaganda arguments that he would have regarded himself "pro-German" if he had not acted as he did. He did not accept without question the entire body of the Allies' propaganda, but on the other hand, he believed enough to endanger American peace. "He was highly susceptible to a righteous cause, and that was where the Allied propaganda struck his most vulnerable point."[1] Although with some misgivings, he accepted the war guilt propaganda. As far as France and Belgium were concerned he accepted their own evaluation of their actions. He wrote to M. Jusserand stating that the loss of Alsace-Lorraine by France "avait été une des tristesses de son enfance."[2] The British claim that they were motivated by the desire to save "poor Belgium" made a deep impression upon him. Josephus Daniels has written that "Mr. Wilson shared the feeling of indignation at the wrongs of Belgium."[3] The effects of the "community of interests" propaganda are likewise noticeable. At one time he even stated to Tumulty, "England is fighting our fight."[4] From time to time it was revealed that many of the other British arguments had become integral parts of his thinking. Perhaps the most effective of all was the propaganda directed against the Hohenzollerns. As a result of Wilson's profound conviction that the German rulers were personally responsible for German actions, he eventually assisted in overthrowing the German monarchy and in turning the control of this restless, expanding nation over to elements which had even less experience.

The basis of Wilson's prejudices may be found in his sources of information and advice. Among newspapers he relied chiefly upon the Springfield *Republican* for a general survey of American opinion.[5] Certain dailies such as the New York *World*, *Times*, and the Washington *Post*, he read with considerable care. Others which were occasionally brought to his attention included the New York *Sun* and *Herald*, the Indianapolis *News*, the Brooklyn *Eagle*, the Chicago *Herald*, and the Louisville *Courier-Journal*.[6]

[1]Arnett, *op. cit.*, 121.

[2]DeVillaneuve-Trans, R., *A l'ambassade de Washington, Octobre 1917-Avril 1919* (Paris, 1921), 49.

[3]Daniels, Josephus, *The Life of Woodrow Wilson 1856-1924* (Philadelphia, 1924), 245.

[4]Tumulty, *op. cit.*, 231.

[5]This publication carried daily reprints of articles from papers representative of various sections of the country.

[6]In the Lansing papers in the Library of Congress may be found notes from Wilson's private secretary in which attention is called to articles from these newspapers. From time to time reference was made to Hearst editorials. These had been

The only European publications which he read were the Manchester *Guardian* and the London *Weekly Times*. It will be noted that every American paper in this list, except the Washington *Post*, was classified by Wellington House as pro-British,[7] and it is unnecessary to comment on the partisanship of the English papers. Certainly such a newspaper diet could not have assisted President Wilson in understanding other than the British view of the war.

As soon as the war broke out, President Wilson isolated himself as much as possible in order to remain free from any influence which the warring governments might attempt to exert. Lord Bryce wrote: Why does Wilson "keep so much to himself and see practically no society?"[8] Representatives of the European powers were unable to meet him informally; to obtain a personal hearing it was necessary to establish contact with a member of his official family. Consequently these individuals close to Mr. Wilson assumed considerable importance.

The President's chief adviser was Colonel Edward Mandell House, a man of no unusual ability or intelligence. Although his importance has undoubtedly been exaggerated, he did influence many of Wilson's decisions, and in his rôle as personal representative of the President, he had considerable opportunity to affect the course of events. It was as a negotiator that Colonel House revealed his naïveté. European statesmen "believed the Colonel to be influential with Mr. Wilson . . . and so they courted him and praised his astuteness and the wisdom of his words."[9] Perhaps because he was the son of an Englishman, he was particularly responsive to the blandishments of British leaders. Edward Grey, Captain Guy Gaunt, Sir William Wiseman, and to a certain extent, Sir Cecil Spring-Rice, were able to make him believe that he was one of their dearest friends. Consequently they

---

reprinted in the Springfield *Republican*, which must have been Wilson's source of information concerning them, since it is understood by this writer that the President did not read Hearst publications — a fact which later research undoubtedly will substantiate.

[7] *Supra*, 161 ff.

[8] James Bryce to Breckinridge Long. In the Breckinridge Long Papers in the Library of Congress.

[9] Lansing Papers, Library of Congress, no date.

were not forced to deal with him as a representative of a foreign power, but as a fellow worker who shared their ideals.

One is impressed by the fact that throughout this entire period Colonel House devoted himself to the advancement of British interests. From the very first he apparently thought that the British cause was "our cause." In 1915, he wrote to Wilson: "The position you have taken with both Germany and Great Britain is correct, but I feel that our position with the Allies is somewhat difficult for we are bound up more or less in their success. . . ."[10] His co-operation with them is rather clearly shown by an incident which occurred in September, 1914. A note had been drawn up in the State Department protesting British infractions of international law. "Its terms made the Colonel's hair rise; instead, however, of merely recommending that it be toned down, he conceived the more remarkable idea of submitting it first to the British Ambassador. The next day he was in secret session with Spring-Rice over the formidable document. . . ."[11] Whenever difficulties arose with Great Britain, House always attempted to secure delay, "and delay was another name for the British diplomacy that was seeking to bring America into the war against Germany."[12] He may not have deliberately attempted to involve the American government in the European conflict, but certainly he was not active in directing policies so that the United States could be kept neutral.[13]

William Jennings Bryan, the Secretary of State, was, next to House, the most important member of the Wilson administration. Bryan was not always sound in his thinking — especially in relation to economics — but during the years of neutrality he appears to have had a clearer understanding of what was involved than any of his contemporaries. He was a deeply religious man and was genuinely disturbed at the thought of the United States taking part in the war. As Secretary of State, he made serious efforts to direct the course of American diplomacy so that neutrality could be preserved. While most of the other members of

[10]Colonel House to President Wilson, May 25, 1916, as quoted in Tansill, *op. cit.*, 208.

[11]Millis, *op. cit.*, 87.

[12]Baker, *op. cit.*, V, 321.

[13]On August 8, 1915, he recorded in his diary his regret that the United States had lost an opportunity to enter the war.

the administration spent their time sympathizing with Belgium, France, and Great Britain, Bryan thought primarily of his own country. He was but slightly affected by the barrage of propaganda, could not be moved by the high-pressure methods of British diplomats, and was perhaps the only powerful individual in the American government who kept his head during the submarine controversy. In the first ten months of the war, he remained a bulwark of neutrality, while other administration leaders followed the crowd to become partisans of the Allies.

Bryan came to hold the opinion that Wilson's policies would lead the United States into war, and did all in his power to persuade his superior to assume a less intransigent attitude. His attempts were blocked at every turn and consequently he felt compelled to resign from office. Perhaps Lane was right when he said that Bryan was "too good a Christian to run a naughty world and he . . . [didn't] hate hard enough."[14]

Robert Lansing, who succeeded Mr. Bryan in the Department of State, has previously appeared as an individual who was seriously preoccupied with the maintenance of America's neutral rights. His published memoirs, however, indicate that his apparent interest in international law was overshadowed by his sympathy for the Allies. He has admitted that his objections to British irregularities were made "half heartedly, as a matter of form, and with no intention" of forcing the issue.[15] He deliberately made his notes to London "long and exhaustive . . . [treatises] which opened up new subjects of discussion rather than . . . [closed] those in controversy. . . . Everything was submerged in verbosity."[16] On the other hand, his notes to Berlin were as short and harsh as possible, and as he has confessed, "short and emphatic notes were dangerous."[17] "In each crisis over the submarine it was . . . [he] who urged strong action against Germany and Wilson who tided it over in the hope of securing peace between the belligerents."[18] Lansing has stated that his policy was to quiet

[14]*Intimate Papers*, I, 459.

[15]Lansing's *Memoirs*, 125.

[16]"It was done with a deliberate purpose." *M. I.*, Part 27, 8264. "Nothing in our controversy with Great Britain must be brought to a head." *M. I.*, Part 27, 8264.

[17]*M. I.*, Part 27, 8264. Lansing's *Memoirs*, 143 f.

[18]Seymour, *American Neutrality*, 141.

dissatisfaction with British naval policy and to educate the American people to the German menace. He remarked: "American public opinion must be prepared for the time, which may come, when we will have to cast aside our neutrality and become one of the champions of democracy."[19]

There is very little evidence to indicate that other members of the Cabinet were able to influence the course of American foreign affairs. Garrison, in the War Department, was perhaps the most bellicose of all the secretaries; he resigned because the President refused to follow all his recommendations regarding preparedness. Although Newton D. Baker, who succeeded him, was a more temperate individual, the British propaganda department reported to Sir Edward Grey that he was "sufficiently pro-Ally." Letters read into the Munitions Investigation Report reveal that the Secretary of the Treasury, William Gibbs McAdoo, was distinctly Anglophile. He interceded for J. P. Morgan and other American bankers in their efforts to induce Mr. Wilson to abandon the policy of withholding loans from belligerents.

Most of the members of the Cabinet were sympathetic with the Allies but preferred that the administration so conduct its relations with all belligerents that the United States would not become involved in the European conflict. With the passing of Bryan, however, there remained no individual in the Cabinet with the courage to oppose the President, and eventually, Wilson became solely responsible for the conduct of American foreign policy.

Among Wilson's diplomatic representatives abroad there were very few who escaped the war hysteria. Walter Hines Page, in London, apparently believed all the propaganda without exception. He wrote home of young girls who had been violated by the Germans, of English soldiers whose noses had been cut off, and

[19]Lansing's *Memoirs*, 21.

"It was Mr. Lansing who transferred this art of war to the quieter atmosphere of American diplomatic correspondence, and who gave it a new turn by using it to delude his own countrymen into the false belief that he was insistent upon the protection of all American rights. His bombardment of the British Foreign Office included all the big guns in international law from Grotius to Westlake, but the range was purposely faulty and the noise of these empty efforts awakened only tardy and muted echoes along the sedate corridors of Number 10 Downing Street. Stage thunder had long been familiar to the personnel of that famous institution." Tansill, *op. cit.*, 168.

of Belgian boys who had been mutilated.[20] He was not merely sympathetic with the Allies, but became such a partisan that he forgot he was an ambassador from a neutral country, and zealously devoted himself to furthering the British cause. Sir Edward Grey wrote as follows: "Page's advice and suggestions were of the greatest value in warning us when to be careful or encouraging us when we could safely be firm"[21] in dealing with the American government. His efforts "went to such astounding lengths that some historians, weighing the documentary record which is now available, insist that the diplomat should have been recalled and tried for treason."[22] The President instructed House to remonstrate with Page concerning his partisanship, and in 1916 called him home for the purpose of giving him "a bath in American opinion." Page, however, remained unaffected by Wilson's desires or instructions. One student of the period has recently stated: ". . . the American Ambassador was wholly unfit to represent the United States at London. Not only did his marked partiality for everything British seriously affect his judgment, but his ignorance of international law as interpreted by the American Government made him a striking example of the futility of drafting journalists into the diplomatic service."[23]

Myron Herrick and Brand Whitlock, American representatives in Paris and Brussels respectively, also raced to the defense of the governments to which they were accredited. Their spectacular partisanship was enthusiastically applauded by the pro-Ally press in the United States and by the Allies' propagandists. Ambassador Herrick declined to leave Paris when the French government moved to Bordeaux, stating that "a dead American Ambassador is worth more to France than a living Ambassador."[24] He encouraged Americans to enlist in the French army and in many other ways rendered actual assistance to the French government. Mr. Whitlock remained in the Belgian capital after its government had departed and became a symbol of American disapproval of Germany. He apparently considered himself something in the nature of a Belgian plenipotentiary to the German

---

[20]Paxson, *op. cit.*, 168.
[21]*The Christian Century*, March 31, 1937, 415.
[22]*Ibid.*, 407.
[23]Tansill, *op. cit.*, 148.
[24]Grattan, *op. cit.*, 76.

army. After the war, the Belgians, French, and British paid trib-
ute to these diplomats for the many services rendered in the years
of neutrality. It is perhaps appropriate that they rather than
Americans should have been the ones to give them honor.

The United States was more adequately represented in Berlin
than in the other European capitals. James W. Gerard handled
a very difficult assignment with a certain degree of capability.
Although he was not especially friendly to the German people or
their government, from time to time he was able to give some
authentic interpretations of the German point of view. David R.
Francis in Petrograd, Frederic C. Penfield in Vienna, and William C. Sharp, who replaced Herrick at Paris, seemed to have
been particularly uninspired.

The American President was not fortunate in his selection of
foreign advisers. They were for the most part well-to-do business
men who had been appointed to their positions because of their
large contributions to party funds. It is known that Wilson deliberately ignored some of the reports of Ambassador Page, and
there are reasons for believing he did not pay a great deal of
attention to the communications of the other ambassadors.[25]

If Wilson paid little attention to many of his official advisers,
he practically ignored the Democratic party leaders in the House
and Senate. The paradoxical aspect of his relationship with Congress lay in the fact that some of his most consistent support on
foreign policy came from the opposition. Throughout the years
of neutrality a large number of the Republican members of Congress, in spite of their desire to maintain an anti-Democratic
front, found themselves in complete accord with Wilson's benevolent neutrality toward the Allies. They nearly always voted to
support him in measures which were favorable to Great Britain
or France. Theodore Roosevelt's almost pathological hatred of
the President was undoubtedly mere envy, while the bitter ti-
rades of Henry Cabot Lodge, James M. Beck, and lesser Repub-

---

[25]It should be mentioned that from time to time very sound reports were
made to Wilson by the non-political appointees in the various European capitals.
Military and naval attachés along with the various chargés d'affaires were quite
often in a better position to understand what was transpiring than their superiors.
Joseph C. Grew was one of the most outstanding of this group. There was also
that peculiar individual, George D. Herron, who from time to time seemed to have
great influence with the President.

lican leaders were the usual attacks made by the "outs" upon the
"ins." If Wilson had worn the Republican label they could have
supported him with their oratory as well as with their votes. Their
only real objection was that the President refused to give unconditional support to the Allies.

The Democratic leaders in Congress during the neutrality
years were distinctly in favor of a more neutral attitude in dealing with the belligerent powers. Champ Clark, the speaker of the
House, naturally had to support the party's leader; privately,
however, he was opposed to Wilson's foreign policy. Henry D.
Flood, chairman of the House Committee on Foreign Relations,
Claude Kitchin, the majority leader of the House, and William
J. Stone, head of the Senate Committee on Foreign Relations, did
all in their power to force Mr. Wilson to assume a less anti-German attitude. Both Kitchin and Stone refused to vote for war in
1917. The desire to be loyal to the party and to work for its success forced the general run of Democratic Congressmen to follow
the President. Even such men as Stone, Kitchin, and Clark were
at times forced to approve, or at least to refrain from disapproving, administration measures for which they had not the slightest
sympathy. The necessity for the Democratic party to maintain a
united front made it impossible openly to oppose the President
and bring on a struggle within the ranks of the party.

Outside governmental and political circles there were, of
course, many attempts to influence the policies of the government. One writer in dealing with the neutrality years has stated
that American bankers and industrialists "had no means of exer-
cising pressure upon the President."[26] The story of the drive for
credits and loans in this country does not seem to bear out this
statement; it would be too much to suppose that what happened
in connection with the lifting of the Bryan ban on loans to belligerents did not also happen to a lesser degree in other cases. But
whether or not other economic interests were able to influence the

[26]Mr. J. P. Morgan led the Munitions Committee to believe that he personally
never tried to influence Mr. Wilson. He stated that he had seen Mr. Wilson but
that he thought "it was before the war broke out." He testified: "I do not think
I saw him after the war broke out at all, except — oh, I do not think I saw him
at all." *M. I.*, Part 25, 7496. This was apparently one of Mr. Morgan's lapses of
memory, for on January 18, 1915, he had interviewed Wilson concerning a Russian loan.

President, it must be conceded that the foreign policies of the Wilson administration were eminently satisfactory to them.

Woodrow Wilson's foreign policies as expressed by himself and his numerous admirers appear to be very commendable. Indeed, they would have been commendable if, in their execution, they had not been given a partisan interpretation. In the carrying out of his policies can be seen the practical results of the British campaign to establish a pro-Ally and anti-German attitude of mind among Americans.

Wilson's policies are usually summarized as follows: (1) To maintain neutrality "in thought as well as in action"; (2) to keep the United States out of war; (3) to act as mediator in an attempt to bring the war to a conclusion; (4) to maintain all the legal rights of the United States as a neutral; (5) to refuse to alter any rules during the progress of the war; (6) to uphold the rights of humanity.

On August 4, 1914, President Wilson issued an official neutrality proclamation. On August 19 he asked for impartiality as well as neutrality, stating, "The United States must be neutral in fact as well as in name during these days that are to try men's souls. We must be impartial in thought as well as in action, must put a curb upon our sentiments as well as upon every transaction that might be construed as a preference of one party to the struggle before another." The immediate response to this call for neutrality was nearly unanimous. House wrote Page: "There is scarcely a dissenting note throughout the country." Even Roosevelt approved it. On being queried by a Belgian woman, "If you were President, what would you do?" Roosevelt replied, "Exactly what President Wilson is doing. The President of the United States can do nothing else at present."[27] Wilson's statement was generally regarded as an attack upon the vociferous pro-Germans. Little serious consideration was given to the idea that it might apply equally well to those who were pro-Ally. On April 20, 1915, Wilson remarked in a public speech: "If I permitted myself to be a partisan in this present struggle, I would be unworthy to represent you."

But his private remarks had no relation to these statements.

[27]Vandervelde, *op. cit.*, 72. Note a contradiction in Roosevelt's later public statements.

In August, 1914, President Wilson said: "Let us pray that Germany will not develop a von Moltke."[28] Later he admitted that he was "heart and soul for the Allies,"[29] and that he had been on their side "since the first day the Germans moved."[30] Even before the sinking of the *Lusitania*, Attorney-General Gregory quoted Wilson as saying "that the ordinary rules of conduct had no application to the situation; that the Allies were standing with their backs to the wall, fighting wild beasts; that he would permit nothing to be done by our country to hinder or embarrass them in the prosecution of the war unless admitted rights were greatly violated and that this policy must be understood as settled."[31] It is now clear that it was his privately expressed opinions rather than his public statements which governed his actions.

The policies (a) to keep the United States out of war and (b) to act as a mediator in an attempt to bring the war to a conclusion, can be identified as Wilson's foreign policies only at the very end of the neutrality period. During the first twenty-one months he did not associate himself with the attempts made to eliminate causes of friction between the United States and the Central Powers. Indeed, he opposed these measures. Serious peace overtures were not made until December, 1916.

The upholding of the legal rights of neutrals occupied a great deal of the attention of the Wilson administration. The sinking of ships without warning and without providing for the safety of passengers quite rightly evoked strong condemnation. War was threatened on this score. Also, the legal rights of Americans to trade and travel were vigorously upheld in so far as Germany was concerned. To Great Britain many protests were sent as a result of the British infractions of international law touching upon trade in wartime. Here, however, the approach was usually quite friendly. Lansing has admitted that the American complaints were made "with no intention to force the issue." Senator Clark has stated that "it is perfectly apparent . . . that the British Government never took the American protests seriously, and

---

[28]Lawrence, *op. cit.*, 140.

[29]*Intimate Papers*, II, 50.

[30]Houston, David F., *Eight Years With Wilson's Cabinet 1913-1920 With A Personal Estimate of the President* (New York, 1926), 221.

[31]The New York *Times*, January 29, 1925.

that Washington, although stating them very forcibly in various communications, never seriously pressed these protests."[32]

The refusal to alter any of the rules of war or neutrality while hostilities were going on was very peculiar in that it left a modern war to be governed by rules formulated during the eighteenth and nineteenth centuries. The policy was used as a justification for the American government to insist on the right of Americans to sell war materials, even though it meant that the United States would become a base of supplies for the Entente Powers. It also served to justify granting belligerent merchant ships the right to carry heavy armament. Negatively, it was the basis for the refusal to grant Germany permission to declare a war zone in European waters. On the other hand, the American government ignored the policy when dealing with the British government's interference with American trade. Ray Stannard Baker has stated that "the Administration defense of American policy was in reality a defense of British blockade, and furnished the British Government with a whole arsenal of arguments against our own criticisms of that blockade." Senator Stone and others brought to the attention of the government its inconsistencies. In certain cases this resulted in the spectacle of America's most idealistic President exculpating himself "with technical appeals to shadowy legalities." Perhaps the most interesting aspect of this general policy is the fact that there were many changes in attitude made by the administration itself.[33]

The policy of upholding the rights of humanity was invoked by the American government in opposing the German submarine warfare. It was maintained that civilians must not be endangered by the actions of the warring powers. If this had been carried out with a full realization of the causes and meaning of the acts of all belligerents, and if the civilians in question had had an uncontested right of immunity in areas in which they were endangered, the policy would have been completely justifiable. However, no serious consideration was given to the inhumane results of the undramatic and illegal British blockade or to the fact that Americans could not rightly claim immunity while traveling on the

---

[32]*M. I.*, Part 27, 8263. Senator Bennett Champ Clark.

[33]Notice that the policy of publishing ships manifests was changed as the British desired. Savage, *op. cit.*, II, 14.

ships of belligerents. Instead, the policy was based entirely upon
opposition to the highly publicized and highly colorful attempts
of the Germans to break the iron ring around them by means of
indiscriminate sinkings of their enemies' ships.

The diplomatic history of the first twenty-one months of neutrality reveal very clearly how the Wilson administration quite
unconsciously adopted the British point of view of the war as its
own point of view. On August 6, 1914, the American government
made its first move to protect its rights of trade. On that date it
was suggested that the belligerents accept the Declaration of
London as a code of maritime law governing shipping in the war
zone. This embarrassed the British a great deal. Naturally if they
intended to evade the existing rules of blockade and contraband,
they would not desire new unambiguous laws which they would
be forced to violate. Their evasions of law were to be difficult
enough to explain without agreeing to any additional regulations.
They replied to Wilson by ostensibly accepting his suggestion.
Actually, however, they attached so many conditions which would
have operated to their benefit that he was forced to acknowledge
that their acceptance was, in effect, a rejection. The American
government stated that under the circumstances it would have to
rely upon the established rules of international law.[34]

Walter Hines Page regarded the suggestion concerning the
Declaration of London as Wilson's first mistake, and was greatly
distressed because he was obliged to handle the negotiations. The
note prepared by Lansing on October 3 was especially annoying
because of the very strong objections made to the illegalities of
British naval practices. According to Page, it "would almost have
been a declaration of war." As a result of pressure exerted by the
administration's advisers, a retreat was made, and the strong
language in the note was replaced by a few weak complaints. All
in all, Page was forced to present four notes on the Declaration
of London, each of which made him more angry until he threatened to resign if the matter were not dropped. Finally Wilson
made his first major surrender to the British and gave up the attempt to have the Declaration of London accepted. This yielding

[34]Page wrote home that the British "quietly laughed at our efforts to regulate
sea warfare." The British did pretend to operate under the Declaration of London
until July 7, 1916, at which time they officially abandoned it.

to British desires was merely the first in a long series of maneuvers in which Wilson virtually approved their economic warfare.

The positive measures to get around the British interference
with American commerce and consequently to reduce causes of
friction with Germany were never successful. A bill was passed
to purchase interned German ships for the purpose of transporting more goods under the American flag. Nothing came of it. Another suggestion was that the United States government should
build ships. This might have gained exemption for many American cargoes. At least it would have made it difficult for the British to keep up their illegal naval practices. This also did not
materialize.

The most important of the suggestions in relation to commerce was that an embargo should be placed on munitions in
order to prevent the United States from becoming a supply base
for the Allies. Sir Edward Grey was constantly haunted by the
fear that Congress would pass an embargo act.[35] "On December
11, 1914, Ambassador Page, from London, telegraphed the Secretary of State: "Sir Edward Grey unofficially expressed the hope
to me that the bill introduced by Mr. Hitchcock in the Senate [to
embargo munitions] . . . will not pass."[36] Very probably Colonel
House's English friends also urged him to oppose such a measure.'
At least, House exerted pressure on Wilson, stating: "If . . . we

[35]Hendrick, *op. cit.*, I, 364; or II, 82, for the same reaction from the Russian
Ambassador, Benckendorff.

An American agent reminded him that the United States had the whip hand
so far as the Allies were concerned if it wanted to exert pressure. *A. P. R.*, August
5, 1916.

"All the congressmen are thinking about re-election. Now if they brought
about an embargo, they would be attacked by the big interests that are supplying
ammunition, and by a considerable number of people who profit by these supplies.
On the other hand, if they vote for an embargo, they may be appealing to a very
large portion of the electorate which consists of ignorant people, who have no
direct interest in the export of ammunition, and who are easily carried away by
high-sounding sentimentalities such as Mr. Bryan is fond of uttering. It is quite
obvious that if the dilemma were presented at present to the congressman, he
would vote against an embargo, but it is not at all safe to assume that this will be
the attitude four or five months hence. . . ." *A. P. R.*, August 5, 1916.

Another report states: "It is felt that unless something is done before the next
session of Congress, the German agents will have brought about a combination
of the cotton growers and the sentimentalists, who, like Mr. Bryan, oppose the
export of munitions of war. Such a combination would be extremely embarrassing."

[36]*M. I.*, Part 27, 8265.

placed an embargo . . . our whole industrial and agricultural machinery would cry out against it."[37]

The English, however, need not have been alarmed. Wilson very definitely did all he could to prevent any restrictions on trade. The American public was told that the placing of an embargo while hostilities were going on would be an unneutral act,[38] and Germany was informed that it was "not within the choice of the Government of the United States . . . to inhibit this trade."[39] "For the Germans . . . the failure of the embargo — the failure, indeed, of every American action or representation which might have disadvantaged the Allies — was but added proof that whatever they were to get they must get by their own exertions."[40]

The possible danger if an embargo were not passed was clearly stated by Professor Charles C. Hyde in a letter to the Secretary of State. He wrote: "While the exportation of war supplies imposes upon our Government no legal duty of prevention, and while the traffic may not as yet have attained a volume sufficient to produce alarm in Germany, it may, by reason of its increasing proportions and its degree of assistance to nations fighting in alliance, lead us to a position where we may be regarded by their foes as a most dangerous participant and hence as an inevitable enemy. Does it not therefore behoove us to be prepared to give the right answer when the time comes, to this final and simple question, which is submitted to your consideration: Is the endeavor to make the resources of the United States win the fight for the Allies worth the price of war with Germany? Or, con-

[37]June 22, 1915. *Intimate Papers*, II, 58.
"Several neutral nations in Europe had imposed embargoes upon exports of war supplies and they had given but little consideration to British protests. Secretary Bryan, however, seemed ever anxious to placate the British Government, and two days after Spring-Rice had addressed his petulant notes to the Secretary of State an assurance was conveyed to Sir Edward Grey that the embargo bills in Congress would not be adopted." Tansill, *op. cit.*, 39. See Bryan letter to Page, January 25, 1915.

[38]Secretary Lansing remarked: "That the United States does have the right in case of need . . . to change the rules and to forbid the sale within its territory of arms to belligerent governments, or to prevent the departure from its territory of such arms may prove of inestimable value." *M. I.*, Part 27, 8267 f.

[39]Oppenheim, L., *International Law, A Treatise* (London, 1921), II, 482. The legal argument on the embargo terminated with the American note of August 11, 1915. Lansing's *Memoirs*, 58.

[40]Millis, *op. cit.*, 147.

versely, is the maintenance of neutrality worth an embargo on munitions of war?"[41]

In direct contrast to the American government's submissiveness to the Allies' blockade was its reaction to Germany's announcement of submarine warfare. Although "the United States [had] declined to join Norway, Sweden and Denmark in a protest" against the earlier establishment of a war zone by the British, the State Department assumed a threatening attitude when Germany announced the setting up of a war zone around Great Britain. It was stated that the United States would hold the German government to "strict accountability" for any acts which resulted in the loss of American lives or ships. The fact that German national existence was at stake seems not to have been given consideration. Wilson apparently expected Germany to give way in the face of American objections, regardless of the consequences to Germany.[42]

Basically, the British blockade and the German submarine retaliation against it were matters which vitally affected only the belligerents. Wilson's insistence, however, that the prosecution of a world war could not be permitted to interfere with American rights of trade and travel, made the United States a party to the struggle. He maintained that Germany could not under any circumstances endanger the lives of American passengers on ships in European waters. It made no difference whether the ships were in a war zone; it made no difference whether the ships belonged to one of the belligerents; it made no difference whether the ships were armed or unarmed. In setting down these rules, the American government assumed a position which was legally untenable, for a ship's immunity is determined by its own nationality and not by the nationality of its passengers. Certainly the presence of a neutral traveler could not be expected to provide exemption from risks which ordinarily fall to a belligerent vessel. Never-

[41]*M. I.*, Part 27, Exhibit 2516, 8473.

[42]Senator Clark: "The Germans constantly pointed out in their exchanges with the United States the fact that the American Government made no concessions to Germany's contention that the use of the submarine weapon was vital in their warfare against Britain's control of the seas with its illegal blockade measures and stoppage of commerce to Germany, while the same Government, the American Government, did very little to insist that Britain observe the rules of international law." *M. I.*, Part 28, 8491.

theless it was the attempt to enforce this fallacious regulation which created troubles between the United States and Germany for which there was no solution.

Wilson was annoyed as well as surprised when the Central Powers declined to submit to American demands and accept his interpretation of maritime law. It seemed to him incredible that the German government should continue its plans for submarine warfare after his ultimatum of February 10, and when shipping actually began to be destroyed, he became indignant. His reaction to the sinking of the *Lusitania* was one of extreme horror. Tumulty reports him as saying: "I dare not act unjustly and cannot indulge my own passionate feelings." "In God's name, how could any nation calling itself civilized propose so horrible a thing?"[43] He did not realize that such an event was inevitable. The act, of course, was horrible, but as long as Germany would not accept the defeat which went with the British blockade and as long as the United States insisted on permitting its nationals to travel through the war zone, it was impossible to avoid an incident which would endanger German-American relations.

Wilson's course of action after the sinking of the *Lusitania* was to threaten Germany with war and to promise the American people that there would be a continuance of peace. That the threat and the promise were irreconcilable apparently did not enter into his mind. He sent a stiff note to Germany without considering what would happen if Germany did not accede to his demands. This thoughtless action pleased the jingoes. On the other hand, he gave his "too proud to fight" speech, which gave the public the impression that he intended to carry on peaceful policies. Roosevelt, of course, was angered by Wilson's "weasel words," and bitterly declared that "for many months our Government has preserved between right and wrong a neutrality which would have excited the emulous admiration of Pontius Pilate." But such was the belief only of Anglophiles — the overwhelming majority of people was insistent upon maintaining neutrality regardless of the admiration it excited.

The next controversy in which the government became in-

---

[43]Tumulty, *op. cit.*, 232. Immediately all official eyes in England were turned upon Wilson. See the correspondence from the Lord Mayor's office in the Buttolph Letters. New York Public Library.

volved was over the arming of merchantmen. In the very remote past, ships had been permitted to mount guns for defense against pirates, but, with the abolition of privateering and piracy, the justification for arming merchantmen had disappeared. During the World War the government of the Netherlands maintained that armed ships were to be excluded from Dutch ports. The United States, on the other hand, placed no such restrictions upon them. "On August 9, 1914, the British Embassy drew the [American State] Department's attention to the fact that there would soon be entering the United States a number of British merchant vessels that were armed...." On August 31 the German Ambassador telegraphed the Department of State from New York that the White Star Liner *Adriatic* had entered that port "armed with cannons and had not left within twenty-four hours...."[44] On September 3 when this boat sailed from New York the Germans were advised that the American government was satisfied that it was a "merchantman." From that time on the United States permitted armed ships to enter American ports and also permitted American citizens to take passage on them.

The attitude of the American government should have been controlled by the *Nereide* decision. In this case Chief Justice Marshall stated that a vessel could not be part neutral and part hostile. "She [the *Nereide*] is an open and declared belligerent; claiming all the rights, and subject to all the dangers of the belligerent character."[45] Marshall also contended that the neutral who availed himself of the protection of armament took "all the chances and hazards of war." The Wilson administration, however, ignored Marshall's decision, and adopted the British argument that because these ships were armed for defense only, they should not be restricted by rules which ordinarily governed ships of war. In defending this stand a garbled version of Marshall's *Nereide* opinion "was widely disseminated, and was used in speeches even in Congress." John Bassett Moore is of the opinion that this "practically involved forgery" because the above mentioned vital parts of the decision were deleted. The administration's attitude was, of course, of great benefit to the Allies. It established a situation in which ships armed to fight submarines

[44]Borchard and Lage, *op. cit.*, 84.
[45]9 Cranch, 430.

were given all the privileges and immunities usually reserved for strictly commercial vessels.

By 1915 the British found that a five or six inch gun could easily sink a submarine. Consequently many merchant ships were armed, and captains were instructed to destroy any U-boat which came within range. Under such circumstances, these commercial vessels should have been classified as men-of-war. Even in the days when vessels were armed against pirates, they were regarded as warships if their governments had furnished the armament.

The result of the increasing aggressiveness of armed merchantmen was a growing unwillingness on the part of submarine commanders to observe the rules of visit and search, which were equivalent to suicide. Before long, even Wilson and Lansing recognized the injustice of the situation. On October 4, 1915, the President wrote to Colonel House: "It is hardly fair to ask submarine commanders to give warnings by summons if, when they approach as near as they must for that purpose they are to be fired upon." On January 2, 1916, Lansing wrote Mr. Wilson: "You will recall the case of the *Baralong* where a German submarine was bombarding a vessel from which the crew had escaped in boats, when a tramp steamer approached flying the American flag. The submarine remained on the surface and awaited the steamer, which on nearing the submarine lowered the American flag, hoisted the British colors, and with a gun mounted on the stern (a defensive armament according to our early definition) opened fire and sank the German vessel killing all the crew. The British Government would urge that this was merely a *ruse de guerre* and entirely allowable, and so it would have been under old conditions, but under the new conditions it presents a strong argument in favor of submarine attack without warning.

"Since we issued the statement of September, 1914, formally, it appears to me advisable to issue a new statement setting forth ... the impossibility of a submarine's communicating with an armed merchant ship without exposing itself to the gravest danger of being sunk by gunfire ... the unreasonableness of requiring a submarine to run the danger of being almost certainly destroyed by giving warning to a vessel carrying an armament, and that, therefore, merchant vessels should refrain from mounting guns large enough to sink a submarine, and that, if they do, they become vessels of war and liable to treatment as such by both belligerents and neutrals."[46]

As an outgrowth of their concern over this matter, Wilson and Lansing formulated a compromise which they felt would be a solution, and communicated it to the belligerents on January 18, 1916. It was proposed that "submarines should be caused to adhere strictly to the rules of international law in the matter of stopping and searching merchant vessels," that they should provide for the safety of crews and passengers, "and that merchant vessels of belligerent nationality should be prohibited and prevented from carrying any armament whatsoever."[47] Lansing wrote: "My Government is impressed with the reasonableness of the argument that a merchant vessel carrying an armament of any sort, in view of the character of submarine warfare and the defensive weakness of undersea craft, should be held to be an auxiliary cruiser and so treated by a neutral as well as by a belligerent government, and is seriously considering instructing its officials accordingly."[48] Such a course would have provided safe-

[46]Savage, *op. cit.*, 431 f. See also *M. I.*, Part 27, 8274 f.

"The *U-27* was struck by several shells from the *Baralong* and sank within a few minutes. Some of the crew were able to swim to the *Nicosian,* which had been abandoned by the British. While hanging to the ropes that dangled over the side of this British vessel, several of them were killed by gunfire from the *Baralong.* Four Germans who succeeded in climbing on board the *Nicosian* were hunted down by British marines, who shot them at sight. The commander of the *U-27,* witnessing this cold-blooded series of murders, seized a life belt and leaped into the sea. There he was shot while his hands were upraised in a signal of surrender." Tansill, *op. cit.*, 379.

[47]Savage, *op. cit.*, 453, Document 156.

[48]Savage, *op. cit.*, 444.

Note the opinion of the Neutrality Board against armed ships. "In its conclusion the Board candidly confessed that the practice of arming merchant ships was a '. . . very questionable one, bristling with possibilities of embarrassment and friction. Save only the possibility of military advantages to a belligerent, it has nothing to commend it and everything to condemn it. . . . Should the General Board (the General Board of the United States Navy) report that the supposed military advantages are illusory, the Joint State and Navy Neutrality Board recommends that the Government of the United States refer the entire question to the next Hague Conference for settlement, and in the meantime that it announce its intention to treat private and armed belligerent vessels by the rules applicable to belligerent vessels of war, or to subject them to other special treatment.' " MS. Opinions of the Neutrality Board, as quoted in Tansill, *op. cit.*, 413.

ty for crews and passengers on ships traveling in the war zone, and would have prevented armed vessels from entering American ports except under rules governing men-of-war.

It is very possible that Lansing's suggestion would have eliminated all reasons for disagreement between the United States and Germany. The British were dumbfounded by this sudden turn of events and returned a categorical rejection to the American proposal. Page reported: "I have only once before seen Sir Edward [Grey] so grave and disappointed, and that was when he informed me that the British had sent the German Government an ultimatum."[49]

There were several important reasons for the British reaction. But, underlying all of them was the realization that a solution of German-American differences would have deprived Great Britain of a potential ally. An immediate objection was that this *modus vivendi* would have removed "the shield of our moralistic humanitarianism" from "between the war supply business and the torpedo." It would no longer have been possible for the Allies to claim immunity for cargoes of munitions and other war supplies merely because the ships in which they were being transported were called merchant vessels. Nor would the presence of neutral passengers have served as protection. Operating under conditions such as those outlined in the American note, the submarines would undoubtedly have been more of a threat to the Allies than ever before. Certainly Great Britain had no desire to protect the lives of people traveling in the war zone at so great a cost to themselves.

In order to defeat the American proposal the British politely threatened to put a stop to the highly profitable war trade which the Allies were carrying on with the United States. Ambassador Page wrote to Lansing: "If no merchantman may carry a defensive gun into an American port, [this] change may precipitate a cutting off of American orders, not from any wish to cut them off, but from fear that other embarrassing acts by us may follow."[50] Suddenly the American government withdrew its plan, declared that it had been only tentative, and issued a statement

[49]Savage, *op. cit.*, II, 449, Document 161.
[50]Tansill, *op. cit.*, 449.

that, "in view of [the] . . . rejection by the Allies this Government had no alternative but to withdraw its proposal."[51]

The note of January 18, 1916, was a great surprise to all belligerents. Its impartiality was distinctly foreign to the usual attitude of the administration, and its presentation at that time is very difficult to understand. Never before had the American government admitted that vital interests of the Central Powers were at stake in the economic struggle of which the submarine warfare was a part. However, even more strange than the note was its hasty retraction. Wilson and his Secretary of State have left proof that they had come to feel that it was of questionable legality to permit heavily armed merchant ships to enter American harbors, and that it exposed the government to criticism. Over night their point of view changed — but why? Who persuaded them to alter their stand? What forces exerted pressure? Was this another case[52] in which financial interests converged on Washington to prevent the government from injuring the very profitable war business with the Allies? Perhaps this idealistic point of view could only have been short-lived and was replaced by Wilson's more fundamental desire to see the Allies win.

Among Wilson's "about faces," the one which was the most ominous for the welfare of the country was his sponsoring of the preparedness campaign. This movement was partially a patriotic American one for defense of the country. In addition, it had become a movement by American Anglophiles to push the United States into the war. Theodore Roosevelt, General Leonard Wood, and the other backers were, almost without exception, the most radical supporters of the Allies. The most important of the organizations which carried on the campaign were the American Rights League, the National Society for Patriotic Organization, the American Legion,[53] the American Defense Society, the Navy League,[54] and the National Security League.[55] All these organizations were dominated by strongly pro-Ally individuals.

[51]One excuse was the fact that Germany declared on February 11 that armed ships were to be considered as war ships. See Tansill, 425, *et seq.*, 463 ff.

[52]Cf. policy on loans, *supra*, 88 ff.

[53]Not the post-war American Legion.

[54]The Navy League was primarily interested in inducing Congress to order more battle ships. Its drive for "unprecedented war ship appropriations did not slack even after Congressman Tavenner disclosed on the floor of the House that

This propaganda was given its most dramatic expression in the Plattsburg camps. These helped to spread a militaristic spirit among the people who attended them, most of whom were drawn from the pro-Ally districts of the East. They provided willing audiences for Wood and Roosevelt when those bellicose Anglophiles attempted to arouse a militaristic spirit among their countrymen.

Great impetus was given to the preparedness movement by the appearance of a certain motion picture.[56] "Into the hands of Commodore J. Stuart Blackton, a leading motion-picture producer of the spectacular school, there had fallen a copy (it seems to have fallen into the hands of nearly every literate person in the United States) of Mr. Hudson Maxim's 'Defenceless America.' The Commodore read it in a night and sprang for the motion picture rights; the result was 'The Battle Cry of Peace.'

"Hundreds of thousands of Americans were to witness this gory piece of incomparable propaganda for preparedness. They were to be thrilled and horrified by its portrayal of an unprepared America overrun by the brutal and licentious soldiery of a foreign power which, though unnamed, uniformed its troops in a strangely close imitation of the Germans. Assisted by tons of smoke powder and regiments of supers, Miss Norma Talmadge and Mr. Charles Richman personified the nation in the agonies of an invasion far more horrible — and more exciting — than anything depicted in the censored films of the real war in Europe. Commodore Blackton's masterpiece, according to an historian of the motion picture, won 'warm endorsement from the belligerently minded, most conspicuously from Colonel Theodore Roosevelt. . . . National exploitation of the picture began'; and it was soon inculcating an enthusiasm for big armament appropriations and fears and hatred for the Germans in theaters throughout the length and breadth of the United States."[57]

At the time this preparedness movement first started, President Wilson was distinctly opposed to it. In his annual message

---

the forwarders of the organization were all personally interested in the manufacture of armor plate." *Christian Century*, March 31, 1937, 408.

[55]Under the leadership of Frederic L. Huidekoper.

[56]*Infra*, Chapter XI.

[57]Millis, *op. cit.*, 217 f.

to Congress in December, 1914, he said: "We shall not alter our attitude toward . . . [preparedness] because some amongst us are nervous and excited." Before, he had said privately that "talk of this sort had been going on since he was a boy of ten."[58] He became "white with passion" when an article appeared in the Baltimore *Sun* saying that the General Staff was preparing a plan in the event of war with Germany.[59]

All this changed in 1915 when Wilson did another of his reversals of policy. As in so many other cases, he surrendered completely to the desires of the Allies' sympathizers and took up the cry of the pack urging a course, the outcome of which could only have led to war. After the third *Lusitania* note, articles appeared in the press stating that means were being taken by the government to prepare the country for "eventualities."[60] On the same day letters were sent to the Secretary of Navy regarding preparations for war.[61] In November, just before House left for Europe, Wilson openly advocated preparedness in his Manhattan Club speech. Finally, beginning on January 27, 1916, he made a series of addresses, usually two a day, preaching preparedness. He spoke in New York City, Pittsburgh, Cleveland, Milwaukee, Chicago, Des Moines, Topeka, Kansas City, and St. Louis.

The very questionable assertion has been made that Wilson joined the preparedness movement in order to deprive the Republicans of a campaign issue in 1916. It is more likely, however, that it was merely another expression of his partisanship. In this particular case, instead of warping government policies for the benefit of Great Britain and France, he was assisting in the educational work to obtain military support for them among the American people.

At first glance, President Wilson's efforts to obtain peace appear to have been diametrically opposed to his support of preparedness. Actually, however, there was no great contradiction. He proffered the good offices of the American government to the warring nations on July 28, 1914, and again on August 4. Once more, after the Speyer dinner in September, Bryan made ineffectual inquiries of the ambassadors in Washington as to the possi-

[58]The New York *Times*, October 20, 1914.
[59]Palmer, *N. D. Baker*, 40.
[60]These were inspired by Wilson.
[61]Tumulty, *op. cit.*, 262 f.

bility of the belligerents' welcoming overtures of peace.[62] Later the demand of Hearst and others for the inauguration of peace negotiations gained a great deal of support among the public, and consequently Wilson sent an informal peace proposal to Germany. The unwillingness of the Allies, however, to enter into a conference under the adverse circumstances in which their armies were to be found caused Wilson temporarily to shelve his idea. He did not wish to offend anyone. Since by December, 1914, both parties appeared more tractable and willing to negotiate, the Kaiser made what Page calls his fourth proposal for peace on the basis of the surrender of Belgium and payment for its restoration.[63]

As a result of these negotiations, early in 1915 Wilson sent Colonel House to Europe to interview diplomats in the belligerent countries. The British courted the Texas Colonel most assiduously, but privately they resented his attempt to act as mediator. They insisted that he should not discuss peace with the Germans until they (i.e., the Allies) had a victory to their credit, but on February 20 Wilson sent his Ambassador Extraordinary a sharp note demanding that he go on to the other European capitals.[64] The interviews which followed in Berlin and Paris were no more fruitful than those in London. The only definite result of House's trip was the beginning of a close friendship with Sir Edward Grey and other Englishmen.

The Allies were tremendously assisted in diverting the attention of the American people and their President away from the peace movement by the timely crises of 1915. The sinking of the *Lusitania* prevented Wilson from making any peace offers during the summer, while the sabotage disclosures and the other incidents had the same effect in the autumn. In October Sir Gilbert Parker reported to his superiors that "any effect detrimental to Great Britain which might have resulted from this [peace

[62]At the Speyer dinner Bernstorff announced that his country was ready for peace. Bryan was elated and hurried to the Allies' ambassadors. He said to Jusserand that the nation refusing this offer would be as culpable as the one starting the war. Then he asked Jusserand what he would say to a return to the *status quo*. Jusserand, *op. cit.*, 26 ff. The latter replied that the only *status quo* acceptable to him must include bringing back to life the Frenchmen who had died in the war. The British Ambassador hid behind Belgium's skirts.

[63]Hendrick, *op. cit.*, I, 426.

[64]Baker, V, 313.

talk] ... has been fully countered by the indignation caused by the barbarous execution of Nurse Cavell."[65]

The transition from neutrality to partisanship in the administration's peace maneuvers occurred in the fall of 1915 when Colonel House devised a plan whereby Germany would be forced to stop fighting or be confronted with military intervention by the United States. This scheme called for a private understanding with Great Britain and France after which Wilson was to issue a "demand that hostilities cease." House explained to the President that "the Allies, after some hesitation, could accept our offer or demand, and, if the Central Powers accepted, we [the United States] would then have accomplished a master stroke of diplomacy. If the Central Powers refused to acquiesce, we could then push our insistence to a point where diplomatic relations would first be broken off, and later the whole force of our Government — and perhaps the force of every neutral — might be brought against them."[66] "I would not let Berlin know, of course, of any understanding had with the Allies, but would rather lead them to think our proposal would be rejected by the Allies."[67]

President Wilson apparently decided to ascertain the practicability of House's suggestion. Early in 1916, therefore, he again sent House to Europe to interview diplomats and prepare the ground for the *coup de théâtre*. In London, House was given a most cordial reception; in Berlin he was pleased to find the Germans "unreasonable." The French were rather unprepared for such an overture from the American government, and must have been astonished when it was accompanied by an unconditional offer of assistance. In addition to the conference plan, House told them that "if they felt they were losing ground ... [Wilson] would intervene to save them and guarantee a settlement based upon justice"[68] and that "the lower the fortunes of the Allies ebbed the closer the United States would stand by them."[69]

---

[65]*A. P. R.*, October 29, 1915. Parker referred to this peace talk as a "form of German intrigue."

[66]*Intimate Papers*, II, 85.

[67]*Ibid.*, II, 91.

[68]*Ibid.*, II, 163.

[69]*Ibid.*, II, 175. This was on February 7, 1916.

House's report to Wilson stated: "In the event the Allies had some notable victories during the spring and summer [which they did not have], you would not intervene; and in the event that the tide of war went against them or remained

The European diplomats could not have been expected to accept House's trick plan[70] for a peace conference after he had promised them unqalified support if the need should arise. However, they did not wish to ruffle the fatuous American's feathers;[71] so they told him that the British Foreign Minister would advise Wilson when it was expedient to issue the "demand for peace."

The famous memorandum as initialed by Sir Edward Grey and approved by President Wilson — with the exception of the word "probably" — was as follows:

"President Wilson was ready, on hearing from France and England that the moment was opportune, to propose that a Conference should be submitted to put an end to the war. Should the Allies accept this proposal, and should Germany refuse it, the United States would probably enter the war against Germany. . . . If it failed to secure peace, the United States would (probably) leave the Conference as a belligerent on the side of the Allies. . . ."[72] This agreement was reached on February 22, 1916, with action deferred until Sir Edward Grey should give the signal.

In a session of the Munitions Investigation Committee Senator Bennett Champ Clark stated: "Here we have an entirely unofficial representative of President Wilson, holding no official position, not confirmed by the Senate in any way . . . agreeing to bring the United States into war . . . without the knowledge of the Congress or any authority for doing so. With regard to the agreement itself, one might be appalled at the extent to which President Wilson had secretly committed this country to war, particularly at a time [February, 1916] when the sentiment of the country was overwhelmingly against war. Comment with re-

---

stationary, you would intervene." *Ibid.*, II, 164. However, "if they made the mistake of waiting until Germany had a decisive victory, or nearly so, they need not expect action from us, for it would be foolhardy for the United States to enter at so late a day in the hope of changing the results in their favor." *Ibid.*, II, 176.

[70]Ambassador Page wrote "the fatal moral weakness of the . . . scheme is that we should plunge into the war, not on the merits of the cause, but by a carefully sprung trick." Hendrick, *op. cit.*, III, 281 f.

[71]Secretary Lansing wrote: "For over two years Colonel House chased the *ignis fatuus* of a negotiated peace." MS entitled *Peace Overtures of 1917*, in the Library of Congress, Lansing Papers.

[72]*Intimate Papers*, II, 201.

spect to the complete unneutrality of such an agreement is hardly necessary."[73]

It is interesting to note that the Germans became suspicious of House's conversations in London and Paris.[74] On February 29 Gerard wrote: "Both the Chancellor and von Jagow say they are convinced America has a secret understanding with England. . . ."[75] A little later it was stated: "English influences are back of the present peace movement and . . . the President will propose terms acceptable to the Allies, but which Germany will be bound to reject, the result being that all blame will fall on Germany."

Perhaps in no other single project of the Wilson administration was the pro-Ally bias more clearly displayed than in this proposal for bringing about peace. The House plan "was tantamount to guaranteeing victory for the Allies."[76] Crudely stated, it meant that the United States was to intervene to take the fruits of victory away from the winner and give them to the loser. It was in no way an impartial proposition, or a "peace without victory." It was a victory peace for the loser.

A recent writer has remarked that "it is not a grateful task to record the diplomacy of the United States during the period 1914-17," for "the conduct of the American Government during that period was a negation of nearly all the requirements of neutrality both in thought and in action."[77] Everything was distorted for the benefit of the British. Certainly this was true in the first twenty-one months of neutrality. In the policies governing peace negotiations, the arming of merchant ships, British restrictions on American trade, the Declaration of London, preparedness, embargo, and loans, there is found a transition from neutrality to hesitant partisanship, and finally to open support of Great

[73]*M. I.*, Part 28, 8489.

[74]During the Munitions Investigation, Senator Clark remarked: "I think it is perfectly apparent from the House-Grey agreement, that the arrangement was that no peace was to be proposed which was not known to be in advance entirely satisfactory to the Allies, and that if the Germans refused to accept such peace, Colonel House was committing the United States to the entry of the war on the side of the Allies." *M. I.*, Part 28, 8517.

[75]*Intimate Papers*, II, 222.

[76]Seymour, American Diplomacy, 146. "The American terms . . . were of positive defeat" for Germany. Grey, *op. cit.*, II, 134.

[77]Borchard and Lage, *op. cit.*, 33.

Britain and her allies. Even the biographer of the British Ambassador concedes that "during the period while America was neutral all the issues in dispute between England and America were decided as England wished."

The sympathies of the American people were, like those of the administration, definitely on the side of the Allies, but unlike those of Wilson and his advisers, they were subordinate to a desire for the maintenance of peace. However, with Bryan out of the way, there existed not a single powerful moderating force within the administration to give voice to the wishes of the public. On November 10, 1914, Professor Muensterberg of Harvard strongly and accurately attacked Wilson's pro-British policies, taking exception more to "the unfriendly spirit than to the actual violation of the law." Wilson wrote to Lansing that the case made out was *"prima facie* very plausible indeed," but as subsequent events proved, it did not cause him to alter his course. William J. Stone, the Chairman of the Senate Committee on Foreign Relations, made strenuous objections to the administration's unneutrality, but he also was unable to influence the president's line of conduct.

Wilson's extravagant partisanship was a product of the idealistic British propaganda which pictured the war as a holy war. When this was accentuated by a growing conviction that he should be the "commander of righteousness triumphant," there ensued a disregard of the public's demand for peace. The administration's course of action was more partisan than that of any other neutral. Also it did not coincide with the wishes of the American people. The reason for the attitude was Wilson's acceptance of the Allies' contention that the war was a crusade against autocracy and militarism. This was, in his mind, justification for distorting neutrality and even for joining the Allies. His sincerity cannot be questioned for a moment. But under such circumstances, sincerity is hardly sufficient.

It has been customary for many to interpret the neutrality years as a period in which the American President patiently struggled to maintain peace, doing all he could to prevent a break in German-American relations. Unfortunately, nothing could be further from the truth. In the first twenty-one months of the war Wilson was not motivated primarily by a desire for peace; above all he wished to see the Allies victorious and did everything in his power to advance their interests. It was this as much as it was the crude actions of the German government which caused the United States to become involved in the war. Wilson probably felt that he could be partial to the Allies without any serious consequences, but he was mistaken. In the last analysis it was the unneutrality of the American government which forced the United States to enter the war. "We were unneutral and we paid the price."[78]

[78]*Ibid.*, 34.

CHAPTER X ☆ WHO KEPT US OUT OF WAR?

DURING the winter of 1915-16 the Wilson administration apparently was considering the desirability of entering the war. From the outset of hostilities various prominent Americans had urged such a course. As early as August, 1914, President Eliot of Harvard was advocating American participation. His excuse was that American help to the Allies would put an immediate stop to the conflict. Interestingly enough, Wilson gave serious consideration to the proposal, although of course he had to reply that public opinion would not support such a move.[1]

But Eliot's suggestion was only the first. At one time Secretary Lansing wrote to a friend: "You can have no idea of the pressure which is being brought to bear on this Government from various elements in this country in regard to our foreign relations."[2] By late summer of 1915 this pressure was even being exerted by Wilson's advisers. Lansing was urging war in August, stating that "our usefulness in the restoration of peace would certainly not be lessened by a state of war between this country and Germany, and it might even be increased."[3] In October Colonel House was expressing unhappiness over the fact that "we had lost our opportunity to break with Germany" and that "therefore we should do something decisive . . . that would bring us in with the Allies."[4]

There are indications that, as a result of the pressure from

[1]Baker, *op. cit.*, V, 69 ff.
[2]August 17, 1915, to A. M. Innes. From the Lansing Papers in the Library of Congress.
[3]Savage, *op. cit.*, II, 376. Document 115, August 24, 1915.
[4]*Intimate Papers*, II, 85.
SENATOR NYE: "It seems to the Chair that the record positively reveals that while our Government was pretending neutrality during those days, it was actually hoping for a break with Germany, inviting that sort of a break, and seems to have been in a frame of mind to welcome the break when it came."
SENATOR CLARK: "I do not think it is justifiable to say, so far as the record shows, that the Government was hoping for a break with Germany, but it was very clearly disclosed that Colonel House, who was acting as a sort of super Secretary of State, on several occasions wanted to have a break with Germany. This is disclosed very clearly by his notes." *M. I.*, Part 28, 8517.

the President's pro-British advisers and also the constant pressure of British propaganda in the American press, Wilson thought the United States should enter the war. He told Colonel House that "he had never been sure that we ought not to take part in the conflict, and if it seemed evident that Germany and her militaristic ideas were to win, the obligation upon us was greater than ever."[5]

At the time that Wilson started on his tour of the country to advocate preparedness, there was no reason for any great excitement. Naturally, British propagandists were rather puzzled by his alarmist speeches. They reported: "There is no evidence that his grave words indicate any new or sudden crisis," and "neither Republicans nor Democrats, with very few exceptions, desire war." Consequently, "if President Wilson were to go as far toward 'preparedness' as some of his recent speeches might suggest he would probably meet with trouble from [the] . . . great body of unorganized pacifists . . ." for "next to 'neutralism' . . . 'pacifism' is the strongest force in the country."[6] The truth of the matter was that the people and their President were not of one mind; the people fervently desired peace, and Wilson was willing to sacrifice peace in order to insure the defeat of Germany.

At this same time the *Lusitania* controversy "was dragged in by the scruff of the neck."[7] The State Department brought it forward suddenly demanding that Germany concede the illegality of her acts. In an interview with Ambassador Bernstorff, Secretary of State Lansing became very imperious in an apparent attempt to bring about a crisis. He even intimated "that further informal negotiations would be useless." Bernstorff was greatly perturbed and finally asked:

"And what would be your course in case my Government will not accede to these terms, which seem harsh?"

Lansing replied: "I see no other course, Mr. Ambassador, except to break off diplomatic relations."

---

[5]*Intimate Papers*, II, 84.

[6]*A. P. R.*, March 3, 1916. Bryan charged that Wilson was "joy-riding with the jingoes." Baker, *op. cit.*, VI, 38 f.

[7]". . . it was necessary to keep alive American disaffection towards Germany. One means of accomplishing this end was to press for an immediate settlement of the *Lusitania* dispute, and to make such demands upon Germany that compliance would be difficult." Tansill, *op. cit.*, 382.

Bernstorff then commented: "I do not see how the matter could stop with the breaking off of diplomatic relations. It would go further than that."

To which Lansing replied: "Doubtless you are correct in this view. I have given the matter most earnest consideration and have discussed it with the President, and I can assure you we do not hesitate to assume responsibility for what may occur in case your Government refuses to accede to our just demands."[8]

In inquiring about advantages to be gained by Germany in return for yielding to the American demands, Ambassador Bernstorff stated:

"As long as [the British] increase their illegal methods instead of relaxing them my Government will hardly be inclined to make any further concessions. Public opinion in Germany would not understand such concessions without any equivalent. I am afraid that if the case of the *Lusitania* is now pressed too much . . . the effect will be contrary to the one you desire. By such pressure my Government might be led to consider that the policy of concessions to the United States for the purpose of obtaining the . . . 'freedom of the seas' was wrong and that it would be better to return to a policy of severe reprisals against Great Britain's illegal blockade."[9]

The German Government for the time being practiced unusual restraint and avoided any acts which would have heightened the crisis. However, it did not give way to the American demands. The German Undersecretary of State for Foreign Affairs insisted that "Germany would not surrender the submarine weapon . . . [and] if the United States wanted a break, Germany could do nothing more to avoid it." He then went on to remark that "the most deplorable part of the whole matter was that there was no real reason for a break."[10] Bethmann-Hollweg also made a public statement in which he said: "I cannot concede a humiliation of Germany and the German people, or the wrenching of the submarine weapon from our hands. . . . There are some things I cannot do."

Elihu Root was right in stating that the American government

---

[8]Savage, *op. cit.*, II, 451. Document 162. January 25, 1916.
[9]*Ibid.*, 417 f.
[10]February 7, 1916, *Foreign Relations Supplement*, 1916, 160.

COUNT VON BERNSTORFF

was not doing so well in the controversy — it was too apparent
that it was a forced issue. However, Wilson was adamant. He did
ask Lansing to delay negotiations, but only "until a letter from
Colonel House arrived on a steamer leaving England on the nineteenth."[11] He remarked: "I have not the least idea what that
letter contains, but I do not think it would be prudent to take
any step towards a diplomatic break before we know what is in
it."[12]

When the message from House arrived, it urged that Wilson
avoid an immediate rupture of relations, stating: "The reason I
am so anxious that you do not break with Germany over the *Lusitania* is that any delay may make it possible to carry out the
original plan in regard to intervention (i.e., by means of a 'peace
conference'). And if this cannot be done because of Germany's
undersea warfare, then we will be forced in, in a way that will
give us the advantage."[13]

All during the month of February House was conferring with
British Cabinet members in an effort to induce them to adopt his
conference plan. On the twenty-second of the month Sir Edward
Grey initialed the agreement.

Meanwhile, in order to curb the trend toward war, bills were
introduced in Congress to warn Americans against taking passage on armed ships. Wilson was strongly opposed to these measures and on the twenty-first he called into conference from the
Senate and the House the majority leaders and the chairmen of
the Committees on Foreign Affairs. These were Senators Kern
and Stone and Representatives Kitchin and Flood. All attended
except Kitchin, who was detained by other duties.

One version of what happened is as follows: "The President
read to them a message which he had prepared and which was to
be dispatched to the German Government. When the reading was·
concluded, one member of the party propounded this question.
'After the delivery of this message, what will be the next step?'
The President answered, 'Germany will break off diplomatic relations.' Some one then asked, 'What will be the next step?' The
President is reported to have answered, 'War!' He then added,

[11]Lansing's *Memoirs*, 151.
[12]Savage, *op. cit.*, II, 477. January 25, 1916, Document 159.
[13]*Intimate Papers*, II, 147. February 3, 1916.

as the account runs, 'that war would not be an unmixed evil, that we would only send our navy to Europe, the war could be ended by midsummer and that we would render a service to civilization, etc., etc.'[14]

"When the President had concluded . . . [Senator Stone] arose [and] emphasizing his remarks by pounding upon the table, said, 'Mr. President, I have followed you in support of your foreign policies, I have followed you when I thought you were right, I have followed you when I doubted your course, I followed you when I did not altogether agree with you, but By God, I do not intend to follow you into this war.' A dramatic silence followed . . . and after a few moments the party filed out."

Part of these remarks of Senator Gore are confirmed in a recently published letter in which a friend of Representative Flood wrote as follows: "I remember Mr. Flood's saying that he and others in the conference asked the President what we, the United States, would do in case we did get in the war, and he said the President replied: 'Well, we will lend the Allies some money and send a few ships over there and wind up the war.' "[15]

Mr. Gore's interpretation of what happened in the conference between the President and the leaders of the two Houses has been strongly questioned by students of the period. It would seem likely that there are errors in his version. One very important one possibly lies in the motivation for the dispute. Where Gore states that "the President read to them a message which he had prepared and which was to be dispatched to the German Government," one is left to believe that the President intended to send the message in order deliberately to provoke the Germans. What probably happened, however, was that the President read a message which he was to send to Germany in case any further action on the part of Germany created a crisis.[16] "What Wilson actually said may forever remain in doubt, but the impression which he gave to his conferees will not." It is certain that the President

[14]Note the similarity of this statement to the advice of President Eliot to Wilson at the outbreak of the war. A friend of Senator Stone has described his categorical denial of Wilson's desire to go to war as "a negative pregnant" as the lawyers say. Senator Gore to the author.

[15]Judge E. Yates to Arnett, November 28, 1935. Kitchin collection. As quoted in Arnett, *op. cit.*, 190.

[16]See Tansill, *op. cit.*, 465.

stopped "speaking English and talked United States." Many of
his words were "not of the sort that fall usually from Presidential
lips."[17] " 'Confidentially,' wrote Kitchin, 'I think the President
is anxious for war with Germany — his sympathies are so strong
with the Allies. . . . I fear . . . [that he] is going to watch for the
first opportunity to strike at Germany and involve this country
in world-wide war. . . . It seems to me a crime against civilization
and humanity for this Christian nation to plunge into the war
and make a slaughter house of the whole world.' "[18] A number of
senators and representatives felt "that the President was pursuing a course too drastic and dangerous, and that he was leading
the country into war."[19]

Although no verifiable report of the interview has been made
public, it is quite clear that Mr. Wilson was not in a peaceful
frame of mind. In the newspapers the meeting was described as
stormy. " 'Perhaps the President talked too frankly,' said David
Lawrence in the New York *Evening Post,* 'or those who saw him
were somewhat indiscreet, but little by little the strong words of
the President got back to Congress generally and yesterday afternoon there was a flurry.' *Flurry* was not the word. *Revolt* it was
mildly called in the *Times,* which reported: 'Veteran legislators
said tonight that not for many years had they seen a situation so
dramatic and sensational.' "[20] "When they returned to their offices on Capitol Hill, Senator Stone was still so excited that he
walked down the corridor of the Senate Office Building 'swearing
like a trooper.' "[21] Members of both parties were "meeting in
excited conferences. When Kitchin learned of what had been said
at the White House, he asked at once for another group-confer-
ence with the President. In fact, White House conferences on the
subject were almost daily, sometimes hourly, occurrences for a
fortnight thereafter."[22]

[17]The New York *Times,* February 24, 1916, as quoted by Tansill, 466.
[18]Kitchin to Rev. Charles H. Nash, February 29, 1916. His position was
stated in the Greensboro *Daily News,* February 25, 29. As quoted in Arnett, *op.
cit.,* 161.
[19]Lawrence, *op. cit.,* 192.
[20]Arnett, *op. cit.,* 159 f.
[21]Tansill, *op. cit.,* 466.
[22]Kitchin to Joseph E. Pogue and to D. T. Wade, February 28, 1916; Greensboro *Daily News,* February 22-26; New York *Evening Post,* February 22, 24,
March 2; New York *Evening Sun,* February 22, 24, March 2. Arnett, *op. cit.,* 160.

On February 24 "it was reported in the press that 'leaders of the House of Representatives virtually served notice on President Wilson this afternoon that unless within forty-eight hours he agreed to warn American citizens that they must not take passage on armed belligerent merchant ships . . . the House by an overwhelming majority would issue the warning in the form of a resolution.' "[23]

"On the afternoon of the 24th, Speaker Clark telephoned to Tumulty that 'the Speaker, Leader Kitchin, and Chairman Flood would like to call on the President as soon as possible to discuss with him the state of affairs' in the House. The President made an appointment for them on the following morning, February 25th, at nine o'clock. It was an uncommonly early hour for official Washington in winter; but Wilson wished to have the conference out of the way before the cabinet met at eleven o'clock. . . . Considering the strong impression it made upon the three congressmen, the conference must have been one of fire and power."[24]

At this second meeting — the "Sunrise Conference" — Wilson reaffirmed his opposition to any abrogation of American rights. As a result, the maintenance of peace seemed to depend upon the action of Germany in carrying out her recently declared "cruiser warfare." This was probably the point which had caused the heated argument in the first conference.

The congressmen became more and more determined to get a measure adopted which would eliminate the possibility of additional trouble over the submarine. "Among various resolutions which had been introduced [in the House of Representatives] there was one which was known to be widely objectionable even among those who favored a warning."[25] This measure, the McLemore Resolution, was apparently chosen because it could be more easily defeated. "Kitchin sought in vain . . . to get a simple,

[23]Baker, *op. cit.*, VI, 166 f.

[24]*Ibid.*, 169 f.

"Champ Clark, Flood, and myself, did have, early one morning, between seven and eight o'clock, *such a conference with the President. At that time he seemed anxious to go to war with Germany immediately. This was in April 1916.*" Italics Arnett's. Kitchin to Claudy, April 2, 1921. As quoted in Arnett, *op. cit.*, 189.

[25]Kitchin to D. A. and W. H. Fishel, March 5; to R. J. Markoe, March 11; to William A. Lucas, March 7, 1916. As quoted in Arnett, *op. cit.*, 174.

straightforward resolution of warning presented; but the above was the only one that the Committee on Rules would report, and the Committee of Foreign Affairs would not report any at all.[26] McLemore himself, when he learned of the objections to his preamble and to a portion of his resolution, 'appeared before the Rules Committee and asked it to strike out all except the warning feature,' but without avail."[27]

The debate which ensued over this resolution and the one introduced by T. P. Gore of Oklahoma[28] in the Senate represented the most vigorous attempt on the part of American pacifists to keep the United States out of the bloody shambles in Europe. For days both houses of Congress engaged in furious controversy. Almost everyone gave at least one speech. In defending his measure, Mr. McLemore reflected the thinking of many of his colleagues. He stated: "The present English plea that an English ship is to be allowed to tote a gun and yet not be considered a fighting ship, is to be allowed all the advantages of armament but be exempt from all the penalties, does not impress my American mind. And if I suspect that England seeks to hide behind the coat tails of Uncle Sam, seeks to lure Americans on her armed ships as they sail out, hoping and praying that they may pot a submarine, and then expects America to step in and do her fighting for her if an American citizen loses his life, then I am quick to resent that conduct, and to resent it to the best of my ability. . . .

"The only answer the English seem to give, when cornered with the question is that Germany cannot be trusted to play fairly. That sounds to me very much like an unmanly whine. I feel very fully convinced that the world is quite tired of the English device of blackguarding her enemies, of calling them names, and spreading about them stories which, for the credit of humanity, I am glad to note have been time after time disproved."[29]

[26]Kitchin to D. A. and W. H. Fishel, March 5, 1916. As quoted in Arnett, *op. cit.*, 177.

[27]Kitchin to H. Q. Alexander, March 9, 1916. As quoted in Arnett, *op. cit.*, 178.

[28]"The Gore Resolution prohibited the issuance of passports to American citizens taking passage on belligerent vessels, and denied protection to those taking such passage without a passport." Borchard and Lage, *op. cit.*, 114.

[29]McLemore quoted from the British Order in Council of August 5, 1914, that "a ship of war shall include an armed ship." He also quoted captured confidential instructions of the British Admiralty in which "it is made manifest there-

Congressman Mondell, among the many other speakers for the resolution, said, "When anyone fully informed contends that an American citizen has a right which should not be denied, curtailed or abridged, to travel on a ship armed to fight, purposed to fight, proposing to fight, and bound into the regions of war ... [he] is either playing politics with the national honor or is disposed to embroil the Nation in war."

The debate in the Senate over Gore's resolution followed very much the same lines as that in the House of Representatives. Senator Norris warned: "The President is leading toward war and Congress is holding back, trying to keep the country at peace. The object of warning our people to keep off of armed vessels is to maintain peace. I fear the course of the President will lead our country into war. . . ."[30]

"Some reporter got hold of the fact that Hamilton Fish, Jr., had wired to Mann and Longworth: 'Thought you would like to know that John Bassett Moore is opposed to President Wilson on the question of armed merchantmen, on the ground that a submarine is a belligerent warship and has the right of visit and search and that guns on merchantmen are for the purpose of defending themselves against the given right of visit and search. He believes in warning Americans.' "[31]

But the partisans of the Allies refused to acknowledge defeat. The President, his advisers, and all the wild-eyed editors of Eastern newspapers flew to the support of those jingoes desirous of maintaining American rights. "Wilson at first demanded that no warning resolution be permitted to come to the floor. He had several conferences with Senator Stone, chairman of the Committee on Foreign Relations in the Senate, and with Representa-

---

from that armed ships do not wait for any actions of German submarines under the laws of the sea, but are to attack them without further ado."

McLemore presented one very interesting argument of the idea back of the arming of merchant ships. He states: "But such ships must not refuse to halt if hailed by an enemy warship and must not resist the exercise of the right of visit and search. If England agrees to that law, as she does, and if England maintains that in arming her merchant ships she does not intend them to violate that law, and she does so maintain, then can any man tell me why England insists on arming such ships?" Hale, *op. cit.*, 71.

[30]*Ibid.*, 43.

[31]New York *Evening Post*, March 7, 1916. As quoted in Arnett, *op. cit.*, 156.

tive Flood, chairman of the Committee on Foreign Affairs in the House. He seems to have urged upon them, first that an open breach between the President and his Congress would certainly be unfavorable and possibly disastrous to the Democrats in the coming election. In fact, he was reported in the press to have said that he would refuse to be a candidate for re-election if Congress failed to support his position in this matter. . . . It is interesting to note how Republican papers, usually condemnatory of Wilson, fervidly came to his side in this matter, and how Democratic papers, prevailingly militant, damned all Democratic Congressmen who refused to take orders from the President."[32] An article in the New York *Times* on March 5, 1916, entitled "The Flag On the Capitol" stated, "It seems as if the Congress . . . [were] ready to haul down the American flag from the capitol, spit on it, run the black, white, and red up in its place."

The principal support of the British in this attempt to stop the American pacifists was given by the President. On February 24 he wrote to Senator Stone: "If the clear rights of American citizens should ever unhappily be abridged or denied by such action, we should, it seems to me, have in honor no choice as to what our own course should be. For my own part, I can not consent to any abridgement of the rights of American citizens in any respect. The honor and self-respect of the nation is involved." This letter reveals the old effective appeal to honor and right — an appeal as old as politics although seldom so carelessly used. The Kingdom of the Netherlands maintained its honor, rights, and peace, but still placed "armed merchantmen on the same footing and under the same restrictions as men-of-war, in accordance with the law that had immemorially prevailed, as declared by our own Supreme Court . . . in the case of the *Nereide*."[33]

On February 29 President Wilson cracked the party whip and drove Democrats to cover. He demanded an immediate vote on the McLemore Resolution. Due to this pressure, the Democrats had to reverse their stand and defeat the bill. Even people who had spoken in favor of the measure voted against it. The 1916 election was coming, and as 1912 had proved, a divided

[32]Arnett, *op. cit.*, 163, 164.
[33]*Ibid.*, 156.

party could win no elections. The Democratic Congressmen discarded their convictions and voted for their jobs.

In the Senate the Gore Resolution met the same fate. Although there were some rather devious political maneuvers in connection with the vote, they only served to confuse an otherwise clear issue.[34] Senator Vardaman has stated: "If the resolutions proposed by the Senator from Oklahoma had been adopted by the Congress as it was originally introduced, in my judgment, the probabilities of war would have vanished as a nightmare from the troubled brain of innocence." With the failure of these two resolutions there disappeared the last hope for American peace.[35]

Sir Gilbert Parker reported to the British Cabinet that if the President of the United States had not fought the measure, it "might have turned out most unfavorably to Great Britain."[36] Others agree that without Wilson's support, the Anglophiles could not have defeated these resolutions. As Senator Gore has remarked, when Wilson gave the word, those in command of the two Houses ran the steam roller over the opposition. The McLemore Resolution was defeated by 276 to 142. There were 183 Democrats and 93 Republicans who voted against the bill while 35 Democrats and 107 Republicans voted for it.[37] The vote tells almost the entire story. In spite of the fact that most of the jingoistic comments in Congress were coming from the Republican side of the House, these advocates of war still could not command a majority of their own party. On the other hand, although these resolutions were Democratic in origin, and had had the support of most of the Democratic leaders, when the vote was taken it was the Democrats who defeated them. It was only by forcing the members of his own party into line that Wilson was able to defeat the measures.

It is impossible to read the speeches in connection with the debates in Congress over these measures without feeling that the sentiment there was decidedly against entering the war. Unfortunately, only a few members of Congress had a full realization

[34]*Ibid.*, 171 ff.
[35]Borchard and Lage, *op. cit.*, 116.
[36]*A. P. R.*, March 3, 1916.
[37]The Gore Resolution in the Senate was tabled by a vote of 68 to 14.

of the meaning of the resolutions. They closed their eyes to the fact that failure of the bills meant the end of American peace.

Champ Clark said at the time of the McLemore debate that the true feeling of the House was two to one against travel by Americans on armed ships.[38] A recent writer has stated that all the Democratic leaders and two-thirds of the members of both Houses favored such a resolution,[39] while a newspaperman of that day remarked that the advantage was about four to one in favor of the measure. The truth of the matter was that Congress, as well as the public, wished steps to be taken which would eliminate the possibility of the United States being involved in the European struggle. But Wilson and the newspapers were shouting against unpatriotic people who were willing to surrender American rights. The President and the press were not reflecting the will of the public and by waving the flag managed to defeat that will.

After these two bills had been defeated, Robert N. Page, a member of Congress, issued an open letter stating, "Where your treasure is, there will your heart be also. The loan of $500,000,-000 to England [sic] by American capitalists, to say nothing of the profits of munitions manufacturers, has destroyed the semblance even of neutrality in the United States and will probably lead us into war." A few days later the New York *Times* ran a cartoon in which Page appeared as a "shade of Benedict Arnold." The logic is not clear, but at least it explains the position of the *Times*.

The individuals in the United States who were espousing the cause of American entrance into the war said that the people opposing Wilson in the armed ship controversy were pro-German. But the British propagandists did not think so. One of them reported: "It is quite untrue to say that this opposition to the President is mainly pro-German. . . . It is the more or less representative expression of the 'pacifist' sentiment, which is a genuine American article, and is very prevalent both in the agricultural districts of the Middle West and in the Far West as a whole."[40] As one of Woodrow Wilson's advisers later expressed it, "there

[38]Lawrence, *op. cit.*, 196.
[39]Arnett, *op. cit.*, 159.
[40]*A. P. R.*, March 3, 1916.

... [was] no time when either his cabinet, the Houses of Congress, or the people, would have supported him in a declaration of war against Germany."[41] The same thought was expressed by Roosevelt who wrote to Lodge stating, "The melancholy thing is the apparently general feeling of satisfaction with Wilson so long as he keeps us out of war." A little later he said, "I am so out of sympathy with what seems to be the prevailing currents of American opinion."[42]

On March 24 a new crisis arose over the attack on the channel steamer, *Sussex*. The boat was not American, and Wilson wrote Lansing that "the proof that the disaster was caused by a torpedo seems to me by no means satisfactory or conclusive."[43] In spite of the uncertainty surrounding the incident, Wilson's advisers were in favor of using it to force the issue with Germany. Lansing, of course, had been advocating a break for some time[44] and

[41]Herron, George D., *Woodrow Wilson and the World's Peace* (New York, 1917), 62.

[42]*Selections from the Correspondence of Theodore Roosevelt and Henry Cabot Lodge, 1884-1918*, II (New York, 1925), 463, 471.

[43]Savage, *op. cit.*, II, 470, Document 177.

"One might well wonder whether the British Government purposely exposed to attack the *Lusitania* and other British passenger vessels carrying American citizens, in order to lead the Germans on to a rash act which might bring the United States into the war.... The same exposure, possibly deliberate, was true in the case of the unarmed cross-channel passenger steamer, *Sussex*.... It was lumbering along, without escort, through a sea littered with the wreckage of recently torpedoed vessels." Bemis, Samuel F., *A Diplomatic History of the United States* (New York, 1936), 610.

"In the journal of Lieutenant Pustkuchen, commander of the *UB-29*, there is a short description of the events leading up to the torpedoing of the *Sussex*. Shortly after 3:30 P.M., on March 24, the *UB-29*, descried a ship that resembled a passenger steamer. This boat, however, had only one funnel and it was equipped with a bridge similar to those carried by warships. It was not following the route prescribed by British Admiralty for merchant ships. Moreover, it did not carry any flag and it was painted entirely in black." Admiral Arno Spindler, *La Guerre Sous-Marine*, III, 170-171, as cited in Tansill, *op. cit.*, 492. "... but in the case of the *Sussex* the usual insignia were missing and the U-boat commander decided to torpedo it without warning." Tansill, *op. cit.*, 492.

[44]As soon as Senator Stone heard of the sinking of the *Sussex*, he wrote to Lansing pleading that no belligerent steps be taken which would result in the American Congress being faced with a *fait accompli*. Lansing replied: "I am in receipt of your letter of today in regard to the alleged torpedoing of the *Sussex* and other vessels and can assure you that I will talk the matter over with you before any definite steps are taken by the Department." March 28, 1916, in the Lansing Papers, Library of Congress.

tried to persuade the President that this was the proper moment. Colonel House stepped in with a new left-handed scheme for entering the war which made even less sense than his first plan. He later confessed that this new idea was "not even good nonsense." It is interesting to note that at this time Wilson did even reconsider the old House-Grey conference plan.

The President finally decided to resolve the crisis by sending an ultimatum to Germany. This note, one of the stiffest he ever wrote, was dispatched on April 18, 1916. It stated that about eighty of the *Sussex's* passengers, "including citizens of the United States, were killed or injured." This was a false statement; no Americans were killed, and only two were injured.[45] Of these one was a music student from Brooklyn, and the other, a Rhodes Scholar.[46] In conclusion the note stated: "Unless the Imperial Government should now immediately declare and effect an abandonment of its present methods of submarine warfare against passenger and freight-carrying vessels, the Government of the United States can have no choice but to sever diplomatic relations with the German Empire altogether." Using the same procedure he followed in 1917, Wilson spoke before a joint session of Congress on the nineteenth advising the members of his action. Apparently expecting a break in relations he asked Page to inquire, confidentially, "the wishes of the British Government, in regard to British representation in Berlin in the event of a severance of relations between the United States and Germany."[47]

On the twentieth the German Ambassador called at the State Department in an effort to avert the impending crisis. He informed Lansing: "I had to telegraph my Government that this Government seemed to offer little opportunity for settlement. . . . Our enemies violate all the rules and you insist on their being applied to Germany." To this Lansing had the customary reply: "You must appreciate that we care more for the lives of our people than we do for the property." In answer Bernstorff remarked,

[45]It was almost a year later that Lansing wrote to the President warning him of his mistake, remarking that no Americans had lost their lives and only one had been injured. April 5, 1917, The Lansing Papers, Library of Congress.

[46]A year earlier Sir Gilbert Parker had quoted the San Francisco *Chronicle* as follows: "Are the lives of American soldiers as sacred as the lives of American tourists?" *A. P. R.*, August 18, 1915.

[47]*F. R. S.*, 1916, p. 241.

"We have the same difficulty — our people are getting to care more for lives."[48]

On the twenty-fifth the German Ambassador interviewed Colonel House. ". . . Bernstorff asked House the question: If we accede to your demands, will the American government 'bring pressure upon Great Britain in regard to the blockade?' "[49] The latter advised him to tell his government not to send a note suggesting a compromise, and, above all, not to raise any question in regard to the blockade. He stated the only safe course to pursue would be to advise the German Government to agree to discontinue submarine warfare pending negotiations. This the Ambassador said he would do at once. . . ."[50]

On April 28 Gerard met the Kaiser and Chancellor. The question was asked: "Would America try to bring peace if Germany met the demands? Gerard was encouraging." While these negotiations were going on Wilson apparently became more and more indignant. On May 3 he talked with House about Germany's part in starting the war and remarked that "those guilty should have personal punishment."[51] In this case the origins propaganda was effective almost to the point of a decision for war.

In order to maintain peace, the Germans finally gave way. Their note of May 4, 1916, is in part as follows:

"The German Government . . . notifies the Government of the United States that the German naval forces have received the following orders: In accordance with the general principles of visit and search and destruction of merchant vessels recognized by international law, such vessels, both within and without the area declared as naval war zone, shall not be sunk without warning and without saving human lives, unless these ships attempt to escape or offer resistance.

"But neutrals can not expect that Germany, forced to fight for her existence, shall, for the sake of neutral interest, restrict the use of an effective weapon if her enemy is permitted to continue to apply at will methods of warfare violating the rules of international law. Such a demand would be incompatible with the

---

[48]Savage, *op. cit.*, II, 480 ff. Document 183.
[49]Baker, *op. cit.*, VI, 192.
[50]*M. I.*, Part 28, 8658.
[51]*Intimate Papers*, II, 239.

character of neutrality, and the German Government is convinced that the Government of the United States does not think of making such a demand, knowing that the Government of the United States has repeatedly declared that it is determined to restore the principle of the freedom of the seas, from whatever quarter it has been violated."[52]

The German note then stated that in consequence of these concessions on their part, they would expect "the Government of the United States . . . [to] demand and insist that the British Government shall forthwith observe the rules of international law. . . . Should the steps taken by the Government of the United States not attain the object it desires, to have the laws of humanity followed by all belligerent nations, the German Government would then be facing a new situation in which it must reserve its complete liberty of decision."[53]

It will be seen that the German government did not surrender completely but merely left matters pending expecting the United States to exert pressure against the British in order to force them to comply with international law.

The German retreat was a smashing diplomatic victory for the American President, but Lansing was not satisfied. He wrote to Wilson that "while I think our note in reply to that of the German Government should be polite, I feel we should omit any expression of relief on having avoided a break with Germany."[54] He also suggested that the reply be made shorter, apparently in line with his general policy of being curt to the Germans.

It was fortunate for Wilson that the Germans gave way. He had gone so far that he could not have retreated without suffering an overwhelming diplomatic defeat. And neither Congress nor the people would have supported him to the extent of going to war over either the sinking of the *Lusitania* or the attack upon the *Sussex*. Secretary of State Lansing wrote to a friend that "the President would have been defeated had he tried to obtain action after either case almost as certainly as night follows day."[55] The

[52]*F. R. S.*, 1916 *Supplement*, 259.
[53]*Ibid.*, 259.
[54]Lansing's *Memoirs*, 143 f.
[55]Lansing to Ed Smith, April 7, 1917, in the Lansing Papers.

British propaganda ministry reported its opinion in almost the same words.

The tumultous events in the first few months of 1916 reveal that the President and his advisers were apparently considering entering the war. It was not, however, a German threat or deed, but the anti-German attitude of mind, which prompted their course of action. The government of the United States had not suffered any great injury; nothing had happened which was overly serious; there was no particular occasion for excitement. The recurring crises in the months from January to April have the appearance of being artificial. In actuality they represented the materialization of British economic pressure, censorship, and formal propaganda.

By April, 1916, nearly all American leaders had been captured and changed from passive to active supporters of the Allies. Over a year was to pass before pressure on public opinion was successful in stirring the more inert mass of the people to join in the cry for war.

PART II ☆ THE LAST YEAR OF PEACE

CHAPTER XI ☆ PROPAGANDA OF THE LAST YEAR OF NEUTRALITY

IN the last year of neutrality British propagandists pursued the same policies which had been formulated at the time they began their work. Wellington House increased its output greatly, issuing approximately two hundred publications in 1916 and four hundred in 1917. The Central Committee for National Patriotic Organizations continued its work along expanding lines. A new organization, the National War Aims Committee, was formed for the purpose of combating the growing pacifist agitation throughout the world. The latter was well supplied with funds from the government, having more than half a million pounds appropriated for its use. By the end of 1917 it had published more than five million pamphlets.

In spite of the success of British propaganda, there apparently arose within government circles considerable dissatisfaction with results being obtained. Charteris wrote at the time that "there seems to be great confusion as to who is responsible" for propaganda.[1] Others contended that the various organizations were inefficient and unable to distribute their material with the requisite speed. These criticisms in reality indicated a behind-the-scene struggle among British leaders to obtain control of the propaganda machine. "The potency of the new engine of warfare was abundantly demonstrable, and powerful figures were seeking opportunities for manipulating its levers."[2] Late in the summer of 1916 Lord Newton was temporarily placed over Masterman, at Wellington House, but he was not particularly successful. With Grey's fall in December, 1916, the importance of Masterman steadily declined, and either at the end of that year, or at the beginning of the next, he was replaced by John Buchan.[3]

Buchan, the Director of Information, reorganized the propaganda work, merging most of the private and semi-private groups

[1] Charteris, *op. cit.*, 157. July 22, 1916.
[2] Squires, *op. cit.*, 34.
[3] The later Lord Tweedsmuir, Governor General of Canada. See Bruntz, G. G., *Allied Propaganda and the Collapse of the German Empire* (Stanford, 1938).

into one central organization called the Department of Information. This Department he subdivided into four bureaus. The first of these, Wellington House, continued its old work of producing and distributing propaganda. The second was a new bureau formed to take charge of the cinema and the entertainment of foreign visitors. The third, the political intelligence department, gathered evidence on the state of public opinion throughout the world. The last, the press bureau, dressed up the news for presentation to the public.

This new centralized organization, at first under the control of the Foreign Office, but later transferred to the War Department, was directed by an advisory committee composed of Lord Northcliffe, Lord Burnham, Mr. Robert Donald, Mr. C. P. Scott, and later, Lord Beaverbrook.[4] It is impossible, of course, to estimate the total expenditures of this organization,[5] but by 1917 it was spending money at the rate of £750,000 a year[6] and asked for £1,800,000 for 1918.[7] The work of Wellington House in the United States continued until the report was received late in 1917 that Americans were determined to take an active part in the war.[8]

The question constantly arises as to whether the British propaganda organization had representatives in the United States comparable to those of the German government. The answer is that there were agents in this country but that their work was not so important to England as the German propagandists' efforts had been to the Central Powers.[9] The Oxford professor, Gilbert

[4]Squires, op. cit., 36. As a result of friction, Sir Edward Carson was put over Buchan early in the autumn of 1917. The final change came in February, 1918, when the Department of Information was abolished. Lord Beaverbrook was then placed in charge of a Ministry of Information. He obtained this as a result of the success of his propaganda in Canada. In 1918 Crewe House was founded under Lord Northcliffe. This organization was devoted to the handling of propaganda within the enemy's lines. A. P. R., January 3, 1917.

In one of the reports of Wellington House under "Intercepted Letters" is given "An American Suggestion for British Propaganda" which was that the British prepare propaganda for German soldiers and drop it behind the German lines from balloons and airplanes. D. R. F. P. Confidential Supplement, December 16, 1916.

[5]"Our propaganda, costing I dare not tell the House how much...." Hansard 5th series, CIV, column 122, March 11, 1918.

[6]Squires, op. cit., 38.

[7]H. C. 132, 36-37, 59-60. As quoted by Squires, op. cit., 38.

[8]Note the comments in A. P. R., of April 11, 1917, et seq.

[9]New York Herald, November 8, 1916. The American Committee on Public Information, set up on April 14, 1917, under George Creel, took care of prop-

Murray, the poet, John Masefield, and others of similar distinction were sent here to report on American opinion and to carry on some propaganda. There were also less prominent people such as a certain Dr. Carlisle who was decorated both by the English and Belgian governments for his "aid in creating sympathy with the aims of the Allies." In February, 1916, Wellington House reported having sent an agent to Washington to obtain information. Later the *American Press Résumé* stated that "our main point of action must be at Washington."[10] In November, 1916, Sir Edward Grey asked Jusserand whether he had changed his mind about handling some of the money being spent for propaganda in the United States.[11] This would seem to indicate that there were also propaganda agents operating from the British Embassy in Washington. After the United States entered the war, the number of agents in this country increased by leaps and bounds. The *Times* of London of November, 1917, stated that there were five hundred officials and ten thousand assistants comprising the British War Mission in the United States. The French and Belgians had similar organizations.

It must be remembered, of course, that these individuals had no great responsibility or importance. There was simply no necessity for the British to engage in the dangerous practice of sending very many propagandists into the field. Such work could be done more effectively at the source of news, that is, in London, or through volunteer American propagandists, who were carrying on the work in the United States for Great Britain.

In spite of French expressions of their innocence as far as propaganda in the United States was concerned, they were also carrying on an intensive campaign. "M. Jusserand's collaborators, secretaries of the embassy and consulates, occasional travelers, and anonymous envoys from France, all followed the same course. Throughout great cities and little villages, towns radiating from the Pacific, smoky centers of the Middle West, land of

aganda work for the United States. A great deal of money was spent, undoubtedly much of it effectively, but Creel's organization is not to be compared with that of Masterman and Sir Gilbert Parker. The volume of propaganda was greatly increased and the technique of distribution was improved but there was no great improvement in the propaganda itself.

[10] *A. P. R.,* May 31, 1916.

[11] Jusserand, *op. cit.,* 69.

Louisiana, and of Pennsylvania, the French gospel resounded. Without fanfare, without announcement, without even the transatlantic cables knowing it, it made itself heard everywhere.

"Almost every evening during the winter which preceded American entrance into the war, one could witness such a scene: in a club, a theatre, a gymnasium, or, most often in a church, the French envoy would come and tell why France fought and bled."[12]

By the middle of 1916 the principal propaganda work in the United States was in the hands of Americans. Anglo-Americans and ordinary Anglophiles from New Haven to San Francisco were doing all in their power to assist the British cause.[13] One of the many American visitors to Europe who had been under Parker's supervision, wrote to him as follows: "Since my return to Richmond I have been kept busy making speeches" to give Americans "a proper appreciation of the aims of the Allies. I hope that my efforts . . . may do some good."[14] One worker for the Allies wrote to a prominent publisher: "I do appreciate the excellent work you are doing in arousing our people and wish you could go to Denver and San Francisco. They need light in the West badly."[15]

The American workers took advantage of every opportunity in order to push the country further and further into the maelstrom. When Major-General Hugh Scott recommended a conscript army, the measure was given widespread support by writers and public speakers who, in the next breath, were condemning the militarism of Germany. In January, 1917, when George Wharton Pepper circulated a petition against a premature peace, many

[12]Lauzanne, Stephane, *Les hommes que j'ai vus — Souvenirs d'un journaliste* (Paris, 1920), 159 f.

At the beginning of 1917 all the French propaganda organizations were consolidated into the "union des grandes associations françaises contre la propagande ennemie" under Ernest Lavisse and Paul Deschanel.

After the United States was in the war, a M. Stephane Lauzanne and a M. Knecht were in charge of French propaganda in the United States. Jusserand, *op. cit.*, 120.

[13]At one time Wellington House mentions "a distinguished and influential British-American citizen of San Francisco who has steadfastly corresponded with Sir Gilbert Parker since the beginning of the war." *A. P. R.*, October 18, 1916.

[14]*A. P. R.*, January 10, 1917.

[15]The Wheeler Papers, December 3, 1916.

preachers and religious journals such as the *Churchman*, gave him hearty support.

The compulsory removal, or deportation of the Belgians to work on German farms and in factories caused great opposition in the United States. Wellington House was pleased to report that there had been a large anti-deportation meeting in Philadelphia and that "other meetings of protest have been held in most of the eastern cities."[16] William R. Thayer, a follower of Theodore Roosevelt, sent the following telegram to certain important Americans: We "are circulating petition supporting President in any steps behalf Belgians even to breaking diplomatic relations. Are telegraphing him sentiment of huge Boston meeting. Will you also telegraph or write. . . ."[17] On April 17, 1916, "An Address to the People of the Allied Nations," signed by eight hundred prominent American citizens, was issued in Boston. This document was an outspoken repudiation of neutrality which openly ranged these American leaders on the side of the Allies, and even intimated their willingness to take up arms.

The principal outlet for British propaganda in the United States continued to be the American press. All in all there were probably well over ten thousand writers — Americans — who were preaching the Allies' cause in newspapers, as well as in books, pamphlets, and magazines. In the words of Ambassador Jusserand, "Ce fut une floraison comme on ne vit jamais la pareille."[18] The regular weekly reports which Parker made to the British Cabinet clearly reveal his satisfaction with the assistance being given him by American newspapermen. The following excerpts are typical of that section of his report entitled, "Influencing the American Press":

"May 31: The American press as a whole is friendly to the Allies and is anxious to give our point of view.

"July 26: The American press . . . made the most of the news communicated to it, and showed itself very ready to take up any hints in the official communiqués, both as to the significance of particular events and as to the general course of the movement.

---

[16]*A. P. R.*, January 31, 1917.
[17]Henry Watterson papers, December 10, 1916.
[18]Jusserand, *op. cit.*, 49.

"August 23: The current week is remarkable for the large number of interviews from British sources.

"September 6: The headlines of newspapers of all shades of opinion have been remarkably open to the military operations of the Allies.

"October 11: The week supplies satisfactory evidence of the permeation of the American press by British influence. . . ."

In spite of the fact that almost all American newsmen were acting (even if, in many cases, unconsciously) as British propagandists, there were occasional members of the American fourth estate who refused to be conscripted to fight the British battle. The outstanding slacker was William Randolph Hearst.[19] To the immense chagrin of the British this publisher did not give that unswerving loyalty to Britain which was characteristic of the New York *Times* and most other American papers. Consequently there must have been many discussions in London as to what to do with this bad boy of the American press. Inasmuch as the ordinary pressure and propaganda did not affect Mr. Hearst, the British found it necessary to adopt more stringent measures. Early in 1916 they apparently delivered a veiled threat to him through a British subject who had been writing articles for the Hearst papers. In reply to this threat Mr. Hearst wrote to his London agent, Mr. W. Orten Tewson, attempting to justify his policies. Sir Gilbert Parker obtained this letter from Mr. Tewson, and included it in his regular weekly report to the Cabinet.[20] The letter is as follows:

My dear Mr. Tewson:

I was much interested in your correspondence with Mr. ————. I don't know whether I ought to be more amused or amazed at his attitude.

It would seem, according to his (ideas?) that my publications have not been sufficiently pro-Ally, and, in order to correct this difficulty, the pro-Ally authors are to cease writing for me.

If I am *against* the Allies, I cannot see where the common sense of his attitude comes in.

[19] *Supra,* 164 ff.

[20] "The following letter from Mr. W. R. Hearst . . . describes his attitude to the war and the cause of the Allies. Mr. Tewson is the permanent correspondent of the Hearst service in England, and has given permission for the use of this letter in this Résumé. We believe this is a fair Statement. . . ." *A. P. R.,* May 25, 1916.

As a matter of fact I am not pro-Ally or pro-German; I am not in favor of those who began the war, or those who unnecessarily protract the war. I think the war is the crowning crime of history, the uttermost imbecility of which the human race is capable.

I am glad that our American people have had intelligence enough and humanity enough to keep out of the war.

I do not sympathize with the homicidal mania of *either* side. I do sympathize most deeply with the thousands of brave men who are being slaughtered in this needless, useless, purposeless war. Regardless of my personal convictions or predilections, however, I believe it is my duty as a publisher to keep our people informed of the acts and utterances of *both* sides.

Mr. Hearst then gave a long list of authors whose pro-Ally articles he had published.[21]

Obviously, therefore, there neither is, nor has been any lack of pro-Ally propaganda in our publications, and through our publications, appeal is made to about twenty million readers.

I have assumed, and I have been directly informed by government and other authorities, that the Allies desire their propaganda distributed through my newspapers, magazines, and other media of distribution.

Mind you, I am not being paid to distribute this propaganda, nor naturally would I consent to do it for pay.

On the contrary, it is I who have paid for the propaganda; paid for its publication and for its distribution. . . .

Now comes the Honorable Hotair ———, expert in strategy and authority on diplomacy, and proposes strategically and diplomatically to amend this situation by denying me the proud privilege of performing these confessed and conspicuous services to the Allies' cause.

The tactical proposition to benefit the Allies' cause by (eliminating?) their propaganda, and to punish me by depriving me of the privilege of paying for their propaganda, is an idea which surpasses in originality anything I have ever seen in any other of Mr. ———'s writings. . . .

Mr. ——— inaugurates his 'spring drive' to influence the public opinion of the United States in the direction of the Allies by proposing to deprive this large proportion of the press and people of the United States of pro-Ally propaganda. This strategic con-

[21]*Supra*, 166.

ception of the successor of Jomini, is enough to cause that departed general to rotate rapidly in his grave.

The London ———— recently published an article, in an apparent effort to surpass in extravagance and ignorance the article which appeared in ————. This . . . article declared that Bryan and I were conspiring to oppose President Wilson, and that I had been moved by our pro-German activities to try to prevent Mr. Wilson's re-election.

Of course I cannot be a co-conspirator with Mr. Bryan. I am not a friend of Mr. Bryan, nor an admirer of Mr. Bryan, nor a supporter of Mr. Bryan, and have not been for many years.

Mr. Bryan has only lately opposed Mr. Wilson, but I was opposed to Mr. Wilson before his nomination for president.

I was opposed to him because I believed he would be a feeble and vacillating president. I have only said of late what I have said before, that he is feeble and vacillating.

The English newspapers, which have no special right to criticize an American president declare that Mr. Wilson is feeble and vacillating, and at the same time these newspapers attack me for criticizing the president and for saying the same thing about him that they say, although I am an American citizen, and have better right to say it.

As a matter of plain fact I am not conducting my newspapers to please either the English or the Germans. I am conducting them to serve Americans and to inform Americans of the exact facts, as nearly as these facts can be discovered and expressed by intelligent observers.

I have been willing to open the columns of my papers for the freest and fullest expression and exploitation of the pro-Ally propaganda, but I have become heartily tired of printing partisan articles either on one side or the other, for which there is not either appreciation or gratitude.

I have received nothing but criticism in return for kindness. I have extended courtesy and been rewarded with calumny.

I am delighted to have the opportunity to dispense with Mr. ————'s articles, and save for better purposes the money that was being wasted on them.

I shall be equally glad to stop publishing or paying for articles by any other purblind and prejudiced writer who shares Mr. ————'s ignorance and ingratitude.

Sincerely,

WILLIAM RANDOLPH HEARST.

Wellington House was willing to consider the matter closed. Parker wrote "that only a good end is served by using the Hearst papers for articles and interviews for the pro-Ally cause. If we could have an article or an interview in the most pronounced paper in the Central Empires we should not hesitate to use the opportunity."[22] The higher officials, however, were not satisfied with the situation and desired to eliminate even the partial opposition in the American field which Hearst was maintaining. Consequently they decided to take steps which would destroy his effectiveness.

The event which served as the excuse for action was the reporting in the Hearst papers of the battle of Jutland. According to Wellington House, part of the article had not been passed by the British censor, and in particular the opening sentence stating: "The British Admiralty tonight admits an overwhelming defeat by a portion of the German High Seas Fleet."[23] As a result Parker reported to the Cabinet that the Hearst press was "prohibited the usual facilities of the British Press bureau and denied the cable service by the British government. . . ."[24] On October 29 France took similar action. "In November the Canadian Government issued an order barring the Hearst newspapers from Canada."[25] It must have been after these measures had been taken that Charteris commented: "The Foreign Office have written to the War Office that our news service to America is admirable and that German news has been swept out of the American press."[26]

When he was first informed of the British action, "Hearst flushed and trembled with anger. He handed the message to his companion who in years of association had never before witnessed the faintest flutter in Hearst's uncanny calm. 'What are

[22]*A. P. R.*, May 25, 1916.

[23]The statement was not exactly correct; nor was it entirely false. It did give an interpretation which the British did not wish to be given.

[24]". . . because of garbling official regular messages passed by the British censorship." *A. P. R.*, October 7, 1916.

[25]Winkler, John K., *W. R. Hearst: An American Phenomenon* (New York: Simon and Schuster, 1928), 264. "Under the terms of the Order in Council no person in Canada shall be permitted, on and after Saturday, the 11th day of November [prophetic choice of date] 1916, to be in possession of such newspaper [or he will be] . . . liable to a fine not exceeding $5000 or imprisonment for any term not exceeding five years, or both fine and imprisonment."

[26]Charteris, *op. cit.*, 161.

you going to do?' asked the employee. 'Do?' exploded Hearst, 'I am going to tell them to go to hell.' "[27] But in spite of any instructions Hearst may have given the British, they, by branding him as pro-German, succeeded in diminishing his influence[28] and in intimidating other intransigent newspapermen.

After the United States had entered the war, the American government found itself confronted with the same difficulties. An official in the State Department wrote to Wilson recommending that a committee be set up to censor American newspapers. In order to make this plan acceptable, he suggested that prominent newspapermen be made members of the committee. The names he mentioned included Adolph S. Ochs of the New York *Times*, Ralph Pulitzer of the New York *World*, George S. Johns of the St. Louis *Post-Dispatch*, Melville Stone of the Associated Press, and Arthur Brisbane of the Hearst papers, "who might be successfully used on the Executive Committee and muzzled." The official stated that "the advantage to the country would be great. Public opinion would respond to proper treatment" and the daily press would automatically become a part of the administration.

Wilson replied that it would be impossible to do this "because of the small but powerful lawless elements among them (i.e., the newspapermen) who observe no rules. . . ." He further remarked that this had been one of the original purposes of the Creel Committee.

The British in 1916 developed several new media for propaganda.[29] One innovation which held great promise, but which was not fully exploited, was the motion picture. In September of 1916 Sir Miles Lampson was placed in charge of Wellington House to handle this work.[30] Later Sir William Jury replaced him. Numerous newsreels and feature length pictures were released in the United States and John Masefield reported that these "cinemas" had been effective. He suggested that "films of Stratford and of other places dear to Americans, such as the old Washington home with troops passing etc. might be shown."[31]

[27]Winkler, *op. cit.*, 264.
[28]See the case INS vs. AP, 245 Fed. 244, for another chapter in this story.
[29]Late in 1917 gramaphone records were issued.
[30]Squires, *op. cit.*, 31.
[31]*A. P. R. Supplement*, April 7, 1916.

It is interesting to note that here as well as in other phases of propaganda, the most effective work was done by Americans. The motion picture entitled "The Battle Cry of Peace," which has already been mentioned, was, in the opinion of Ambassador Jusserand, more effective than an army of conferences.[32]

Cartoons, always popular with the public, were issued in great numbers. Raemakers, the Hollander, immortalized the atrocity stories, and other cartoonists of much less fame contributed their bit towards objectifying the Allies' cause. More dignified drawings were turned out by Muirhead Bone, who was the first of many official artists at the front appointed by Wellington House.[33]

A tremendously important department of the American Ministry of Information was that which issued photographs. These were "distributed through the International Film Service, the American Press Association, and other agencies."[34] One propagandist wrote: "Opportunities for utilizing official photographs seemed to increase every day. In addition to supplying the necessary illustrations for all our official books and pamphlets and our own lavishly illustrated publications, either conducted or subsidized by Wellington House, we sent forth countless thousands of prints for reproductions in newspapers, magazines, and periodicals outside Great Britain in neutral and allied countries, and in the British Empire."[35]

This pictorial department of Wellington House supplied the American press very liberally with photographs.[36] It issued "a monthly illustrated magazine called *The War Pictorial*, which was sent out every month in . . . [a] bewildering variety of languages. . . ."[37] In his report of August 16, 1916, Parker was able to say that "pictures supplied by Wellington House to the American papers are conspicuous in the Sunday editions, and on front pages of papers of every locality."[38] The following week he gave a tremendously long list of weeklies and dailies which carried photographs emanating from Wellington House.

[32] Jusserand, *op. cit.*, 817.
[33] Nicholson, *loc. cit.*, 600. Wellington House also published maps, diagrams, and drawings.
[34] *A. P. R.*, August 5, 1916.
[35] Nicholson, *loc. cit.*, 579.
[36] *A. P. R.*, August 23, 1916.
[37] Nicholson, *loc. cit.*, 596.
[38] *A. P. R.*, August 16, 1916.

Propagandists who issued photographic material found that they could use effectively the same technique which the writers of propaganda employed. Questionable and even false interpretations were given to pictures just as they were given to news stories. For instance a picture of marching German troops was captioned: "The Germans Retreat"; atrocity photographs which had been taken in 1905 were re-dated 1915, and given titles which placed the blame on Germans; a snapshot of a carpet beater was issued as a picture of a whip used in German prison camps; some interned French and English prisoners lined up were said to be German workers in a bread line; a picture of a German soldier helping a wounded Russian was given the title: "German Ghoul Actually Caught in the Act of Robbing a Russian"; a pre-war picture of German cavalry officers with their trophies of competition was entitled "Three German Cavalrymen Loaded with Gold and Silver Loot;" a picture of three men happy to return home in Germany was captioned as men happy to become French prisoners of war.[39] The British and French not only gave false titles to news pictures; they also doctored them.[40] The French were especially competent in this branch of propaganda.[41]

The propaganda appeals continued along much the same lines as in the early days of the war. However, by this time an entirely different situation confronted the propagandists. In the first place, although American opinion had been won over almost completely to the side of Great Britain and France, a number of difficulties had to be taken into consideration. For instance, the Germans were not so generous in making blunders as they had been in 1914 and 1915. There were no more Louvains, Edith Cavells, or *Lusitanias*. The British also found it impossible to arouse any new indignation over German activities in the United States since the propaganda and sabotage work of the latter had

[39]Ponsonby, *op. cit.*, 135 ff. Ferdinand Avenarius did the original research in this matter. His *Die Weltkarikatur in der Völkerverhetzung* (Munchen, 1921), is a classic.

[40]The British Naval Censor shows how photographs themselves were doctored — for other than propaganda purposes. The results are astounding. Presenting the picture before and after being doctored one has the feeling of being in the hands of a magician — now you see it and now you don't. Brownrigg, *op. cit.*, 16, 80, 144, 176, 240, 256.

[41]*Hinter den Kulissen des französischen Journalismus* (Berlin, 1925), 226.

been practically eliminated. Another thing which detracted from British effectiveness was the fact that improved radio facilities brought considerable German news to the American press, including "the radiograph transmission of the full reports of American correspondents in Berlin and on the German fronts."[42]

During the last year of neutrality, the British propagandists also found it necessary to overcome obstacles erected by Americans. First of all, they had to defeat the efforts of pacifists or neutralists who wanted to keep the United States out of the war. Secondly, they had to undo the work of those who were attempting to induce Wilson to call a peace conference. And finally there was the necessity for overcoming the opposition to British naval policy.

The Irish question was particularly difficult for British propagandists. In an official report to Parker, John Masefield remarked: "It is most important that some authoritative loyal Irish member [of Parliament], preferably a Catholic, should go over as soon as may be [possible] . . . to silence the Irish-American party, who exude poison from every pore."[43] Others also recommended propaganda for this purpose. Consequently Wellington House persuaded Mr. John Redmond, Mr. Horace Plunkett, and other "loyal Irishmen" to give interviews and write articles in defense of Great Britain in the hope of tempering the virulence of Irish-American opposition.

The execution of Sir Roger Casement[44] and the Easter Rebellion naturally aroused feeling to a white heat, but, as Parker reported, "it would . . . [have been] silly to pretend or to fear . . . [that these occurrences would] imperil the general pro-Ally, or even the pro-British, sentiment in America. That . . . [was] secure beyond trivial damage."[45] "The [Irish] insurrection inspired [hostile] flaring headlines in the Western and Middle-Western press." "On the other hand, the huge headlines of the Chicago *Herald* . . . were most satisfactory. . . ." Parker must have been pleased to write: "The Chicago *Herald,* which has

[42]Seymour, Charles, *Woodrow Wilson and the World War: A Chronicle of Our Own Times* (New Haven, 1921), 160.

[43]*A. P. R. Supplement,* April 7, 1916.

[44]*A. P. R.,* June 7, 1916. "It seems to be taken for granted . . . that almost all Irish-American feeling has been irretrievably alienated by the executions. . . ."

[45]*A. P. R.,* May 31, 1916.

taken a very pro-British view of the insurrection, opens its editorial by remarking: 'Curiously enough, the very morning on which the news of the outbreak in Dublin appears, brings into the *Herald* office a book on "The Irish at the Front," with an introduction by Mr. John Redmond. . . .' " Parker added: "The book in question was received from Wellington House."[46]

From time to time the Jewish problem assumed large proportions on the propaganda scene. The various pogroms which had featured Russian history were only too well remembered, and naturally Jews did not wish to assist the side on which Russia was fighting. There were numerous attempts made to disarm this opposition. The New York *Times* even tried to explain the Russian anti-Semitism by stating that "the reactionary elements in Russia . . . [were] mostly of Teutonic origin."[47] A final solution was devised in November, 1917, when Mr. Balfour laid the foundations for a Jewish national home in Palestine.[48]

In 1916 the British found that their greatest difficulty lay in making the victory propaganda appear convincing. To their dismay, the big plans for defeating the Germans apparently were not working. The best that could be done was to boast that the Germans had not defeated them. Parker, who was usually alarmed by peace talk, was greatly relieved when the attention of the American press was diverted from the Roumanian disaster to agitation for peace. He stated this was fortunate "because the operations on the Roumanian front are little understood in America, and have lately gained too much attention."[49] A suggestion was made to him that "it might be well to turn various writers . . . in the big American monthlies" to answering the question "what has England done."[50] The resulting articles did a little to counteract the effects of military defeats.

The victory propaganda also encountered difficulties in the field of finance. The Kipling interview[51] and the American questioning of the ability of the Allies to pay for the war compelled

[46]*A. P. R.*, May 19, 1916.
[47]*A. P. R.*, November 8, 1916.
[48]Wanderscheck, *op. cit.*, 40.
[49]*A. P. R.*, January 17, 1917.
[50]The reports of April 21 and May 12 show that this suggestion was carried out.
[51]*Supra*, 105.

Wellington House to issue counter-propaganda on the soundness of the British financial structure. Parker arranged for a vast flood of speeches, interviews, pamphlets, and inspired newspaper articles for American consumption. The reactions were fairly satisfactory.

The pity campaign or the attempt to exploit American sentimentality continued unabated. Advantage was taken of every opportunity to extract tears from American eyes over "poor ruined Belgium,"[52] or heroic France. One of Parker's American agents recommended the "writing-up of Belgium and the devastated parts of France rather more particularly than . . . [had] been done."[53] Perhaps as a result of this suggestion numerous articles and interviews tending to evoke sympathy appeared in the American press. Parker found these to be successful as late as 1917. He remarked that "any allusion to Belgium is assured of an instant response from American opinion."[54]

In the field of atrocities, considerable new material was developed. Lord Bryce issued another excellent collection of stories, this time on Armenia.[55] Parker was able to report that "The New York *Times*, Philadelphia *Public Ledger,* and the Chicago *Herald* . . . devoted much space to the advance sheets of 'these Armenian horror stories.' "[56] Unfortunately they did not have the cordial reception given to the earlier Bryce Report. In spite of the fact that Americans greeted the Armenian reports with apathy, they still maintained a strong interest in any stories of violence which might come out of Belgium or France. In the middle of 1916 Parker commented: "It is remarkable to notice how instant is the response in the United States to every fresh German atrocity." "It might have been expected . . . [that] German atrocities would have by this time become somewhat stale. But this is not the case. There seems to be no more certain appeal to the American public than through the medium of such atrocities."[57]

[52]"The *Saturday Evening Post* published an illustrated article on the work of the Belgian Relief Committee." *A. P. R.,* November 15, 1916.

[53]*A. P. R. Supplement,* April 7, 1916.

[54]*A. P. R.,* July 18, 1917.

[55]Note Morgenthau's misrepresentation of Armenian atrocities and of German action regarding them. Grattan, *op. cit.,* 254 f.

[56]*A. P. R.,* November 1, 1916.

[57]*A. P. R.,* August 30, 1916. The propagandists were never quite able to understand why the American public did not react favorably or unfavorably to events

Even in 1917 it was stated that they "still hold a very prominent place in American public writing."[58]

Air attacks upon defenseless cities continued to provide material for the pity propaganda. Sir Gilbert Parker noted that "air raids upon London . . . [were] supplying a most desirable tonic to American opinion."[59] In this particular propaganda, as in that connected with gas, there occurred a somewhat changed attitude in cases where the efficiency of the Allies was comparable with that of the Germans. On June 26, 1916, the Corpus Christi procession at Carlsruhe in Germany was bombed by planes belonging to the Allies. Five women and sixty-five children were killed.[60] A little later Munich was attacked. In these two cases the American press reacted quite satisfactorily, in some cases even complimenting the Allies. The New York *Herald's* headline stated: "Munich Bombed By Daring French Flier In Great Feat." Here the atrocity, when done by a French aviator, became a commendable action.[61]

One of the most successful of the propaganda attacks in 1916 dealt with the Belgian deportations. The hostile population behind the German lines had presented a difficult problem ever since August, 1914. Sabotage and attacks upon individual soldiers were not troublesome after the Germans had undertaken reprisals, but the shortage of food and other supplies in 1916 along with German distrust of the enemy at their rear, prompted them to start deporting Belgians into Germany to work on farms and in factories, especially as the blockade became more effective. Although deportation was not unprecedented,[62] Wellington House found that it provided a good means for arousing American sympathy.

---

in eastern and southern Europe. "American public opinion will be interested, but will not be much affected by any developments that may take place with regard to Greece." *A. P. R.*, June 21, 1916.

[58]*A. P. R.*, May 23, 1917. A month later "air raids and atrocities of all kinds still continue profoundly to affect American opinion." *A. P. R.*, June 27, 1917.

[59]*A. P. R.*, July 18, 1917.

[60]Demartial, *op. cit.*, 21.

[61]Some adverse criticism was secured in the United States when a British boat, the *King Stephen* did not pick up the survivors of the German Zeppelin Z-19.

[62]Some 80,000 Germans were deported by France in 1870 and since the armistice 120,000 Germans have been deported from Alsace-Lorraine. Allen, *op. cit.*, 40.

SIR WILLIAM WISEMAN

British propaganda of the last year of neutrality was characterized by continued attempts to establish the conviction in
the minds of Americans that their interests and aspirations were
directly involved in the Allies' cause.[63] The native propagandists
were contending that the war was "our war," that the Allies were
fighting "our fight." It was hoped by Parker that the activity of
the *U-53* near the American coast would be very helpful in this
propaganda. He felt that it destroyed some of the remoteness of
the war for Americans, stating: The "startling proximity of the
occurrence is bound to be of far-reaching and beneficial influence.
It frightened a good many people rather badly, which . . . was a
most desirable result. I wish [the Germans] had thought of doing
something of the sort long ago."[64] Unfortunately he had to admit
a little later that the *U-53's* exploits had not produced the reaction for which he had hoped.

An Anglo-American friend of Sir Gilbert Parker, and also of
Theodore Roosevelt, thought he was being original when he suggested that Wellington House should "publish an article by a
well known British authority . . . on the subject of Anglo-American relations, in order to show that the interests of the United
States and of the British Empire run parallel in most parts of the
world."[65] In April, Bonar Law[66] gave an interview, at the instigation of Parker, on the danger of a German invasion of the United
States. It will be remembered that this was the tenor of the motion picture "The Battle Cry of Peace." In May, Lord Cromer
gave an interview entitled "England's Defeat, Our Defeat."[67] In
order to establish a belief in the identity of interests of Great
Britain and the United States, John Masefield even suggested:
"A big application of the idea of the Rhodes scholarships" along
with public mark of thanks to Yale or Harvard for their sons who
have served the Allies, might be of great value. He commented,
"Some few scraps of autograph by famous English writers would
be ample for the purpose."[68]

[63]Note the speeches of John Buchan in the United States in 1937.

[64]*A. P. R.*, November 1, 1916.

[65]*A. P. R.*, May 12, 1916.

[66]*A. P. R.*, April 21, 1916.

[67]*A. P. R.*, May 19, 1916.

[68]*A. P. R. Supplement*, April 7, 1916. One wonders if a "scrap of autograph"
by Masefield would have been satisfactory.

Closely akin to the "our fight" arguments was the propaganda of democracy. The injection of this issue into World War propaganda was a brilliant maneuver. It created a façade behind which the real issues of the war could be hidden, and invalidated adverse criticism of the related propaganda. It was not only an appeal to the American belief in democracy; it was an exploitation of the age-old hatred of everything foreign — in this case a foreign type of government. Many Americans had the idea that history is the story of man's struggle for a voice in his own government, and when they were told that this was the issue in the World War, their interest and sympathy were immediately enlisted.

Although the British made use of this propaganda of democracy as early as 1914, they had to be cautious because of the presence of Russia among the Allies. It was not until the Czarist regime was overthrown in February, 1917, that they were freed of the embarrassment caused by that autocratic government. As a matter of fact, democracy was never an issue in the war and to state that it was a remedy for European troubles was utterly naïve. Each government is an expression of national needs and national aspirations; as nations are different, so governments must differ. But in spite of its falsity, the democracy argument was most effective. It exploited American provincialism and idealism, ignorance, and self-interest; it provided a semi-religious appeal which Wilson was to immortalize with the phrase "the world must be made safe for democracy."

The propaganda of the last year of neutrality was not colorful, nor was it new. Not much happened that could be sensationalized, and, after a year and a half of writing and talking about the war, very little that was original remained to be said. The major task of Parker and his legion of volunteer assistants in the United States was to maintain the advantages which had already been won. This was accomplished largely through repetition of the propaganda arguments devised at the beginning of the war. Incessant reiteration of these ideas until they became an integral part of American thought patterns made possible the final conversion of the American public from passive to active adherents of the Allies.

The resulting climate of opinion made it impossible for those

Americans who desired to keep out of the war to express their views. Their warning cries were drowned out by the pro-Ally tub-thumping. Even the most timid isolationists were accused of being pro-German and immediately muzzled. On the other hand, those Americans who were expressing the fashionable pro-Ally sympathies were able to be violently partisan without encountering the slightest criticism. Anglophiles and Francophiles had all the fervor of religious converts and looked upon anyone who disagreed with them as utterly devoid of decency. Propaganda had thus created an intolerance in America comparable with that in any of the warring nations. This attitude of mind made possible and inevitable the American course of action in April, 1917.

CHAPTER XII ☆ PRESSURE OF ECONOMICS IN THE LAST YEAR OF NEUTRALITY

THE economic warfare of the last year of neutrality affected the United States even more than it had in 1914 and 1915. Charles A. Beard has said that "war is not made by a *deus ex machina,* but comes out of ideas, interests, and activities cherished and followed in the preceding months and years of peace."[1] This is proved very definitely by the events in the year immediately preceding American entrance into the war. The British blockade and the German retaliation against it became more severe, and each became more important from the American point of view. The prevention of German purchases in the United States and the monopoly of the American market by the Allies also came to have a larger effect upon American policies. Each phase of the economic struggle tended to involve the American government more and more in the military struggle.

Throughout 1916 and 1917 the British government continued its cavalier treatment of international law whenever that law interfered with its plan for starving Germany into submission. In April, 1916, the distinction between conditional and absolute contraband was abolished, and in addition, a change was made in the rules of evidence, "throwing on the cargo owner the burden of proving that the goods would never reach Germany."[2] On July 7 the Declaration of London was laid to rest. It should be said that although the British actually ignored the rights of neutrals and belligerents engaged in maritime commerce, they made a great show of rendering lip service to legality.

One of the most effective measures adopted was the restriction on bunker coal. The following summarizes what they had to say to neutrals in this matter: "If you want bunker coal . . . you must supply us with a list of all your ships and their charter parties and bind yourselves not to allow any of them to trade with

[1]Beard, *op. cit.,* 28.
[2]Borchard and Lage, *op. cit.,* 15.

an enemy of Great Britain."[3] What this actually meant was that neutrals were compelled to work for Great Britain or else be subjected to what was in reality a blockade of their own ports. "Thenceforth . . . the Allies were only willing to revictual the neutrals in so far as the latter were willing to lend their merchant fleets to make good the losses sustained in submarine warfare."[4] Those neutrals who were so rash as to refuse to comply with British demands were denied bunker coal, blacklisted, and forced to stay in port. Those who agreed and were placed on the white list became an integral part of the British merchant marine and participants in the war against the submarine menace.

Eventually any ship sailing from a neutral port had to have a certificate from a British consul before it could be assured immunity from British interference on the high seas.[5] When this was done, it can be seen that the blockade of Germany was complete.

In dealing with the small neutrals who were doing business with the Central Powers even more ruthless policies were followed. Great pressure was exerted on the Greek government in an attempt to force it to enter the war on the side of Great Britain and France. French and British forces refused to evacuate the Greek port of Salonika. "An Allied base also was established on the *neutralized* Greek island of Corfu. When Constantine protested these violations of Greek neutrality and compared them to Germany's violation of Belgium, the Allies rejoined that Greek neutrality had not been guaranteed by treaty."[6] In December, 1916, they even demanded that Greece turn over her supply of arms and ammunition to the Allies. Naturally the Greeks refused. One American editor wrote: "The pro-German position of King Constantine of Greece once again is indicated clearly by his refusal to accede to the demands of the Entente Powers that all

[3]Guichard, *op. cit.*, 89. "Pressure was therefore applied to induce neutral vessels to accept employment useful to the Allies by making this a condition of their supply with bunker coal." Salter, James Arthur, *Allied Shipping Control* (London, 1921), 105.

[4]*Ibid.*, xv.

[5]*Ibid.*, 117.

[6]Langsam, Walter C., *The World Since 1914* (New York: The Macmillan Company, 1936), 29.

guns and ammunition of the Greek army be surrendered."[7] The
Allies then, resorting to still more radical measures ... established
a blockade, demanded the demobilization of the Greek army, recognized a Venizelist Government at Salonika, and in the summer
of 1917 ordered the dethronement of the king and the abdication
of his eldest son. The Allied army, moreover, marched on Athens
— the capital of a state which still was neutral. On June 12, 1917,
Constantine finally abdicated in favor of his second son, Alexander. Thereupon, Venizelos was called to head a new government
and all known German sympathizers were exiled. On July 2, 1917,
Greece officially became one of the Allied Powers."[8]

In the middle of 1917 the British began to operate against
the Liberian government, compelling its officials to eliminate all
business connections with Germany or with the Germans who
lived in Liberia. An American State Department official reported
that "as soon as the German subjects ... have been carried away
and the ... minister states that the German firms are being closed,
the restrictions which were placed on trade with Liberia in order
to wreck German enterprises there will be cancelled."[9] The Liberian officials were then told that they might be required to declare war against Germany. On August 4, 1917, Liberia joined
forces with the enemies of the Central Powers.

The foregoing incidents were not important from the point
of view of public opinion in the United States for the reason that
Americans had little interest in countries other than those in
northwestern Europe. Antagonistic reactions were encountered,
however, as soon as American interests were adversely affected.
This was especially true in connection with British censorship of
the mail which was developed into a vital part of the blockade
against Germany. An enterprising staff "perceived ere long that
their powers could be developed and turned to account ... in
stifling the commercial activities of the Central Powers in the
western hemisphere. It truly became a great and potent weapon
of attack."[10] The British censor wrote: "I am doubtful if any

[7]*Commercial and Financial Chronicle, loc. cit.,* CIII, December 2, 1916.
[8]Langsam, *op. cit.,* 29.
[9]Breckinridge Long Papers, Report to U. S. State Department, June 23, 1917,
Library of Congress.
[10]Callwell, Major-General, Sir C. E., *Experiences of a Dugout 1914-1918*
(New York, 1920), 143.

more powerful weapon in enforcing the blockade and ruining the enemy's over-seas trade ever existed."[11]

Americans considered this interference with their mail an outrageous procedure. Complaints made to the government were numerous and not devoid of vigor. Eventually many suspected that the mail of some business houses was being intercepted for the benefit of their British competitors.[12] In spite of American objections, there are reasons for believing that when the United States entered the war, she also interfered with neutral mail.[13]

Indignation in this country became positively violent as a result of the next move made by the British. This was the issuance on July 18, 1916, of a blacklist, compiled by the censor, of eighty-five American firms which had been doing business with the Central Powers. It was at first kept secret, and surreptitious efforts were made to bankrupt these blacklisted firms. However, the great prosperity in the United States prevented such pressure from being effective. As soon as the blacklist was made public, bankers refused to issue drafts to firms whose names were upon it, while the thousands of firms doing business directly or indirectly with the Allies naturally hesitated to become in any way associated with the outlawed companies.

Americans were infuriated by these attacks on business being carried on within the boundaries of the United States. Frank L. Polk wrote to his superior, Secretary of State Lansing: "This week has been absolutely hideous. The Danish treaty made trouble, but the blacklist has caused an awful row. The innocent and the guilty have come down here together, wildly protesting. It was an extraordinarily stupid move on the part of the British and both Jusserand and Spring-Rice threw up their hands over it."[14] Wilson wrote to House that "the blacklist is the last straw. I am at the end of my patience with the Allies." It should be

[11]Brownrigg, *op. cit.*, 183.

[12]Lansing's *Memoirs*, 125, 127. Naturally this was not lost on the British, as one report states: "The most serious aspect of the resentment against British naval policy is a widespread suspicion that Great Britain is using her maritime power to gain undue trade advantage over neutrals." *A. P. R.*, April 7, 1916. Also *A. P. R.*, October 4, 1916. See also Silber, J. C., *The Invisible Weapons* (London, 1932).

[13]For instance, the "Executive Postal Censorship Committee" in San Antonio, Texas, censored all the mail between the two neutral countries, Spain and Mexico. Breckinridge Long Papers in the Library of Congress.

[14]*M. I.*, Part 28, 8660.

borne in mind that here again the American government was itself guilty of the practices against which it objected so strenuously. "Before the end of 1917 ... [the United States] had adopted a blacklist ... and ... surpassed England in the vigor with which the policy was enforced."[15]

British propagandists were distinctly alarmed by these violent American objections. They reported to the Cabinet: "The real extent of agitation against the 'Blacklist' cannot be gauged by studying the newspapers, because many of its most serious opponents are prevented by their economic relationship with the Allies from publicly voicing their opinions. Thus it comes about that the pro-Ally papers are for the most part silent about the 'Blacklist.' "[16] Nevertheless each week reports showed evidence of the increasing resentment within the United States, and even friends of the Allies were of the opinion that the British were violating international law.[17] In November Parker reported that Edwin S. Corwin had written a magazine article entitled "Sea Rights and Sea Power" which was a most vigorous attack on British conduct at sea. He confessed that the article displayed "a very extensive knowledge of international law" and had "no evidence of German bias."[18] British propagandists were forced to admit to themselves that there was "real depth of genuine and unbiased American resentment" against these British policies.[19]

Even the Wilson administration became indignant. The President wrote to House: It is an "altogether indefensible course Great Britain is pursuing with regard to trade."[20] "Can we any longer endure their intolerable" conduct?[21] At the behest of the

15Nowell, Charles E., *The British Blacklist And The United States* (Stanford, 1927), vi.

16*A. P. R.*, September 13, 1916.

17The consistently pro-British Indianapolis *News* was quoted as saying, "The Entente Powers have shown little or no respect for neutral rights." *A. P. R.*, October 4, 1916.

18*A. P. R.*, November 1, 1916.

19Wellington House was constantly making suggestions to the Cabinet in connection with this outbreak of American opinion. For instance, it was recommended that the blockade be featured as a policy of all the Allies rather than as a British blockade. *A. P. R.*, April 21, 1916. At another time it was recommended that British officials stop quoting Civil War precedents. *A. P. R.*, April 28, 1916.

20Seymour, *American Diplomacy*, 74.

21Seymour, *American Neutrality*, 118.
On January 12, 1916, Wilson cabled to House: "It now looks as if our several

President, Lansing sent several strong notes to the Allies. Concerning one of them he remarked: "It could not be made much stronger and be polite, and of course we must observe our manners."[22] House commented in his diary: "We think the British foolish not to give way on the blacklist and to arrange for less rigorous censorship of the mails. It is a question how far the President will be justified in straining our relations with Great Britain rather than consent to their insolent methods of conducting their blockade. A note has just come from Great Britain about the blacklist which Polk considers offensive, although Lansing thinks otherwise. . . . The State Department will try to suppress the note until after the election. Polk thinks the President is likely to give them a jolt which will not increase good feelings toward us. He suggests two methods to bring them to their senses. One is the restriction of further loans and [the other, restriction of] the exportation of gasoline. He thought we might do both under pretext of domestic necessity and in a way which would not justify retaliation."[23]

At this point the Allies' program faced considerable danger. A British official commented at the time: "You can play tricks with neutrals whose fighting potentialities are restricted, which you had better not try with non-belligerents who may be able to make things hot for you."[24] The question was how far could the Allies go without causing retaliation on the part of the American government.

In this last year of neutrality it is quite clear that a considerable change came over Wilson. He did not become sympathetic with the Germans but the British actions made him lose much of his sympathy for them. He no longer looked at the war through British eyes. In July Wilson wrote to House that he was seriously considering asking Congress for authority to prohibit loans and restrict exports to the Allies, stating, "Polk and I are compound-

---

difficulties with Germany will be presently adjusted. As soon as they are, the demand here, especially from the Senate, will be imperative that we force England to make at least equal concessions to our unanswerable claims of right. This is just." Seymour, *American Diplomacy*, 73.

[22]Viereck, George Sylvester, *The Strangest Friendship in History — Woodrow Wilson and Colonel House* (New York, 1932), 145.

[23]*M. I.*, Part 25, 7638.

[24]Callwell, *op. cit.*, 110.

ing a very sharp note."[25] On September 8, 1916, the President was granted some feeble discretionary powers to retaliate against the British blockade. "Congress also proceeded to vote the largest naval appropriation ever passed by any legislative body of a state not at war."[26] These immediately aroused the fears of the English. Parker reported to the Cabinet: "It is not possible to discover from the newspapers alone how far these ... [measures] are designed for political purposes ... [or] whether they are to be used at all." In order to be sure that they would not be used, the British hinted at retaliation. Spring-Rice wrote to Lansing: "It is only fair that a warning should be given as to the probable effects on the good and friendly relations" between the United States and Great Britain if the President should enforce these measures.

In reply to the President's inquiry concerning the possible effectiveness of the new retaliatory powers, the Department of Commerce reported: "We can attack their commerce but our own commerce will unavoidably suffer in consequence even more than it has suffered from the restrictions placed on it by the countries at war. There is little likelihood by these means of obtaining the withdrawal of the objectionable regulations. Counter reprisals would be almost inevitable.

"We have suffered the effect of embargoes and Orders in Council for a long period — under protest but without retaliation. ... But the weapon — an embargo on war munitions and supplies — has now become dulled."[27]

Senator Clark stated before the Munitions Investigation Committee: "The effect of the Secretary of Commerce document was that our own high public officials recognized that the powers of retaliation conferred upon the President by Congress could not be invoked without endangering this huge, abnormal wartime trade in the face of the great vested interest in war traffic which had grown up in the United States by that time." "The awakening on the part of the President very obviously came too late, because a vested interest had been created in the shape of this war trade which was too formidable to be tampered with by the

[25]Wilson to House, July 23, 1915, Seymour, *American Diplomacy,* 76-77.
[26]*Intimate Papers,* 316.
[27]*M. I.,* Part 28, 8670 f.

President, particularly at a time when he was facing an election."[28] Seymour has contended that "it would certainly have ruined not merely the 'war babies' of industry, but the cotton and wheat growers, the copper producers, the iron and steel workers and have thrown the country back into the bleak depression and unemployment from which it had just emerged."[29]

According to Bernstorff, Colonel House told him that "Wilson no longer had the power to compel England to adhere to the principles of international law. That the reason for this was that American commerce was so completely tied up with the interests of the Entente that it was impossible for Wilson to disturb these commercial relations without calling forth such a storm of protest on the part of the public that he would not be able to carry out his intentions."[30] Spring-Rice wrote to Lord Cecil in the same tenor, stating: "The reason why there has been no embargo on arms and ammunition is not sympathy with us but the sense that the prosperity of the country on which the Administration depends for its existence would be imperiled by such a measure. There may be a breaking point." "If it approaches, you may have to concede a point or two."[31]

But nothing whatsoever was done with the retaliatory powers and what is more, the British knew that nothing would be done. Mr. Lloyd George wrote: "We know how Mr. Wilson stands and we may feel very sure that he will do nothing of a serious nature to interfere with the blockade or the export of munitions."[32]

It must not be assumed that because American officials criticized British actions, that they were to remain without sin. Mr. Polk, of the American State Department, remarked to the British Foreign Minister in 1917: "Mr. Balfour, it took Great Britain three years to reach a point where it was prepared to violate all the laws of blockade. You will find that it will take us only two months to become as great criminals as you are."[33]

[28]*M. I.*, Part 28, 8498, 8499.
[29]Seymour, *American Neutrality*, 13. See *M. I.*, Part 27, 8182.
[30]*Official German Documents*, I, 234.
[31]Spring-Rice, *op. cit.*, II, 345.
[32]*M. I.*, Part 28, 8508.
[33]Hendrick, *op. cit.*, II, 265.
Wellington House smilingly quoted the Springfield *Republican* in the report of June 6, 1917. "In the brief space of a single month many Americans seem to have forgotten absolutely that the United States was ever a neutral and a champion

The British economic warfare was tolerated in the United States because Americans were afraid to annoy their best foreign customer. They had invoked the evil genie of war prosperity and then found that they had become his slave. The "blood soaked boom" came to be the governing force throughout the country. Not only did it restrict the thoughts and actions of people engaged in the munitions business, it channeled the thinking of all business men from coast to coast, and prevented the government from taking any steps against the British. When the President was given power to retaliate against their high-handed conduct, the bonds of interest prevented him from using it. "Faced with the choice of working havoc on the whole financial and commercial structure of this country, which by that time was inseparably bound up with the Allied cause, and which Wilson's pro-Ally policies, [from] 1914 to 1916, had very definitely fostered, the President was forced to back down. What had been intended as a 'club for Great Britain if they . . . [did] not give real relief on trade interference' . . . would have been a club against United States commerce and industry in this abnormal war trade which had been developed. The result was that the club was never used."[34]

The huge volume of business enjoyed by the United States during this last year of neutrality reveals rather clearly why no action was taken against Great Britain. Exports jumped from over two and one-half billion dollars to four and one-third billion dollars.[35] "The total amount of American exports during these neutral years to the four great Allies, Great Britain, France, Russia, and Italy, were seven billions of dollars.[36] Of that not over two billions were in what were called munitions of war. The other

---

of neutral rights. The very people who most stridently demanded war on the ground that the rights of this country as a neutral were infringed, are now assuming that a neutral has no rights which a belligerent is bound to respect." *A. P. R.*, June 6, 1917.

A little later they stated: "The American papers have quite forgotten their former anxiety for the rights of neutral trade." *A. P. R.*, August 8, 1917.

[34]Senator Bennett Champ Clark. *M. I.*, Part 28, 8498.

[35]Noyes, *op. cit.*, 117.

[36]"It was seven billion dollars' worth of prosperity. Well, according to the estimates of President Coolidge, participation in the World War cost the people of the United States, besides death and suffering, at least $100,000,000,000, counting outlays to come for pensions, bonuses, and other war charges." Beard, *op. cit.*, 104.

five billions were in commodities, foodstuffs, cotton, raw materials, metals, [and] manufactured goods of a general order."[37] (See Appendix B.)

Naturally such statistics meant prosperity for individual American firms. For instance, Worth Brothers Company earned $4,013,184 on a capitalization of $250,000, a return of 1605 per cent. The Bethlehem Steel Company announced that it had earned $24,821,408 in 1915. At the end of 1916 the company's business had reached the astonishing figure of $61,717,309. In the first quarter of 1916 United States Steel earned over $81,-000,000, and for the entire year, $348,000,000. "The rough total of all of J. P. Morgan & Co.'s business with the Allies [was] ... 3 billion dollars."[38]

This increased business was not enjoyed by munitions firms alone. Big dividends and unbelievable profits were reported in all branches of industry and commerce. Meat packers,[39] mining companies,[40] and oil firms joined in the pursuit for profits and more profits. American incomes increased in all brackets[41] caus-

[37]M. I., Part 27, 8158.

The total munitions shipments in 1914 had amounted to $40,000,000; in 1915 they increased to $350,000,000; and in 1916 the figure was $1,290,000,000. Hanighen, Frank C., and Engelbrecht, G. C., Merchants of Death (New York, 1934), 174.

On December 3, 1916, the New York Times' headlines read as follows: "Five Liners Depart For Europe In A Day," "They Carry Thousands of Tons of War Supplies for Allies." The Mid-Week Pictorial of January 25, 1917, showed pictures of the quays of France jammed with American goods. "For the vital points for us are that this country should serve as a base of supplies. . . ." Spring-Rice, op. cit., II, 282.

[38]M. I., Part 25, 7793 f.

[39]The big four among the meat packers in 1915 earned $17,000,000, in 1916, $36,000,000, and in 1917, $68,000,000 — all over the profits made in the pre-war period. "In the three war years from 1915 to 1917 their total profits . . . reached the astounding figure of $140,000,000 of which $121,000,000 represents excess over their pre-war profits." The New York Times, December 14, 1934.

There had been a conflict between the British government and the Chicago meat packers earlier in the war. However, as the Allies came to absorb more and more of their output, that animosity was eliminated. In 1916 Wellington House reported: "According to Mr. Brooks [of the Daily Mail] no further trouble need be apprehended from the packers, and their immense influence and resources throughout the West may confidently be relied upon in support of another Anglo-American loan." A. P. R., April 21, 1916.

[40]Calumet and Hecla Company, a mining firm, made a profit of 800 percent in 1917.

[41]The number of people with incomes of $50,000 to $1,000,000 increased from

ing widespread speculation. It was not unusual during the summer of 1916 to have million share days on the New York stock exchange, and at the end of the year two million share days were common. It suddenly became evident that "the West was immensely enriched by the enormous export of its food products,[42] the East by the steel trade's spectacular activities, and at length the South by a profitable cotton crop."[43]

There naturally arose a great deal of criticism of this money making, both in Europe and in the United States. Maurice Low remarked: "The only statesmanship the [American] public understood was peace with war profits."[44] Charteris said, "I can see no reason at all why America should join either us or Germany. She stands exactly where many of our own people wanted us to stand, with a front seat on the ropes of the ring and drawing all the gate money. . . . The U. S. A. is the U. S. A., Ltd."[45] LaFollette wrote in 1916: "Never in the history of this nation has there been a year like the past year for 'surplus millions,' 'melons,' 'extra dividends,' for the rich and powerful few."[46] Charles Lindbergh, Sr., shouted: "Amid all this confusion the lords of 'special privilege' stand serene in their selfish glee, coining billions of profit from the rage of war."[47]

All this new wealth soon began to create a problem for the American banking system. From June 30, 1914, to September 12, 1916, the resources of the national banks increased $2,929,000,-000 while their loans and discounts increased $1,429,000,000.[48] It became imperative for the banks to obtain a market for this money, and at the same time it was essential for Great Britain

---

7,449 in 1914 to 16,879 in 1916. The number of people with incomes of $3,000 to $50,000 increased from 350,000 in 1914 to 412,316 in 1916.

[42]At the beginning of 1916 it could be reported that "California had no such share in the profitable side of the war" as had the East (*A. P. R., Supplement,* January 28, 1916), but by the end of the year the tide of prosperity had reached the Pacific.

[43]Noyes, *op. cit.,* 124.

[44]Low, A. Maurice, *Woodrow Wilson, An Interpretation* (London, 1919), 180.

[45]Charteris, *op. cit.,* 135.

[46]*LaFollette's Magazine,* February, 1917.

[47]*Congressional Record,* LIII, App. 497.

[48]Report of John Skelton Williams in the Lansing Papers in the Library of Congress.

to secure money to pay for the huge purchases being made in the United States. The outstanding indebtedness of all the Allied countries in the United States on June 1, 1916, was $899,000,-000. On December 1 of the same year it had risen to $1,794,-000,000. It should not be surprising that when the Allies and the United States found themselves confronted with such a situation, they did all in their power to facilitate loans. In this period Great Britain marketed three loans totalling $800,000,000: the first on September 1, 1916; the second on November 1, 1916; and the third, on February 1, 1917. France floated two $100,000,000 loans: the first on August 1, 1916; the second on April 1, 1917. Russia obtained a loan of $11,000,000 in April, 1916, and one for $50,000,000 in June of the same year. The total of all loans made to the Allies prior to American entrance into the war, excluding loans made to Canada, amounted to $2,262,827,544.[49] Loans made to Great Britain totaled $1,476,511,566.[50] The number of American investors in the Allies' cause was estimated by Mr. Lamont at "possibly 500,000."

In connection with one of the loans to Russia, the American Ambassador in Petrograd wrote: "I am rendering all the assistance I consistently can toward the consummation of this loan. . . ."[51] But the State Department nervously wired him to stop his activity saying: "Such participation is contrary to the accepted rule of international law that neutral Governments should not lend their assistance to the raising of war loans by belligerents."[52] Francis was able to reply that he had maintained nominal neutrality.[53]

Late in 1916 Germany attempted to obtain money from the American market. On November 23 House wrote to the President: "Baruch tells me that Kuhn, Loeb & Co. are preparing to make a loan to the German cities just as they did some time ago to the French cities. Before doing it they want to be sure that our relations with Germany are satisfactory, otherwise they will re-

[49]*M. I.*, Part 29, 8981.
[50]*M. I.*, Part 29, 8981. Loans to France, $675,315,988; loans to Russia, $86,-000,000.
[51]Savage, *op. cit.*, II, 498, Document 194.
[52]*Ibid.*, 504, Document 196, June 8, 1916.
[53]*Ibid.*, 505, Document 197.

fuse to go on. I am wondering what, if anything, you want done in regard to this."

Wilson replied that "our relations with Germany are now in a very unsatisfactory and doubtful state, and . . . it would be most unwise at this time to risk a loan."[54]

In order to facilitate loan operations between the United States and England, negotiations were inaugurated in an attempt to establish closer co-operation between the Bank of England and the American Federal Reserve Board. It was desired that each organization act as agent for the other. In a memorandum prepared by the Federal Reserve Board August 29, 1916, the following questions were raised: "(1) Are the actions contemplated by the Federal Reserve Bank of New York, under the plan of operations with the Bank of England, unneutral in character, and (2) if they are unneutral, is the Government of the United States involved in such a way as to render the actions of the bank improper?" Based partially on the contention that the Federal Reserve was not a government institution, the board decided that such an agreement would be permissable. Nevertheless action was deferred until after the election because of fear of "rocking the boat." Late in December, 1916, arrangements were finally completed.[55]

In spite of the fact that the British received great financial co-operation in the United States, they were faced with many difficulties in the flotation of new loans. In the first place the "investment community in America would not . . . buy any more unsecured obligations." The three United Kingdom loans for $800,000,000 were backed by $960,000,000 worth of collateral.[56] "The British Government kept producing more and more of these available resources. They put . . . fresh legislation into effect . . . requiring the further mobilization of American securities from all their people. They began to ship those over, [and] . . . at the end of December 1916 they had over $700,000,000 of available securities, the greater part of which were not at all utilized."[57] They

[54]*M. I.*, Part 28, 8569.

According to Senator Clark German-American relations were "more satisfactory than they had probably been at any time during the war."

[55]*M. I.*, Part 27, 8239-8252, 8428.

[56]*M. I.*, Part 28, 8632, 8642.

[57] *M. I.*, Part 28, 8524. See also *M. I.*, Part 25, 7597.

shipped a great deal of gold into this country and also accumulated British municipal bonds and Canadian railroad bonds totaling hundreds of millions of dollars.[58] They were apparently even considering turning over to the American market their holdings in South American and Indian companies.[59] One of their greatest difficulties lay in marketing the bonds even after proper securities had been provided. Friends of the Allies began to display a reluctance to absorb more of these loans. Mr. Lamont cabled London in January, 1917: "We cannot look to the munitions manufacturers for heavy subscriptions, as heretofore. In all the issues till now we have pressed them vigorously, and most of them still have on hand the notes of former issues which they have been unable to liquidate at cost. In fact, we believe it is not too much to say that the only munition makers who have liquidated their interests have been those who have been willing to do so at a loss. All of them who have not heretofore taken their loss are still carrying notes at figures far below cost.

"Therefore we must rely more upon the individual investor and must devise some scheme that will appeal to him. We have in the last three weeks canvassed and discarded a large number of plans, all with the same end in view."[60]

As usual, the scheme which offered most promise of success was propaganda. Both the Morgan firm and Wellington House did their utmost to get the proper educational material before the American public. On November 24, Morgan cabled to Paris: "We want you to know that we are engaged in steady educational work"[61] to prepare the way for another French loan. Mr. Davison, one of the Morgan partners, was especially interested in keeping the Federal Reserve and the government from interfering with their work. He kept in constant touch with members of the board and occasionally even called upon the President.[62] The

---

[58]*M. I.*, Part 28, 8593.

[59]During the munitions investigation, Mr. Raushenbush made the following significant statement: "If Britain had had to turn over the Royal Dutch or Argentine railways or Indian cotton mills and all the things she had, that would have amounted to turning her industrial empire over to the hands of the United States. She would have lost her industrial empire while she was winning a military war." *M. I.*, Part 28, 8612.

[60]*M. I.*, Part 28, Exhibit 2665, 8801.

[61]*M. I.*, Part 28, Exhibit 2585, 8719.

[62]*M. I.*, Part 28, Exhibit 2596, 8730.

British Chancellor of the Exchequer was "greatly impressed with [the] skill and usefulness of . . . [Davison's] propaganda."[63]

The American press, of course, was most co-operative. Mr. Warburg recorded: "There has been going on quite an active press campaign, the object of which was to show that unless we granted foreign credits quite freely, the country ran the risk of being choked with gold with the attendant consequences of inflation of prices and credits."[64] After reporting to the Cabinet that the financial press in America was "preparing the way for fresh loans to the Allies" Sir Gilbert Parker added the interesting information that "the *Financial and Commercial Chronicle* has supported all the loan operations of the Allies. . . . The paper has . . . special affiliations with Standard Oil interests."[65]

The British found it necessary not only to use propaganda, but also to spend vast sums of money to hold up the prices of their securities and exchange.[66] This was essential in order to quiet the fears of American speculators and to make them believe that these new loans were sound. Between May and December, 1916, Morgan and Company spent four hundred and fifty million dollars to peg the exchange. In the one month of December they spent two hundred and ten million dollars, and Mr. Whitney testified that on a single crucial day between forty and fifty million dollars was spent.[67]

As the war progressed and the needs of the Allies grew to unbelievable proportions, it was found that in spite of all efforts to make these loans attractive, they were not being well received. In November, 1916, Morgan cabled London: "Hardly a single one of recent issues of any account is selling above issue price, and this applies to both countries."[68] Many bankers found they could not resell the securities. One of them reported in March, 1916: "It must be borne in mind that the banks in this country that have taken part in the European loans have not been able to pass their participation along to individuals to any appreciable

[63] *M. I.*, Part 28, Exhibit 2584, 8718.
[64] *M. I.*, Part 28, 8549.
[65] *A. P. R.*, November 29, 1916.
[66] *M. I.*, Part 28, 8520 f.
[67] *M. I.*, Part 28, 8542.
[68] *M. I.*, Part 28, Exhibit 2585, 8719. See also 8544 f.

extent. . . ."[69] The pressure was increasing. The Allies were pushing one issue after another upon the American public without waiting for the previous ones to be completely absorbed.[70] Foreign government securities held by national banks increased from $10,000,000 to $192,272,000 with the greatest increase occurring in the sixty days preceding September 12.[71]

The magnitude of the Allies' requirements created great concern in financial circles of the United States. As banking houses became heavily involved, this concern turned into alarm. Even the President and the Secretary of State began to listen to the urgings of Paul M. Warburg who was advocating retreat before it was too late. The Federal Reserve Board became particularly alarmed with a new form of security known as Treasury Bills and advised the Morgan firm of their uneasiness. "Governor Harding . . . [of the Federal Reserve Board] pointed out to Mr. Davison that there was some danger of a creditor becoming so much involved with one debtor that finally, no matter whether the creditor wanted to or not, he would have to go in deeper and deeper. In other words, while you thought you had the bull by the tail, as a matter of fact, the bull had you by the tail. In this case, it is John Bull who would have us by the tail."[72]

Finally Mr. Wilson became so disturbed over the situation that he requested the Federal Reserve to take some action. Consequently on November 28, 1916, the board issued the following statement: "The Board deems it . . . its duty to caution the member banks that it does not regard it in the interest of the country at this time that they invest in foreign treasury bills of this character.

"The United States has attained a position of wealth and of international financial power, which, in the natural course of events, it could not have reached for a generation. We must be careful not to impair this position of strength and independence.

"The Board does not share the view frequently expressed of late that further importations of large amounts of gold must of necessity prove a source of danger or disturbance to this country.

[69]*M. I.*, Part 28, Exhibit 2578, 8713.

[70]*M. I.*, Part 28, 8546.

[71]Report of John Skelton Williams in the Lansing Papers in the Library of Congress.

[72]*M. I.*, Part 28, Exhibit 2603, 8732.

"In these circumstances, the Board feels that member banks should pursue a policy of keeping themselves liquid."[73]

Needless to say, this caused great excitement in England,[74] and in certain parts of the United States. Mr. Lamont cabled to Morgan in London: "Statement of Federal Reserve Board cabled you last night prominently displayed in our newspapers all over country and has caused great excitement in financial circles here. . . . Regardless of the motives lying back of statement, we must recognize this as the most serious financial development in this country since the outbreak of the war and one likely to be of far reaching consequence. Please make this fact plain to the authorities so that they may consider whole situation in its grave aspects. . . . At present outlook is very dark.

"Exchange situation is, of course, very grave, and we have bought for you today almost £4,000,000 of exchange. We cannot, of course, maintain this pace even for a few days.

". . . despite our most strenuous efforts this Federal Reserve Board statement has brought about . . . a radical change for the worse in the whole situation."[75]

For once the pro-Ally press made no outburst. The situation was too serious for that. Parker commented: "It is, of course, satisfactory that the principal papers friendly to the Allies should be so emphatic in explaining away the action of the Federal Reserve Board. Yet, the very emphasis and anxiety with which they write, point to a serious feeling in the opposite sense which they are eager to stem."[76] André Tardieu later remarked that "if this decision had been maintained, the defeat of the Allies would have been merely a question of months, as they could neither have supplied their armies nor have fed their peoples."[77]

It is true that the resources of France and Great Britain were large, but nevertheless the war was proving to be unbelievably expensive. It would perhaps have been impossible for them to continue if the United States — a neutral — ceased to finance the war. On March 5, 1917, Ambassador Page wired Washington

---

[73]*M. I.*, Part 28, 8734 f. See also *M. I.*, Part 28, 8552 ff.
[74]*M. I.*, Part 28, 8567.
[75]November 28. *M. I.*, Part 28, 8556 f.
[76]*A. P. R.*, December 20, 1916.
[77]Tardieu, *op. cit.*, 141.

bluntly stating that the United States government would have to save the credit of the Allies[78] as their financial situation was becoming more and more critical.[79] When Mr. Wilson mentioned liberal credits in his war message, a reporter noticed the "diplomats grouped to the right of the President sat up and looked as if they would like to have applauded. . . ." "When we finally did enter the war, we became the principal sustainers of Allied economic interests which in such large measure had become our own."[80] In July, 1917, Bonar Law cabled Secretary McAdoo: "Resources of the United Kingdom which are available for payments in the United States are exhausted. Unless the government of the United States can fully meet our expenses in America, including exchange, the entire financial fabric of the alliance will collapse. This conclusion will be a matter of days, not months. . . . If matters continue on the same basis as they have during the past few weeks, it will not be possible to avoid a financial disaster of the first magnitude."[81] Naturally only a few people in the highest positions really knew how desperate was the Allies' situation. In 1916, of course, not the slightest intimation was given to Americans that Great Britain and France would be faced with a financial crisis in the following year.

Immediately after the Federal Reserve issued its warning, pressure began to be exerted to obtain reconsideration of its action. Both government and business officials realized that the United States had gone too far to retreat. The American financial structure had become so thoroughly tied up with that of Great Britain and France that more money had to be loaned to the Al-

[78]This "was actually done when the overdraft of $400,000,000 owed by Great Britain to J. P. Morgan and Company was eventually underwritten by the United States Government." Grattan, *New Republic, loc. cit.*, 372.

[79]"The pressure of this approaching crisis, I am certain, has gone beyond the ability of the Morgan financial agency for the British and French governments. . . . It is not improbable that the only way of maintaining our present trade position and averting a panic is by declaring war on Germany." Hendrick, *op. cit.*, II, 271.

[80]Grattan, *New Republic, loc. cit.*, 372.

[81]McAdoo, *op. cit.*, 413 f.

As loans were brought forward for discussion in Congress, the French and British newspapers started discussing changing these loans into gifts. This has been continued ever since. James Arthur Salter wrote: "With America's entry, therefore, finance ceased to be a crucial factor in the conduct of the war." Salter, *op. cit.*, 3.

lies in order to save that which had been previously advanced to them. In other words, what Warburg feared had already materialized.

Colonel House, as usual, came to the assistance of the British. He advised the French Ambassador to cable his government "that we are trying to undo the harm which the Federal Reserve Board has done regarding their credits." Immediately a reversal in procedure was noticed. The Federal Reserve Board began to soften and qualify its public statement. On December 26 it changed the previous ruling on the Bank of England credit which had been under negotiation for so long. On February 1 a new loan was floated by the British.

The retreat on the matter of the Federal Reserve warning was similar to the numerous retreats which the Wilson administration had made in 1915 and in the early part of 1916. The attempt to restrict loans, however, was not abandoned because of Wilson's pro-British attitude. By the winter of 1916 American interests had become so completely involved with those of Great Britain that an economic partnership had been formed between the two countries. Consequently the American government and American finance were no longer free agents.

At the first of 1916 it was said that "just as an early peace, favorable to the Allies, is the object of the best hopes of legitimate American finance, so the avoidance of American intervention in the war seems also to be hoped for in Wall Street."[82] By the end of the year, however, intervention had become a lesser evil. Britain's economic warfare, her vast purchases in the United States, and the attendant loans, had created a situation in which the American people and the American government lost their freedom of action. Von Tirpitz remarked: "It follows that the United States, whether they desire to be so or not, are directly interested in our defeat, and have become a direct enemy of Germany."[83] The economic tentacles of Great Britain had fastened on every branch of American business and made American business dependent upon a British victory. Early in 1917 *The New Republic* wrote: "We have already been playing a part in the war and behaving so as to promote the success of one group of bellig-

[82]*A. P. R.*, January 7, 1916.
[83]*Official German Documents*, II, 1126.

erents and the failure of another. We have been conniving at British illegality and penalizing that of Germany. It springs from an ultimate community of situation and disposition."[84]

The stock market reports throughout 1916 reveal strikingly the close economic relationship between the United States and the Allies. The news of the German victory at Jutland[85] caused a big drop in the market while the exploits of the *U-53* created a temporary panic in which $500,000,000 was lost in fifteen minutes. Early in December the New York *Times* recorded that the German peace offer had sent all stocks down. The next day prices rose because there was no "fear of peace." At the time of the Wilson peace offer, the New York *Times* stated: "Sales of more than 300,000 shares force most violent slump known in fifteen years."[86]

When Ambassador Bernstorff was given his passports the newspapers carried headlines: "Stocks Rise on News of Break with Germany."[87] The reaction in the economic circles to the declaration of war was reported by Wellington House as follows: "The entry of the United States into the war would seem, to judge from the press, to have been nowhere more welcome than in the financial districts of New York, Chicago, Boston, and Philadelphia. In London, British bankers received from their American friends and correspondents numerous cables expressing satisfaction at the new situation. These cables were all of the same nature, full of relief as well as satisfaction that the United States found themselves about to fight side by side with the nations with whom their financial relations were already so intimate."[88]

---

[84]*A. P. R.*, March 1, 1917.

[85]*A. P. R.*, June 14, 1916.

[86]Baruch admitted clearing $476,168.00 as a result of this slump.

[87]The New York *Times*, February 4, 1917.

[88]*A. P. R.*, April 28, 1917.

The New York *Sun* made this statement: "Leading bankers expect that the entrance of the United States into the war will result in a material increase in orders placed here for shells and other munitions. One banker pointed out that the Allies have reduced their purchases of shells and finished munitions in the United States owing to the desire to curtail the heavy expenditures. Munitions companies which have been closing their plants and discharging employees by the thousands are expected to resume operations on a larger scale." The *Wall Street Journal* offered further confirmation. The first sign of a big *Government loan*, it said, would give new life to all the war-orders companies. New York *Sun*, April 4, 1917; *Wall Street Journal*, April 3, 1917; Arnett, *op. cit.*, 220 f.

The tie-up between the United States and the Allies angered the Germans a great deal and was partially responsible for their willingness to go to war with this country. The fact that this country was being used as a base of supplies not only for munitions, food, and equipment, but also for money with which to buy them, caused this anti-American feeling to become very strong. It was heightened by the fact that although many concessions had been made to the United States in connection with submarine warfare, there had been no serious attempt on the part of the American government to compel the British to revise their naval policy.

As the blockade of Central Europe became increasingly effective, German officials became more and more alarmed. Zimmermann felt that the food situation had become so bad that Germany could not possibly hold out another year.[89] His prophecy was just about correct as is proved by the following reports to the American State Department:

"September 15, 1916: Although the open-air restaurants are full of people who at first sight seem to be not only well but happy, yet it needs but little close inspection to see the marked depression underlying all. Almost all of the faces are pale and denote bad or insufficient food."[90]

"July 23, 1917: Economic conditions are not only lamentable, they are tragic. There is scarcity of all articles of the first necessity. If the Allies turn the screws a little tighter the entire structure will tumble down like a house of cards.

"August 6, 1917 [reporting an interview with an American by the name of Lang]: The class of people Lang associated with were practically on the verge of starvation all the time. Hundreds drop in the streets faint from hunger. He has heard reports of hundreds having died from lack of food. Newspapers never report such cases, but say the people died of typhoid, or smallpox, etc. Lang weighed one hundred and twenty pounds and he had formerly weighed one hundred and seventy-five pounds.

"August 13, 1917: The death rate among old people is huge, as it is with very small young children. There is great discontent in the navy among the sailors. The food is very bad.

[89]*F. R. S.*, 1917, 103.
[90]*M. I.*, Part 28, 8672.

"August 20, 1917: The food crisis has reached tremendous proportions. . . . There exists a food shortage which approaches famine to within a very narrow margin. The mortality of persons over 45 years of age is immense. The average loss of weight is 35 to 40 pounds."[91]

A natural accompaniment of all this privation in Germany was the spread of disease. Abram I. Elkus reported that "there was a great increase in tuberculosis cases because of the lack of sufficient proper food."[92] At another time it was said that there were thirty thousand cases of smallpox in Northern Germany alone.[93] Wellington House noted on January 4, 1917, that the Germans were "having epidemics of typhus, scarlet fever and diphtheria and a terrible number of people . . . [were] dying." There was also a report of widespread sickness among children in the city of Hamburg.

By the end of the war disease and starvation had taken a heavy toll among Germans. It is estimated that seven hundred and sixty-three thousand lives were lost as a result of the blockade, and "to say that Germany was really emaciated in 1918 is no figure of speech."[94]

Faced with such a situation, the German government again began to consider unrestricted submarine warfare. Hindenburg informed the government: "We are counting on the possibility of war with the United States and have made all preparations to meet it. Things cannot be worse than they are now. The war must be brought to an end by the use of all means as soon as possible."[95] At a meeting at Pless in September, 1916, it was tentatively decided to inaugurate a new submarine campaign the following spring. Final decision was made on January 9, 1917.

People are inclined to ask why the Germans risked so much

---

[91]"There is more starvation in Turkey than in any other country; out of 300,000 persons in Lebanon, it is estimated (conservatively) that 200,000 have died." Breckinridge Long Papers, July 30, 1917.

[92]*M. I.,* Part 28, 8672.

[93]*F. R. S.,* 1917, I, 74.

It was probably this same privation which caused the appearance in Spain of an epidemic of grippe. First reports of this disease appeared in June, 1918. Before it had run its course, this Spanish influenza was responsible for more fatalities than was the war.

[94]Guichard, *op. cit.,* 294.

[95]*Official German Documents,* II, 1319.

on the submarine. The answer is that, as far as they were concerned, it was not a risk. Their desperate situation seemed to hold more danger than any possible reactions to an unrestricted submarine warfare. And also many believed that the submarine could force Great Britain to her knees. It was felt that if enough ships were destroyed, either Great Britain would be starved into submission, or else her lack of materials would make possible a German victory on land. "If the submarines could sink 350,000 tons a month, working under restrictions, was it not reasonable to suppose that when freed from restrictions they would succeed in bringing the rate up to 600,000 a month — a rate which would certainly be fatal to Great Britain."[96] "The decision of the German Government to embark on the intensive campaign in 1917, with its consequent effect on America, has often been spoken of as a reckless and foolish gamble, but not by anyone who was concerned in countering it."[97]

The submarine campaign was undertaken principally with the hope of damaging the economic structure of Great Britain and her allies to such an extent that they would be unable to continue the war. In order to do this the United States, as a base of supplies, had to be cut off from Europe; the vast flood of American agricultural and manufactured products must be prevented from reaching the Entente Powers. The Germans desired to stop this traffic, and, by means of the submarine, to turn the tables on Great Britain, and starve her into submission.

The possibility of the United States entering the war did not prevent German officials from giving free reign to the submarine. They felt that there was not a great deal to choose between the United States as an open enemy and the United States as a neutral, that every policy of the American government had been anti-German, and that they could hope for no impartial action from the American President. General Falkenhayn wrote to Bethmann-Hollweg on May 4: "So far as this [submarine] situation is concerned, America's step from the secret war in which it has long been engaged against us, to an openly declared hostility can

[96]Newbolt, Sir Henry, *A Naval History of the War, 1914-1918*, IV (London, 1920), 350.

[97]Salter, *op. cit.*, 6.

effect no real change."[98] One editor wrote: "Are we actually fighting England, France, and Russia, or are we in reality only fighting America?"[99] Another German wrote: ". . . every time the warrior strikes the sword from the hand of the enemy, a so-called neutral comes running from behind and places a new weapon in the hand of the defeated foe."[100] In the last analysis, the decision of the Germans to undertake unrestricted submarine warfare turned upon their trust, or rather, distrust of Wilson. Some even felt that he would enter the war regardless of circumstances, if he thought the Germans were winning. Ludendorff has remarked: "I had reckoned on [the United States entering the war] . . . provided the balance of war continued in our favour, even if the unrestricted campaign had never been opened."[101] A seeming confirmation of this view can be found in the testimony of President Wilson before the Senate Committee on Foreign Relations. It is as follows:

SENATOR McCUMBER: "Do you think if Germany had committed no act of injustice against our citizens that we would have gotten into this war?"

THE PRESIDENT: "I do think so."

SENATOR McCUMBER: "You think we would have gotten in anyway?"

THE PRESIDENT: "I do."

The strangle hold which Great Britain had obtained upon Germany naturally caused bitter resentment in the Reich. When there was added to this the apparent intention of the American government to condone British actions, the resentment was directed toward the United States. As American industry, commerce, and finance became active participants in the war against Germany, that which had been resentment turned into violent anger. The situation was satisfactory to England. It was satis-

---

[98]*Official German Documents,* II, 1152.

[99]Kunstwart und Kulturwart, May, 1915, XXVIII, 105-106, as cited in Tansill, *op. cit.,* 60.

[100]*Amerikas Waffenausfuhr und Neutralitaet,* 9, as cited in Tansill, *op. cit.,* 62.

[101]Ludendorff, Erich von, *My War Memories 1914-1918,* II (London, 1919), 415.

factory to the United States, but it was definitely objectionable to Germany. Under the circumstances, Germans rather looked forward to the possibility of striking back at their neutral enemy. It was hardly within the bounds of reason for Americans to expect to continue their course unmolested, and yet they could not retreat from their advanced position. They had permitted their interests and their sympathies to become inextricably involved, and it was inevitable that they should have to suffer the consequences.

CHAPTER XIII ☆ THE ELECTION OF 1916

THE election of 1916 was an extraordinary event. It developed into a referendum on the question of American entrance into the war, and might have resulted in drastic changes in American foreign policy. It greatly influenced the actions of the members of Congress and Senate as well as those of the President, and came to be especially important to the officials of belligerent governments in Europe. The British propaganda ministry made regular reports on the progress of the election, and, from time to time, expressed considerable anxiety as to its outcome.[1] To Parker's organization, the significance of this quadrennial American circus lay chiefly in the attitude of the successful candidate — which attitude might be very detrimental to Great Britain. In the last analysis the election would determine how successful British propaganda in the United States had been.

It was a foregone conclusion that Wilson would be the nominee of the Democratic party, and with the great prestige which accompanies an incumbent, there was a good chance that he would win the contest. He, quite rightly, was considered strongly pro-Ally. "A personal friend of the President," in a letter to Parker pointed out that, "but for the friendly patience of Mr. Wilson and the sympathy of the American people, the millions of German and Irish irreconcilables would almost certainly have forced . . . [the President's] hand." In spite of pressure "to take action against Great Britain" Mr. Wilson had done nothing.[2] The British felt that this type of benevolent neutrality must be continued, and they had every reason to believe that under Wilson it would be continued. One of Parker's native volunteers in the United States gave the following forecast:

[1] In one of these early reports Sir Gilbert Parker commented that one of his "valued" correspondents "who understands the intricacies of American politics, reports that he is confident that the future attitude of the American public will be favorable to Great Britain; but he warns us that there will be a vast amount of loose thinking, and still looser talking [in the campaign] which, though it may appear unfavourable, must not be regarded too seriously." *A. P. R.*, October 29, 1915.

[2] *A. P. R. Supplement*, November 29, 1916.

"Wilson is likely to adhere to his present policy, carefully avoiding, if possible, war with Germany, and favouring the Allies, so far as compatible with legal neutrality. There is a tendency to forget the many ways in which Mr. Wilson, as President, might have injured Great Britain, without being unneutral, if he had wished to do so: (1) Congress, but for the restraining hand of Mr. Wilson, might well have sanctioned an embargo on the export of munitions; (2) President Wilson might have placed obstacles in the way of the Allied loans in the United States; (3) [He] . . . might have given way to some at least of the German contentions with regard to submarine warfare."[3]

Quite unlike the Democrats, the Republicans had great difficulty in finding a candidate. In order to bring the Progressives back into the party, some prominent individual had to be chosen who had not participated in the 1912 revolution. In addition, he had to be acceptable to the jingoes of the Roosevelt stripe, and yet not unacceptable to the pacifists of the Middle West. The person who seemed to satisfy all these requirements was Charles Evans Hughes, a member of the Supreme Court since 1910. He was supposed to be a liberal, he had been identified with neither Taft nor Roosevelt, and had taken part in none of the controversies over neutrality. He was the perfect candidate — an enigma to the American people, to the Republican party, and for a while, to the British government.

There was great speculation as to just where Hughes stood in regard to the war. The British in particular were eager to know.[4] Did the support of Roosevelt mean that the Hughes administration would be dominated by the former Progressive? Would Hughes adopt the Rough Rider's belligerent anti-German attitude? Or did the similarity in temperament between Wilson and Hughes mean that the latter was merely a "whiskered Wilson?" A British intelligence officer wrote: "There is no more difference between . . . [Hughes and Wilson] than a barber could remove in ten minutes." Was this true? Was it to be expected that Hughes would continue Wilson's pro-Ally policies? On the other hand, if Hughes followed neither Roosevelt nor Wilson, would he pursue a course which would be satisfactory to the Allies?

[3]*A. P. R.*, November 1, 1916.   [4]*A. P. R.*, October 18, 1916.

Wellington House made great efforts to obtain information which would answer these questions. Each week during the period before the election careful reports were made to the Cabinet concerning the two candidates. In October Parker noted that Hughes' ideas were not necessarily the same as Roosevelt's. One of his correspondents wrote: "Mr. Roosevelt is for Hughes simply because he wants to beat Wilson. . . . It is extremely unlikely that . . . [he] will have any influence on the conduct of affairs at Washington if Mr. Hughes is elected." At the same time this report intimated that Hughes, unlike Wilson, would not fight Britain's battles in the United States. "I believe that Mr. Hughes is absolutely neutral as regards the war. I have had some conversation with him, and I do not really think he is very much interested in the war, or cares very much which side wins. He is far more interested in internal American politics."[5]

All of Parker's observers began to fear Hughes would take neutrality seriously rather than shape his policies for the benefit of the Allies as had Mr. Wilson. One of them reported to London that Hughes had said: "We propose that we shall protect and enforce American rights on land and sea without fear and unflinchingly with respect to American lives, American property, and American commerce." The correspondent then remarked: "These words in the mouth of Mr. Wilson would not mean very much, but in the mouth of Mr. Hughes they mean a good deal. . . . It might be supposed that he will be prevented from taking any retaliatory steps [against Great Britain], but I do not think it is safe to take this view. . . . The Foreign Office ought to be thoroughly informed as to the change that is likely to take place in the attitude of Washington if Mr. Hughes is elected." "The situation is more fraught with danger now than it has ever been before."[6] A later report stated: "It is difficult to see what form a new policy could take, unless it should be a less friendly attitude to Great Britain. . . ."[7] The anxiety of these agents was caused by the fear that the very helpful Wilson partisanship would be replaced by a neutrality which would be disastrous to the Allies.

[5] *A. P. R.*, October 18, 1916.
[6] *Ibid.* "It is to remembered that Mr. Hughes has a legalistic mind. . . ."*A. P. R. Supplement*, November 29, 1916.
[7] *A. P. R.*, November 1, 1916.

There is no evidence that the British took any part in the actual election. As far as can be ascertained, the course of events was determined by the state of American feeling and by the political perspicacity of the parties to the struggle.

The Hughes campaign was not conducted with any considerable astuteness or good fortune. In the first place the Republican leader was handicapped by the support of reactionaries. The backing of Eastern industrial leaders and the apostate head of the Progressive Party alienated many liberals. Hughes was also embarrassed by the widespread impression that he and his party stood for war. Without question the Republican candidate's "greatest liability was the support of Roosevelt." In addition to these inherent difficulties, the Republican campaign was at fault in many ways. Hughes' speeches were disappointing throughout. A totally different type of oratory is needed for the hustings from that used on the bench. The Republican candidate was unable to make the transition successfully. The junket of Eastern society women also contributed to the general dissatisfaction with the Republicans. Hughes made the crowning error when he snubbed Hiram Johnson in California — an error which cost him the presidency.

After Wilson had taken over preparedness, it apparently became the intention among Republicans to make foreign policy the issue of the campaign. But here great difficulties were encountered. In the first place it was impossible to demand a sterner attitude toward the belligerent powers, because that might mean war, and the American public was revealing unequivocally that it desired peace. Still they could not advocate a less intransigent foreign policy. That would have seemed to imply a weakness on their part. Hughes could not state that he favored either a stronger attitude or a weaker one. Nor could he contend that Wilson's course of action had resulted in failure, for the concessions obtained from Germany in the *Sussex* pledge appeared to have been a decisive victory. In the end, it became difficult for the Republican candidate to deal with anything but generalities. One wag commented that Hughes was convincing until he touched on the *Lusitania,* then "he spent most of his time clearing his throat." By October, Republican efforts to make an issue of foreign policy had collapsed.

The Democratic campaign progressed much more happily. In the first place some degree of success was obtained in attacking the "hyphenates." One of Parker's observers in the United States reported: "It will be noticed that the German voters are, for the most part, not included in any of these classes whom the President must not alienate, being Republicans out of sympathy with the policies of the Republicans in the East. It may be expected, therefore, that President Wilson will adopt as strong an attitude towards Germany as he can so long as such an attitude does not immediately threaten a rupture of peaceful relations."[8] The accuracy of this particular opinion is borne out by Lansing's advice to Wilson at a much earlier time. He had said: "I believe the pro-German vote in this country is irrevocably lost to us and that, no matter what we do now, we can never win back any part of it. If this view is correct, we ought not from the political standpoint lose the support of the Americans hostile to Germany."[9] Wilson was particularly anxious to use the German-Americans as a whipping dog. At one time he stated: "There is disloyalty active in the United States, and it must be absolutely crushed."[10] When Jeremiah O'Leary wrote Wilson accusing him of being pro-British, the President took advantage of this opportunity to attack the "hyphenates."[11] But otherwise he was unsuccessful in pushing the issue.

The outstanding success of the Democratic campaign was achieved in the field of foreign affairs, where, accidentally, those individuals who favored keeping out of the war made the Wilson campaign their own. They, quite mistakenly, thought Wilson shared their desire to maintain neutrality. But the strong pacifist stand taken by the convention in St. Louis was not Wilson's work. In fact it was contrary to his wishes. It is important to notice that his strong statement on American rights was deleted from the platform and, "with the plank that represented the strong peace feeling of the convention, Wilson personally had nothing whatever to do."[12]

[8]*A. P. R.*, March 17, 1916.

[9]Savage, *op. cit.*, II, 415, November 19, 1915.

[10]The Public Papers of Woodrow Wilson, IV, 209.

[11]Wilson's telegram was as follows: "I would feel deeply mortified to have you or anybody like you vote for me. Since you have access to many disloyal Americans and I have not, I will ask you to convey this message to them."

[12]Baker, *op. cit.*, VI, 256.

The pacifist movement became powerful early in the convention. Martin H. Glynn of New York in making his introductory speech, inadvertently began to dwell upon the incidents in American history when presidents managed to maintain peace in spite of the aggressive actions of foreign governments. The reaction was astounding:

" 'When Grant was President, during the war between Spain and the Spanish West Indies, a Spanish gunboat seized the vessel *Virginius* . . . flying the American flag. . . .'

" 'But we didn't go to war.'

"The orator cited cases of violations under Harrison and Lincoln:

" 'But we didn't go to war.'

"He cited precedents under Pierce, Van Buren, Jefferson, Adams, Washington:

" 'But we didn't go to war.'

"The crowd was delirious with joy. Their faith in their chief and his course of action was being completely justified.

" 'Go to it, Glynn. Give them some more!'

"One auditor, in the press gallery, the 'peerless leader,' William J. Bryan, was weeping with emotion at this recital of the victories of peace: but the party leaders who had wanted to stress Americanism were aghast. The convention was getting wholly out of control. It looked like a demonstration for pacifism. Senator John Walter Smith of Maryland rushed to the platform to confer with McCombs. Something must be done to check the stampede. McCombs hastily scrawled on a sheet of paper, 'but we are willing to fight if necessary,' and passed it over to Glynn, who was waiting for the delirium to subside.

" 'I'll take care of that,' he called back — and, intoxicated with his own oratory, roused to a still higher pitch the ardour of his vast audience."[13]

The climax came on the second day in the speech of Senator Ollie James of Kentucky who declaimed:

" 'Without orphaning a single American child, without widowing a single American mother, without firing a single gun, without the shedding of a single drop of blood, he wrung from the most militant spirit that ever brooded above a battlefield an acknowl-

[13]*Ibid.*, 251 f.

edgment of American rights and an agreement to American demands.'

"The crowd roared with delight. 'Repeat it, repeat it!'

"When the orator ceased, the cheering was tumultuous and long continued. Nor was there anything bogus about it. Every delegate was on his feet; the Marylanders in the front row stood on their chairs; and women as well as men paraded in the aisles.

"Nothing could better have expressed the deep feeling of the delegates than the shout that went up from every part of the great auditorium for 'Bryan, Bryan!' They wanted still more oratory on the peace theme: and they wanted it from the silvery tongue of the Old Warrior."[14]

In spite of administration desires, this note of pacifism was the only thing which stirred the convention. "It was a 'stampede'; it was also a revelation. The Democratic managers themselves could not have realized the true depth and power of the pacifist sentiment in the country — so long obscured by the outpourings of the editorial war-hawks or the romantic patriotism of the upper classes."[15]

All this pacifist feeling was epitomized in the phrase "he kept us out of war." It appeared in the Democratic platform, but its author remains unknown. The phrase was marvelous propaganda in itself — it was incisive and easily remembered. The single-syllable words were forceful and easily pronounced. But this again was not Wilson's doing. "It was certainly never the President's intent to rest the most important recent phase of his record — his attitude toward the European war — upon the naïve generality that he had kept us out of war (with the implication that he would continue to do so). There are, indeed, many evidences that he did not like the phrase. . . ."[16] But in spite of Wilson's attempt and the attempt of other speakers to emphasize to the public that the administration was ready to go to war under certain circumstances, Americans closed their ears and dwelt upon that one phrase — "he kept us out of war." Wherever Democratic speakers appeared, they found that there was only one sure means of gaining applause, and that was by dwelling upon

[14]*Ibid.*, 253 f.
[15]Millis, *op. cit.*, 319.
[16]Baker, *op. cit.*, VI, 257 f.

the pacifist argument that "he kept us out of war." No matter what else was said, those simple words crowded out all other appeals. They did not accurately interpret the policy of the administration — past, present, or future — but they did interpret the policy of the American people.

The outcome of the contest between Wilson and Hughes was as remarkable as the campaign itself. In the nineteen page special report prepared for the British Cabinet, Wellington House called it "an astonishing election."[17] It was astonishing because after it had become generally believed that Wilson had lost the election, it was found that he had won it. With the announcement that New York had gone for Hughes, there was jubilation in Republican headquarters. Newspapers throughout the country and in Europe were issuing extras proclaiming a Hughes victory. Soon, however, reports from the West put his election in doubt. The returns from California were late in arriving. When they were finally recorded, it was found that the Republican Hiram Johnson had been elected by a huge majority, while the Republican Hughes had been defeated by a few thousand votes. The loss of California meant the loss of the election. An American agent reported to Parker that "future histories will not err if they put down 1916 as the date of the Discovery of California."[18]

The vote in the electoral college revealed the division in the nation which had been observed so many times during the preceding years — a division between those who desired to assist the Allies and those who wished to remain neutral. It was the East versus the West and Middle West, and the East was defeated. It was one of the few times that a President of the United States was chosen contrary to the desires of the voters in the great financial and industrial centers of the nation. The support of the pacifists was, of course, largely the result of Bryan's campaigning.[19]

[17]A. P. R., Supplement, November 29, 1916.

[18]A. P. R., Supplement, November 29, 1916.

[19]See Tansill, op. cit., 602. Wilson wrote Bryan: "May I not say how much I have admired your part in the campaign and what a vast deal of effective work you seem to me to have done in the very part of the country which has now aligned itself with the forces of progress? I think all Democrats are grateful to you. Certainly I am." President Wilson to Mr. Bryan, November 17, 1916, Bryan MS, as quoted by Tansill, op. cit., 603.

The foreign influence in the campaign of 1916 was not a determining factor. Sir Gilbert Parker has stated that the "German vote was not solid, and had no decisive effect on the election."[20] It was true that German-Americans who sympathized with the Central Powers cordially disliked President Wilson, but like the average American, they feared that a Hughes victory would mean a Roosevelt victory, and hence war against Germany. Consequently many of them voted the Democratic ticket. "The conclusion was inescapable that the 'hyphenates' had after all exercised little influence, and the Cincinnati *Volksblatt* frankly admitted that Hughes had polled his biggest vote where the hyphenates were weakest."[21] On November 20, Colonel House wrote to Wilson that he had "indisputable evidence that Bernstorff used in a quiet way what influence he could bring to bear in favor of your election."[22]

In another letter to Wilson, Colonel House quoted Roy Howard as saying that "Germany almost to a man is wishing for your defeat and that France and England are almost to a man wishing for your success. Lloyd George, Northcliffe, and others are particularly keen to have you win."[23] But English opinion was far from being unanimously pro-Wilson. In spite of the realization in many quarters that Wilson had done everything that he legally could do for the Allies, there was great personal dislike for him. Wellington House remarked at one time that "constant reference has been made to the grave harm which offensive and thoughtless criticism by the English press has done to the Allied cause in the United States. Accumulating evidence merely confirms all that has been said."[24] Just before the election Sir Horace Plunkett wrote E. M. House: "I hope you will not be annoyed, if the President's re-election is badly received by British public opinion."[25] When Wilson read the English newspapers which were published at the time it was thought that he had been defeated in the election, he soon found that Plunkett, and not Howard had correctly interpreted British opinion. He, of course, should not have been

[20]*A. P. R., Supplement*, November 29, 1916.
[21]Wittke, *op. cit.*, 110.
[22]Baker, *op. cit.*, VI, 363, footnote.
[23]*Ibid.*, VI, 363.
[24]*A. P. R.*, March 3, 1916.
[25]Baker, *op. cit.*, VI, 364.

surprised, for he had been attacked by the English press since the outbreak of the war, and attacks against him were to continue until the United States broke off relations with Germany.[26]

Sir Gilbert Parker reported to the Cabinet that Wilson's re-election should be attributed: (1) "To his personality. He is a tried leader." (2) "To the growing radicalism of a part of the United States in domestic politics." (3) "To the unexampled prosperity of the United States." (4) "To his policy of peace."[27]

To a large extent the nine million people who voted for Wilson did so because of the phrase "he kept us out of war." They made a surface assessment, decided for themselves that the choice was between war and peace, and consequently voted for peace. Even J. P. Morgan has conceded that the election "certainly showed that the majority of the people did not want us to go into the war."[28] In its official report the British propaganda ministry stated: "But, however strong may be the sympathy of the American people for the Allies, it is impossible to view the election without realizing how decisively the American people favor a peaceful policy."[29]

To Americans a vote for Wilson had meant a vote for peace. Through the only medium available to them they had expressed their unmistakable desire to keep out of the European conflict.

[26]One Wellington House agent reported that "as nothing but an unforeseen mischance could deprive President Wilson of office during the continuation of the war, it is important that British public opinion should not allow itself to be in any way associated with any opposition to the President." *A. P. R.*, May 30, 1917.

[27]*A. P. R.*, November 15, 1916.

[28]*M. I.*, Part 26, 7814.

[29]*A. P. R., Supplement*, November 29, 1916.

CHAPTER XIV ☆ THE RACE BETWEEN A NEGOTIATED PEACE AND UNRESTRICTED SUBMARINE WARFARE

THE winter of 1916-17 was the climax of the war in Europe, and the climax of the struggle in the United States over participation in that war. The outcome of both contests turned upon the success or failure of Woodrow Wilson's efforts to obtain a negotiated peace. The American President, whose attitude during the last year of neutrality appeared to change noticeably, wished to bring the war to an end in order to forestall the German threat of unrestricted submarine warfare. The Allies, on the other hand, wished to see the United States forced into the war against Germany; they desired not a negotiated peace, but a victorious peace. Consequently they did all in their power to defeat Wilson's attempt to bring an immediate end to hostilities.

In September, 1914, President Wilson, at Bryan's suggestion, had considered making an open proposal for the calling of a peace conference. However, Colonel House and others discouraged a Wilsonian intervention. Lord Bryce personally wrote the American President opposing any such move. Page objected, stating that if Wilson would only wait, the British would be glad to have him act as mediator at a later time. "The wishes of the Allies were heeded"[1] and Wilson made no offer of peace.

During the winter of 1915-16 House evolved his trick plan for a peace conference which actually would have given victory to the Allies. In order to explore its possibilities, he went to Europe in January to confer with statesmen in London and Paris. On February 22 Sir Edward Grey tentatively agreed to the proposition, but with the proviso that a conference was not to be called until he had decided that the time was opportune. On March 7 Wilson formally agreed to go ahead with the plan as soon as Grey indicated that he was ready. In the meantime the Gore-McLemore debate and the *Sussex* crisis intervened to oc-

[1] Baker, *op. cit.*, V, 291.

cupy the attention of the American President. However, in spite
of these events, he retained his interest in the peace plan and
waited patiently for word from the British government. House
cabled Grey on April 7 urging that action be taken soon. On
April 19 Wilson threatened war with Germany over the sinking
of the *Sussex,* and on May 4 the German government temporarily
acceded to his demands concerning submarine warfare. Meanwhile, the British Foreign Minister did not give the necessary
signal for Wilson to send out the suggestion for the calling of a
peace conference. Finally, on May 12, Grey lamely backed out of
his agreement. He did announce "adherence to the principle of
a league to keep peace, predicating it, however, on Allied victory. . . ."

"On the eve of the great Somme offensive Sir Edward thought
that the 'time for durable peace' would come only after the British army had made 'its effort and its sacrifice.' " When the offensive was finished the British sacrifice amounted to more than
400,000 casualties. All these lives went to secure a piece of land
thirty miles long by seven miles deep — territory which was of
no strategic value. The total casualties of British, French, and
German reached over 1,100,000. And still there was no desire for
peace among the statesmen. The new argument was that nothing
less than the crushing of Germany would be acceptable.[2]

Wilson now fully appreciated the seriousness of the situation
confronting him as a result of the German reply to his ultimatum.
In a letter to House dated May 16, 1916, he stated: "We are
plainly face to face with this alternative, therefore. The United
States must either make a decided move for peace (upon some
basis that promises to be permanent) or, if she postpones that,
must insist to the limit upon her rights of trade and upon such
freedom of the seas as international law already justifies her in
insisting on as against Great Britain, with the same plain speaking and firmness that she had used against Germany. And the
choice must be made immediately. Which does Great Britain
prefer? She cannot escape both. To do nothing is now, for us,
impossible." In other words, the American President realized
that he would be faced with renewed submarine warfare if he
did not immediately effect a change in British illegalities or if the

[2]See Tansill, *op. cit.,* 586, 587.

war were not brought to an end. As a way out of this dilemma, Wilson began to give serious thought to the initiation of a peace move. On May 27, 1916, before the League to Enforce Peace, he implied that the American government would be glad to act as mediator. It was in this speech that he expressed a willingness to abandon the American policy of isolation and to participate in a league of nations.[3]

In England and France press comment on Wilson's speech was limited primarily to expressions of indignation over a phrase he had used stating that American interests were not identical with those of the Allies.[4] Naturally this denial of the "our fight" propaganda annoyed Allied newspapermen. In so far as it was discussed, the idea of American co-operation was well received, but no great interest was aroused by the suggestion for the establishment of a league of nations. Nor was any attention given to the intimation that Wilson would be willing to act as mediator. At least no European statesman rushed forward to ask the American President to call a conference.

The cool reception given by the Allies to the offer to join in a league of nations as well as their apparent lack of sincerity in connection with the House proposal, annoyed President Wilson greatly. "From this period dates his suspicion of Allied motives in the War, which was not entirely dissipated by co-partnership against Germany after 1917 and was intensified during the Peace Conference."[5] He began to wonder if their aims were not almost as sordid as those of the Central Powers.[6] In June he told House that he could see no justification in helping the Allies "to destroy Germany politically and economically, so that France and Rus-

[3]In his outline of fundamentals on which this league would operate, is found the basis of the fourteen points.

[4]"With its causes and its objects we are not concerned."

[5]*Intimate Papers,* II, 304.

[6]In the spring of 1916 an agreement was arrived at between Great Britain, France, and Russia with regard to their spheres of influence in Asiatic Turkey. On July 3, 1916, Japan and Russia agreed to keep others out of China. In February, 1917, Russia agreed to support France on the Alsace-Lorraine question, the Saar Valley and a neutral Rhine state — in other words the dismemberment of Germany. In return France recognized Russia's "complete liberty in establishing her western frontiers." Cocks, F. Seymour, *The Secret Treaties and Understandings* (London, 1918).

sia might divide the dictatorship of the Continent and Great Britain be rid of German naval and commercial competition."[7]

As a matter of fact, at this time there was appearing the deep struggle between the propaganda of hate and the propaganda of enlightened war aims. By the time of the peace conference the former had won out and was responsible for the vicious aspects of the Treaty of Versailles. Nicolson has stated that "by arousing popular emotion during the war" the Allies "had created a Frankenstein" which held them helpless in 1919. This was responsible for what he has called the "appalling hypocrisy" of the peace conference.

As the summer of 1916 wore on, the high-handed conduct of the British in connection with censorship and the blacklist turned Wilson's suspicion into anger. Before long he was stating: "How difficult it is to be friends with Great Britain without doing whatever she wants us to do."[8] "We must now get down to 'hard pan' with the Allies." Their attitude has been "altogether indefensible" and "intolerable." When Page came home to get a "bath in American opinion," he found that Mr. Wilson "was utterly cold, utterly unresponsive, interested only in ending the war." "He spoke of England's having the earth and of Germany's wanting it."[9]

Early in the summer Wilson had remarked: "We are holding off not because we do not feel concerned, but because when we exert the force of this nation we want to know what we are exerting it for." A similar expression is to be found in his Memorial Day address at Arlington when he stated: "We are not going to devote our nationality to the same mistaken aggressive purposes that some other nationalities have been devoted to." His peroration intimated rather clearly that he was referring to the Allies as well as to the Central Powers. Sir Cecil Spring-Rice reported to his government that at Buffalo Wilson had "compared the war to a drunken brawl in a public house. This is the view which he is taking, and which the people of this country cordially share."[10]

The reports of Wellington House throughout 1916 display

[7]October 10, 1916, The Papers of Colonel House (Yale University).
[8]Baker, *op. cit.*, VI, 331.
[9]Hendrick, *op. cit.*, II, 196 f.
[10]Spring-Rice, *op. cit.*, II, 356.

very clearly the progressive decline of British prestige among the rank and file of Americans. Comments began to appear such as:

"*February 12*: British cause has recently suffered a slight setback in the United States.

"*May 25*: ... prestige of Great Britain in this country is at the lowest ebb since the war began.

"*May 31*: ... during the current week British prestige in the United States has fallen even lower; in the Far West [it] is indeed becoming serious.

"*June 7*: It seems to be taken for granted ... that almost all Irish-American feeling has been irretrievably alienated by the executions arising out of the Easter Rebellion.

"*September 6*: There is no doubt that pro-British sympathy in the United States ... has recently undergone considerable modification.

"*October 18*: The outstanding feature of American opinion at the present time is the growing feeling against Great Britain. Also relations between Japan and the United States are not improving."

The widespread character of this criticism will be realized when it is noticed that even Colonel House, that staunch supporter of all things British, became impatient with his European friends. In December he remarked: "The United States had practiced benevolent neutrality which the Allies in no way appreciated. We had gotten the enmity of Germany and had not received corresponding benefit from the Allies."[11]

The reappraisal of the Allies by the American President and the American people was caused by a number of factors. Among these were the widespread questioning of the Allies' motives,[12] anger at their attitude towards neutral rights, and the belief that they intended to continue the economic warfare against the Central Powers even after the military struggle had been brought to an end.[13] Above all this change in feeling was the result of the

[11]*M. I.*, Part 28, 8751.

[12]Parker reported in October: "It is to be feared that there is a growing tendency ... to throw doubt upon the ideals for which the Allies are fighting." *A. P. R.*, October 4, 1916.

[13]"The President on July 10 transmitted to Congress Lansing's report on the Allies Economic Conference held at Paris in June. The agreement, Lansing had

growing conviction that a stalemate had been reached, and that neither the Allies nor Germany could win the war.[14] In January, 1916, an American observer reported that in the United States the feeling was widespread that a negotiated peace was the only peace the Allies could hope for.[15] By December Mr. Wilson had become positively convinced that neither side could win. Ambassador Bernstorff wrote home: "One hears constantly the view expressed by members of the Cabinet and by others of the President's friends who are in his confidence" that our enemies can never conquer us.[16] As a matter of fact there is considerable doubt as to whether the Allies could have maintained even a stalemate without the assistance of the United States.

A direct outgrowth of these changed attitudes was the American public's desire to have steps taken which might bring an end to the war. From many sources in the country pressure was exerted against Wilson to force him to call a peace conference. And added to this were urgings from the German government. At first Wilson was noncommittal. However, some time after March 27, he did request House to ask the Allies to state that their peace terms would be unselfish. If House carried out the suggestion, it brought no results. On May 11 Bethmann-Hollweg warned Gerard that Wilson had better do something about British illegalities or else the U-boats would have to be again released. In the summer months, probably because of the election, the Germans marked time.

In September von Jagow warned Gerard that if Wilson did not hasten with his peace move, "German public sentiment would compel the government to give in to the demands" for ruthless submarine warfare.[17] After this there was a temporary easing, within Germany of criticism of the United States and discussion

pointed out, anxiously, proposed 'to continue the war industrially after actual warfare ceases,' and he drew the conclusion that it would 'cause the Central Powers to hesitate in taking steps toward a restoration of peace.' " Lansing to Wilson, June 23, 1916. Baker, *op. cit.*, VI, 313.

[14]As early as August of 1915 Page reported: "I hear that neither side can win in France." Again in May of 1916 he wrote: "The English fear that they can never win a real victory but only a draw." Hendrick, *op. cit.*, III, 252, 295.

[15]*A. P. R., Supplement,* January 28, 1916.

[16]To Bethmann-Hollweg, December 11, 1916. *Original German Documents,* II, 1029.

[17]Baker, *op. cit.*, VI, 356.

of the renewal of submarine warfare, in order "to avoid embarrassing the President should he desire to act" for peace.[18] On October 19 the Kaiser himself prepared a memorandum in an attempt to hasten Wilson's offer of a peace conference. This memorandum addressed to Ambassador Gerard stated: "Your Excellency hinted to His Majesty in your last conversation at Charleville in April that President Wilson possibly would try towards the end of the summer to offer his good services to the belligerents for the promotion of peace. The German Government has no information as to whether the President adheres to this idea and as to the eventual date at which his step would take place. Meanwhile the constellation of war has taken such a form that the German Government foresees the time at which it will be forced to regain the freedom of action that it has reserved to itself in the note of May 4 last and thus the President's steps may be jeopardized."[19]

The Allies of course became very disturbed at the prospect of intervention on the part of Wilson. In December, 1914, Clemenceau had discounted American intervention, stating, "peace must be the concern of the belligerents only, with no outside mediation or interference."[20] As early as January, 1915, the British had informed Page that they did not like Wilson's suggestion that he act as mediator. They were also disturbed by his speech on April 20, 1915, before the Associated Press in which he indicated that he would like to be the peace maker. Lord Bertie remarked: "Let the Americans mind their own business and keep their own Germans in order."[21] Spring-Rice told House that "it would not do for the President to make any proposals" as to terms of peace.[22] The renewed rumors in 1916 annoyed the Allies even more. On

[18]F. R. S., 1916, 293, 297.

[19]Official German Documents, II, 987.

[20]Bertie, Francis Leveson, The Diary of Lord Bertie of Thame 1914-1918, I (New York, 1924), 821.

In the secret Treaty of London, Italy, in return for the many things she obtained from that treaty, agreed to keep the Pope from making peace offers. Article XV reads as follows: "France, Great Britain, and Russia undertake to support Italy insofar as she does not permit the representatives of the Holy See to take diplomatic action with regard to the conclusion of peace and the regulation of questions connected with the war." This was signed by Benckendorff, Imperiali, Cambon, and Grey.

[21]Hendrick, op. cit., III, 213.

[22]Intimate Papers, I, 326.

May 24, 1916, Grey made an impromptu speech in Commons, declaring "that the time had not come to make speeches about peace."[23] In June of that year Ambassador Page wrote to his son of British annoyance, stating: "If anyone should talk about peace, or doves, or ploughshares here, they'd shoot him."[24]

On June 22, 1916, Wilson wrote to House: "They are in danger of forgetting the rest of the world, and of waking up some surprising morning to discover that it has a positive right to be heard about the peace of the world. I conclude that it will be up to us to judge for ourselves when the time has arrived for us to make an imperative suggestion. I mean a suggestion which they will have no choice but to heed, because the opinion of the non-official world and the desire of all peoples will be behind it."

On September 19, 1916, Briand declared "the idea of peace by negotiation as 'an outrage against the memory of so many heroes who had fallen for France.' "[25] In a public article Walter Hines Page wrote that Britain would not tolerate intervention. On September 25 Colonel House recorded in his diary: "Walter Page called this afternoon. . . . He said the British resent our trying to bring about peace."[26] On October 11 Asquith stated that the war "cannot be allowed to end in some . . . dishonouring compromise, masquerading under the name of Peace,"[27] and Lloyd George gave a speech "warning neutrals from dallying with mediation."

Wellington House also gave expression to the anxiety caused by these rumors of peace. As early as August 6, 1915, it was stated: "In the near future a serious effort will become necessary to counteract the peace propaganda in the United States. The task may be difficult."[28] There is "a very great danger in this peace talk with its consequent stimulation of the peace longing." Regularly after this time additional warnings were made until the report of November 29, 1916, which stated: "Peace talk is vastly upon the increase." "If, therefore, it is desired to prevent

[23]Baker, *op. cit.*, VI, 219.
[24]Hendrick, *op. cit.*, I, 431.
[25]Baker, *op. cit.*, VI, 355.
[26]As quoted in *M. I.*, Part 28, 8493.
[27]Baker, *op. cit.*, VI, 359.
[28]*A. P. R.*, August 6, 1915, 4.

or counteract the further growth of peace sentiment in the United States, it may be necessary to take timely and definite steps."[29]

Although the Germans were anxious that Wilson issue a call for peace, they did not want him to have anything to do with terms. Throughout all these discussions it is very clearly stated that Wilson must have nothing to do with the actual mediation. In Bethmann-Hollweg's telegram of August 18, 1916, he made it clear that he wanted Wilson's assistance in opening peace negotiations, but he definitely did not want any intervention by the American President concerning terms. He confirmed this in his message to Bernstorff on October 14. In the German reply to Wilson's peace message of December 18, 1916, it was stated unequivocably that terms must be decided upon by the belligerents, and that Wilson would be welcomed only at a second conference which was to formulate means to preserve peace. The Germans, of course, looked upon Wilson with a deep and bitter distrust. They felt that in any peace conference, he would do all in his power to injure them.

By the summer of 1916 the unleashing of the submarine, which was ultimately to drive the United States into the war, turned upon one of two questions: first, would there be an easing up of the attempt to starve Germany into submission; and second, was there any possibility of successful peace negotiations being inaugurated? The solution of either or both of these depended upon the actions of the American President. The economic situation of the Allies had become so difficult that Wilson, by means of an embargo, could have compelled them to eliminate the most glaring of their illegalities from their blockade procedure. Their economic dependence upon the United States would also have forced them to enter into peace negotiations if Wilson applied pressure. The Allies "were dependent on American supplies." "They could not go on with the war without a continuous flow of supplies from America, for which they could no longer pay in cash, or in repatriated securities, or in temporary bank loans."[30] In November, Lloyd George wrote: "Our dependence

[29]*A. P. R.*, *Supplement*, November 29, 1916.
[30]Baker, *op. cit.*, VI, 366 f.

upon America is growing for food, raw material and munitions. We are rapidly exhausting securities negotiable in America."[31]

In 1915 McAdoo had suggested that loans might be used as a club over the British, but nothing was done with his suggestion at that time. In June, 1916, Wilson decided to secure authority from Congress to prohibit loans and restrict exportations of supplies to the belligerents. In spite of House's objections,[32] Wilson obtained from Congress on September 8 an act which placed in his hands the "vastly potent weapon of economic reprisal." Wilson told Page "that he wouldn't do anything with the retaliatory act till after election lest it might seem that he was playing politics. But he hinted that if there were continued provocation afterward [in case he were elected] he would."[33] A report from the Department of Commerce on the probable effect of retaliatory measures stated that such action on the part of the American government would undoubtedly result in injuring the very prosperous American war business. Perhaps as a result of this report, Wilson discarded the thought of using the weapon of reprisal. He even intervened to temper the language of the State Department notes on censorship and the blacklist.[34]

In November the issuance of the Federal Reserve warning, at the suggestion of Wilson, appears to have been another contemplated method, by means of financial pressure, of forcing the Allies at least to consider peace negotiations. Qualifications, however, which were soon made in this pronouncement, demonstrate that if pressure had been contemplated, it was very soon discarded. After considering the entire situation, one is inclined to believe that American economic entanglements with Great Britain and France, and Wilson's own intense personal sympathies for those countries, prevented him from using any economic pressure.

At the time that Wilson may have been dallying with the

[31]*War Memoirs of David Lloyd George,* II, 340.

[32]Baker, *op. cit.,* VI, 315 f.

[33]Hendrick, *op. cit.,* II, 186.

[34]Baker, *op. cit.,* 316. ". . . when President Wilson was disposed to employ drastic measures against the Allies' lack of respect for our rights, he discovered that the tremendous commercial and financial involvements of this country in the Allied cause rendered drastic action against the Allies impossible, rendered him powerless to affect any change. . . ." *M. I.,* Part 28, 8487.

PRESIDENT WOODROW WILSON AND COLONEL E. M. HOUSE

thought of utilizing pressure to force a conference of the belligerents, the Central Powers were becoming more and more anxious for a peace offer to be made. On September 8 Bernstorff advised his home office that Wilson would move for peace before the end of the year, if he were re-elected.[35] On September 25 the Germans again asked Wilson to call a peace conference. On October 8 they warned him that if he did not act soon they would have to reconsider unrestricted use of the submarine. "It it clear that the administration, of course, was well informed of the situation in Germany, the struggle between the civil faction which wanted to avoid a break with the United States and the military and naval faction, which insisted that the war could only be ended by the renewal of indiscriminate submarine warfare."[36] At a later time, British agents informed their government that the New York *World,* at the suggestion of the administration, was preparing the American public for "possible adverse developments"[37] in connection with the submarine.

On November 9 Bethmann-Hollweg — not Sir Edward Grey — accepted Wilson's League of Nations proposal and agreed to the general ideas of disarmament, freedom of the seas, and compulsary arbitration. Meanwhile Sir William Wiseman and Captain Guy Gaunt were exerting pressure on House to have him prevent Wilson from taking any steps looking toward peace.[38] On November 14 House was in Washington to see the President. Wilson told him that either he had to move immediately for peace or else the Germans would commence unrestricted submarine warfare and thus force the United States into the war. House objected to peace overtures, stating that "the Allies would consider it an unfriendly act." It is interesting to note that at this time he was giving the German Ambassador an entirely incorrect impression. Bernstorff reported to his government: "House is continually urging Mr. Wilson to take action."

The situation in Germany was becoming tense, and on November 16 von Jagow wrote Bernstorff impressing upon him that

---

[35]It is interesting to note that instead of working for peace, Secretary of State Lansing at this time was urging a reopening of the *Lusitania* controversy.

[36]*M. I.,* Part 28, 8503.

[37]*A. P. R.,* January 3, 1917.

[38]Incidentally House was using Captain Gaunt as his messenger to Sir Edward Grey.

it was "desirable to know whether the President was willing to take steps toward negotiation, and if so, which and when."[39] On November 21 and again on November 25 Wilson wrote House saying things were ready to break and something had to be done. By the twenty-fifth the President, having completed the first draft of his proposed demand for peace, wrote to House: "I think things are thickening and we should choose our course at once." On the twenty-seventh House was in Washington to see the note. Being mainly desirous of not irritating the British he objected to Wilson's continued questioning of what the British were fighting for. To please him, the President eliminated the phrase "the causes and objects of the war are obscure." "House next urged him to add something 'which would make the Allies believe he sympathized with their viewpoint.' The document itself shows that Wilson refused."[40] On November 29 Wilson had a note sent to the German government requesting that it stop Belgian deportations and the sinking of ships so that public opinion in the United States would quiet down enough to allow him to make a move for peace.[41]

On November 30 House wrote Wilson: "I have been thinking a lot of your proposed note to the belligerents and I cannot bring myself to believe that it should be done immediately or without further preparation...." "And Lansing, to whom Wilson submitted a [revised] draft of the note on December 1st, damned it with faint praise; it was 'far less objectionable than the one originally proposed.'"[42] During all this period "Ambassador Jusserand was incessantly beseeching President Wilson not to undertake any peace mediation."

House apparently wrote Wilson during the first week of December suggesting his original peace conference scheme be again attempted. In reply Wilson sent the following letter: "The time is near at hand for *something!* ... But that something is not mediation such as we were proposing when you were last on the other side of the water, and therefore I do not think that it would be wise to send the letter you were kind enough to submit to me

[39]Bernstorff, *op. cit.*, 304.
[40]Baker, *op. cit.*, VI, 387.
[41]*F. R. S.*, 1916, 70 f.
[42]Baker, *op. cit.*, VI, 388.

to Lloyd George. We cannot go back to those old plans. We must shape new ones."

In Germany the situation had become critical. The government had postponed decision on unrestricted submarine warfare because the Chancellor was able to "hold out some hope that peace might be arranged if Germany did not go forward with this policy."[43] But months had passed, and Wilson had done nothing to start peace negotiations. Finally, giving up all reliance upon the American President, German officials decided to issue their own peace note, and, if that did not succeed, to turn loose the submarine. A call for peace carried with it the danger of giving Germany's enemies the impression that she was weakening. The necessity, however, for either breaking the blockade or ending the war, was so imperative that all else became of minor importance. The Kaiser wrote: "Trusting God I shall risk it. Submit the notes to me at an early date and make everything ready."[44]

The request for peace, issued on December 12, stated that Germany and her allies were willing to enter into a conference to discuss the possibility of ending the war. The Allies and their sympathizers in the United States were greatly disturbed by this German offer and were unsparing in their attacks upon it. Wilson apparently saw that the sands had just about run out. Either he had to do something immediately or the U-boats would drive the United States into war. On December 13 it was reported from Berlin that "if the peace offer should fail, as is generally expected, the Chancellor would be subjected to greater pressure than ever before to reopen the ruthless submarine campaign."[45] Consequently, without consulting Colonel House, President Wilson determined to send out his own request for peace.

Although Wilson had been considering the issuance of a peace message for some time, the form which his note actually took in December, 1916, was suggested by *The New Republic*. The editors of this magazine had recommended that the warring governments be asked to state terms upon which they would be willing to cease fighting. Wilson's acceptance of the idea was based upon his belief that the people in the belligerent countries did not share

[43]I. C. Gerard to the Secretary of State, October 16, 1916. *M. I.*, Part 28, 8675.
[44]Lutz, *op. cit.*, I, 394.
[45]*F. R. S.*, 1916, 89.

the territorial and political ambitions of their leaders. He felt that if European statesmen were forced to make known their war aims, public opinion within their own countries would compel them to make those aims reasonable. Thus, with moderate terms of peace published by both sides, would it not be possible to establish a basis upon which the war could be brought to an end?

On December 18 Wilson's peace note was dispatched to the belligerent governments. It was in part as follows:

"The suggestion which I am instructed to make the President has long had it in mind to offer. He is somewhat embarrassed to offer it at this particular time, because it may now seem to have been prompted by the recent overtures of the Central Powers. It is, in fact, in no way associated with them in its origin, and the President would have delayed offering it until those overtures had been answered but for the fact that it also concerns the question of peace and may best be considered in connection with other proposals which have the same end in view. The President can only beg that his suggestion be considered entirely on its own merits and as if it had been made in other circumstances.

"The President suggests that an early occasion be sought to call out from all the nations now at war such an avowal of their respective views as to the terms upon which the war might be concluded. . . .

"He takes the liberty of calling attention to the fact that the objects, which the statesmen of the belligerents on both sides have in mind in this war, are virtually the same, as stated in general terms to their own people and to the world. . . .

". . . Never yet have the authoritative spokesmen of either side avowed the precise objects which would, if attained, satisfy them and their people. . . .

"It may be that peace is nearer than we know; that the terms which the belligerents on the one side and on the other would deem it necessary to insist upon are not irreconcilable as some have feared. . . .

"The President is not proposing peace; he is not even offering mediation. He is merely proposing that soundings be taken in order that we may learn, the neutral nations with the belligerent, how near the haven of peace may be. . . ."

In Europe the effect of the Wilson peace note was tremendous, especially the statement: "He takes the liberty of calling attention to the fact that the objects, which the statesmen of the belligerents on both sides have in mind in this war, are virtually the same, as stated in general terms to their own people and to the world. . . ." This questioning of the war aims propaganda was another "frightful staggerer." "The British read his words with dismay and consternation. Their feeling of outraged virtue at once sought an outlet in personal attacks."[46] The "corpse factory" man wrote: "We are all rather aghast." "To Lord Robert [Cecil], as to every member of the Government, the President's note, with its equivocal phrases, had been a terrible shock." Bertie recorded in his diary: "We shall be obliged to reply with civility and suppressed anger." Page wrote that there was "sorrowful consternation," a "feeling of disappointment and in many quarters even of anger," and that "the people are mad as hell." "The king wept."[47]

In the United States the reception was somewhat different. Wellington House reported: "The President's note had a curious reception in the Entente press. All the papers hastened to assure their readers that the note was neither pro-Ally nor pro-German, but pro-American and that the President was not offering mediation."[48] The New York *Times*, as might be expected, interpreted the note as being meant for Germany and not the Allies.[49] The New York *World* wrote: "Whatever comes of President Wilson's suggestions, they cannot be ignored."[50] The public sincerely applauded the note, but the army of Anglophiles and Francophiles attacked it bitterly. General Wood, at a banquet in New York thundered: "Gentlemen, we have no leadership in Washington." Roosevelt declared "the net results of the President's peace efforts has been to ruin stock investors."[51]

Any effect which the Wilson note might have had upon the warring nations was destroyed by an interview given by Secretary of State Lansing. Perhaps with the idea in mind of threatening the Germans and reassuring the Allies of American sympathy,

[46]Baker, *op. cit.*, VI, 400.
[47]*F. R. S.*, 1916, 108 f., *Supplement*.
[48]*A. P. R.*, January 10, 1917.
[49]*D. R. F. P.*, *Neutral Press Supplement*, January 12, 1917.
[50]*A. P. R.*, December 27, 1916.
[51]The New York *Times*, January 4, 1917.

Lansing intimated to newspaper reporters that the United States was on the brink of war. This statement immediately caused an uproar, and at Wilson's suggestion, he gave another interview in which he stated that he had been misinterpreted. To a friend he wrote: "I have been generally criticized by the press but I do not blame the editors as on the face of it they are right. Unfortunately I cannot make public the real reasons now. For the present, however, I must bear the blame of having made an unpardonable blunder, and I do so with perfect equanimity knowing that my action accomplished what it was intended to accomplish."[52]

What Lansing accomplished was the creation of great cheerfulness among the Allies and the feeling among their statesmen that they need pay no attention to any peace offers. Why bother with Wilson's demands if the United States were on the brink of war? Spring-Rice remarked that Lansing's statement was "the only thing that saved the situation as far as his government was concerned." A French historian said that "such a declaration, coming as a commentaire on the note, could not disturb the Entente. We had never menaced America."[53] Among the Central Powers, the interview also created an unwillingness to consider the Wilson peace offer. "Officials in Berlin decided that mediation by Wilson was more than ever a thing to beware of." On the twenty-third von Hindenburg wrote to Bethmann-Hollweg: "I regard Wilson's suggestions as being inspired by England in order to delay the submarine campaign."

The official replies of the Entente statesmen to the German peace note was one of furious rejection. One official remarked: "Russia . . . will not talk peace with Germany until right and justice win triumph." The statesmen of France, Italy, and Great Britain joined in denouncing the German offer.

The Wilson peace message was handled differently. The Germans acknowledged the message with vague generalities, but declined to trust him with any terms. The Allies, on January 10,

[52]To E. M. Smith, January 21, 1917. Lansing Papers, Library of Congress.

[53]Mermeix, *Les Négociations Secrètes et les Quatres Armistices* (Paris, 1921), 61.

At about this time House wrote: "I have noticed recently that . . . (Wilson) holds a tighter rein over his cabinet and that he is impatient of any initiative on their part."

1917, gave a crushing response. They named terms, but they were meant to be unacceptable. "The reply was obviously expected to put an end to any further talk of negotiations."[54]

In spite of the adverse reception given Wilson's message, the latter went ahead with his effort to find a basis for peace. This time he decided to try secret diplomacy. On December 29 House saw Bernstorff, and the latter reported to Berlin "that in Wilson's opinion a peace conference could not be brought about in the absence of preliminary [understandings]. . . . This communication . . . was accompanied by an invitation for us to take part in absolutely confidential negotiations."[55] To House, Wilson wrote: "If Germany really wants peace she can get it, and get it soon, if she will but confide in me and let me have a chance."[56] But before this the Germans had lost all confidence in the American President.

At the approach of the new year they found it imperative to reach a decision on the submarine question. Conditions in Germany and in England would not permit further delay. If unrestricted warfare were to be effective in 1917 it had to be started before new supplies were received by Great Britain from overseas. But this would mean that the United States would enter the war. On the other hand, if the U-boats were not turned loose, Germany would be starved into submission unless President Wilson either persuaded or forced the Allies to enter into a peace conference. In this case there was the strong possibility that Wilson in conjunction with England and France, would force upon Germany a humiliating peace treaty — a treaty which would deprive her of wealth, and destroy her position and power.

The response of the Allies to the peace note of President Wilson and to that of Germany greatly influenced the latter's decision for unrestricted warfare. The final decision, of course, rested upon German distrust of the American President. In a message from von Jagow to Bernstorff on June 7, 1916, the comment was made: "The fact is that we entertain but little hope for the result of the exercise of good offices by one whose instincts are all in favor of the English point of view, and who, in addition

[54]Baker, *op. cit.*, VI, 419.
[55]*Original German Documents*, II, 1010.
[56]Viereck, *The Strangest Friendship in History*, 170.

to this, is so naïve a statesman as President Wilson."[57] In the post-war inquiry conducted by the German government, one official stated: "As a mediator . . . [Wilson] would exert all his influence against us." Bernstorff remarked: "It is perfectly clear that this conception was, in a word, the one which was generally entertained here; and it is made even more plain by the fact that we did not accept peace mediation by Wilson but launched the U-boat war instead of so doing."[58] By the beginning of the new year the Kaiser had decided to place absolutely no reliance on Wilson's peace move.[59]

From general headquarters at Pless on January 9, 1917, the following confidential instructions were given: "I order that the unrestricted submarine war be launched with the greatest vigor on the 1st of February. You will immediately take all the necessary steps, taking care, however, that this intention shall not prematurely come to the knowledge of the enemy and the neutral powers. . . . WILHELM I. R."

Even before Wilson made his next move the British knew that he could be ignored. By that time they were fully acquainted with the German decision and realized that it was only a question of time before the United States would be plunged into war with the Central Powers.

Knowledge of the German action was obtained by their very successful Naval Intelligence Department under the direction of Admiral Sir William Reginald Hall. The British were well informed as to German plans. They knew of the meeting held at Pless in September, 1916, for the purpose of discussing the submarine; they knew of the urgings to President Wilson to call a peace conference; on January 16, 1917, they learned that, com-

[57]*Official German Documents*, II, 977.

Gerard gave as his interpretation of the reasons for the inauguration of the submarine campaign: "first, the desire to torpedo ships carrying grain from Argentina; second, food situation here; third, threatened great Allied offensive; fourth, public demanding use of submarine weapon and contempt and hate for America." *M. I.*, Part 28, 8680.

[58]*Official German Documents*, II, 283.

Roosevelt wrote to Henry White: "Moreover, I think Germany has made up her mind quite rightly that Wilson, as an enemy, is hardly more redoubtable, than Wilson as a friend." "The Government of this country inspires nothing but contempt."

[59]*Official German Documents*, II, 1106. Von Lersner to the German Foreign Office, January 16, 1917.

mencing February 1, the Central Powers would inaugurate un-restricted submarine warfare. They also intercepted on this same date, a second message — the Zimmermann note.[60] The first of these two dispatches carried with it the message to Bernstorff: "I know full well that by taking this step we run the danger of bringing about a break and possibly war with the United States. We have determined to take this risk."[61]

With this information at hand, the British knew that they had only to hold on and the American campaign would be won. On January 26 Sir William Wiseman called on Colonel House. Although he neither then nor later told the President's adviser what had been discovered, "his whole tone had changed, he said the atmosphere had cleared wonderfully since yesterday."[62]

Totally unaware of the impending crisis, Wilson made an-other effort to secure peace. This was his plea for a peace without victory — an idea which had been expressed much earlier by William Jennings Bryan.[63] Both Lansing and House, as usual, objected to certain parts of the original drafts of the speech, but Wilson made no important change in the document. It was given before the Senate on January 22, 1917.

"GENTLEMEN OF THE SENATE:

"On the eighteenth of December last I addressed an identic note to the governments of the nations now at war requesting them to state, more definitely than had yet been stated by either group of belligerents, the terms upon which they would deem it possible to make peace. . . . The Central Powers united in a reply which stated merely that they were ready to meet their antag-onists in conference to discuss terms of peace. The Entente Pow-ers have replied much more definitely and have stated, in general terms, indeed, but with sufficient definiteness to imply details,

[60]Bernstorff forwarded the Zimmermann note to Mexico on the nineteenth. The British government permitted the United States to believe that it was this message — the one sent to Mexico — which they had intercepted. As a matter of fact, the note was picked up in four different places.

[61]*Official German Documents*, II, 1019.

[62]Baker, *op. cit.*, VI, 441.

[63]Early in the war Bryan wrote to Wilson: "It is not likely that either side will win so complete a victory as to be able to dictate terms and if either side does win such a victory, it will probably mean preparations for another war. It would seem better to look for a more rational basis for peace." Baker, *op. cit.*, V, 285.

the arrangements, guarantees, and acts of reparation which they deem to be the indispensable conditions of a satisfactory settlement. We are that much nearer a definite discussion of the peace which shall end the present war. . . .

"I have sought this opportunity to address you because I thought that I owed it to you, as the counsel associated with me in the final determination of our international obligations, to disclose to you without reserve the thought and purpose that have been taking form in my mind in regard to the duty of our Government in the day to come when it will be necessary to lay afresh and upon a new plan the foundations of peace among the nations.

"Is the present war a struggle for a just and secure peace, or only for a new balance of power? If it be only a struggle for a new balance of power, who will guarantee, who can guarantee the stable equilibrium of the new arrangement? Only a tranquil Europe can be a stable Europe. There must be, not a balance of power, but a community of power; not organized rivalries, but an organized common peace. . . . The statesmen of both of the groups of nations now arrayed against one another have said, in terms that could not be misinterpreted, that it was no part of the purpose they had in mind to crush their antagonists. . . . They imply, first of all, that it must be a peace without victory. I am seeking only to face realities and to face them without soft concealments. *Victory would mean peace forced upon the loser, a victor's terms imposed upon the vanquished. It would be accepted in humiliation, under duress, at an intolerable sacrifice, and would leave a sting, a resentment, a bitter memory upon which terms of peace would rest, not permanently, but only as upon quicksand.*[64]

The appalling truth of these words has been brought home to the victors of 1918-19, and most of them now know that a peace with victory actually meant a victory without peace. From this part of the message Wilson went on for the first time giving terms of peace, generalities that were later to be the fourteen points. He spoke of an "independent and autonomous Poland," "government by the people," "an outlet to the sea for every nation as far as possible," "freedom of the seas," and "that modera-

[64]A draft of this speech was sent to Page on January 13. Lansing's *Memoirs*, 193.

tion of armaments which makes of armies and navies a power for order merely, not an instrument of aggression or of selfish violence." In closing, he appealed to the American people and to all liberals to give him support. "These are American principles, American policies. We could stand for no others. And they are also the principles and policies of forward looking men and women everywhere, of every modern nation, of every enlightened community. They are the principles of mankind and must prevail."

Few people were prepared for this speech, and especially for the "peace without victory" phrase. The dismayed statesmen and editors of France and England did not hesitate to express their angry resentment. They classified the phrase "peace without victory" as another of Wilson's unfortunate mistakes. Germans expressed satisfaction at some of the statements. The British propaganda report of American reactions stated: "Roosevelt proceeded to curse, and Jeremiah O'Leary to bless, without apparently taking any trouble to read the document they were criticising."[65] Here again Wellington House labored under the illusion that Wilson did not mean what he said. Roosevelt could curse and O'Leary could bless, quite appropriately. Wilson did mean what he said, and a great body of people realized how truly he had read the future.

Unlike the officials in Berlin, Bernstorff believed Wilson was sincerely attempting to be impartial, and, on January 27, he addressed to them a final plea saying: "Wilson offers in the first place, in confidence, peace mediation based on his message to the Senate, that is, without interfering in the matter of the territorial conditions of peace. . . . House related to me in detail the following line of reasoning of the President: That our enemies had publicly announced their peace conditions, which were impossible of acceptance; that, in direct opposition to this, the President had thereupon announced his program; that from now on we too were under the moral obligation of disclosing our peace conditions, because otherwise, our intentions with regard to peace would not be looked upon as genuine. . . . The President was of the opinion that the Entente note to him was a bluff and, for that reason, need not be taken into consideration; that he hoped with reason to be

[65]*D. R. F. P.*, February 2, 1917.

able to bring about peace conferences and, indeed, at such an early date that unnecessary bloodshed in the spring offensive could be avoided. . . . In the meantime, I urgently beg leave to make the following suggestion: If the U-boat war is commenced forthwith, the President will look upon this as a slap in the face, and war with the United States will be unavoidable. The war party on this side will gain the upper hand, and we shall not be able, in my opinion, to tell when the war will end, since the resources of the United States are, in spite of all statements to the contrary, very great. . . . In any event, my view of the situation is that at this time we can get a better peace by means of conference than if the United States should join our enemies."[66]

There was much to indicate that Wilson was sincere and that he would have been fair at a peace conference. He had changed a great deal since the first of 1916. A certain von der Lancken wrote to Count Montgelas: "Whitlock is convinced that Wilson does not believe that the destruction, or even a very material weakening of Germany on the political side, is to the interest of the United States . . . that Wilson said that such a people must be allowed to maintain the level which they had gained."[67] Again on January 26 Cobb, of the New York *World,* the administration paper, wrote: "Nor could anybody in his right mind expect the United States to help guarantee a peace that dismembered Germany and Austria-Hungary and left them prostrate." But the Germans refused to reconsider. On the sixteenth of the month the Kaiser had stated: "Matters cannot be changed; we shall go ahead."[68]

The outcome of the World War turned upon the economic struggle being carried on between Great Britain and Germany. Each was attempting — the one by means of the blockade, the other by the submarine — to undermine the enemy's economic ability to continue fighting. British operations were never seriously questioned by the American government, but German actions were immediately challenged. As a result, in 1915 and 1916,

[66]*F. R. S., Supplement,* 1917, I, 31 ff.
[67]*Official German Documents,* II, 1284.
[68]*Official German Documents,* II, 1106.

the Central Powers were forced to restrict the use of the submarine.

At the beginning of 1917, German officials felt that the state of economic and military affairs had become so critical that all restrictions on the submarine must be removed even at the risk of American participation in the war. There could be no more yielding on the part of Germany. At this point Wilson found that he had entered a blind alley from which there was no retreat. He attempted to extricate himself by making peace overtures, but he failed — quite largely as a result of the same pro-Ally attitude which had created the situation in the first place. His partiality had become so obnoxious to the Central Powers that they placed no confidence in his offer of mediation.

CHAPTER XV ☆ DECISION FOR WAR

O N JANUARY 31, 1917, at ten minutes past four, Ambassador Bernstorff appeared at the State Department and gave to Secretary Lansing papers announcing the resumption of unrestricted submarine warfare: "Since the Entente Powers . . . have made it impossible to come to an understanding based upon equality of rights of all nations, as proposed by the Central Powers, and have instead declared only such a peace to be possible, which shall be dictated by the Entente-Allies and shall result in the destruction and humiliation of the Central Powers, Germany is unable further to forego the full use of her submarines . . . the now openly disclosed intentions of the Entente-Allies give back to Germany the freedom of action which she reserved in her note addressed to this Government of the United States on May 4, 1916.

"Under these circumstances Germany will meet the illegal measures of her enemies by forcibly preventing after February 1, 1917, in a zone around Great Britain, France, Italy and in the Eastern Mediterranean all navigation, that of neutrals included, from and to England and from and to France etc. etc. All ships met within that zone will be sunk."[1]

Secretary Lansing read the note with amazement. His account of the interview with Bernstorff reveals that both men were greatly disturbed. Lansing has written: "As I finished my deliberate perusal of the papers, I laid them on the desk and turned toward von Bernstorff. 'I am sorry,' he said, 'to have to bring about this situation but my government could do nothing else.'

"I replied . . . 'but you must know that it cannot be accepted.'

" 'Of course; of course,' he said, 'I understand that. I know it is very serious, very, and I deeply regret that it is necessary.' "[2]

On leaving, Bernstorff extended his hand to Lansing, who took it "with a feeling almost of compassion for the man, whose

[1] There were rather humiliating provisions made whereby regular American passenger steamers would not be molested after this unrestricted submarine warfare went into effect.
[2] Lansing's *Memoirs*, 221.

eyes were suffused and who was not at all the jaunty carefree man-of-the-world he usually was. With a ghost of a smile he bowed . . . and, turning, left the room."[3]

Lansing immediately notified Wilson's secretary, but the President did not receive the message until after eight o'clock that evening. Tumulty has recorded Wilson's reaction as follows: "As I entered . . . he looked up from his writing, casual inquiry in his eyes. Without comment I laid the fateful slip of paper on his desk, and silently watched him as he read and re-read it. I seemed to read his mind in the expressions that raced across his strong features; first, blank amazement; then incredulity. . . ."[4]

In spite of the many warnings that Germany would take this step, Wilson was dumbfounded. "He felt as if the world had suddenly reversed itself . . . and that he could not get his balance." "The sudden *volte face* aroused in him a resentment against the German Government such as had not resulted from any previous German action."[5] But, in spite of his anger, and in spite of the fact that this must mean war — still he hesitated. The Secretary of State was amazed to hear the President say that he "was not yet sure," that "we must think it over." The change which had taken place in Wilson's thinking now made his decision difficult. He realized that the actions and aims of the Allies were not entirely praiseworthy. Again he feared that Japan might come out of the war so powerful that she might, in the future, be as much of a problem as Germany was at that time. In other words, there apparently came a realization that the simple solutions embodied in the propaganda arguments accepted in the United States were not solutions at all. Wilson had been "more and more impressed with the idea that white civilization and its domination over the world rested largely on . . . [American] ability to keep this country intact. . . ." The memory of Japan's twenty-one demands still

[3]*Ibid.*, 212.
[4]Tumulty, *op. cit.*, 254 f.
[5]*Intimate Papers*, II, 439.
It is possible that his decision to carry on the war "without stint" grew out of this resentment. Bernstorff has said: "The President's spiteful censure and treatment of us both during the war and at Versailles, may be explained psychologically by the fact that we rejected his efforts as a mediator, and declared the U-boat war." Bernstorff, *op. cit.*, 369.

rankled in his mind.[6] He was also irritated at the rumors of the British giving merchantmen heavy guns. And he was still impatient over British disregard for neutral rights. "Nothing could induce him to break off relations unless he was convinced that, viewed from every angle, it was the wisest thing to do."[7]

The next day, February 1, Lansing called on the President again and pleaded for war, saying that "peace and civilization depended on democracy and this would be impossible if Prussian autocracy controlled Germany after the war. The President said he was not sure of this, as it might mean the disintegration of German power and the destruction of the German nation."[8] Nevertheless, Lansing left the conference convinced that Wilson had decided to break off relations.

On February 2 Wilson held a cabinet meeting in which the entire situation was discussed. Although no decision was reached, it was generally agreed that there would have to be a break with Germany. He then had a conference with Senator Stone, as he had previously agreed to do. He also saw other political leaders and went over the situation with them. Most of them were in favor of breaking off relations with Germany.

Wilson made his decision on February 3. He arranged to appear before Congress that afternoon to explain in person what had occurred. In his speech he did not ask for war, but stated: "Notwithstanding this unexpected act of the German Government . . . I refuse to believe that it is the intention of the German authorities to do in fact what they have warned us they will feel at liberty to do. . . . Only actual overt acts on their part can make me believe it even now."[9] Wilson did announce that the American Ambassador in Berlin was being withdrawn, and that Bernstorff had been given his passports. By so doing he lost all control of the situation.

On the Western Front, Repington wrote: "Tonight came the great news that America had broken off relations with Germany

---

[6]To Wellington House went the report in 1915: "There is undoubtedly wide distrust of Japanese aspirations, and America fears for her colonies." *A. P. R.,* July 8, 1915.

[7]Lansing, Robert, "War Days in the White House," *Saturday Evening Post,* August 8, 1931, 90 f.

[8]*Ibid.,* 90.

[9]See *Intimate Papers,* II, 441.

CAPTAIN GUY GAUNT

and had sent Bernstorff his passports." Admiral Hall "uttered just two words, 'Thank God!' " It was he who brought Ambassador Page the news. Captain Gaunt wired London: "The Barber gets his papers at 2 P.M. and I'll probably get soused."[10]

The American people, however, did not react in the same manner. The President and his advisers kept a close watch on public opinion, and found but few expressions of satisfaction or pleasure.[11] House wrote that Durant of General Motors "has just returned from the far West and insists that he met only one man between New York and California who wanted war."[12] British reports of American opinion show very clearly the widespread reluctance to fight Germany. Immediately after February 1 it was stated: "All the press comments to hand bear out the impression conveyed by the telegraphic news that the American people stand solid behind the President; but they also show that the vast majority of the nation has little or no interest in anything except the danger to American lives and the humiliation to American self-esteem involved in the German commands and menaces." In some places satisfaction was expressed that the United States was entering the war on the right side, "but nowhere . . . with any enthusiasm." "The leading papers of the South approved Mr. Wilson's action but showed little interest in any issue save that of America's legal rights."[13]

A careful check of opinion during the weeks that followed dis-

[10]According to Page, Gaunt had cabled: "Bernstorff has just been given his passports. I shall probably get drunk tonight."

[11]"The psychology of the situation is the real problem which has to be solved. I wish this was not so and that no question existed as to the attitude of all the American people in the present crisis. Unfortunately this is not the case. Whatever our inclinations may be we cannot act without carefully feeling out the ground in advance." February, 1917, Lansing to Edward N. Smith.

It is interesting to note the coincidence of Wilson's waiting two months before declaring war, and Germany's request that she be given two months in an attempt to secure peace. One February 1 Gerard telegraphed Wilson as follows: "Zimmermann gave me the reckless submarine note and memorandum and maps at six today. He said . . . that Germany was compelled to take this step, and that he hoped that the President will stay quiet for *two months* in which time he was sure they could by submarine war compel England to ask for terms, that Lloyd George was a wild man and was now the real head of the Entente, that if peace was not made there would be an exhausted Europe and that we would be confronted by Japan and other yellow races." *F. R. S.*, 1917, Part I, 37. Italics mine.

[12]*Intimate Papers*, II, 448.

[13]*A. P. R.*, March 1, 1917.

played that there was never manifested any great desire to enter the war. The British report of February 9 revealed that (1) the Roosevelt press was afraid Wilson would not fight; (2) the independent press wanted strong action but still thought negotiations could be carried on; (3) the San Francisco *Chronicle* urged that nothing be done until the United States was injured; (4) *The New Republic* became strongly anti-German; and (5) Hearst was unfriendly to the Allies but ready to follow the President — he was for negotiation.[14] The report of March 9 displayed that (1) the official press was settling down to a belligerent attitude; (2) the anti-administration press was torn between distrust of Wilson and desire for dictatorial action; and (3) the New York *American* [Hearst] was for lone action.[15]

The confidential report to the Cabinet of March 7 stated that there was a "remarkable lack of excitement or enthusiasm." "The cleavage in opinion between East and West seems to be more marked than ever. . . ."[16] "The whole American people . . . appear to endorse the President's policy firmly, though without enthusiasm." "There is no indication . . . of any pro-Ally enthusiasm except among that body of ardent pro-Allies intellectually important, but numerically far less important, which has shown its warm sympathy from the very beginning of the war."[17]

The pacifists exerted themselves mightily in an attempt to prevent the final step into the war. Every possible expedient was tried. Emergency Peace Federations sprang up all over the country and attempted to counteract the work of the jingo press, but they were, of course, much too late.

Wilson apparently still had some illusions that he might keep out of war through the calling of a peace conference. "He even went so far as to prepare a draft of the bases of peace, which he purposed to submit to the belligerents if they could be induced to meet in conference."[18] On February 8 he sent a note to Page who presented it to the British government: "The President still believes . . . were it possible for him to give the necessary as-

[14]*D. R. F. P.*, February 9, 1917.
[15]*D. R. F. P.*, March 9, 1917.
[16]*A. P. R.*, March 7, 1917.
[17]*A. P. R.*, March 14, 1917.
[18]Lansing, *op. cit.*, 16.

surances to the Government of Austria, which fears radical dismemberment and which thinks that it is now fighting for its very existence, he could in a very short time force the acceptance of peace upon terms which would follow the general lines of his recent address to the Senate [i.e., the peace without victory speech] regarding the sort of peace the United States would be willing to join in guaranteeing."[19]

In reply Lloyd George said he could not consider a peace proposal and that Britain's allies had to get compensation from Austria as their part in the general booty. He was, of course, most diplomatic and even told Page that Wilson's assistance as a mediator was essential. He said: "We want . . . [Wilson] to come into the war not so much for help with the war as for help with peace." From this he went on in an almost lyrical note, saying if Wilson did not enter the war and sit at the peace table, "even Great Britain, who wants nothing for herself, will be prevented from returning the German colonies. South Africa and Australia will not permit the giving back of lands that would make them neighbors to German subjects and give Germany secret submarine bases throughout the whole world."

Later, around the twentieth of the month, the new Prime Minister was forced to reverse his stand, partially as a result of pressure from Curzon and the army. At that time he agreed to consider a peace proposal if it were presented privately. His idea was to get a separate peace with Austria-Hungary. The Dual Monarchy, however, refused to desert its ally, and peace discussions were brought to an end.

Wilson's continued efforts to obtain a peace conference were, of course, not known to the public. If they had been, he would very probably have received the same savage criticism which the pacifists were getting. For in spite of the fact that the general public had not become excited, the army of native propagandists was doing its utmost to make Americans lose all vestiges of reason. The cabinet became insistent upon a declaration of war. Lane, McAdoo, Houston, Redfield, and, of course, Lansing and

---

[19]*F. R. S.*, 1917, Part I, 40 ff. At the time the American Ambassador read this message Admiral Hall had apparently already deciphered it and given it to the British Prime Minister, for as Page expressed it, "Before I could mention details . . . [Lloyd George] answered every question I had prepared to ask him."

House, were urging participation. There was even some suggestion that Houston and McAdoo would threaten resignation if the President did not act.

The pro-Ally press immediately turned upon all those who dared to speak of peace and lashed them unmercifully. "Referring to the position of the anti-war groups in general, and of Bryan in particular, the Philadelphia *Inquirer* declared, 'It comes perilously close to the border-line of treason.' The New York *World* called it 'a form of moral treason'. . . [stating], 'What is called peace propaganda is of necessity a pro-German propaganda. . . . The pacifists who advocate peace are in reality advocating nonresistance for the benefit of German militarism.' "[20] The great newspapers were apparently trying to rush the country into the struggle, "the yearning for an 'overt act'. . . [being] manifested in large sections of the Eastern press."[21] "It is difficult to say which were more insane, the mobs who beat up 'pacifists' or the editors of militant dailies."[22] "Even the pulpits of the nation resounded with sermons which would have delighted the pagan gods of war. The astonished President exclaimed . . . 'I think our ministers are going crazy.' "[23]

With the breaking off of German relations, British propaganda immediately took on a new aspect. In England, of course, Wellington House and other organizations continued to operate, but there were numerous significant changes in personnel. Sir Gilbert Parker resigned; Strachey, who had been acting as host to American newswriters in London, enjoyed a diplomatic illness and was able to terminate his activities; Captain Guy Gaunt was soon to be transferred; and Sir Alfred Ewing, in charge of the deciphering of wireless messages, gave up his work. As far as these men were concerned, the campaign had been won. It was now primarily up to the American volunteers to "carry on."

In this last period, the British carried out their most successful propaganda maneuver, which gained the support of the western part of the United States. Throughout the many months of

[20]Arnett, *op. cit.*, 213.

[21]Borchard and Lage, *op. cit.*, 45.

[22]Arnett, *op. cit.*, 213.

[23]Baker, *op. cit.*, VI, 461. On October 30, 1916, he wrote of a prominent New York minister: "The action of the rector was absolutely inexcusable. These cannot in fact be ministers of God."

neutrality the chief handicap of the Allies had been the reluctance on the part of the Middle West and Far West to become
enthusiastic over joining in the war. On January 16, however,
the British found a means of defeating the Western and Middle
Western pacifists. This was a message from the head of the German Foreign Office, Alfred Zimmermann, to the German Minister in Mexico, which stated:

"On the first of February we intend to begin unrestricted
submarine warfare. In spite of this, it is our intention to endeavor
to keep neutral the United States of America.

"If this attempt is not successful, we propose an alliance on
the following basis with Mexico: That we shall make war together and together make peace. We shall give general financial
support, and it is understood that Mexico is to reconquer the lost
territory in New Mexico, Texas, and Arizona. The details are
left to you for settlement.

"You are instructed to inform the President of Mexico of the
above in the greatest confidence *as soon as it is certain that there
will be an outbreak of war with the United States* and suggest
that the President of Mexico, on his own initiative, should communicate with Japan suggesting adherence at once to this plan;
at the same time, offer to mediate between Germany and Japan.

"Please call to the attention of the President of Mexico that
the employment of ruthless submarine warfare now promises to
compel England to make peace in a few months.

ZIMMERMANN."

It is quite obvious that no mature student of politics would
have been surprised at a belligerent's effort to obtain allies. The
reaction of the public, however, to this particular move might be
quite different. With them such an overture would have tremendous propaganda possibilities. Henry Cabot Lodge wrote: "It
seemed to me of almost unlimited use in forcing the situation."[24]
Nevertheless Admiral Hall was somewhat embarrassed. He obtained the telegram on January 16 before the Germans had publicly declared unrestricted submarine warfare. If he had then
released it, would not the Germans have reconsidered their action

[24]*The Correspondence of Theodore Roosevelt and H. C. Lodge,* II, 499.

and thus kept the United States from going to war? And even if he had released it after relations had been broken, would not Americans have looked upon it merely as a British trick? There was, of course, at all times the possibility of their considering it a fake. Because of these factors the note was withheld for over a month.

When it was turned over to the American government, on February 24, Wilson's cabinet, according to Jusserand, was in favor of "an immediate declaration of war." Most probably these American statesmen had never thought of the idea that by taking part in Europe's wars their country's territory would run the risk of being considered spoils of war. Here again one gets the impression that no thought was given as to the consequences. There apparently existed no realization that to gain their ends they would have to be willing to pay a high price.

The note was released to the public on March 1. Great indignation was immediately aroused throughout the country, and most important was the fact that the West and Middle West joined in the expressions of anger. The fact that the Central Powers were supposedly threatening the West naturally made Westerners ready to fight back. It brought the war home to them and completely defeated the work of the pacifists. It made the identity of interest propaganda effective west of the Alleghanies. The propaganda value of the telegram was at first diminished by the suspicion that it was not genuine. However, to the immense relief of the British, Zimmermann acknowledged authorship. The American newspapers made the incident even more effective by omitting discussion of the note's most salient feature — that it was to apply only *in case of,* and *after,* the United States had declared war against Germany. The note turned out to be the "overt act" for which the war hawks had been waiting, and the highest hopes of Admiral Hall were realized.

Wellington House reported: "The timely revelation of the proposed German alliance with Mexico, and the gift to Mexico of these states of the Union, appears to have aroused feeling considerably, and it seems to have stirred precisely that part of the country which was most indifferent to American rights at sea."[25]

[25]*A. P. R.,* March 7, 1917.

"The one factor which . . . has convinced the people that war with Germany is necessary, is the German intrigue in Mexico."[26]

The absurdity of Zimmermann's idea apparently never dawned upon Americans nor upon the German government. It was, of course, Zimmermann's duty as Foreign Minister to arrange for the eventuality of American entrance into the war. He was not at fault in trying to secure an ally; he was at fault for being found out. The episode must be now considered as one of history's classic stupidities — a blunder from which the British reaped great profit.

On February 24 news of the Zimmermann note was received at the White House, and on the twenty-sixth President Wilson appeared before Congress to ask authority for the arming of merchant ships: " 'I request that you will authorize me to supply our merchant ships with defensive arms, should that become necessary, and with the means of using them, and to employ any other instrumentalities or methods that may be necessary . . . to protect our ships and our people . . . on the seas.'

"LaFollette threw up both hands instinctively as though hope were gone. Lodge unclasped his fingers and gently tapped the points of them together, not, apparently, in applause, but as one would say, a little cynically, 'Well, well.' "[27]

"The Republicans in the Senate [had] held a caucus February 23rd to consider plans for delaying legislation and thereby compelling an extra session. . . . Republicans who yearned for war were determined not to leave a 'pacifist' President in control for nine months. On the other hand, it soon appeared that those who wanted peace were equally determined on forcing an extra session to prevent any war move on the part of the President."[28] Wilson's proposal provided the opportunity for both of these groups. Fortunately for the Republicans, the pacifists took the onus of opposition to the arming of merchantmen. In order to force passage of the bill, on March 1 Wilson released the Zimmermann message, and, as a result, the House ratified the measure almost unanimously. In the Senate, however, a filibuster was started by Norris, LaFollette and Stone. Some in the group were

[26]*A. P. R.*, April 4, 1917.
[27]Baker, *op. cit.*, VI, 476 f.
[28]*Ibid.*, VI, 472 f.

Democrats. The filibuster was kept up until the sixty-fourth Congress automatically expired, thus forcing a special session.

"Wilson was thoroughly angry.... He commented on the 'vanity' of LaFollette and the 'slipperiness' of Stone." "Late that evening ... [he] issued the angriest, least premeditated, statement of his career — which he was afterwards to regret:"[29]

". . . the Congress has been unable to act either to safeguard the country or to vindicate the elementary rights of its citizens.

"A little group of willful men, representing no opinion but their own, have rendered the great Government of the United States helpless and contemptible."[30]

But these willful men did represent opinions other than their own — primarily those of people who had voted for Wilson in 1916 on the slogan "he kept us out of war." The President's diatribe against these senators marked a very important break in his career, for they were the men who had supported his liberal program.[31]

Meanwhile the pacifists gained a foretaste of the treatment to be meted out to anyone daring to oppose war. They were pursued "with malicious falsehood and recklessly libelous attacks." An example of this can be found in the remarks of Theodore Roosevelt about Senator LaFollette. "LaFollette as a type is considerably inferior, in morality and capacity, to Robespierre."[32] "I abhor Germany. I abhor the Hun without our gates, but more I abhor the Hun within our gates."[33] In another place he displayed some interesting logic when he said that "the public man who did not consider first of all the real and permanent welfare of the working man [presumably as between war and peace] was no friend of democracy." "The most sinister enemy of democracy in the United States is Senator LaFollette." LaFollette had voted against war.

During this period, between neutrality and war, one event in Europe had great influence upon Wilson. This was the Russian

[29]*Ibid.*, VI, 481.

[30]This "little group of willful men" included Geo. W. Norris, Robert M. La-Follette, Wm. J. Stone, M. E. Clapp, A. B. Cummins, W. S. Kenyon, A. J. Gronna, J. D. Works, W. F. Kirby, Harry Lane, J. A. O'Gorman, and J. K. Vardaman.

[31]Baker, *op. cit.*, VI, 462.

[32]*Correspondence of Theodore Roosevelt and H. C. Lodge*, II, 494.

[33]The Toledo *Blade*, September 29, 1917.

Revolution. He could now truthfully say that it was a combination of liberal governments against autocratic governments. Circumstances thus made the propaganda of democracy appear logical.[34] It was also thought that a democratic Russia would be a stronger ally than the former imperial Russia. One otherwise sane Cabinet member wrote: "The lovable, kindly Russians are not to be conquered . . . and it makes me rejoice that we are to be with them."[35] It was now possible to contend that the United States was entering the war for the preservation of democracy.

Another occurrence which possibly had some influence upon the administration's course of action was the piling up of goods in Atlantic ports owing to the refusal of ship owners to send out their vessels. "Freights were snarled, goods were spoiled, business was menaced with a complete tie-up."[36] This may have been brought about by fear of the submarines, but it is not improbable that the effect of such a tie-up on the administration had been given consideration by ship owners.

At the end of the two-month period following the breaking of relations, Americans were still not anxious to enter the war. The two and one-half years of propaganda and economic penetration had broken down their resistance, but it had not created any enthusiasm. The jingoes had destroyed all vocal opposition to joining the Allies. They had not succeeded in creating positive support among the public as a whole. In March, the Springfield *Republican* analyzed American opinion as follows: "(1) the overwhelming majority of the American people still desire most earnestly to avoid war; (2) Americans approve the President's measures and if necessary approve force to uphold rights; (3) they wish no entangling alliances and would prefer measures short of war; (4) a majority of the American people would insist that in upholding American rights the United States should *not* join the Entente; (5) they oppose sending American soldiers to Europe."[37]

The British were particularly alarmed by the American unwillingness actually to participate in the war. Wellington House

[34]Lansing stated in his memoirs that he had been talking to Wilson for six months "about the struggle between autocracy and democracy."

[35]Lane, *op. cit.*, 243.

[36]Seymour, *American Neutrality*, 11.

[37]*A. P. R.*, March 21, 1917.

reported: "There is in the Western and Middle Western States a very strong reluctance to join the Allies in the event of war. . . ." "In time, the more provincial parts of the United States may become reconciled to joint naval and military operations. Meantime, Eastern papers . . . such as the New York *Outlook* and *Colliers Weekly* . . . are endeavoring to educate opinion."[38] Other magazines and newspapers took up this campaign so that in another fortnight it was said: "The week was remarkable for the spread of the movement" for co-operation with France and England.[39] This problem was so important to the British that an entire section of their propaganda report dealt with the question: "Will the United States join the Allies." It also caused them to continue their activities in the United States until the autumn of 1917, when they felt definitely assured of the participation of American armed forces.

By the spring of 1917 the reluctance of the American people to enter the war was no longer of great importance. Those individuals who opposed entrance into the conflict were labeled unpatriotic or pro-German; consequently their influence was eliminated. Only the war hawks dared speak out without restraint. Under such circumstances the government could enter the war without paying much attention to the public. In actuality this meant that the President alone would make the decision for the nation.

During the period from February 1 to April 2 Wilson gradually came to the conclusion that the conflict between his policies and those of Germany left him with no choice: he must declare war. Early in February he wrote: ". . . I am doing everything that I honorably can to keep the country out of war. . . ."[40] But as the weeks wore on, the success of the submarines disturbed him more and more. In the first month of unrestricted warfare they sank 781,500 tons of shipping. In addition, the Allies' financial situation became precarious; Wilson was now faced with the possibility of a German victory. On February 23 the trend of his thinking was revealed in the comment: "We could not afford to

[38]*A. P. R.,* March 28, 1917.

[39]*A. P. R.,* April 11, 1917. In the report of March 14, 1917, Wellington House wrote disapprovingly of "a very unfriendly article" in which Hearst made a very accurate prophecy of the future course of events.

[40]Baker, *op. cit.,* VI, 464.

let Germany dominate us or cut England off and then crush France."[41] House wrote to him on March 9 enclosing a letter from Arthur H. Frazier. He stated: "What Frazier says is disturbing, and I fear is true. If France should cave in before Germany it would be a calamity beyond reckoning."[42] When the perilous position of the Allies was fully comprehended, "the Administration was a bit aghast."[43]

"Woodrow Wilson's valley of decision, the most critical, the most heart-breaking, of the entire period of his leadership of the American people, was in the three weeks from March 12th, when he ordered the arming of ships to meet attacks of German submarines, to April 2nd, when he asked Congress for a declaration of war."[44] His decision was taken on March 20. On that date a cabinet meeting was held in which the entire situation was considered. The cabinet members expressed the belief that public opinion favored war. To which the President replied: "We are not governed by public opinion in our conclusion." "I want to do right whether it is popular or not."[45] He apparently "had no idea of calling Congress together earlier than the 16th [of April] but was persuaded to call it on the 2nd . . . because of the unanimous opinion of the Cabinet that he should do so."[46] The meeting adjourned without the President's having told his advisers what he intended to do. Nevertheless the opinion was generally held among the cabinet members that he had decided on war. Meanwhile the Cabinet unanimously favored war with Germany, and this unanimity had great weight with the President.[47]

On March 24 House wrote: "Lansing has no idea what the President has in mind to say in his address to Congress when it convenes." A few days later he quoted Wilson as saying: "We must put excited feeling away." On March 27 House wrote: "The President asked whether I thought he should ask Congress to declare war, or whether he should say that a state of war exists and

[41]Houston, David F., "Wilson As A War President," *The World's Work*, June, 1926, 34.
[42]Baker, *op. cit.*, VI, 496.
[43]*A. P. R.*, June 13, 1917.
[44]Baker, *op. cit.*, VI, 486.
[45]Daniels, Josephus, *Our Navy at War*, 32.
[46]*Intimate Papers*, II, 461.
[47]Tansill, *op. cit.*, 656.

ask them for the necessary means to carry it on."[48] On the first of April Lane wrote: "The die is cast — and yet no one has seen the message." Wilson is for "recognizing war and taking hold of the situation in such a fashion as will eventually lead to an Allied victory over Germany. But he goes unwillingly."[49]

On April 1 President Wilson said to Frank I. Cobb that "a declaration of war would mean that Germany would be beaten and so badly beaten that there would be a dictated peace, a victorious peace." It means, he said, "an attempt to reconstruct a peace-time civilization with war standards, and at the end of the war there will be no bystanders with sufficient power to influence the terms. There won't be any peace standards left to work with. . . . Once lead this people into war and they'll forget there ever was such a thing as tolerance. To fight you must be brutal and ruthless, and the spirit of ruthless brutality will enter into the very fiber of our national life, infecting Congress, the courts, the policeman on the beat, the man in the street." "If there is any alternative, for God's sake, let's take it."[50] But there was no alternative. He had closed the door to negotiation in the note of February 10, 1915.

On the evening of April 2, before an excited Congress, President Wilson made his request for war. A French newspaperman said, "La voix . . . est froide." The very famous speech expressed his ideals in the loftiest manner, but it was defeat that was recorded rather than victory. This is clearly shown in his closing statement:

"It is a distressing and oppressive duty, Gentlemen of the Congress, which I have performed in thus addressing you. There are, it may be, many months of fiery trial and sacrifice ahead of us. It is a fearful thing to lead this great peaceful people into war, into the most terrible and disastrous of all wars, civilization itself seeming to be in the balance. But the right is more precious than peace, and we shall fight for the things which we have always carried nearest our hearts — for democracy, for the right of those who submit to authority to have a voice in their own Govern-

[48]*Intimate Papers*, II, 462, 464.
[49]Lane, *op. cit.*, 242.
[50]*Cobb of "The World," A Leader In Liberalism*, compiled by John Heaton (New York, 1924), 269 f.

ments, for the rights and liberties of small nations, for a universal dominion of right by such a concert of free peoples as shall bring peace and safety to all nations and make the world itself at last free. To such a task we can dedicate our lives and our fortunes, everything that we are and everything that we have, with the pride of those who know that the day has come when America is privileged to spend her blood and her might for the principles that gave her birth and happiness and the peace which she has treasured. God helping her, she can do no other."[51]

The applause in the crowded chamber was tumultuous. Supreme Court members, the Allies' diplomats, and ordinary men and women visitors joined the legislators in applauding the President. "The approval was indeed all but unanimous. But LaFollette, opposition in every grim look, was silent, arms folded high on his chest, contemptuous of the defeat that the moment held for him."[52] Kitchin, Stone, Norris, and a few others who refused to be swept along in the general hysteria, sat quietly, fully aware of the impossibility of blocking Wilson.

The next day discussion was started in the two chambers on the war resolution. There was a surprising lack of excitement, and among some, even a frivolous attitude. The Speaker of the House was forced to remind the members that they were not "at a vaudeville performance." Opposition had been beaten down thoroughly. Claude Kitchin was one of the few who dared openly to oppose the advocates of war. His comments were typical of the pacifists in the House of Representatives: " '. . . let me at once remind the House that it takes neither moral nor physical courage to declare a war for others to fight.' 'War upon the part of a nation is sometimes necessary and imperative. But here no invasion is threatened. Not a foot of our territory is demanded or coveted. No essential honor is required to be sacrificed. No fundamental right is asked to be permanently yielded or suspended. No national policy is contested. No part of our sovereignty is questioned. Here the overt act, ruthless and brutal though it be, is not aimed directly at us. The purpose of the proposed enemy is not our injury, either in property or life. The whole aim and purpose and effort are directed at a powerful enemy with which

---

[51]Borchard and Lage, *op. cit.*, 237.
[52]Baker, *op. cit.*, VI, 515.

she is in a life and death struggle.' 'The causes for which we are now asked to declare war could have been given with equal — yea, greater — force thirty days or ten days after the first step taken by the German Army in its march toward Paris.' "[53] The vote in the House was 373 to 50.

In the Senate there was a more dignified atmosphere. LaFollette spoke hopelessly against the resolution. Senator Stone of Missouri stated: "Even now I lift my voice in solemn warning against this blunder." "I shall vote against this mistake, to prevent which, God helping, I would gladly lay down my life." The vote in the Upper Chamber was 82 to 6.

American intervention was the only thing that saved the Allies. "The simple fact was that both the French and the British armies were practically bled white."[54] "One of the French ministers told Hoover that they had fixed on the first of November as their last day, if the United States had not come in."[55] "For God's sake, get your men over" they urged General Slocum. "You have got to finish it."[56]

It is quite often said that Americans entered the war with the greatest enthusiasm, but this is not true. The Eastern newspaper people, ministers, professors, and the upper classes throughout the country were, of course, strongly in favor of the move. But they had been partisan from the outset. On the other hand, among the common people who would have to fight the war, there was no rejoicing in spite of the fact that their sympathies were with the Allies. At the time of the war message, Wellington House reported: "Telegraphic dispatches suggest that something akin to war fever is now apparent, at any rate in the Eastern States. This may be true. . . . However, the American newspapers now arriving in this country do not give any previous intimation of such a development . . . editorial comment as a whole, indicates resignation rather than jubilation, compliance with necessity rather than fervour. . . . The fact seems to be that the pacifists in the

[53]Arnett, op. cit., 227, 233.
[54]Hendrick, op. cit., II, 363.
[55]Lane, op. cit., 253.
[56]Hendrick, op. cit., II, 363.

West were a larger and more important body than was commonly assumed in England. . . ."[57]

In the days that immediately followed, British propaganda agents continued to report that there were still "no indications of enthusiasm except in a few Eastern papers."[58] "Without much enthusiasm, except in certain Eastern quarters . . . the American Press has gone into the war. . . ."[59] Privately, even members of the administration conceded that the people were not with them whole-heartedly. The Secretary of State wrote to a friend: "The vote in the House must indicate the conditions under which we have long been laboring. We have known the state of mind in the House and realized that it was not as 'clear sailing' as many people seem to think. . . . I really believe that there were a number of others who would have voted against the [war] resolution if they had dared.

"It is my judgment that if the same resolution had been presented in February the House would have shown three times as great opposition, and if it had been voted on last summer its passage would have been so close as to show a divided country. Indeed, it might have entirely failed. . . . The only course practicable was to wait. . . . It was to wait the time when there could be no question but that a substantial majority favored war."[60]

The Wellington House reports of May and June, 1917, showed that Americans continued to be apathetic toward the war:

"*May 16*: It would seem . . . that the enthusiasm which these missions [headed by Joffre and other heroes] have aroused in Washington and New York has not entirely pervaded the Western States.

"*May 23*: There is evidence that in many localities the people have only entered the war with reluctance, and with a feeling of its inevitability rather than with any enthusiasm, and the Admin-

---

[57]*A. P. R.*, April 4, 1917.
[58]*A. P. R.*, April 18, 1917.
[59]*A. P. R.*, May 2, 1917.
[60]April 7, 1917, to Edward N. Smith.
Congressman Flood canvassed the House in December, 1916, and found a majority against a declaration of war. In his memoirs, Lansing states an earlier attempt to enter the war would have resulted in "irreparable disaster to the cause of the Allies" presumably because it would have been defeated and would have encouraged the opponents of war. Lansing's *Memoirs*, 24.

istration seems to be ahead of public opinion. Moreover, there is still much ignorance as to the causes and progress of the war.

"June 27: In spite of the President's assurances, doubts still appear in some quarters as to why the United States is in the war, and what she is fighting for."

One very interesting aspect of this period was the fact that although the Easterners had been shouting for war, when it came time to enlist, their enthusiasm was not so apparent. For two and one-half years the editors, teachers, preachers, bankers, lawyers, and American society leaders had scolded the West for its lack of patriotism. When the test actually came, however, enlistments in the West surpassed those in the East. Wellington House reported: "There are indications that it is now necessary to revise former estimates of American opinion based upon a geographical sub-division into East and West. The recruiting figures show that the response of the West has been more satisfactory than that of the East; moreover now that the West is in the war, it seems to be settling down to a determined prosecution of it."[61]

The New York *Post* was quoted as saying: "It had become customary hereabouts to speak of the Western States as far behind us in vigilant and vivid patriotism. They were comparatively cold about the war in Europe. . . . But it looks now as if the West would have to send missionaries East as the converts there put to shame the preachers here."[62] This would tend to make one believe that the pacifists were the only real patriots.

The total figures on enlistment in the army from the first of April to the sixteenth of May "only reached 73,000."[63] The lack of enthusiasm displayed by these figures made it necessary for the American government to raise a conscript army.

The administration became somewhat embarrassed by the continued disinterestedness of the public. Secretary Tumulty wrote to Colonel House: The people's " 'righteous wrath' seems not to have been aroused. . . . A speech by Mr. Whitlock about

[61]*A. P. R.*, May 30, 1917.

[62]*A. P. R.*, June 13, 1917.

[63]*A. P. R.*, June 6, 1917.

"These figures supply evidence that American enthusiasm for the war has been in some quarters exaggerated. . . ." From April 1 to June 30, 117,974 men enlisted in the regular army. In July enlistments amounted to 34,926; in August 28,155; in September 10,557.

German outrages in Belgium [i.e., atrocities] would help the
people to visualize just what poor Belgium has suffered and what
our own people might suffer if German autocracy should triumph."[64] Lansing commented: "I have felt that the American
people were not wholly convinced of the real menace of Germany."[65]

In order to arouse the "righteous wrath" of the American
people, President Wilson, on April 14, 1917, set up the Committee on Public Information. This American "Wellington House"
had as its objective the transmuting of the sympathy for the Allies — the product of two and one-half years of effort on the
part of European propagandists — into an active or even violent
force. By the end of 1917 Mr. Creel and his colleagues were
showing results. Mr. Wilson, of course, had even more influence
than Mr. Creel. In the period after 1917 "he became the greatest
propagandist the modern world has known."[66] In 1918 Americans were responding cordially to the propaganda appeals. By
that time they were enjoying the war thoroughly and hating the
Germans in a very satisfactory manner.

[64]Lansing Papers, May 31, 1917.
[65]Lansing's *Memoirs*, 208.
[66]Low, *op. cit.*, 181.

CHAPTER XVI ☆ CONCLUSION

THE reasons back of the American decision of April, 1917, were not unlike those which had governed the European nations in the crisis of August, 1914. There was the same overcharged atmosphere of hate and distrust; there was the same helplessness resulting from an entanglement of interests; and there was the same stubbornness and political ineptitude on the part of the statesmen. Even the immediate cause for American entrance into the war was brought about by a political impasse similar to that of 1914. Like Grey, Poincaré, and the Kaiser, the American and German officials had taken an extreme position from which they could not retreat without a loss of prestige to themselves and their nations. Wilson, like his European contemporaries, chose war rather than accept a diplomatic defeat, and, again like them, justified himself by claiming that the United States was entering the war to uphold peace, liberty, democracy, and the rights of small nations.

The most important of the reasons for the American action in 1917, however, was none of these things — it was instead the attitude of mind in this country — the product of British propaganda. People under the influence of the propaganda came to look upon the struggle of 1914-18 as a simple conflict between the forces of good and evil; they felt that all that was wrong was that certain malevolent individuals had gained control of an autocratic government and were attempting to dictate to the rest of the world. In the minds of American leaders there was developed a blind hatred of everything German. After this hatred had distorted American neutrality, it created a willingness to sacrifice American youth in an attempt to punish the hated nation.

But, even if the propaganda version had been true, no entire nation or race can justly be punished for the actions of single individuals or leaders. Such a course means that the innocent are to be made to pay for the misdeeds of the guilty. In spite of this truth the concept of retaliation was applied in making up the peace treaty and was responsible for making that document vicious. That which made it unworkable also stemmed from the propaganda. Out of an untrue interpretation of what was happening American leaders arrived at an utterly fallacious conclusion as to what could be achieved. In other words the propaganda was not only responsible in a large degree for American entrance into the war, but it was also responsible for the temper and irrationality of the peace treaty and the vindictiveness of the post-war years.

The overwrought nature of post-war events is, of course, but a reflection of the extravagance of wartime propaganda, but it is in addition a direct outcome of the warped interpretation of the meaning of the war embodied in that propaganda. The propaganda blinded men completely to the actual forces at work. Economics, nationalism, power politics, and the rise and decline of nations came to mean nothing. American leaders thought that the appalling political crudities of the Germans were the cause for Europe's difficulties instead of realizing that they were merely the outward manifestation of a deep historical force, of a shift in political power. They failed to see that the war was merely one in the long series of wars which the European set-up makes inevitable — that it was a natural concomitant of the political transition caused by Germany's rise to power.

It is now clear that Europe is going to remain unsettled until a new balance of power is completed. But even then there can be no permanent peace in Europe because there will always be some new rising power to act as a disturbing force. The particularism and vitality of the European people makes war on that continent inevitable. It is not something strange and unusual and personal, but a natural outcome of Europe's political, ethnographic, economic, and geographic configuration.

It is useless to criticize Great Britain for the propaganda — for spreading falsehoods and exaggerated interpretations of their own and their enemy's actions. Locked in a life-and-death struggle it was only natural that she should have vilified her enemy and have done everything in her power to gain help. The United States would do the same thing. Criticism can only be directed against America's leaders for failing to see that the propaganda arguments were largely irrelevant and that the causes for Europe's troubles were not given in these arguments.

But the propaganda was accepted largely at face value. With

President Wilson it was especially important, influencing him to such an extent that he subordinated the American desire for peace to his own desire for an Anglo-French victory. It caused him to be unneutral, perhaps unconsciously, until it was too late for him to exert pressure to bring about a just peace. It caused him, in the first twenty-one months of the war, to defeat most of the attempts at neutrality which might have been disadvantageous to the Allies.

In order to remove the causes for German submarine warfare, some Americans desired that pressure be exerted on Great Britain forcing her to relax the illegal blockade of the Central Powers. Wilson, however, refused to do anything which would embarrass the Allies. Many Americans wished an embargo on munitions; Wilson objected. Bryan prohibited loans to the warring nations; Wilson lifted the ban. Bryan asked for permission to warn Americans from traveling on foreign ships; Wilson refused. Congress tried to pass a bill preventing Americans from traveling on the armed ships of belligerents; Wilson personally defeated the measure. The President's partisanship was so apparent that even the British stated: "During the period while America was neutral all the issues in dispute between England and America were decided as England wished."

Although no serious attempt was ever made to compel Great Britain to comply with international law, notes were sent to Germany threatening war if she infringed upon what Wilson called American rights. The public was told that the argument with Great Britain was concerned with property while that with Germany was concerned with lives. This served to hide the actual claims on the part of Mr. Wilson which today seem almost fantastic. He was not insisting that Americans were privileged to travel on American ships in peaceful waters. And no Americans were killed on American ships previous to February, 1917, under circumstances which would have justified war. What he was insisting on, at the price of war, was the right of Americans to travel in the war zone (1) on foreign ships of belligerent nationality, (2) on foreign ships which were armed, and (3) on foreign ships carrying munitions and other supplies of war. Wilson contended that these were absolutely inviolable, and that they must be given precedence by the warring powers even when those nations were struggling for their very existence. He refused to make any concessions whatsoever — ignoring the fundamental rule of politics, that people and nations live together only by a patient adjustment of interests.

By 1917 the situation was beyond his control and "he was unprotected from his own ultimata, which never would have been issued had peace been his policy. But when finally the dilemmas and confusion led him into the war, no suggestion appeared that the mishandling of the American case might have had something to do with our misfortunes. On the contrary, the American position was pictured as unchallengeable — a malevolent aggressor had dragged the American people into war. The debâcle was then rationalized not as a defense of the freedom of the seas, even against submarine attack, but as a great crusade to end war, a championship of democracy against autocracy, a kind of religious war which laid the foundation for that current conflict of ideologies which threatens new wars.

"It is thus that credulity and misinformation can set in motion hysterical forces incalculable in their capacity for destruction."[1]

In the last analysis the American government was forced to join the Allies in 1917 because it had previously surrendered to them all its material, diplomatic, and moral support. Norway, Sweden, Denmark, and Holland refrained from such unneutral conduct and, in spite of the fact that they suffered a great deal more than did this country, they escaped becoming involved.[2]

---

[1]Borchard and Lage, *op. cit.*, 58.

[2]". . . the official Norwegian records show that by February 1, 1917 — two days before America broke off relations with Germany — 247 lives had been lost on Norwegian vessels." Borchard and Lage, *op. cit.*, 231.

Counting the 128 Americans who lost their lives on the *Lusitania*, there was a total of only 179 American casualties as a result of the submarine warfare from March, 1915, to February, 1917, when relations with Germany were broken off. As has already been mentioned, only three lost their lives as the result of an attack on an American ship (the *Gulflight*). Of the remaining forty-eight — aside from the American casualties on the *Lusitania* and *Gulflight* — twenty-one were members of the crew of a boat operated by the British Admiralty on official service, which boat resisted attack (the *Armenian*). Eight were on ships attempting to escape (the *Falaba*, the *Iberian*, and the *Englishman*). One of these casualties was a muleteer who was already in bad physical condition as a result of "a protracted course of dissipation." Seven were on armed vessels (the *Marina*, and the *Persia*). Of the remaining twelve, two were on the British liner *Arabic*, the sinking of which Germany disavowed and offered indemnity. One American, undoubtedly a member

Certainly if the United States had emulated their self-restraint, she also could have remained at peace. The reason she did not act in the same way was because of the tremendously effective British propaganda campaign. In Europe the agents of Wellington House had to compete with the propagandists of the Central Powers. In the United States, however, they had a free field and controlled public opinion almost as closely as they did within their own boundaries. Consequently there was developed within the United States a climate of opinion which influenced finance, industry, and government.

To some the history of the "neutrality" period demonstrates that the United States cannot keep out of war. But the facts do not bear out any such contention. What it does prove is that it is impossible to be unneutral and keep out of war.

---

of the crew, was on the Italian horse transport *Palermo*. Nine were on the Italian steamer *Ancona* which was sunk by an Austrian submarine. This sinking was subsequently disavowed and indemnities were offered.

"... America's total loss of life, wherever situated, on April 6, 1917, amounted to 266 — including the forty foreigners on American vessels, for whom America was responsible." Borchard and Lage, *op. cit.*, 230.

APPENDICES

APPENDIX A

I

Nov. 4, 1914	$10,000,000	French credit
Feb. 1, 1915	25,000,000	Russian acceptances
April 1, 1915	26,000,000	French loan
May 1, 1915	10,200,000	Russian
June 26, 1915	44,436,395	Rothschild-Freres
Sept. 5, 1915	20,000,000	Brown—French credit
Oct. 15, 1915	25,000,000	Italian
Oct. 15, 1915	500,000,000	Anglo-French
Nov., 1915	50,000,000	British bank credit
Dec. 1, 1915	100,000,000	Canadian
	45,000,000	Bonbright—French credits
April, 1916	11,000,000	Russia
April 1, 1916	75,000,000	Canadian
June 18, 1916	50,000,000	Russian
August 1, 1916	100,000,000	American Foreign Securities
August, 1916	25,000,000	Brown Bros., French credits
Sept. 1, 1916	250,000,000	First U.K. Loan (British)
Sept. 15, 1916	12,380,000	French—Seligman loan
Oct. 1, 1916	100,000,000	Canadian
Oct. 15, 1916	50,000,000	City of Paris
Nov. 2, 1916	3,881,683	French du Pont treasury note
Nov. 1, 1916	36,000,000	French Tri-City
Nov. 1, 1916	300,000,000	Second U.K. Loan
Nov. 11, 1916	50,000,000	French industrial credit

†1,919,098,078

* American loans to the Allies.

† Above total does not allow for reduction of approximately $134,636,395, which had been redeemed by December 1, 1916.

There were other loans made before the United States entered the war:

Date	Amount	Description
Feb. 1, 1917	250,000,000	United Kingdom
April 1, 1917	100,000,000	French Republic

Taken from the *Munitions Hearings*,
Part 28, p. 8708. Exhibit No. 2570.

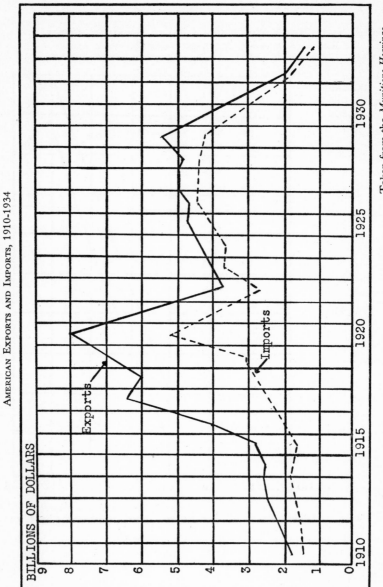

II

AMERICAN EXPORTS AND IMPORTS, 1910-1934

Taken from the *Munitions Hearings,*
Part 26, p. 7930. Exhibit No. 2150.

III

UNITED STATES TRADE WITH CERTAIN ALLIED COUNTRIES: FRANCE, ITALY,
RUSSIA, (EUROPE AND ASIA) AND UNITED KINGDOM, EXCEPT
CANADA, 1911-1918

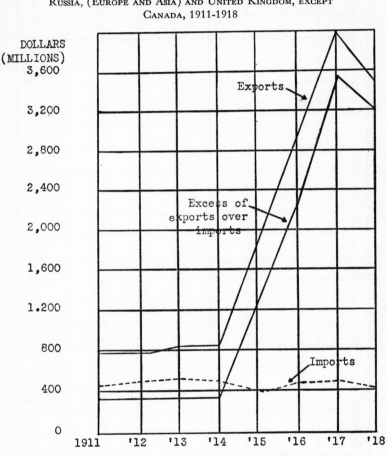

Taken from the *Munitions Hearings*,
Part 26, p. 7931. Exhibit No. 2151.

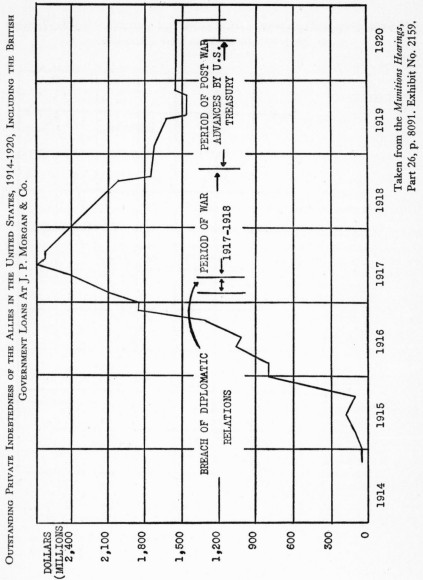

IV

Outstanding Private Indebtedness of the Allies in the United States, 1914-1920, Including the British Government Loans At J. P. Morgan & Co.

Taken from the *Munitions Hearings*, Part 26, p. 8091. Exhibit No. 2159.

V

GEOGRAPHICAL DISTRIBUTION ON A NUMERICAL AND DOLLAR VOLUME BASIS
OF THE J. P. MORGAN & CO. WAR CONTRACTS

(From the British contract records of the export dept. of J. P. Morgan & Co.)

STATE	DOLLAR VOLUME	NO. OF COMPANIES
New York	718,158,016	118
Delaware	399,255,709	5
Pennsylvania	372,125,800	53
Connecticut	115,660,705	32
Massachusetts	66,181,033	38
Ohio	56,876,686	41
Illinois	16,398,518	29
Maryland	14,557,469	2
Missouri	14,126,130	6
West Virginia	12,024,601	2
Michigan	6,994,648	5
New Jersey	3,074,322	27
Alabama	2,250,045	2
Iowa	2,228,382	2
Tennessee	1,423,869	2
Wisconsin	1,120,759	6
Washington, D. C.	161,280	1
Indiana	122,510	4
Vermont	90,321	3
Louisiana	88,134	1
Ontario	82,797	3
California	39,315	3
Minnesota	32,488	1
Mexico	18,500	1

Taken from the *Munitions Hearings*,
Part 26, p. 8103. Exhibit No. 2182.

APPENDIX B

UNITED STATES FOREIGN COMMERCE COMBINED EXPORTS, 1914-1916

	DOLLARS	INDEX (1914 = 100)
A. To Allied Countries, England, France, Italy, Russia:		
1914	$ 824,860,237	100.0
1915	1,991,747,493	241.0
1916	3,214,480,547	389.7
B. Central Powers, Austria-Hungary, Germany:		
1914	169,289,775	100.0
1915	11,878,153	7.0
1916	1,159,653	0.68
C. Neutrals (Northern), Denmark, Holland, Norway, Sweden:		
1914	187,667,040	100.0
1915	330,100,646	175.8
1916	279,786,219	149.0

Taken from the *Munitions Hearings*,
Part 28, p. 8701. Exhibit No. 2561.

APPENDIX C

I

French Loans Outstanding in the United States, April 7, 1917

MATURITY	LOAN	AMOUNT
1. May 1, 1917	Schneider credit, 1st of 2nd series....	$5,000,000.00
2. June 1, 1917	Schneider credit, 2nd of 2nd series...	5,000,000.00
3. July 1, 1917	Schneider credit, 3rd of 2nd series...	5,000,000.00
4. Sept. 10, 1917	Brown Bros. credit.................	5,000,000.00
5. Sept. 24, 1917	Brown Bros. credit.................	5,000,000.00
6. Oct. 2, 1917	Brown Bros. credit..................	5,000,000.00
7. Oct. 10, 1917	Schneider credit, 1st of 3rd series	5,000,000.00
8. Oct. 10, 1917	Brown Bros., credit................	5,000,000.00
9. Oct. 16, 1917	Seligman loan.....................	10,072,706.22
10. Nov. 2, 1917	Du Pont Treasury note.............	3,787,008.60
11. Nov. 9, 1917	Schneider credit, 2nd of 3rd series ...	5,000,000.00
12. Nov. 12, 1917	Brown Bros., credit................	5,000,000.00
13. Dec. 12, 1917	Schneider credit, 3rd of 3rd series....	5,000,000.00
14. Dec. 15, 1917	Du Pont Treasury note.............	2,716,769.60
15. Mar. 15, 1918	Du Pont Treasury note.............	2,739,503.97
16. Apr. 10, 1918	Schneider credit, 1st of 4th series *...	5,000,000.00
17. May 7, 1918	Schneider credit, 2nd of 4th series*...	5,000,000.00
18. June 7, 1918	Schneider credit, 3rd of 4th series*...	5,000,000.0
19. July 18, 1918	French industrial credit............	50,000,000.00
20. Apr. 1, 1918	2-year 5½% loan	100,000,000.00
21. Aug. 1, 1919	Amer. For. Sec. Co. loan	100,000,000.00
22. Nov. 1, 1919	Three Cities Loan	36,000,000.00
23. Oct. 51, 1920	Anglo-French loan, French share.....	250,000,000.00
24. Oct. 15, 1921	City of Paris loan	50,000,000.00
	Total.......................	675,315,988.39

* Although the drafts for the 4th Schneider credit were all dated after April 17, 1917, the credit was established on March 12, 1917, and can therefore be regarded as outstanding on April 7.

Taken from the *Munitions Hearings*,
Part 29, p. 9205. Exhibit No. 2778.

II

British Loans Outstanding in the United States April 7, 1917

MATURITY DATE	LOAN	AMOUNT
On demand	Overdraft at J. P. Morgan & Co......	$345,000,000.00
June 20, 1917	British banks credit.................	50,000,000.00
Oct. 2, 1917	DuPont Treasury notes..............	15,950,000.00
Dec. 15, 1917	DuPont Treasury notes..............	12,986,600.75
Feb. 1, 1918	U.K. No. III, 1-yr. $5\frac{1}{2}$'s of Feb. 1, 1917...........................	94,887,000.00
Mar. 15, 1918	DuPont Treasury notes..............	17,829,403.93
July 7, 1918	Canadian Northern notes............	5,700,000.00
Sept. 1, 1918	U.K. No. I, 2-yr. 5's of Sept. 1, 1916..	194,688.000.00
Sept. 18, 1918	Metropolitan Water Board notes......	6,300,000.00
Dec. 1, 1918	English Sewing Cotton Co. Treas. notes	4,900,000.00
Feb. 1, 1919	U.K. No. III, 2-yr. $5\frac{1}{2}$'s of Feb. 1, 1917	143,654,000.00
Feb. 1, 1919	Bethlehem Steel Co., Treasury notes ..	37,300,000.00
Apr. 2, 1919	Bliss Treasury notes................	2,225,000.00
Apr. 30, 1919	Marlin Treasury notes..............	1,953,561.66
July 14, 1919	Treasury notes.....................	1,100,000.00
Oct. 21, 1919	Remington-Winchester Treasury notes.	27,332,000.00
Nov. 1, 1919	U.K. No. II, 3-yr. $5\frac{1}{2}$'s of Nov. 1, 1916	131,117,000.00
Oct. 15, 1920	Anglo-French Loan (British share)....	250,000,000.00
Nov. 1, 1921	U.K. No. II, 5-yr. $5\frac{1}{2}$'s of Nov. 1, 1916	131,589,000.00
(?)	American Locomotive Co., Treas. notes	2,000,000.00
(?)	Treasury notes, various contractors....	(?)
	Total........................	1,476,511,566.34

Taken from the *Munitions Hearings*,
Part 29, p. 9205. Exhibit No. 2777.

III

RUSSIAN LOANS OUTSTANDING IN THE UNITED STATES APRIL 7, 1917

MATURITY DATE	LOAN	AMOUNT
May 1, 1917	5% Treasury notes................	$11,000,000.00
June 18, 1919	Three-year 6½%................	50,000,000.00
Dec. 1, 1921	Five-year 5½%.................	25,000,000.00
	Total........................	$86,000,000.00

Taken from the *Munitions Hearings*,
Part 29, p. 9206. Exhibit No. 2779.

BIBLIOGRAPHY

BIBLIOGRAPHY

I. BIBLIOGRAPHIES

Bulkley, M. A., *Bibliographical Survey of Contemporary Sources For the Economic and Social History of the War*, Oxford, 1922.

Dearle, N. B., *Dictionary of Official War-Time Organizations*, London, 1928.

Hall, Hubert, *British Archives and the Sources For the History of the World War*, Oxford, 1925.

Lutz, Ralph H., "Studies of World War Propaganda 1914-1933," *Journal of Modern History*, 1933, Volume V, pp. 496-516.

Weltkriegsbücherei, *Bibliographie zur englischen Propaganda im Weltkrieg*, Stuttgart, 1935.

Young, Kimball and Lawrence, Raymond I., *Bibliography on Censorship and Propaganda*, University of Oregon Publications, Journalism Series, Vol. I., No. 1, March, 1928.

II. MANUSCRIPT COLLECTIONS, PROPAGANDA REPORTS

Alliance Française, *Bulletin*, 1914-1917.

Buttolph Letters (New York Public Library).

Central Committee For National Patriotic Organizations, *Report of 1916*.

Forster Papers (New York Public Library).

France, *Bulletin periodique de la presse américaine*.

Great Britain, General Staff, War Office (also issued by the Foreign Office), *Daily Review of the Foreign Press* 1915-1917. Numerous supplements were also issued. The most important were the *Confidential Supplement* and the *Neutral Press Supplement*.

Great Britain, Foreign Office, *American Press Résumé* (also issued by the War Office) ("For Use of the Cabinet"), London, 1915-1917.

Great Britain, *Report of the Committee on Alleged German Outrages* (Lord Bryce's Report), London, 1915.

Herron, George D., *Papers* (Hoover War Library).

Kanner, Dr. Heinrich, *Papers* (Hoover War Library).

Knox, Philander, *Papers* (Library of Congress).

Kriegsministerium, *Die Beschiessung der Kathedral von Rheims*, Berlin, 1915.

Lansing, Robert, *Papers* (Library of Congress).

Long, Breckinridge, *Papers* (Library of Congress).

Mitchell, Peter Chalmers, *Report on the Propaganda Library* (Great Britain War Office — probably 1917).

Parker, Sir Gilbert, *Letter* in the Hoover War Library.

Watterson, Henry, *Papers* (Library of Congress).

Squier, George O., *Diary* (Library of Congress).

Wheeler, E. P., *Letters* (New York Public Library).

White, Henry, *Papers* (Library of Congress).

Wellington House Schedule of British Propaganda.

In addition to the above there exist numerous collections of papers which are of interest to the student of this period. The Bryan Papers in the Library of Congress and the House Papers at New Haven represent two of the largest collections. In addition there are incidental items in the Hoover War Library, the Clark University War Library, the British Museum, and the British War Museum. Some of these may not be quoted.

III. GOVERNMENT DOCUMENTS

Congressional Record.

Official German Documents Relating To The World War, published by the Carnegie Endowment for International Peace, Oxford University Press, New York, 1923.

Mixed Claims Commission, *United States and Germany Administrative Decisions and Opinions,* Washington, 1925.

Savage, Carlton, *Policy of the United States Toward Maritime Commerce in War,* Vol. II, 1914-1918, Washington, 1936.

Senate, U. S., Judiciary Committee Hearings on *Brewing and Liquor Interests and German Propaganda,* Washington, 1919.

Senate, U. S., *Hearings Before The Special Committee Investigating The Munitions Industry,* Washington, 1935-37.

Senate, U. S., *Hearings Before The Committee on Foreign Relations Concerning the Treaty of Peace With Germany,* Washington, 1919.

State Department, U. S., *Supplements, Papers Relating To The Foreign Relations of The United States,* 1914-17, Washington, 1927-31.

State Department, U. S., *Diplomatic Correspondence With Belligerent Governments Relating To Neutral Rights and Commerce,* Washington, 1915-18. (4 vols.)

IV. BOOKS

Abrams, Ray H., *Preachers Present Arms*, New York, 1933.

Allen, William C., *War! Behind The Smoke Screen*, Philadelphia, 1929.

Arnett, Alex Mathews, *Claude Kitchin And The Wilson War Policies*, Boston, 1937.

Avenarius, Ferdinand, *Die Weltkarikatur in der Völkerverhetzung*, Munich, 1921.

Baker, Ray Stannard, *Woodrow Wilson Life and Letters*, Garden City, New York, Vol. V (1935), Vol. VI (1937).

Baudrillart, Mgr. Alfred, *Une campagne française*, Paris, 1917.

Beard, Charles A., *The Devil Theory of War*, New York, 1936.

Beaverbrook, Lord, *Politicians and The Press*, London, 1927.

————, *Politicians and the War 1914-1916*, London, 1928.

Bernstorff, Count von, *My Three Years in America*, New York, 1920.

Bertie, Lord, *The Diary of Lord Bertie of Thame, 1914-1918*, New York, 1924.

Bomert, E. A., *Truth — A Path To Justice and Reconciliation*, London, 1926.

Borchard, Edwin M. and Lage, William P., *Neutrality For The United States*, New Haven, 1937.

Bornecqui, Henri and Drouilly, J. Germain, *La France et la guerre, Formation de l'opinion publique pendant la guerre*, Paris, 1921.

Briggs, Mitchell P., *George D. Herron and The European Settlement*, Stanford University, 1932.

Brownrigg, Rear-Admiral Douglas, *Indiscretions of The Naval Censor*, London, 1920.

Bruntz, George G., *Allied Propaganda and The Collapse of The German Empire in 1918*, Stanford University, 1938.

Bryan, W. J., *The Memoirs of W. J. Bryan*, Chicago, 1925.

Callwell, Major-General C. E., *Experiences of A Dug-Out 1914-1918*, New York, 1920.

Capek, Karel, *President Masaryk Tells His Story*, London, 1935.

Charteris, John, *At G. H. Q.*, London, 1931.

Cocks, F. Seymour, *The Secret Treaties And Understandings*, London, 1918.

Consett, Admiral, *The Triumph of Unarmed Forces 1914-1918*, London, 1928.

Cook, Sir Edward Tyas, *The Press in War-Time*, London, 1920.

Creel, George, *How We Advertised America*, New York, 1920.

————, *The War, The World and Wilson*, New York, 1920.

Dahlin, Ebba, *Public Opinion on Declared War Aims in France and Germany 1914-1918* (Ph.D. dissertation), Stanford University, 1931.

Daniels, Josephus, *The Life of Woodrow Wilson 1856-1924*, Philadelphia, 1924.

DeChambure, A., *Quelques guides de l'opinion en France pendant la grande guerre 1914-1918*, Paris, 1918.

Demartial, Georges, *La guerre de 1914. Comment on mobilisa les consciences*, Paris, 1922.

Dewey, John, *The Public And Its Problems*, New York, 1927.

Doob, Leonard W., *Propaganda, Its Psychology and Technique*, New York, 1935.

Dumba, Constantin, *Memoirs of A Diplomat*, Boston, 1932.

Gerard, James W., *My Four Years in Germany*, New York, 1917.

Gibson, R. H. and Prendergast, Maurice, *The German Submarine War 1914-1918*, New York, 1931.

Got, Ambroise, *The Case of Miss Cavell*, London, 1920.

Grattan, C. Hartley, *Why We Fought*, New York, 1929.

Grey, Sir Edward, *Twenty-Five Years 1892-1916*, London, 1925.

Guichard, Lieutenant Louis, *The Naval Blockade 1914-1918*, New York, 1930.

Hale, W. B., *Peace or War*, New York, 1916.

Hanotaux, Gabriel, *Pendant la grande guerre*, Paris, 1916.

Hansen, Ferdinand, *Pillory and Witness-Box*, Hamburg, 1930.

Heaton, John (editor), *Cobb of "The World" A Leader in Liberalism*, New York, 1924.

Hendrick, Burton, *The Life and Letters of Walter H. Page*, New York, 1922-25.

Henschel, A. E., *The "Lusitania" Case*, New York, 1915.

Herron, George D., *Woodrow Wilson And The World's Peace*, New York, 1917.

Hollis, Christopher, *The American Heresy*, New York, 1930.

Houston, David F., *Eight Years With Wilson's Cabinet*, Garden City, New York, 1926.

Hovelaque, Emile, *Les États-Unis et la guerre, De la neutralité à la croisade*, Paris, 1919.

Hoy, Hugh Cleland, *40 O.B. or How The War Was Won*, London, 1932.

Irwin, Will, *Propaganda and The News*, New York, 1936.

Jusserand, J., *Le sentiment américain pendant la guerre*, Paris, 1931.

Landau, Captain Henry, *The Enemy Within*, New York, 1937.

Lane, Franklin, *The Letters of Franklin K. Lane*, New York, 1922.

Lansing, Robert, *War Memoirs of Robert Lansing, Secretary of State*, Indianapolis, 1935.

Lasswell, Harold D., *Propaganda Technique in The World War*, New York, 1927.

Lauriat, Charles E., *The Lusitania's Last Voyage*, Boston, 1915.

Lauzanne, Stephane, *Les hommes que j'ai vus, Souvenirs d'un journaliste*, Paris, 1920.

Lawrence, David, *The True Story of Woodrow Wilson*, New York, 1924.

Lechartier, Georges, *Intrigues et diplomaties à Washington 1914-1917*, Paris, 1919.

Logan, Marshall, *Horrors And Atrocities of The Great War*, Brantford, Ontario (c. 1917).

Low, A. Maurice, *Woodrow Wilson, An Interpretation*, London, 1919.

Lowell, A. L., *Public Opinion in War and Peace*, Cambridge, 1923.

Lumley, Frederick E., *The Propaganda Menace*, New York, 1933.

McAdoo, W. G., *Crowded Years, The Reminiscences of William G. McAdoo*, Boston, 1931.

Masaryk, Thomas G., *The Making of A State*, London, 1927.

Mermeix (Pseud.) (Terrail, Gabriel), *Les négociations secrètes et les quatre armistices*, Paris, 1921.

Meyer, Edouard, *Der amerikanische Kongress und der Weltkrieg*, Berlin, 1917.

Millis, Walter, *The Road To War, America 1914-1917*, Boston, 1935.

Nitti, Francesco, *They Make A Desert*, London, 1924.

Notter, Harry, *The Origins of The Foreign Policy of Woodrow Wilson*, Baltimore, 1937.

Noyes, Alexander D., *The War Period of American Finance*, New York, 1926.

Nowell, Charles E., *The British Blacklist and The United States* (Ph.D. dissertation), Stanford, 1927.

Palmer, Colonel Frederick, *Newton D. Baker — America At War*, New York, 1931.

————, *With My Own Eyes*, New York, 1934.

Pareto, Vilfredo, *The Mind and Society*, New York, 1935.

Paxson, Frederick L., *American Democracy and The World War — Pre-War Years 1913-1917*, Boston, 1936.

Playne, Caroline E., *Society at War 1914-1916*, Boston, 1931.

Ponsonby, Sir Arthur, *Falsehood in War-Time*, New York, 1928.

Ribot, Alexandre, *Lettres à un ami, Souvenirs de ma vie politique*, Paris, 1924.

Riddell, G. A. R., *Lord Riddell's War Diary 1914-1918*, London, 1933.

Riegel, O. W., *Mobilizing For Chaos, The Story of the New Propaganda*, New Haven, 1934.

Rintelen von Kleist, Franz, *The Dark Invader*, London, 1933.

Salter, James Arthur, *Allied Shipping Control*, London, 1921.

Seymour, Charles, *American Diplomacy During The World War*, Baltimore, 1934.

———, *American Neutrality 1914-1917*, New Haven, 1935.

——— (editor), *The Intimate Papers of Colonel House*, Boston, 1926.

Silber, J. C., *The Invisible Weapons*, London, 1932.

Spring-Rice, Sir Cecil, *The Letters and Friendships of Sir Cecil Spring-Rice* (edited by Stephen Gwynn), Boston, 1929.

Sprott, Mary Esther, *A Survey of British War-Time Propaganda In America Issued From Wellington House* (Master's Thesis), Stanford, 1921.

Squires, James Duane, *British Propaganda At Home and In The United States From 1914 to 1917*, Cambridge, Mass., 1935.

Strachey, J. St. Loe, *The Adventure of Living*, London, 1922.

Stuart, Sir Campbell, *Secrets of Crewe House*, London, 1921.

Tansill, Charles C., *America Goes To War*, Boston, 1938.

Thimme, Hans, *Weltkrieg ohne Waffen*, Stuttgart, 1932.

Thwaites, Norman, *Velvet and Vinegar*, London, 1932.

Tumulty, Joseph P., *Woodrow Wilson As I Knew Him*, New York, 1921.

Turlington, Edgar, *Neutrality — The World War Period*, New York, 1936.

Turner, John Kenneth, *Shall It Be Again*, New York, 1922.

Vandervelde, Lalla, *Monarchs and Millionaires*, London, 1925.

Van Langenhove, Fernand, *Comment naît un cycle de légendes*, Paris, 1917.

Vic, Jean, *La littérature de guerre*, Paris, 1923.

Viereck, George Sylvester, *Spreading Germs of Hate*, New York, 1930.

———, *The Strangest Friendship in History — Woodrow Wilson and Colonel House*, New York, 1932.

Villeneuve-Trans, R. de, *À l'ambassade de Washington octobre 1917-avril 1919*, Paris, 1921.

Wanderscheck, Hermann, *Weltkrieg und Propaganda*, Berlin, 1936.

Winkler, John K., *W. R. Hearst: An American Phenomenon*, New York, 1928.

Wittke, Carl, *German-Americans and The World War*, Columbus, Ohio, 1936.

V. MAGAZINES AND NEWSPAPERS

Archibald, J. F., "Ambassador Dumba's Recall," *Current History Magazine,* November, 1931.

Aston, Sir George, "Propaganda and The Father of It," *Cornhill Magazine,* May, 1931.

Bailey, Thomas A., "The Sinking of The Lusitania," *The American Historical Review.*

———, "German Documents Relating To The Lusitania," *Journal of Modern History,* September, 1936.

Baker, Newton D., "Why We Went To War," *Foreign Affairs,* October, 1936.

Borchard, Edwin M., "Dragging America Into War," *Current History,* July, 1934.

"Censorship in France," *Outlook,* June 13, 1917.

Child, Clifton J., "German-American Attempts to Prevent The Exportation of Munitions of War 1914-1915," *The Mississippi Valley Historical Review,* December, 1938.

Grattan, Hartley C., "Fools Highway," *The New Republic,* May 8, 1935.

Hapgood, Norman, "Atrocities," *Harpers' Weekly,* July 10, 1915.

Houston, David F., "Wilson As A War President," *The World's Work,* June, 1926.

Lamont, Thomas, "Partner In The House of Morgan," *Time,* January 20, 1936.

Lansing, Robert, "War Days In The White House," *Saturday Evening Post,* August 8, 1931.

"Militarismus Abroad and At Home," *Edinburg Review,* January, 1915.

Moore, John Bassett, "America's Neutrality Policy," New York *Times,* Book Review, May 17, 1937.

Nicholson, Ivor, "An Aspect of British Official Wartime Propaganda," *Cornhill Magazine,* May, 1931.

Norris, George W., "After Twenty Years," *The Christian Century,* March 31, 1937.

Parker, Sir Gilbert, "The United States and The War," *Harpers' Monthly Magazine,* March, 1918.

Redfield, William C., "Glimpses of Our Government in War and Peace," *Saturday Evening Post,* October 11, 1924.

Schieber, Clara Eve, "The Transformation of American Sentiment Towards Germany 1870-1914," *Journal of International Relations,* July, 1921.

Van Alstyne, Richard W., "Private American Loans To The Allies," *The Pacific Historical Review,* June, 1933.

Newspaper and magazine articles covering the neutrality years are so numerous that it is impossible to mention more than a few of the more important ones. A view of how the period looked to contemporaries may be found in the New York *Times,* the New York *World,* the Chicago *Tribune,* and the Los Angeles *Times* or *Examiner.* Magazines which will be found helpful are the *World's Work,* the *Review of Reviews,* the *New Republic, Life, LaFollette's Magazine,* the *Fatherland,* the *Commercial and Financial Chronicle, Harpers' Magazine,* and the *Atlantic.*

INDEX

INDEX

ACCEPTANCES, 94 f.
Albert, Dr. Heinrich, 143 f., 147
Albert portfolio, 154 f.
Alliance Française, 32
American Press Résumé, 23
Anglo-French Commission, 101
Arabic, 132
Archibald, J. F., 155

BACON, ROBERT, 21
Battle Cry of Peace, 202
Beck, James M., 24, 30, 39, 62
Belgian baby without hands, 59
Belgian neutrality propaganda, 45 f.
Belgian Relief, 66
Bernstorff, Count Johann von, 156 fn.,
   204 fn., 212, 223 f., 299, 303 f., 305
Bethlehem Steel Company, 91 f.
Bethmann-Hollweg, Theobald von, 291,
   293
Blacklist, British, 251 ff., 286
Black Tom explosion, 148
Blockade, British, 74 f., 80 fn., 191, 195
Bone, Muirhead, 239
Bosch Magneto Company, 145
Boy-Ed, Captain, 147, 156
Bridgeport Projectile Company, 144 f.
British War Mission, 231
Bryan, William Jennings, 86, 127 ff.,
   131, 178, 183 f.
Bryce, Lord, 10, 58 f.
Bryce Report, 53 ff., 58 fn.
Buchan, John, 229 f.
Burke, Frank, 154

CALIFORNIA, 1916 election in, 280
Casement, Sir Roger, 241
Cavell, Edith, 39, 41, 61 fn.
Censorship, mail, 14 f., 286
Censorship, press, 12 ff.
Central Committee for National Patri-
   otic Organizations, 19
Clark, Bennett Champ, 206, 216
Coal, bunker, 248
Committee on Public Information, 230
   fn., 325
Contraband, 72 f., 248
Corpse factory propaganda, 59
Credits, British, 88 fn., 89 f.
Crewe House, 230 fn.

"Crucified Canadian," 57
Czech National Alliance, 152 f.

DAILY REVIEW OF THE FOREIGN PRESS,
   23
Damnation propaganda, 67
Declaration of London, 192 f.
Democratic Convention, 277 ff.
Department of Information, 230 fn.
Deportation of Belgians, 233, 244
Dernburg, Bernard, 136, 141
Dumba, Constantin, 155 f.
Durant, Kenneth, 20

ECONOMIC WARFARE, BRITISH, 77 f., 108,
   248
Economic warfare, German, 109, 270
Election, 1916, 273 ff., 193 fn.
Eliot, President Charles W., 210
Embargo, food, 73
Embargo on war munitions, 177 f., 193
   f., 193 fn., 194 fn., 254
Exchange crisis, 91, 98 fn., 99, 100, 107
   fn., 134
Exports to the Allies, 256 ff., 257 fn.
Exports, German resentment towards
   American, 266, 270 f.

Falaba, 116 fn., 18
Federal Reserve, 93, 260, 263 ff., 292
Flood, Henry D., 214, 323 fn.
Ford, Henry, 178 f.
"Foreignness" propaganda, 37 f.
Fryatt, Captain, 39

GAS WARFARE PROPAGANDA, 63 f.
Gaunt, Captain Guy, 152 f., 182
Gerard, James W., 187
Glynn, Martin H., 278
Gore Resolution, 217 fn., 220
Gore, Thomas P., 214, 217
Greece, Allies occupation of, 249 f.
Grellings, Dr. Richard, 39
Grey, Sir Edward, 29, 30, 41, 193
Gulflight, 117

HALL, SIR WILLIAM REGINALD, 15, 152
Hearst, William Randolph, 165 f., 234
   ff., 237
Herald, New York, 162

Herrick, Myron, 186
Horn, Werner, 149
House, Colonel E. M., 29, 182 f., 204 ff., 223, 281
Hughes Campaign, 276
Hughes, Charles Evans, 274 ff.
Hyde, Charles C., 194
Hyphenates, 173 f., 178, 277, 281

IDENTITY OF INTERESTS PROPAGANDA, 35 f.
Igel, von, 157
Information service, propaganda, 22, 136 f.
Irish, 193, 241

JAGOW, GOTTLIED E. C. VON, 293 f.
James, Senator Ollie, 278 f.
Japan, 307
Jewish problem, 242
Johnson, Hiram, 276, 280
Jusserand, M., 231

KIPLING, RUDYARD, 105
Kitchin, Claude, 188, 215, 217, 321

LAFOLLETTE, ROBERT M., 31, 63, 129 fn., 177, 315 f., 321 f.
Lansing, Robert, 88, 184 f., 199, 210, 222, 225, 277, 297, 307 f.
Liberia, Allies pressure on, 250
Loans, 95, 102, 105, 259 ff., 265 fn.
Loans, policies on, 88 f., 96, 99 f., 103
Loans, restrictions on, 87 f.
London, Declaration of, 248
Louvain propaganda, 60
Lusitania, 117 ff., 118 fn., 26
Lusitania cargo, 120 f.
Lusitania casualties, 125
Lusitania, crew, 123 ff.
Lusitania incident, reactions, 121, 125, 170, 196
Lusitania passenger list, 119 f.

MCADOO, WILLIAM GIBBS, 98
McGuire, James K., 138
McLemore, Jeff, 217
McLemore Resolution, 216, 219 f.

MAIL, BRITISH INTERFERENCE WITH, 250 f.
Maison de la presse, 232 fn.
Masefield, Sir John, 21
Masterman, Charles, 16, 18
Materials, raw, 75
Merchantmen, arming of, 114 fn., 117 fn., 197 ff.

Mercier, Cardinal, 28, 41
Mersey Report, 37, 122 fn., 123
Militarism, propaganda of, 46 ff.
Ministry of Information, 230 fn.
Moore, John Bassett, 197, 218
Morgan, J. P., 21, 43, 44, 84 ff., 91, 95 ff., 155, 257
Morgan Report, 58 fn.
Muensterberg, Professor Hugo, 208
Muenther, Eric, 149 ff.
Munition makers, 104

NATIONALISTIC PROPAGANDA, 29
National Security League, 31
National War Aims Committee, 229
"Native" propagandists, 25, 32
Naval Policy, British, 252 f.
Navy League, 31, 201 f.
Nederlandsche Overzeetrust Maatschappij (N.O.T.), 76
Nereide decision, 197
Neutral flags, 114
Neutrality Proclamation, 189
Newspapermen, propagandizing, 25 ff.
Newspapers, California, 164
Newspapers, foreign language, 166 f.

O'LEARY, JEREMIAH, 277

PACIFISM, 177 f., 278, 310
Page, Robert N., 221
Page, Walter Hines, 43, 45, 185 f., 192
Palmer, Frederick, 24
Papen, Franz von, 21, 144, 156
Parker, Sir Gilbert, 16
Peace overtures, 288 ff., 311
Peace Plan, House-Grey, 205 f.
Peace without victory, 301 f.
Pearson, Colonel G. S. H., 14
Pilgrim's Society, 32
Pity propaganda, 64 ff., 243 f.
Plattsburg Camp, 202
Poor Belgium propaganda, 65 ff.
Preparedness campaign, 201 ff.
Press, American, 7 f., 159 ff., 167, 233 f., 323
Press bureaus, 27
Professors, propagandizing of, 29
Propaganda, air raid, 64
Propaganda atrocities, 51 ff., 243, 324 f.
Propaganda, cartoons, 239
Propaganda, cinema, 238
Propaganda, French, 32 ff.
Propaganda, German, 134 ff., 150 fn.
Propaganda, loan, 104 f., 261 f.
Propaganda, photographic, 239 f., 240 fn.

Propaganda technique, 37 ff.
Prosperity, war, 256 ff.
Purchases, Allies', 91 f., 105, 256 ff.
Purchases, German, 143

RAEMAKERS, LOUIS R., 239
Rathom, John R., 153
Reactions to war, American, 169 f., 171 f., 174 ff., 323 fn.
Religious propaganda, 28
Reports of world opinion, 23
Republican, Springfield, 181, 317
Reservists, German, 153 f.
Revolutionary plots, 150
Rheims propaganda, 60 f.
Rintelen, Franz, 146 ff., 156
Roosevelt, Theodore, 29, 30, 170, 196, 275
Russian Revolution, 316 f.

SABOTAGE, GERMAN, 147 ff., 171, 146 fn.
Scheele detonator, 147 fn.
Schwab, Charles M., 92
Schwieger, Captain Walther, 121 ff.
Shipping losses, 116
Slogans and phrases, 68 f.
Société Suisse de Surveillance (S.S.S.), 76
Spring-Rice, Sir Cecil, 72, 182
Starvation policy, 83, 268 f.
Stock Market, 87, 89, 96 ff., 107, 267
Stone, William J., 188, 208, 215, 222 fn.
Strachey, John St. Loe, 27
Strict accountability, 111
Submarines, British, 92
Submarine policy, German, 269 f.
Submarine warfare, 109, 115, 270, 291, 293, 299, 300 fn.
Submarine warfare, reactions, 195 f.

Sunrise conference, 216
Sussex, 222 f.

Times, New York, 6, 161 f., 181
Too proud to fight, 127
Travel in war time, right to, 112
Treaty of London, 50 fn., 289 fn.
Treitschke on militarism, 49
Tribune, New York, 162
Tumulty, Joseph P., 17, 30
Turner, William Thomas, 124

U-20, 121 f., 125
U-27, 199 fn.
U-53, 245

VERSAILLES TREATY, 286
Victory propaganda, 42

WAR AIMS PROPAGANDA, 50 f.
War, conduct of, propaganda, 51 ff.
War decision, reactions to, 308 ff., 312, 317
War guilt propaganda, 43 ff.
War Pictorial, 239
War zones, 110
Wellington House, 16 f., 231, 237, 252 fn., 290, 314
Whitlock, Brand, 186
Wilhelm, Kaiser, 41 f., 289, 300
Wilson's foreign policy, 189 ff.
Wilson, Woodrow, 9, 10, 127, 180 ff., 201, 203, 205, 208, 211, 213 f., 218 f., 273 ff., 283 ff., 288, 294 ff., 301 f., 318 ff.
Wiseman, Sir William, 152
World, New York, 162, 181

ZIMMERMANN, ALFRED, 313 ff.
Zimmermann note, 301, 301 fn., 313, 315

PROPAGANDA FOR WAR

THE CAMPAIGN AGAINST AMERICAN NEUTRALITY, 1914-1917

BY H. C. PETERSON

HAS BEEN COMPOSED ON THE LINOTYPE IN 11 POINT

OLD STYLE NO. 7 WITH ONE POINT LEADING

THE PAPER IS OLD STYLE WOVE

UNIVERSITY OF OKLAHOMA PRESS

NORMAN, OKLAHOMA